ROYAL HISTORICAL SOCIETY

STUDIES IN HISTORY

New Series

AFTER THE SHOCK CITY

PAST & PRESENT
a journal of historical studies

AFTER THE SHOCK CITY

URBAN CULTURE AND THE MAKING OF
MODERN CITIZENSHIP

Tom Hulme

THE ROYAL HISTORICAL SOCIETY

THE BOYDELL PRESS

First published 2019

A Royal Historical Society publication
Published by The Boydell Press
an imprint of Boydell & Brewer Ltd
PO Box 9, Woodbridge, Suffolk IP12 3DF, UK
and of Boydell & Brewer Inc.
668 Mt Hope Avenue, Rochester, NY 14620–2731, USA
website: www.boydellandbrewer.com

ISBN 978-0-86193-349-5

ISSN 0269-2244

A CIP catalogue record for this book is available
from the British Library

The publisher has no responsibility for the continued existence or accuracy of
URLs for external or third-party internet websites referred to in this book, and
does not guarantee that any content on such websites is, or will remain, accurate
or appropriate

This publication is printed on acid-free paper

Typeset by Fakenham Prepress Solutions, Fakenham, Norfolk NR21 8NL

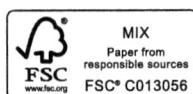

MIX
Paper from
responsible sources
FSC
www.fsc.org   FSC® C013056

Printed and bound in Great Britain by
TJ International Ltd, Padstow, Cornwall

FOR HOWARD AND SUSAN HULME

Contents

List of figures   viii

Acknowledgements   x

Abbreviations   xii

Introduction: after the shock city   1

1   Citizenship and the interwar city   18

2   Urban utopias and education   47

3   Celebrating the city   71

4   History, progress and community performance   107

5   The citizen of tomorrow   136

6   Civic culture and welfare   167

Conclusion: after the citizenship city   198

Bibliography   215

Index   245

List of Figures

1. A civics class in progress at Association House in Chicago
(c. 1930s), Chicago History Museum, ICHi-030505   59

2. The Pageant of Progress under construction on Chicago's
Municipal Pier (1921), Chicago History Museum, ICHi-020785
(N. McDonald, photographer)   75

3. Entertainment during the Pageant of Progress (1921), Chicago
History Musuem, ICHi-014116   75

4. Manchester's gothic Town Hall (1877) and contemporary extension
(1938) (photograph Tom Hulme, 2018)   80

5. Mayor Miles Ewart Mitchell and civic dignitaries opening
Manchester Civic Week (1926), Manchester City Archives,
Photographs of Port Canal activities, GB124.B10/3/2177   82

6. Mayor Miles Ewart Mitchell beginning the opening parade
of Manchester Civic Week (1926), Manchester City Archives,
Photographs of Port Canal activities, GB124.B10/3/2177   83

7. Commemorative brochure of municipal government published for
Chicago's Jubilee (1937), Chicago History Museum, ICHi-173728   95

8. The 'Civic Tree' that grew from Manchester's 1838 incorporation
(1938), Manchester City Archives, *Pictorial Finance*, Manchester
1938, 4, M68/21/3/9   99

9. Model showing ratepayers 'where the money goes' during
Manchester's centenary celebrations (1938), Manchester City
Archives, Incorporation Centenary Exhibition, m07359   101

10. Illuminated bus during Manchester's centenary celebrations (1938),
Manchester City Archives, Illuminated bus municipal centenary,
m48240   101

11. Post-impressionist style front cover of the Manchester Historical
Pageant programme (1938), Manchester City Archives, *Manchester
Historical Pageant*, Manchester 1938, B127.M740/2/8/2/39   111

12. Father Time leads weary children away from the city in the
Manchester Historical Pageant (1938), Manchester City Archives,
Manchester centenary celebrations, M61984   115

13. From ancient Africa to modern America on the cover of O, Sing a
New Song (1934), Chicago History Museum, ICHi-089150   129

14. Group associated with early Bud Billiken Parade: Noble Sissle, David Kellum, Duke Ellington, Nathan McGill, unidentified, Earl Father Hines, and unidentified (c. 1930s), Chicago History Museum, ICHi-038800   131

15. University of Manchester Settlement's 'Round House', Manchester City Archives, Manchester University Settlement, Ancoats, Round House, M08520   152

16. Boys waiting in line to enter the YMCA in Chicago (Dec. 1933), Chicago History Museum, ICHi-173723 (N. C. Drevalas, photographer)   153

17. Children in front of Association House (c. 1930s), Chicago History Museum, ICHi-173725   154

18. Acrobats on a float during the Chicago Boys' Week opening parade (1923), Chicago History Museum, ICHi-173727   155

19. Reserve officers' training corps procession during Chicago Boys' Week Federation (1923), Chicago History Museum, ICHi-173727   156

20. Boys playing ping pong at the YMCA in Chicago (c. 1930s), Chicago History Museum, ICHi-173724 (N. C. Drevalas, photographer)   156

21. Youths in the gym of the Grove House Lads Club (c. 1937), Manchester City Archives, Grove House Lads Club, GB124. DPA/2421/20   160

22. Typical 'slum property' in Miles Platting area of Manchester (c. 1930s), Manchester City Archives, Miles Platting, Barratt Street, m29756   186

23. Substandard housing in Chicago's Near North Side, proposed site of Frances Cabrini homes, Chicago History Museum, ICHi-17372   187

24. Blackley Housing Estate in Manchester (c. 1920s), Manchester City Archives, Blackley, Victoria Avenue, M14790   192

25. Trumbull Park Homes in Chicago (opened 1938), Chicago History Museum, Hedrich-Blessing Collection, HB-12520-C   193

The author and publisher acknowledge with thanks the following for permission to reproduce material in their collections: the Chicago History Museum for the cover illustration and for figures 1–3, 7, 13–14, 16–20, 23 and 25; and the Manchester City Archives for figures 5–6, 8–12, 15, 21–2 and 24. Every effort has been made to trace the copyright holders for all images; apologies are offered for any omission, and the publishers will be pleased to add any necessary acknowledgement in subsequent editions.

Acknowledgements

This book began its life in Leicester almost a decade ago, and throughout the (far too many) years it has taken me to finish it I have relied on the support of many colleagues, friends and family members. Three people deserve special mention at the outset. Simon Gunn has been an exceptional source of encouragement for over a decade, believing in me when I was an undergraduate and pushing me to achieve my best in the years since. Without his mentoring, I am certain that I would not be writing these acknowledgements at all. Paul Readman has also been central to my academic development. He gave me my first job, but went above and beyond simply being a 'boss' by helping me navigate the difficult postdoctoral world. Both have given more help than I could have possibly imagined. The final thanks should be given to Roey Sweet, though, who introduced me to urban history as an undergraduate and set me on this path.

Many other friends and colleagues have kindly commented on earlier versions or drafts of the manuscript: Miriam Cady, Mark Freeman, Dion Georgiou, Katie Palmer Heathman, George Lewis, Peter Mandler, Gisela Mettele, Nik Ribiansky, Douglas Tallack, Zoe Thomas, Frank Trentmann, Martha Vandrei, Melli Velazquez and Keira Williams. Any oversights are still, of course, my own. Bernhard Rieger and Christine Linehan, on behalf of the Royal History Society Studies in History series, have both given me vital advice in preparing the manuscript. Colleagues at the Centre for Urban History (University of Leicester), King's College London, the Centre for Metropolitan History (University of London) and Queen's University Belfast have provided support and advice.

Friends in Belfast, Buxton, Chicago, Leicester and London have listened as I've fretted and moaned about writing (or, at least, facilitated my avoidance). Too many to mention, but a few should be picked out: Gill Murray and Gary Davies, who were brilliant office mates in Leicester; Mikey Fox, Daniel Bailess and Alexey Morozov, who are always reliable drinking pals in London; Greg Lash, Jonathan Grossman, Charles 'Chuck' Edwards, Melissa Rose and Caitlin Kuzik, who helped me settle into American life; Jack Gregory, Dan Bradd, the Mellor brothers and many more in Buxton who always make going home such fun; and new friends in Belfast, a place where I knew no one when I left England, particularly Kieran Connell and Floris Verhaart. Special mentions, however, must go to Joe Frazer, who has been a constant rock of support, and Cormac McAteer, who has made settling down into my new Northern Irish life so enjoyable.

Material from chapters 2 and 4 has previously appeared in 'Putting the city back into citizenship: civics education and local government in Britain,

1918-1945', *Twentieth Century British History* xxvi/1 (2015), 26–51; 'Putting the city back into citizenship: civics textbooks and municipal government in the interwar American city', in Michael Fortner and Amy Bridges (eds), *Urban citizenship and American democracy: the historical and institutional roots of local politics and policy*, New York, NY 2016; and '"A nation of town criers": civic publicity and historical pageantry in interwar Britain', *Urban History* xliv/2 (2017), 270–92. My thanks to Oxford University Press, SUNY Press and Cambridge University Press respectively for permission to include the same material here. Photographs are reproduced with the permission of the Chicago History Museum and the Manchester City Archives. Thanks also to the Economic and Social Research Council, which funded the first few years of this research (no. ES/I903089/1).

My interest in the focus of this book started with Manchester Civic Week – a spectacular festival that took place in October 1926. A year either side of this celebration, my Granddads – Joe Hulme and Ken Brown – were taking their first breaths just twenty or so miles away in Derbyshire. They both passed away in the final months before this book was finished, and so did not live to see me in print. I hope that they would have been proud.

Tom Hulme
December 2018

Abbreviations

CHM	Chicago History Museum
MCA	Manchester City Archives
CD	*Chicago Defender*
CT	*Chicago Tribune*
EHR	*English Historical Review*
HJ	*Historical Journal*
JAH	*Journal of American History*
JBS	*Journal of British Studies*
JUH	*Journal of Urban History*
MG	*Manchester Guardian*
P&P	*Past & Present*

Introduction: After the Shock City

On a March afternoon in 1921 an unusual scene unfolded in front of the city hall of Chicago. As a brass band played, onlookers stopped to watch four elephants marching down the street. On the flank of each was a sign advertising an upcoming 'Pageant of Progress'.[1] Masterminded by the city's eccentric mayor, William 'Big Bill' Thompson, this event took place over fifteen days on the Municipal Pier that jutted out into Lake Michigan. Several hundred of Chicago's firms presented exhibits that illustrated the strides in science and industry made in the three decades since the city's famous World's Fair of 1893. Entertainments, such as diving competitions, street parades and Venetian singing, took place alongside the exhibition. Billed locally as 'the greatest national exposition ever held', it was a characteristic testament to the 'I Will' spirit of Chicago – though onlookers may have seen it as just another brass claim from the 'Windy City'.[2] Five years later, and over 3,800 miles away across the Atlantic Ocean, a strikingly similar event was held in the British city of Manchester. If the announcement of 'Civic Week' lacked the extravagance of elephants, a banner hung from the town hall proclaimed a comparable message: 'The City keeps open house and provides a wealth of attractions. Invite your friends and tell them to bring their curiosity.'[3] Mancunians from all sections of society could tour municipal buildings, utility works, factories and a textile exhibition. The programme of events also included entertainment, from singing and dancing to pageants and parades. Mayor Miles Ewart Mitchell boasted that 'No city in the world has greater resources for such a display' and claimed that the Civic Week would 'attract universal attention'.[4]

If civic leaders in Manchester and Chicago were outwardly confident, the economic background of each celebration was gloomier. Both cities depended on industry and commerce and had suffered big falls in production and trade when the brief post-war boom ended. Unemployment was accordingly rising rapidly. Each mayor assured local industrial employers, and the public more generally, that the events would stimulate business, create a demand for labour and help to solve the downturn.[5] Urban boosterism – the decision to promote

---

[1]   'Pageant', *Chicago Tribune*, 27 Mar. 1921, 5.

[2]   'No end of spectacular events' (1921), and 'The Pageant of Progress Exposition: a typical Chicago exhibition' (1921), in Pageant of Progress Exposition miscellaneous pamphlets, CHM, F38MZ.1921.P14.

[3]   'City's open house', *Manchester Evening News*, 7 Sept. 1926, 8.

[4]   'Manchester's "Civic Week"', MG, 9 June 1926, 13.

[5]   'William Thompson letter to businessmen' (1921), in Pageant of Progress Exposition miscellaneous pamphlets, CHM, F38MZ.1921.P14; 'Report of the first meeting of the Civic

place for financial gain – provided the immediate catalyst.[6] But this was not the only purpose. Mitchell, in the Civic Week official handbook, insisted that 'the real wish of all concerned' was for local people to 'see the customary conduct of the establishment', and he frequently explained how the success of the Week depended on the cooperation and enthusiasm of all in the city.[7] Big Bill's Pageant of Progress also went further than just economic goals. The *Chicago Tribune*, not a slavish supporter of the mayor by any means, still described how the exposition would awaken both the country and the wider world 'to the importance of the city'.[8] The people of Chicago were, for Thompson, the direct target: the 'great educational force' of the pageant would, he argued, combine their 'thousands of minds' into 'a new and harmonious civic spirit'.[9] These festivals were, in the eyes of their supporters, a popular and participatory way to build urban community.

Chicago and Manchester shared more in this period than just their decision to host ambitious celebrations. Each could make a claim to contemporary national importance, and even second city status, as regional *entrepôts* and engines of national economic growth. Coupled with this commercial power, in the eyes of their champions, was a proud sense that they were cities of culture in art, theatre, music and more. For the historians Asa Briggs and Harold Platt they also occupied a mutual historical position as 'shock cities': new industrial and mercantile giants that were distinctly different from older trade centres and imperial capitals, and places that heralded the coming of a new social, economic and political age.[10] Their journey and arrival at this status took place at different times, though, and at speeds and intensities that reflected broader national patterns and timeframes of urbanisation as well as their own histories.

Manchester claimed pre-modern heritage back to the Romans and was already an important proto-industrial town and provincial centre of the north of Britain by the late eighteenth century, with a population of around 76,000 in 1791. The industrial revolution, however, transformed the town into a city and 'Cottonopolis': a place of national importance. By 1831 its population

Week Advisory Committee', 23 Mar. 1926, 3, in Miscellaneous souvenirs of Manchester Civic Week, MCA, MSC942.7391.

[6]   See Stephen V. Ward, *Selling places: the marketing and promotion of towns and cities, 1850–2000*, London 1998.

[7]   *Manchester Civic Week: official handbook*, Manchester 1926, 27, MCA, M68/11.

[8]   'Pageant, trade born, rises to heights of art', CT, 21 July 1921, 17. The *Tribune* criticised Thompson for his corruption and idiocy, and for making 'Chicago a byword for the collapse of American civilization': Lloyd Wendt, *Chicago Tribune: the rise of a great American newspaper*, Chicago, IL 1979, 545.

[9]   'William Thompson letter to businessmen'; *Greater Chicago 1*, no. 7 (Mar. 1921), 4, CHM, F38AP.g79.

[10]   Asa Briggs, *Victorian cities* (1963), Berkeley, CA 1993; Harold Platt, *Shock cities: the environmental transformation and reform of Manchester and Chicago*, Chicago, IL 2005.

had grown to 187,000, and to 316,000 just twenty years later.[11] Britain, by the mid-nineteenth century, was unchallenged in its status as the first industrial nation. Between 1801 and 1841 the urban population doubled and, by the mid part of the century, over 40 per cent of the population lived in cities of more than 100,000 people.[12] Manchester's 'shocking' moment consequently came early, in the 1830s. Some, such as Friedrich Engels, were horrified by the filth, poverty and segregation of the classes; whereas others, such as James Kay-Shuttleworth, were concerned about a perceived growing immorality. More generally, as the century went on and urbanisation continued, hysterical commentators began to see the industrial poor as a race apart, and a cause-and-effect of social breakdown that could even threaten the ascendancy of both nation and Empire.[13]

Chicago, at the point that Manchester was declared a frightening harbinger of the world to come, was just a small Midwest settler's town of a few thousand. By the 1840s, however, the city had begun to grow, serving as a gateway between the industrialising north-east and the rural frontier west. By the 1860s its population had reached over 100,000, as it absorbed growing immigration from the Old World to the New as well as internal migration from rural to urban. In the next few decades Chicago's population increased at a world-leading rate: 503,000 in 1880, over 1,000,000 by 1890 (overtaking Philadelphia to become the second largest city in the country) and 2,200,000 by 1910.[14] As with Manchester in Britain, Chicago encapsulated the transition of the US to a fundamentally and irreversibly urban nation – a position officially reached in around 1920 when over 50 per cent of the population was defined as 'urban' by census takers.[15] In the 1880s and 1890s, with entwined problems of political corruption, crime and ethnic conflict, Chicago accordingly became America's own 'shock city'. When the visiting British journalist W. T. Stead, in an 1893

[11]   Alan Kidd, *Manchester* (1993), Edinburgh 2002, 14, 1–10, 13–29.

[12]   Pamela Sharpe, 'Population and society, 1700–1840', in Peter Clark (ed.), *The Cambridge urban history of Britain*, II: *1540–1840*, Cambridge 2000, 501.

[13]   Briggs, *Victorian cities*, 89–96; Platt, *Shock cities*, 3–23. For contemporary accounts see Alexis de Tocqueville, *Journeys to England and Ireland*, trans. George Lawrence and K. P. Mayer, ed. J. P. Mayer, London 1957, 104–10; James Kay-Shuttleworth, *The moral and physical condition of the working class employed in the cotton manufacture in Manchester*, London 1832; and Friedrich Engels, *The condition of the working class in England in 1844*, London 1892. As historians have pointed out, this impression of the working class tended to miss the diversity of their lives. See 'Introduction' to Andrew Davies, Steven Fielding and Terry Wyke (eds), *Workers' worlds: cultures and communities in Manchester and Salford, 1880–1939*, Manchester 1992, 1–20.

[14]   John F. McDonald, *Chicago: an economic history*, Abingdon 2016, 24–84; William Cronon, *Nature's metropolis: Chicago and the great West*, New York, NY 1991.

[15]   David E. Kyvig, *Daily life in the United States, 1920–1939: decades of promise and pain*, Westport, CT 2002, 8–9. Defined as any place with 2,500 residents or more. Of the 54,000,000, 27,000,000 lived in cities of over 100,000, with another 17,000,000 in places of 10,000 to 100,000.

best-selling *exposé*, wondered 'If Christ came to Chicago' what 'would He think of us and of our lives', he colourfully captured broader fears about racial 'purity', immorality and the future direction of the US as an emerging world power.[16]

The local response to rapid urbanisation in Manchester and Chicago, at the different times that they emerged as most 'shocking', was similar. Coalitions of voluntary associations and municipal reformers, often supported by the emerging central state, recognised the prosperity and national pride that came with commercial success, and so did not reject the city. Instead, they aimed to overcome the worst excesses of unregulated economic growth by forging a superior urban culture, one which guided the lives of the working classes or immigrants through the physical and moral improvement of the city.[17] Such civic action, by the end of the nineteenth century, became part of a wider exchange of intellectual and practical thinking on cities that 'intercrossed' the Atlantic. A convergence of experience and ideology, from sanitary experts to town planners, meant that a broad sense of urban problems and solutions could be articulated by politicians, academics and reformers.[18]

There were, of course, also key differences between the two cities. Chicago's population started at a significantly lower point in the nineteenth century yet still outstripped Manchester to become one of the largest cities in the world by 1900. More pressing for Chicago's reformers than the speed of growth was the stench of political corruption that hung over the youthful metropolis. Proponents of civic betterment also had to contend with an entrenched and often *laissez-faire* business leadership, and a general culture that viewed public ownership with suspicion.[19] Manchester, in contrast, boasted a solid municipal tradition by 1900 – and one that was increasingly supported by an interventionist state at the central level too.[20] Most importantly, when it came to defining who was included in the urban community, was the issue of race and immigration. In the USA, and in cities such as Chicago especially, consideration of the European immigrants pouring into the 'melting pot' – as well as those that were legally denied assimilation, such as Asians and African

---

[16] See W. T. Stead, *If Christ came to Chicago: a plea for the union of all who love in the service of all who suffer*, Chicago, IL 1894.

[17] For a British overview, including Manchester, see Tristram Hunt, *Building Jerusalem: the rise and fall of the Victorian city*, London 2004, 189–380. For the US see Frederic Cople Jaher, *The urban establishment: upper strata in Boston, New York, Charleston, Chicago, and Los Angeles*, Urbana, IL 1982. This volume includes a chapter on Chicago.

[18] Daniel T. Rodgers, *Atlantic crossings: social politics in a progressive age*, London 1998.

[19] Gail Radford, 'From municipal socialism to public authorities: institutional factors in the shaping of American public enterprise', *JAH* xc (2003), 874. See, for an overview, Jon Teaford, *The twentieth-century American city: problem, promise and reality*, Baltimore, MD 1986, 31–44.

[20] Arthur Redford, *The history of local government in Manchester, III: The last half century*, London 1940.

4

Americans – steered the discussions of society and citizenship.[21] There was a 'Britannic melting pot' effect at play in the industrial cities of Britain, with the migration of Irish Catholics and, later in the nineteenth century, Jews as well, leading to some inter-ethnic conflict.[22] But British cities were certainly not as diverse as American cities, and – apart from a few small communities in London and other ports – lacked a significant black population. If direct clashes were less apparent, however, racial 'othering' and categorisation was still a part of how the establishment constructed the essence of national identity and citizenship in the age of empire.[23]

A path of comparative civic stability and consolidation in these two cities, despite these key differences in context and timeframe, can be traced from the nineteenth into the twentieth century. Enough reform had taken place by the 1920s to mean that, when coupled with the increasing familiarity of modern urban life, a rhetoric of urban transformation had a sufficient anchoring in reality in both countries. A similar story of progress could feasibly be told by civic elites in events such as Civic Week or the Pageant of Progress – one in which municipal and voluntary action had triumphed over the unruly and unhealthy city of the past.[24] But the earnestness of interwar city elites to fashion this narrative suggests that they retained some of the doubts of their civic forebears about urban society.[25] For many observers, from sociologists to civic reformers, the modern city continued to be damaging: a threat to community and good citizenship rather than its natural home. Aftershocks of the nineteenth- and early twentieth-century city combined with new social and political fears in the 1920s – such as enfranchisement, political radicalism, the continued growth of mass leisure and shifting gender relations – as both countries readjusted to peace after the First World War.

Utopian planners, and the movements that they inspired, romanticised the countryside and hoped to mitigate city problems by constructing more rational planned settlements far beyond the urban boundary. Replacing the city, they argued, would create healthier and more virtuous citizens. Apart from some small successes in decanting the urban population, however, such as Letchworth Garden City in England or the New Deal-era Greenbelt towns in the US, large industrial cities continued to grow.[26] It was a more realistic

---

[21] Gary Gerstle, *American crucible: race and nation in the twentieth century*, Princeton, NJ 2001, chs i–iii.

[22] Hugh Kearney, *The British Isles: a history of four nations*, Cambridge 1989, ch. ix.

[23] See, for example, Catherine Hall, *Civilising subjects: metropole and colony in the English imagination, 1830–1867*, Chicago, IL 2002.

[24] See W. Barker (ed.), *Your city: Manchester, 1838–1938*, Manchester 1938, and Chicago Association of Commerce, *Survey of Chicago: twenty-first anniversary of the Chicago Association of Commerce*, Chicago, IL 1925.

[25] Andrew Lees, *Cities perceived: urban society in European and American thought, 1820–1940*, Manchester 1985, 105–88.

[26] See Stephen V. Ward, 'The Garden City introduced', Frederick H. A. Aalen, 'English

prospect for experts, officials and volunteers to remake urban culture, a process that had begun in the previous century, than it was for them to dismantle and relocate the city. It is on this process of reshaping the city and its culture that this book focuses. Detailing the pursuit of urban community building can encourage historians to reassess the importance of the local and the urban within the national paradigm, and to historicise the trajectory of citizenship ideology in the twentieth century in a distinctly different way.

Putting the city back into citizenship

Prioritising the importance of the city to citizenship in the twentieth century is something of a revisionist argument. With the global turn in the final decades of the twentieth century, scholars have often stripped cities of their primacy in citizenship debates in favour of a national/global dichotomy that gives little relevance to locality. Late medieval and early modern European states, where membership of the social body was linked to the locality through rank or profession, are often seen to be a high point of local citizenship. The eighteenth century, however, heralded the 'dawn of the age of nationalism', after which distinctly national membership categories began to take over.[27] Certainly, by the late nineteenth and early twentieth centuries, citizenship was a term used to denote membership of the nation state. Corresponding rights (such as medical provision or the vote) and responsibilities (such as taxes or military service), whether granted through birth or earned through naturalisation, were usually enshrined in national law.[28]

Legal membership of the nation also came with parallel social and cultural characteristics that affected the understanding and articulation of citizenship. In Britain, a gendered and racialised sense of 'Englishness' had begun to challenge localism and provincial identity by the early twentieth century and was put to work by politicians and elites who were trying to mould a responsible working

---

origins', and Daniel Schaffer, 'The American Garden City: lost ideals', in Stephen V. Ward (ed.), *The Garden City: past, present and future*, London 1992, 1–27, 28–51, 127–45.

[27] Benedict Anderson, *Imagined communities: reflections on the origin and spread of nationalism*, London 1983, 11. For the early modern period see Andreas Fahrmeir and H. S. Jones, 'Space and belonging in modern Europe: citizenship(s) in localities, regions, and states', *European Review of History* xv/3 (2008), 243–53. For criticisms of how the national and global turn has obscured or undervalued the urban see James Holston and Arjun Appadurai, 'Cities and citizenship', *Public Culture* viii (1996), 188, and William Whyte and Oliver Zimmer, 'Introduction', in William Whyte and Oliver Zimmer (eds), *Nationalism and the reshaping of urban communities in Europe, 1848–1914*, Basingstoke 2011, 1–16.

[28] For essays on historical interpretations of citizenship see Gershon Shafir (ed.), *The citizenship debates: a reader*, Minneapolis, MN 1998. For contemporary theorising see Peter Dwyer, *Understanding social citizenship: themes and perspectives for policy and practice*, Bristol 2004; Keith Faulks, *Citizenship*, London 2000; and Derek Heater, *What is citizenship?* Cambridge 1999.

class – one that was 'safe' to participate in increasingly democratic political systems.[29] National and imperial identities also persisted in new forms in the 1920s and 1930s, altered, but not necessarily diminished, by the First World War. Public remembrances such as Armistice Day, and new institutions such as the BBC, bolstered the feeling of a national character, while yearly celebrations such as Empire Day (institutionalised in 1904) continued. Citizenship lost the more aggressive aspects of imperialism that had been common in the Edwardian period, but the nation and its empire remained important markers of identity in the 1920s.[30] In the US, too, allegiance to the nation was growing. Fears about mass immigration, coupled with a wave of popular patriotism during the First World War, shaped a resurgent sense of national identity in the opening decades of the twentieth century – one that focused on 'American' cultural values, symbols and practices.[31] Conservative organisations and movements for both men and women, such as the American Legion and its women's auxiliary or the Women's Patriotic Conference on National Defense, encouraged a citizenship based on literacy, patriotic rituals and 'a reverential, unquestioning view of American history'.[32] Following the end of the war, demands for '100 percent Americanism', a term coined by Theodore Roosevelt in 1915, continued. Signs of cultural or economic nonconformity – such as labour strikes and communism – were portrayed as being contrary to what it meant to be a 'true' American. This led to a rabidly nationalistic and paranoid atmosphere of 'hyper-patriotism' in the 1920s – one that surged again in the late 1930s in response to the prospect of another global conflict.[33]

A growth in national feeling, however, did not equate to an eclipse of the local, and cities were still central to citizenship in the first half of the twentieth

---

[29]   Brian Doyle, 'The invention of English', in Robert Colls and Philip Dodd (eds), *Englishness: culture and politics, 1880–1920*, Beckenham 1986, 113–40; Stephen Heathorn, *For home, country, and race: constructing gender, class and Englishness in the elementary school, 1880–1914*, Toronto 2000, 4–25.

[30]   See Richard Weight and Abigail Beach (eds), *The right to belong: citizenship and national identity in Britain, 1930–1960*, London 1988; Brad Beaven and John Griffiths, 'Creating the exemplary citizen: the changing notion of citizenship in Britain, 1870–1939', *Contemporary British History* xxii/2 (2008), 211–12; Julia Stapleton, 'Citizenship versus patriotism in twentieth-century England', *HJ* xlviii/1 (2005), 164–6; and Jim English, 'Empire Day in Britain, 1904–1958', *HJ* xlix/1 (2006), 247–76. Not all historians are convinced by the contemporary power of imperial discourse in British culture, however: see Bernard Porter, *Absent-minded imperialists: what the British really thought about empire*, Oxford 2004.

[31]   Christopher Capozzola, *Uncle Sam wants you: World War I and the making of the modern citizen*, Oxford 2008.

[32]   Christina A. Ziegler-McPherson, *Americanization in the States: immigrant social welfare policy, citizenship and national identity in the United States, 1908–1929*, Gainesville, FL 2009, 10. For the conference see Christine K. Erickson, '"So much for men": conservative women and national defense in the 1920s and 1930s', *American Studies* xlv/1 (2004), 85–102.

[33]   Cecilia E. O'Leary, *To die for: the paradox of American patriotism*, Princeton, NJ 1999; William E. Leuchtenburg, *The perils of prosperity, 1914–1932*, Chicago, IL 1993; John Higham, 'Hanging together: divergent unities in American history', *JAH* lxi/1 (1974), 27–8.

century. This was for three linked reasons. Firstly, as Linda Colley has so aptly put it: 'Identities are not like hats. Human beings can and do put on several at a time.'[34] Pride in the local community was often complementary to national or imperial ideas of patriotism. Identity, in a sense, worked as a form of 'nested citizenship'.[35] Individuals could see themselves as belonging to their neighbourhood, city, nation and empire as well as religious, ethnic or classed communities, and act on behalf of each of those groups – sometimes singularly, sometimes in combination. Urban elites, for their part, neither sought nor expected the rejection of non-urban ideas of belonging – though city dwellers were sometimes asked to prioritise their home town over other competing loyalties. In the main, however, there was no conflict between being loyal to Manchester or Chicago as well as to England and Britain or the USA. On the contrary, it was in the local and the city that national understandings of identity and belonging could find expression.[36] Those that attempted to create citizenship in the city did so by forming an emotive narrative of urban identity and progress – past, present and future – and connecting it to broader beliefs in national advancement. If nations are 'imagined' because of the inability of their members to meet or know each other, as Benedict Anderson so famously reasoned, the city was an environment where the imagined could be made more real.[37]

Secondly, the urban context directly informed the strategies of intervention that were used to shape citizenship. Reformers, investigators and sociologists consistently sought to understand the effects, both positive and negative, of urban life on health and behaviour. Though each country had accepted its urban future by the interwar period, large cities could still be labelled as a cause of social disintegration. Yet, for pragmatic shapers of citizenship, pride

[34] Linda Colley, *Britons: forging the nation, 1707–1837*, London 1994, 6.

[35] Peter Kivisto and Thomas Faist, *Citizenship: discourse, theory, and transnational prospects*, Oxford 2007, 122. They specify 'nested citizenship' as the levels of legal citizenship above the nation; I contend, however, that it also applies to levels below – and for belonging and identity as well.

[36] For comparable examples see the combination of local politics and boosterish interests with national patriotism in the siting of American historical monuments in John E. Bodnar, *Remaking America: public memory, commemoration, and patriotism in the twentieth century*, Princeton, NJ 1992; how local citizenship fed into larger narratives of national and imperial duty in Portsmouth in Melanie Bassett, 'Regional societies and the migrant Edwardian Royal Dockyard worker: locality, nation and empire', in Naomi Lloyd-Jones and Margaret M. Scull (eds), *Four nations approaches to modern 'British' history: a (dis)United Kingdom?* London 2018, 189–214; and the intersection of local and national patriotic identities during wartime in David Monger, *Patriotism and propaganda in First World War Britain: the National War Aims Committee and civilian morale*, Liverpool 2012, ch. iii. See also case studies from across Europe, the Americas and Asia in Michael P. Smith and Thomas Bender (eds), *City and nation: rethinking place and identity* (2001), New York, NY 2017, and Whyte and Zimmer, *Nationalism*.

[37] Anderson, *Imagined communities*, 6. See also Timothy J. Lombardo, 'Making urban citizens: civility and civic virtue in the modern metropolis', *JUH* xli/1 (2014), 143–51.

in the city and its success could still be the way to transform society. Those that attempted to form community and belonging in Britain and the US accordingly continued to work in the city in the first half of the twentieth century: firstly, through urban organisations and networks, from municipal councils to voluntary or charitable bodies; and secondly, in response to the physical environment, whether the civic centre and downtown or the shame of the slums. Local and national government saw intervention in the lives of the working classes especially as a way to mould a citizen that measured up to economic and military goals in an increasingly competitive global environment. The everyday 'terrains' of government – such as leisure, welfare and education – were still under the jurisdiction of municipal councils until at least the 1940s, even if larger governmental units played an important role in setting the political framework.[38] Civic elites, through these different areas of life, had access to the minds and bodies of urban dwellers and worked on both to create healthy citizens.

Finally, urban life encouraged the mixing of people and their identities in ways that could also change the rules, meanings and practices of citizenship.[39] The city was a place where rights and responsibilities were received and enacted yet also negotiated and challenged. Public and semi-public space, from streets and stadiums to classrooms and club rooms, framed how individuals and groups could display or perform their membership of the urban and national community – or, indeed, challenge the basis of their exclusion. Municipal government and local reformers alike believed that 'active citizenship', the contribution of the individual to improving both themselves and society, functioned better when it came in response to the city in which one lived and worked. Consequently, they encouraged enthusiastic action from participants in their projects of civic pride. But life in the modern metropolis was a ceaseless struggle between the control or 'production' of space by the governors of the city and the subversive or adaptable responses by those that were being governed.[40] Urban elites may have sought to regulate urban life to invoke civic feeling, but their power over that response was rarely assured or unchallenged; when this conflict became apparent, understandings of citizenship could be reshaped.

An active civic culture of government and associations attempted to mould a sense of citizenship at multiple units and levels, from families and home to

---

[38]   Engin F. Isin, 'The city as the site of the social', in Engin F. Isin (ed.), *Recasting the social in citizenship*, Toronto 2008, 273.

[39]   Holston and Appadurai, 'Cities and citizenship', 88.

[40]   Scholarship on urban space has shifted from builders or architects and toward the 'vernacular' of how ordinary people shaped or 'produced' urban life: Geoff D. Zylstra, 'Productions of space, productions of power: studying space, urban design, and social relations', *JUH* xliii/3 (2017), 562–9. For the theorists that have set the agenda see, in particular, Michel de Certeau, *The practice of everyday life*, Berkeley, CA 1984, and Henri Lefebvre, *The production of space*, Oxford 1991.

neighbourhoods and the whole city. The combination of these three areas of citizenship debate and construction - identity, intervention and practices - meant that the city was still vital across the late nineteenth to mid-twentieth century. This book traces urban identity and belonging across several areas of life and concentrates on the 1920s and 1930s especially - a period when urbanity was assured in Britain and the US, yet the experience of past shocking growth continued to shape the discourse of citizenship. To more specifically theorise this experience of continuity and change from the nineteenth century into the twentieth, it is useful to return to debates, awakened by the postmodern turn, about the when, where and what of the tricky concept of 'modernity'.

Urban modernity and transnational history

Historians have come relatively late to the conceptualising of modernity, only contributing substantially to the discussion since the early 1990s.[41] In the years since, however, this concept has grown in popularity and been historicised in a variety of places, periods and forms - from the Enlightenment understanding of knowledge to the interwar *avant-garde* of modernist art, literature and architecture. This outpouring means that scholars have begun to challenge 'the study of the process of modernisation or one monolithic modernity or process' and are now more likely to investigate 'modernities'.[42] If a crude generality can be drawn across the competing definitions or conceptualisations, it is an element of rupture: a distinctive and often conscious break with the past.[43] Little wonder, then, that writers in the past understood modernity through the turbulent changes that accompanied industrialisation and urbanisation. For thinkers at the turn of the twentieth century, such as Georg Simmel and Walter Benjamin, it was the intensification of the relationship between capitalism and urban growth in the nineteenth century that led to the emergence of a new and distinctly modern experience - and a different urban-dweller as a consequence. Disconnected from the intimacy of traditional rural or small-town life, and socially and mentally adrift in the maelstrom of urbanity, the individualised metropolitan inhabitant sought meaning and pleasure in a spiralling demand for the stimulation of their senses.[44]

---

[41] Simon Gunn, *History and cultural theory*, Harlow 2006, 107–8.

[42] Bernhard Rieger and Martin Daunton, 'Introduction', to Martin Daunton and Bernard Rieger (eds), *Meanings of modernity: Britain from the late-Victorian era to World War II*, Oxford 2001, 4.

[43] Lynn Hunt, *Measuring time, making history*, Budapest 2008, 47–91.

[44] See Georg Simmel, 'The metropolis and mental life' (1903), in Donald N. Levine (ed.), *On individuality and social forms: selected writings of Georg Simmel*, Chicago, IL 1971, 324–39 and Walter Benjamin, 'Paris, capital of the nineteenth century' (1939), *Perspecta* xii (1969), 163–72.

In more recent years, theorists and historians have reasserted the importance of the city. For the influential writer Marshall Berman, it was also the taking root of capitalism in cities that created a different mindset. Drawing directly on Marx and his *Communist manifesto*, he typified modernity as an urban experience: 'to find ourselves in an environment that promises us adventure, power, joy, growth, transformation of ourselves and the world – and, at the same time, that threatens to destroy everything we have, everything we know, everything we are'.[45] Lyn Hollen Lees and Andrew Lees, writing in the British socio-economic urban history tradition, have similarly argued that cities were 'the places where modernity began and where it reached its zenith'.[46] James Vernon, recently reacting against the confusion brought by the turn towards multiple 'modernities', has specifically foregrounded rapid population growth as the central facilitator of modernity. Both the increased mobility of that population and, vitally, its urban concentration, created a new and distinctly modern 'society of strangers' in Britain. This process, he argued, began to reshape social relations in the eighteenth century, from the level of the individual to the state that governed them, with the full nature of its effects becoming apparent by the mid-nineteenth century.[47] If modernity, then, can be best understood as a consequence of sustained urban growth, rapidly swelling industrial cities played a particularly important role: it was in these places that the 'shock of the new' was most keenly felt.

Though an important part of modernity was the sense of a historical break, 'the past' did not disappear with the urban transformations of the nineteenth and early twentieth centuries. In large and rapidly growing industrial places it was the origins of the modern city that provided the logic for the reform of urban culture. Contemporaries understood the present problems and solutions of urban life in a long perspective. The historic 'character' of the city – its seeming ability to adapt and evolve in response to rapid change and dislocation – provided the framework for urban redevelopment. This 'ongoing dialogue between past and present', and the 'remaking' of the former to serve as a 'restitutive link' to the latter, happened across many different aspects of urban culture in the first half of the twentieth century.[48] From the continuing centrality of historic civic architecture and established municipal rituals, to the stories told about an engrained civic character that had survived the 'shock', the transition to modernity was never as simple as a rejection of the urban

---

[45] Marshall Berman, *All that is solid melts into air: the experience of modernity*, New York, NY 1982, 15.

[46] Andrew Lees and Lynn Hollen Lees, *Cities and the making of modern Europe, 1750–1914*, Cambridge 2007, 2.

[47] James Vernon, *Distant strangers: how Britain became modern*, Berkeley, CA 2014, 1–7.

[48] Richard Dennis, *Cities in modernity: representations and productions of metropolitan space, 1840–1930*, Cambridge 2008, 1. For the 'restitutive link' see George Behlmer, discussed in Peter Mandler, 'How modern is it?', *JBS* xlii/2 (2003), 277.

past. For cities, 'history, modernity, and particularity' were 'inseparable and mutually constituted'.[49]

To put it simply, the distinctive history of the shock city continued to shape its experience of modernity in the period that followed. By the end of the nineteenth century the popular understanding of the modern condition surpassed a focus on the direct consequences of industrial development, and took account of the social, political and cultural effects of living in an industrial society.[50] As increased population and capitalist processes defined the physical form and experience of the city, there were corresponding active responses to reshaping urban space and culture. These began in the nineteenth century, but clearly continued in the twentieth, with ramifications for the representation, performance and practice of urban belonging.[51] As Vernon points out, the new forms of governmental or bureaucratic abstraction and estrangement that modernity enabled also 'catalysed attempts to re-embed social, economic, and political life in local and personal relations'.[52] Understanding citizenship in an urban and modern context can be achieved, then, by concentrating on two linked areas: firstly, the novel contemporary modes of understanding and portraying city life and identity, both present and past and the important links between them; and secondly, the new spaces and practices of citizenship that were forged in response to these understandings and representations.[53]

Looking between cities and across national borders is one way to untangle this urban modernity, homing in on specificities and the uniqueness of one city's experiences while still uncovering the fundamental aspects of urban life.[54] This study limits itself to Britain and the US. Partly this is due to reasons of space and time, and, for this author, limitations in geographic expertise and language. There is certainly value in studying or comparing experiences of modernity in dissimilar places and social and political regimes – as can be seen

---

[49]   Thomas Bender, 'Reflections on the culture of urban modernity', in Alev Çınar and Thomas Bender (eds), *Urban imaginaries: locating the modern city*, Minneapolis, MN 2007, 267.

[50]   Rieger and Daunton, 'Introduction', 2.

[51]   For the nineteenth century see Simon Gunn, *The public culture of the Victorian middle class: ritual and authority in the English industrial city, 1840–1914*, Manchester 2000, and Daniel Bluestone, *Constructing Chicago*, New Haven, CT 1993; for the twentieth century see Keith D. Revell, *Building Gotham: civic culture and public policy in New York City, 1898–1938*, Baltimore, MD 2003, and Charlotte Wildman, *Urban redevelopment and modernity in Liverpool and Manchester, 1918–1939*, London 2016.

[52]   Vernon, *Distant strangers*, 7.

[53]   Richard Dennis takes a similar approach, but without the focus on citizenship: *Cities in modernity*.

[54]   Nicholas Kenny and Rebecca Madgin, '"Every time I describe a city": urban history as comparative and transnational practice', in Nicholas Kenny and Rebecca Madgin (eds), *Cities beyond borders: comparative and transnational approaches to urban history*, Abingdon 2015, 7–11.

in scholarship on continental Europe.[55] But there is also a logic to studying modern urban citizenship in Britain and the US in tandem. As will become clear in the following chapters, these two countries had a degree of shared experience. Firstly, activists and intellectuals believed that the problems facing the two countries – of mass urban centres, industrial-corporate power and organised working-class discontent – were similar. A transnational exchange of information 'criss-crossed the Atlantic' in response to these problems in the first three decades of the twentieth century.[56] Secondly, and somewhat conversely, they arguably shared a similar relative stability – at least in comparison with the rest of Europe – between the 1870s and the 1930s. In terms of constitutional government, global power, industrial supremacy, the domestic effects of war and the lack of revolution, they had more in common than difference.[57]

The theorising, representation and reshaping of the city, then, was often analogous in Britain and the US. Manchester and Chicago, too, had a comparable national status and experience of rapid industrialisation that made them a lens through which contemporary observers understood the past, present and future. By 1914, the point at which Platt concludes his comparative study, they were 'typical of large metropolitan areas' and 'second-rank industrial cities'. But the novelty of their history meant that other industrial cities shared important attributes that 'made them all little Manchesters and Chicagos'.[58] This book uses these two cities to understand the consequences of the 'shock city' in a longer perspective, taking the story into the middle decades of the twentieth century. It explores how urban culture was understood, critiqued and remade, and the effects that the industrial city – in terms of both its governance and social experience – had in shaping citizenship and belonging. I emphasise the similarity of this experience, especially when it was the result of transnational intellectual and practical exchange, and analyse movements, policies and manifestations that were common to both countries. But I do not seek to collapse the differences between each city nor the nations to which they belonged: the ideology, policy and experience of urban citizenship was as fundamentally altered by distinctive civic and national cultures as it was by the transmission of urban knowledge across the Atlantic.[59]

---

[55] See the discussion in Rieger and Daunton, 'Introduction', 1, and examples at pp. 15-16 nn. 1-3.

[56] Marc Stears, *Pluralists, and the problems of the state: ideologies of reform in the United States and Britain, 1906-1926*, Oxford 2002, 1-2. See also James Kloppenberg, *Uncertain victory: social democracy and progressivism in European and American thought, 1870-1920*, Oxford 1996.

[57] For differences between Britain and continental Europe see Rieger and Daunton, 'Introduction', 9-13.

[58] Platt, *Shock cities*, 493.

[59] This approach falls under the concept of 'histoire croisée', which emphasises empirical intercrossings between different units of analysis within a framework that also acknowledges the multiplicity of viewpoints and divergences that also shape historical events: Michael Werner and Bénédicte Zimmerman, 'Beyond comparison: *histoire croisée* and the challenge of reflexivity', *History and Theory* xlv/1 (2006), 30-50.

In the chapters that follow, the contours of citizenship will be traced through the theorising of local belonging, the representation and performance of civic community and the public-private policies of intervention in urban culture. The civic response of the interwar period will be linked back to the nineteenth century to show how the experience of the 'shock city', and the ideals and solutions that reformers proposed, continued to evolve and exert power in the ongoing experience of modernity that followed. Three framing questions are kept central. Firstly, what was the relationship between the individual, the voluntary association and municipal government? Secondly, how were people encouraged – or compelled – into urban citizenship? Finally, who was included in the vision of civic community, how was power negotiated and who was ultimately excluded? Answering these three questions in tandem reveals the continued importance of urban notions of citizenship, yet also points towards the concept's inherent problems and eventual decline after the Second World War.

Chapter 1 begins by locating an ideological moment of urban citizenship in the latter part of the nineteenth century and unravels its evolution over the following five decades. The problems of the industrial city were explicitly linked to the future of the nation. As both countries experienced or adapted to rapid urbanisation, and the state grappled with the need to ensure a healthy productive workforce as international competition and conflict grew, the perceived effects of urban living became increasingly important. Reformers and critics took part in a transnational critique of the immoral degenerate culture of cities and articulated civic responses. In Britain, idealist thought – building on the philosophy of Thomas Hill Green – shaped a new enthusiasm for local community building. Some of this ideology transferred directly to the US, where it was absorbed into the growing Progressive movement and, in the case of citizenship especially, the theories of the influential thinker John Dewey. Both countries had an enthusiasm for rural visions of identity and citizenship – whether the Jeffersonian small-town democracy in the US or pastoral village life in Britain. But, rather than encouraging a return to the countryside, they imagined a new city – and one governed by a benevolent municipal government. Improved health and active citizenship would, they believed, be the result. Aspects of this ethos remained in the 1920s and 1930s but evolved to meet new problems and possibilities. Sociologists, politicians and reformers adapted to mass democracy, changing leisure patterns, inter-ethnic and racial conflict and the growing purview of the central state. Now taking a more 'scientific' approach, the hysterical tone of urban critique softened and was replaced by a balanced understanding of how urban problems could have civic solutions: a society bonded by its commitment to civic betterment, urban pride and cooperative community.

The focus on ideology continues in chapter 2 but its practical expression begins to come to the fore. In civics education, a didactic method of teaching citizenship that was used with both children and adults, students were taught that they received and enacted the rights and responsibilities of citizenship through their locality. At the same time, civics articulated local identity as a key contributor to national patriotism in an example of 'nested citizenship'. Civics was institutionalised locally through the work of municipal councillors, associations and philanthropists. I trace citizenship education across these interest groups but also pay attention to how these narratives of urban progress could be challenged, falter or fail. A notable cadre of educators, enthusiastic about municipal study and local citizenship, could be found in both cities. But they could clash with a disinterested (or antagonistic) central educational culture, as in Britain, or a hostile and politically powerful class of anti-public ownership businessmen, as in the US. Even when there was support for civics ideology, urban inequality meant that the message could fall flat. For working-class tenants crammed into unsanitary housing, or African Americans confined to poorly serviced districts, their benevolent city government seemed far away indeed.

The reach of local citizenship education was limited, but the discourse that it reflected was resilient. Chapter 3 shows how civics was popularised beyond the classroom in large urban festivals. Alliances of local government, businessmen and civic associations used these celebrations to construct narratives about the past, present and future of the city. They visualised the work of government through models, and encouraged visits to important infrastructural sites. Combining entertainment with education, civic elites hoped that urban inhabitants would develop a greater respect and pride in their local authority. The very fabric of the city, both historic and new, was embellished and celebrated. Parades of municipal leaders and employees, beginning at key civic sites and winding their way through chosen areas, identified what, where and who was considered to be important in the life of the city. But these festivals also offered opportunities for demotic inclusion. By the 1930s especially, organisers preached a message of general civic inclusion. In the US this was the result of a growing 'consensus' about what it meant to be American – one that incorporated, at least rhetorically, different ethnicities and religions. In Britain, the 'ordinary' or 'everyday' inhabitant of the city, usually a euphemism for the working classes, also found themselves closer to the heart of civic stories. Local groups could match the democratising of citizenship discourse by parading, celebrating and generally 'taking part'. But hierarchies of race, gender and class remained, and civic festivals often inadvertently revealed the tensions in urban society that they were attempting to control.

This representation of how the city had emerged victorious from the shock of industrialisation and urbanisation received more nuance in historical pageants staged as educational entertainment. In these popular and participatory events, the subject of chapter 4, amateur casts of thousands were recruited to colourfully re-enact a chronological series of episodes. Historical pageantry exploded onto the British social scene in the early 1900s, and quickly transferred across to North America. Scriptwriters and 'pageant-masters', employed by civic elites, used the prism of history to reflect on contemporary understandings of urban belonging, inclusion and exclusion. Like civics, in both its ideological and popular form, this was an opportunity to construct a narrative that demon-strated how urban power had emerged, and how local places contributed to national greatness. In Manchester, given the city's ancient roots, this was over a long period of time – before, during and after industrialisation. In Chicago, because of the city's relative youth, the distant past – and Native American legitimacy – were rejected in favour of a nineteenth-century story of wilderness to civilisation. In both cases, pageants portrayed an adaptation to modernity rather than a rejection. Public theatre, though, was not just the preserve of civic elites trying to smooth over contemporary problems. Less powerful groups could also challenge hierarchies through performance – as demonstrated by 'alternative' ethnic and political pageants of the 1930s, from African re-enactment in Chicago to Communist Party parades in Manchester. These events allowed those who were ignored, excluded or demeaned in civic narratives to shape their own sense of citizenship: one that looked to identities, places and epochs beyond the British or American modern city.

The size and success of pageants and festivals hints at the extent of local organisation that existed to coordinate citizenship-creating activity. In the final two thematic chapters, I look at the day-to-day activities of civic culture to show how urban problems and civic solutions were consistently a part of how citizenship – for both local voluntary activists and their targets – was framed and experienced. In chapter 5 the focus is upon an attempt to reimagine youth culture in the interwar city. Understandings of urban degeneration that focused on the health and behaviour of the young were a key part of the eruption of late nineteenth-century debates about 'national efficiency' in Britain or 'race suicide' in the US. Into the 1920s and 1930s, however, moralists' laments and predictions about the downfall of society were superseded by more nuanced sociological critique. This was especially the case in the US, home to the influential Chicago School of Sociologists. Researchers posited that there was something distinctive about the modern city – in its geography and the relationships that it encouraged or enabled – that was particularly damaging to youth citizenship. These concerns filtered down to the civic associations that shaped adolescent civic training. In Britain, though lacking a comparable 'urban studies' sociology, voluntarists were coming to similar understandings based on their observance of modern urban leisure. Reflecting the emphasis on health and morality, and the perceived effects of the First World War, this was partially about regulating sexuality and conditioning boys and girls into gendered societal roles: strong male workers for city and nation, and wives and mothers of future citizens. It was also, however, about creating a sense of community, as character training moved away from individual moral improvement and toward a softer comradely 'team spirit'.

Citizenship was also affected by the expansion and evolution of state-given welfare relief. Chapter 6 demonstrates how, as central and local state provision grew and national citizenship rights became more important, new opportu-nities for urban voluntary organisations paradoxically blossomed. In the US, this process was catalysed by the Great Depression and ensuing New Deal legislation of the 1930s. Old organisations in Chicago, struggling financially and desperate for volunteers, were rejuvenated by federal money and brought further into a cooperative private-public sphere of citizenship creation. They became the first line of defence in the fight to quell any signs of social or political unrest brought on by the dislocation of the economic crash. In Britain, the rise of the state was more of a long-term and piecemeal process in which the responsibilities of local associations gradually shifted. Some in Manchester did not survive, their functions taken over by local and then central government. Others, though, adapted to the new model of centrally distributed benefits. Associations now attempted to ensure that welfare was not given without a corresponding commitment to personal uplift and civic responsibility – a renewed emphasis on much older voluntarist understandings of charity. The chapter ends with a case study of public housing: a moment when the coalition of voluntary associations and the state used welfare architecture to shape better citizenship in the working classes. Though the programme for public housing in Britain started much earlier than in the US and was greater in its scope, the ideology – if not the exterior design – was shaped through transnational communication between the two countries.

Urban modernity fashioned the understanding of citizenship in the opening decades of the twentieth century. But local identity and belonging was also altered by shifts taking place at the national level. The concluding chapter traces how, by the 1950s and 1960s, these changes signalled the city's failure to respond to both new and old problems of conflict. At this point, a departure in the comparable experience of citizenship between these two nations occurred. Urban elites continued to encourage a sense of urban pride and belonging but were met with an increasingly apathetic local population. In Britain, as power was centralised in the welfare state from 1945, municipal governments found their prestige and autonomy waning. Urban populations, at the same time, became less enthusiastic about city-centre living and entertainment and more enamoured with the space, opportunity and privacy of the growing suburbs. The result was a decline in civic cohesion and identity in the country's older industrial cities especially. In the US, some of the same challenges to urban sustainability, especially in the northern industrial cities, were apparent. It was, however, the inability of civic culture to respond effectively to segregation and racism, and the consequent political mobilisation of a more determined racial consciousness, which made urban citizenship less viable. Instead of looking to the city hall, black activists sought the bestowal of civil rights from the national courts. Before reaching the end of our story, though, we return to the beginning: the question of modern citizenship after the birth of the 'shock city'.

1

Citizenship and the Interwar City

Britain and the US had clearly urbanised by the turn of the twentieth century, and towns and cities continued to grow into the interwar decades. It is generally accepted that landscape, culture, politics and daily life was consequently transformed – and that cities were both 'exemplars of a changing order and also engines for the creation of that order'.[1] Until now, however, the question of the specifically urban aspects of citizenship have been somewhat underplayed. Cities were getting bigger, more numerous and setting the agenda in terms of politics and governance, yet questions of belonging and civic identity, the prevailing historiography suggests, were supposedly becoming less important or apparent by the end of the nineteenth century. This chapter outlines, explains and critiques this seeming paradox, and offers an alternative: that the city still had an important role to play in the theories and practices of citizenship right into the 1930s.

To achieve this rethinking I take a long perspective. I begin by tracing how historians have emphasised the political and legal definitions of citizenship. Britain and the US experienced similar developments in the nineteenth and early twentieth centuries that shaped the articulation and response to societal questions: the creation of a mass electorate, changing fortunes in global power, the growth of the state and internal challenges to the social and political order. I then turn to the place of the 'shock city', and the urban more broadly, in late nineteenth-century understandings of citizenship. Reacting against urban degeneration in the industrial city, and fearing the decline of society and national power, civic reformers and municipal governments increasingly intervened to shape a better (if still hierarchical) local community. Rather than following historians who have seen the decline of urban solutions in the interwar period, however, I emphasise continuity. Progressivism may have faltered in the US by 1920, British cities might have continued to lose civic leaders to the suburbs, and political debate and practice did partially move to the national in both countries. But cities were still, nevertheless, conceptualised as a key site of community building. This opinion is tracked across a range of thinkers on urban life in the 1920s and 1930s. Urban critique, in comparison to the often-shrill denunciations and predictions of the 1880s and 1890s, now softened. Commentators still acknowledged urban problems but argued that a proper civic pride could shape a citizenry up to the task of securing the stability

---

[1]   Lees and Lees, *Cities and the making of modern Europe*, 2. For the US see Teaford, *The twentieth-century American city*.

of both local and national. The chapter ends by looking more closely at how Chicago and Manchester encapsulated this evolved critique, demonstrating their value as case studies for understanding urban citizenship in the variety of ways that the book goes on to examine.

Citizenship, society and the city, 1850s–1920s

The declining importance given to the urban variable in citizenship is an understandable assumption that has resulted from the value historians have given to other factors. Political rights and responsibilities, the most commonly articulated aspect of the legal sense of citizenship, certainly shifted dramatically from the nineteenth to the twentieth century. Extensive franchise reorganisation in Britain began modestly with the 1832 Reform Act – a response more to the underrepresentation in parliament of large towns and cities than it was an attempt to democratise the vote. After the rise and fall of the mid-century Chartist movement, and the emergence of organisations such as the Reform League, calls for the extension of the franchise grew. The Second Reform Act in 1867, passed by the Conservative Party, was a political manoeuvre that attempted to enfranchise the 'respectable' new urban working class to the party's benefit – though it failed in the short-term.[2] With the political mood shifting, however, further extensions took place in 1884–5, with the vote now given to householders in the counties to create a mass electorate. But it was the Representation of the People Act in 1918 that created a truly representative electorate. Before the war, just over 7,500,000 people in Britain had been eligible to vote; in 1918 this had risen to over 21,000,000. All men over twenty-one were now enfranchised, and women over thirty, though still with property qualifications, were also eligible. In 1928 the property qualification and age inequality were removed.[3] Older ideas of who deserved the vote had lost legitimacy by the 1920s. Victorian ideas of the ballot being limited to the respectable head of the household and man of the community, when soldiers of all classes were returning home after experiencing the horrors of the First World War, were harder to justify.[4] Women, too, after years of tireless suffrage campaigning, had done their wartime 'duty' by providing 'the blood of their sons'.[5] By also undertaking dangerous munitions work, and castigating those who refused to sign up, they displayed their patriotic loyalty. National duty,

---

[2]   The Conservatives lost in 1868; in 1874, however, they won their first majority since 1841.

[3]   For these acts see Derek Heater, *Citizenship in Britain: a history*, Edinburgh 2006, 107.

[4]   Anna Clark, 'Gender, class and the nation: franchise reform in England, 1832–1928', in James Vernon (ed.), *Re-reading the constitution: new narratives in the political history of England's long nineteenth century*, Cambridge 1996, 253.

[5]   Nicolleta C. Gullace, '*The blood of our sons': men, women and the renegotiation of British citizenship during the Great War*, Basingstoke 2002.

rather than manhood, had become, if only for a short time, a key qualification for citizenship in Britain. Political rights increased correspondingly – with long-lasting effects.

In the US, two years after the British government began to enfranchise women at the national level, the Nineteenth Amendment to the Constitution also prohibited the exclusion of voting rights on account of gender after a campaign that had lasted, with ebbs and flows, for almost seventy-five years. The fight started before the Civil War and was thus tied to other shifts in American government and democracy, such as slavery, constitutionalism, modernisation and nation-building. The movement for suffrage reached the height of its power in the first two decades of the twentieth century, as more women were mobilised on social issues. For American suffragists the vote was the means to a greater end: the improvement of the life and rights of women in all areas. Obtaining and exercising this democratic right had become the key symbol of legitimacy and inclusion in American society.[6] The First World War also provided an opportunity for American women to shape a public image of duty.[7] After suffrage was achieved, political parties in both countries stepped up their competitive efforts to gain allegiance, taking advantage of new forms of mass media and communication. At the same time women responded by organising into new associations of civic and social action, building on networks that had been in action since the middle decades of the nineteenth century.[8]

The course of racial and ethnic enfranchisement in the US was less uniform. The tumult of the Civil War, and the immediate Reconstruction Era (c. 1863–77), had led to a partial renegotiation of African American citizenship. After the Emancipation Proclamation in 1863 and the Thirteenth Amendment in 1865, and thus the formal abolition of slavery, the question

[6]   Jean H. Baker (ed.), *Votes for women: the struggle for suffrage revisited*, Oxford 2002; Liette Gidlow, *The big vote: gender, consumer culture, and the politics of exclusion, 1890s–1920s*, Baltimore, MD 2004.

[7]   Positions of power for women in government or the military did not open up, but there was an acknowledgement that mobilisation depended on women's loyal voluntarism: Lettie Gavin, *American women in World War I: they also served*, Niwot, Co 1997; Susan Zeiger, *In Uncle Sam's service: women workers with the American Expeditionary Force, 1917–1919*, Philadelphia, PA 1999.

[8]   For the US see Douglas B. Craig, *Fireside politics: radio and political culture in the United States, 1920–1940*, Baltimore, MD 2000, and Charles E. Merriam, *Civic education in the United States*, Chicago, IL 1934. For Britain see David Jarvis, 'British Conservatism and class politics in the 1920s', *EHR* cxi/440 (1996), 59–84, and Laura Beers, 'Education or manipulation? Labour, democracy, and the popular press in interwar Britain', *JBS* xlviii/1 (2009), 129–52. Works on civic associational responses to enfranchisement are numerous. For a start see Caitriona Beaumont, 'Citizens not feminists: the boundary negotiated between citizenship and feminism by mainstream women's organisations in England, 1928–39', *Women's History Review* ix/2 (2000), 411–29, and Nancy F. Cott, 'Across the great divide: women in politics before and after 1920', in Louise A. Tilly and Patricia Gurin (eds), *Women, politics, and change*, New York, NY 1990, 153–76.

of enfranchisement ascended to paramount importance. The Civil Rights Act of 1866, first enacted by Congress the previous year but vetoed by President Johnson, was the first US federal law to define citizenship, stipulating that race and previous condition of servitude were no longer barriers: legally, African Americans were to be given the same rights as whites. Four years later, the Fifteenth Amendment prohibited the excluding of voting rights for the same reason. Yet even as the entrance to full membership in the nation had seemingly been made wider, it was soon being closed off. The 'egalitarianism' and 'inclusiveness' of the 1860s and 1870s was followed by a political, intellectual and legal embracing of 'renewed ascriptive hierarchies' during the Gilded Age (c. 1870s–1900). The 'cultural hegemony' of white Anglo-Saxon Protestants was now cemented at the expense of most of the other groups of society.[9]

Civic nationalism, which argued for equal rights for all individuals who proclaimed American allegiance, regardless of race and ethnicity, was now challenged by racialised nationalism.[10] This was a reaction to the shifting demographics of the nation, and its cities especially, away from their perceived Northern European and Protestant roots. Pluralistic citizenship was now replaced with nativism, common blood and whiteness. Immigration bans on those from southern and eastern Europe (and consequently Catholics and Jews), and other bans and legal restrictions on the rights of East and South-East Asians, were created from the 1880s to the 1920s, and reached their culmination in the National Origins Quota system that became law in 1924. At the same time, complex and discriminatory electoral systems, and more broadly the rolling-back of Reconstruction-era reforms, limited the ability of African Americans to take up the rights that they had ostensibly been given.[11] By the time that women's suffrage was granted, African American voting rights had thus been heavily circumscribed. Enfranchisement, then, was never balanced nor complete in the opening decades of the twentieth century, and reflected deeply-embedded white supremacy, racism and discrimination. As Linda K. Kerber succinctly puts it: 'the American dream of equal citizenship has always been in tension with its nightmares'.[12]

Some historians have seen this increased emphasis on the franchise, regardless of its limitations in both countries, as signifying a decline in 'active citizenship' in the first half of the twentieth century. Civic participation had become secondary to performing the simpler, or at least more passive, duty of voting – shifting the model of citizenship, in a sense, from republican to

[9]   Rogers M. Smith, *Civic ideals: conflicting visions of citizenship in US history*, New Haven, CT 1997, 347–409, quotation at p. 348.

[10]   Gerstle, *American crucible*, chs ii and iii.

[11]   Evelyn Nakano Glenn, *Unequal freedom: how race and gender shaped American citizenship and labor*, Cambridge, MA 2002, 26.

[12]   Linda K. Kerber, 'The meanings of citizenship', *JAH* lxxxiv/3 (1997), 836.

liberal-democratic.[13] Developments in political citizenship – where engagement was positioned in terms of national politics and the vote – were, by the interwar period, certainly important. For this reason, according to many of the existing histories of citizenship, it was in the previous century that the city had been most obviously linked to citizenship. In Britain, the high point of Victorian civic liberalism saw a public culture based on an interplay of self- and urban improvement. Prosperous and altruistic businessmen dominated civic life, proving their civic spirit by both literally and figuratively building up the culture of their cities. A similar ethos was evident in the US from the Jacksonian period up to the Progressive Era (c. 1900–20), when elites maintained charitable and cultural institutions in an attempt to culturally and morally uplift the poor and working classes. The 'top tier' of citizenship, however, was limited to wealthy men, who had not just the inclination, but the time, money and social standing to engage in remaking urban culture.[14]

Toward the end of the nineteenth century there was a growing realisation that more needed to be done to close the gaps, both in terms of bodily health and community, between the better and worse off in society. In Britain, as social scientists such as Charles Booth revealed alarming levels of poverty, faith in the ability of liberal political economy (and its central tenet of free trade) to ensure the vitality of Britain began to falter.[15] At the turn of the twentieth century, a moment of panic about 'national efficiency' across political divides – amplified by the poor fitness of Boer War recruits and the growth of competing empires – led to a renewed awareness of the problems that urban living was fostering.[16] Some voluntarist associations and reformers now renewed their efforts of urban reform. Settlements, such as Samuel Barnett's Toynbee Hall (1884), followed by others such as the Manchester University Settlement (1895) in the working-class district of Ancoats, attempted to facilitate better relations between classes in the new social life of the modern industrialised city. Middle-class settlement volunteers, including women, could not only prove their own citizenship by actively participating in civic life, but could also 'civilise' and bring the urban working classes into citizenship too, through character development and emulation of the middle classes. A new 'Civic Gospel' also aimed to transcend competing loyalties in Britain, especially class, by emphasising

[13]   Michael Schudson, *The good citizen: a history of American civic life*, New York, NY 1998, 173; Anne B. Rodrick, *Self-help and civic culture: citizenship in Victorian Birmingham*, Farnham 2004, 149–50, 208; Siân Nicholas, 'From John Bull to John Citizen: images of national identity and citizenship on the wartime BBC', in Weight and Beach, *The right to belong*, 36–58. See also D. L. LeMahieu, *A culture for democracy: mass communication and the cultivated mind in Britain between the wars*, Oxford 1988.

[14]   For Britain see Rodrick, *Self-help and civic culture*, and Gunn, *The public culture*. For the US see Kathleen D. McCarthy, *Noblesse oblige: charity and cultural philanthropy in Chicago, 1849–1929*, Chicago, IL 1982, and Jaher, *The urban establishment*.

[15]   See James Vernon, *Modern Britain: 1750 to the present*, Cambridge 2017, 268–91.

[16]   Geoffrey R. Searle, *The quest for national efficiency: a study in British politics and political thought, 1899–1914*, Oxford 1971.

a spiritual civic brotherhood that was nurtured by progressive municipal government.[17]

This focus on working-class health and behaviour, and a sense of urban community, also signalled another shift in ideas of citizenship and government: a move away from individualism, self-help and *laissez-faire* attitudes and toward collective, community-focused and often state-encouraged goals. Community grew to be a crucial concept for liberalism in Britain in the Victorian period, despite the doctrine's foregrounding of personal rights and individual liberty. For John Stuart Mill, transposing the republican model of Ancient Athens to the present day, it was through civic duty and collective political engagement that liberals believed that individual liberties would be ensured.[18] In the Idealist philosophy of Thomas Hill Green, an inheritor in many ways of Mill's mantle, this idea was given powerful expression. His lecture 'Liberal legislation and freedom of contract' (1861) saw civic engagement as a necessary and beneficial consequence of liberty, and positioned the state as the maintainer of conditions that encouraged liberty to flourish.[19] Green's theories were readily adopted and enlarged by late nineteenth- and early twentieth-century reformers, legitimising criticisms of the non-interventionist state, and influenced both socialist politics and the 'New Liberalism' of the early twentieth century.[20] Second, and relating to this focus on community and poverty, was a concentration on the healthy physical body as a key attribute of citizenship. Both state intervention and associational culture turned away from merely encouraging individual morality or 'character', and towards a societally-focused 'common good'. Arthur Newsholme, the chief medical officer of health of the Local Government Board, aptly summarised this in 1908: redefining the environment from a 'social standpoint' had emphasised 'a vision of the whole' or 'the collective' rather than the personal or individual.[21]

---

[17]   Beaven and Griffiths, 'Creating the exemplary citizen', 205-7. For Barnett see Helen Meller, 'Introduction and Note', in S. A. Barnett and Patrick Geddes, *The ideal city* (1905–6), ed. Helen Meller, Leicester 1979, 9–53, and Standish Meacham, *Toynbee Hall and social reform, 1880–1914: the search for community*, London 1987.

[18]   Eugenio F. Biagini, 'Introduction: citizenship, liberty and community', 2–3, and 'Liberalism and direct democracy: John Stuart Mill and the model of ancient Athens', in Eugenio Biagini, *Citizenship and community: liberals, radicals and collective identities in the British Isles, 1865–1931* (1996), Cambridge 2002, 21–44.

[19]   Thomas H. Green, 'Liberal legislation and freedom of contract' (1861), in Thomas H. Green, *Lectures on the principles of political obligation and other writings*, ed. Paul Harris and John Morrow, Cambridge 1986, 194–212.

[20]   See Matt Carter, *T. H. Green and the development of ethical socialism*, Exeter 2003, and Michael Freeden, *The New Liberalism: an ideology of social reform*, Oxford 1978.

[21]   Arthur Newsholme, 'Some conditions of social efficiency in relation to local public administration', *Public Health* xxii (1908), 403-15. See Ina Zweiniger-Bargieloska, *Managing the body: beauty, health, and fitness in Britain, 1880–1939*, Oxford 2010, and Mark Freeman, 'The provincial social survey in Edwardian Britain', *Historical Research* lxxv/187 (2002), 73–89.

In the US debates followed a somewhat similar – though more heavily racialised – pattern. To critical observers, it seemed that the older population of Protestant Northern Europeans could be surpassed by southern and eastern European immigration, and Catholic and Jewish people especially, into cities. As pseudo-scientific understandings of innate capacity developed, a fear grew among the elite classes that the Anglo-Saxon 'race' was thus declining, taking with it the physical strength of the nation.[22] The settlement movement was transplanted from Britain to the US in the 1890s, as Progressive Era reformers were more broadly energised by the urban problems nurtured by unfettered capitalism and corrupt urban government. Jane Addams and her Hull House settlement (founded 1889) in Chicago, for example, had been directly inspired by Toynbee Hall.[23] In the American context, settlements, whether responding to racialised fears or out of a more benevolent belief in social uplift, attempted to create loyalty and understanding between immigrants and the cities in which they now lived. The Christian women who staffed these settlements understood that, in order to spiritually redeem the city, they first had to provide for the material and social needs of urban dwellers.[24] In doing so, they also constructed a central place for a maternal instinct that legitimised the role of educated women in public life.

A range of other American initiatives in this fertile period of social planning could be included in this shift in urban governance: the Social Centres Movement, which tried to create a democratic public from below; the top-down City Beautiful movement, which aimed to engender civic pride and loyalty in urban populations through monumental civic beautification; and the improvement of working-class housing by a responsible local state which, it was argued, would banish crime and vice.[25] Progressives, in an ambitious moment, believed that their vision of professional scientific expertise and municipal-led civic betterment was the way to safeguard the whole nation. As the prominent reformer Frederic Howe speculated in 1905, in part looking to the example of municipal councils in Britain, the city could be 'The hope of democracy' – the place where political and social

---

[22]   Richard Hofstadter, *Social Darwinism in American thought* (1944), Boston, MA 1964, remains an excellent introduction. More recently see Mike Hawkins, *Social Darwinism in European and American thought, 1860–1945: nature as model and nature as threat*, Cambridge 1997, 104–22.

[23]   Addams visited Toynbee Hall in 1888 with Ellen Starr; they set up Hull House in Chicago the following year. For an introduction to Addams see Allen F. Davis, *American heroine: the life and legend of Jane Addams* (1973), Oxford 2000, and Jean B. Elshtain (ed.), *The Jane Addams reader*, Chicago, IL 2002.

[24]   Mina Carson, *Settlement folk: social thought and the American settlement movement, 1885–1930*, Chicago, IL 1990.

[25]   Kevin Mattson, *Creating a democratic public: the struggle for urban participatory democracy during the Progressive Era*, Philadelphia, PA 1998; Rodgers, *Atlantic crossings*; Janice Metzger, *What would Jane say? City-building women and a tale of two Chicagos*, Chicago, IL 2009.

answers to industrial modernity would be found in effective and democratic urban government.[26]

Progressive thinkers and reformers in the US, though not a homogeneous group, thus experienced a similar evolution in thought to the British as discussions about freedom, liberty and the role of the state criss-crossed the Atlantic.[27] But there were also other specifically American and anti-urban ideas at work. For many Progressive Era reformers, the breakdown of 'community' in the city reflected a decline of the active civic virtue of the eighteenth-century Jeffersonian small-town democracy under the isolating experience of modern industrial urban living. Coupled with this was the resilience of a 'country-boy myth' that compared the 'local rural genius' and 'country-bred men of integrity' of the prairies of the middle west with 'the slick sophistication' and 'sharks and paupers' of the cities.[28] Rather than destroying the city, however, experiments such as settlements sought to recreate the neighbourly communication and ideals of the pre-industrial past, and their own idealised rural upbringing, in the modern urban centre.[29] For John Dewey, the influential American pragmatist philosopher, it was pointless to merely complain about the changes wrought by industrialisation and urbanisation. Education, instead, could encourage the creation of a new society: one held together by 'working along common lines, in a common spirit, and with reference to common aims'.[30] Most important, however, was how the powerful camp of Progressive reformers beyond Dewey confirmed the centrality of racialised understandings of this 'common' ethos: cultural homogeneity, Anglo-Saxon domination, gendered distinctions, fears around immigration and limitations to black enfranchisement. Even if Dewey's vision was democratic and cosmopolitan, he too was still 'often embarrassingly reticent' on issues of race and ethnicity.[31] Cooperative behaviour and societal transformation on an inherently hierarchical model, rather than individual-istic improvement or rights, were seen by the majority as the route to stability and national power.

---

[26] Frederic C. Howe, *The city: the hope of democracy*, New York, NY 1905, and *The British city: the beginnings of democracy*, New York, NY 1907. See Thomas Bender, 'Intellectuals, cities, and citizenship in the United States: the 1890s and 1990s', *Citizenship Studies* iii/2 (1999), 203–20.

[27] For the various shades of Progressivism see Smith, *Civic ideals*, 412–24. For this transatlantic discussion see Stears, *Pluralists, and the problems of the state*.

[28] Briggs, *Victorian cities*, 77; Richard Wohl, 'The country boy myth and its place in American urban culture: the nineteenth-century contribution', *Perspectives in American History* iii (1969), 107–21.

[29] See Jean B. Quandt, *From the small town to the great community: the social thought of progressive intellectuals*, New Brunswick, NJ 1970, and Paul K. Conkin, *Puritans and pragmatists: eight eminent American thinkers*, Bloomington, IN 1968, 345–90.

[30] John Dewey, 'The school and social progress', in John Dewey (ed.), *The school and society*, Chicago, IL 1899, 11.

[31] Smith, *Civic ideals*, 413.

These ascendant discourses about the role of the state, the nature of biological degeneration and of building community explicitly depended on ideas about the best way to promote urban belonging and civic engagement. Many historians, however, have seen the interwar period as marking the end of this urban sense of citizenship. In this interpretation, socialisation through the city and urban improvement led by the middle classes came to be seen as no longer a realistic response to questions of national or imperial decline. Even if there had been an enthusiasm for solving urban problems through civic culture, so the dominant historiography argues, shifts in urban governance by the interwar period had also rendered this a dead end. In Britain, improved transport and a newly acquired affluence enabled an elite and middle-class flight to the suburbs, while improved communication and a rising patriotism helped active citizens to think of themselves in a national rather than just a local context. As Tristram Hunt, Simon Gunn and John Garrard have argued, there was a perception that civic leadership had declined in industrial cities such as Manchester, and that municipal activists had abandoned the fight for the city.[32]

Much the same point has been made for the US. Historians such as Frederic Cople Jaher and Michael Schudson have highlighted how the upper-class civic elite was lured away to a more salubrious suburban existence and began to socialise at exclusive resorts or country clubs rather than in the centre of the city.[33] In Chicago, as Marcus Gräser and others have explained, this left the city centre dominated by ethnic and immigrant groups with less mainstream political power compared to their white predecessors. The middle-class progressives left behind struggled to challenge the machine politics that consequently proliferated.[34] In the US more generally, according to Thomas Bender, as gains against city council corruption were lost, Howe's earlier hopes for a new political citizenship seemed unrealistic, and the focus of social politics moved away from the city and towards the nation.[35] In

[32]　See Gunn, *The public culture*; Hunt, *Building Jerusalem*; John Garrard, '1850–1914: the rule and decline of a new squirearchy?', *Albion: A Quarterly Journal Concerned with British Studies* xxvii/4 (1995), 583–621; R. J. Morris, 'Structure, culture and society in British towns', in Martin Daunton (ed.), *Cambridge urban history of Britain*, III: *1840–1950*, Cambridge 2001, 395–426; and, most recently, Andrew J. H. Jackson, 'Civic identity, municipal governance and provincial newspapers: the Lincoln of Bernard Gilbert, poet, critic and "booster", 1914', *Urban History* xlii/1 (2015), 113–29. For a broader argument about the move to the national in Britain after 1900 see José Harris, *Private lives, public spirit: a social history of Britain, 1870–1914*, Oxford 1993, 18–19.

[33]　Schudson, *The good citizen*, 175; Jaher, *The urban establishment*, 538; Sam Bass Warner, Jr, *The urban wilderness: a history of the American city*, New York, NY 1972, 108–9.

[34]　Marcus Gräser, 'A Jeffersonian skepticism of urban democracy? The educated middle class and the problem of political power in Chicago, 1880–1940', in Ralf Roth and Robert Beachy (eds), *Who ran the cities: city elites and urban power structures in Europe and North America, 1750–1940*, London 2007, 222.

[35]　Bender, 'Intellectuals, cities, and citizenship', 214. In general, historians of the

both countries, then, the secondary literature could be summarised by John Griffith's contention that 'citizenship discourse had left the city, soon to be followed by civic leaders'.[36]

Cities, of course, did not vanish and nor did, for the most part, the cooperative networks of civic associations or the administrative machinery of the local state. More recently, historians such as Daniel Amsterdam and Charlotte Wildman have begun to reassess the adaptability and resilience of a progressive civic culture until at least the Great Depression in the US and the late 1930s in Britain.[37] In terms of citizenship, it is true that national legislation and a concentration on exercising the vote weakened the idea of active civic responsibility in one way, with political corruption and demographic change affecting belonging in another. But the strength of citizenship ideology in terms of the collective state of the nation, expressed through its citizens and the community of which they were part, continued to be important. Fears about the physical fitness of the population, and especially of the working classes, did not disappear in the 1920s and 1930s. Philosophy and political thought that gave a central place to the city, germinating from the last two decades of the nineteenth century, also continued to shape citizenship discourse and practice well into the interwar years. The question of how and where individuals were brought into a social model of citizenship, then, remained paramount. A degree of continuity, rather than total divergence, marked the passage from late nineteenth- and early twentieth-century progressivism to the 1920s and 1930s. Even with all its faults – indeed, because of its faults – the city still had a vital role to play.

Urban problems and civic solutions in the interwar period

If there were a place for the city after the First World War, it was, for many planners and social thinkers, still a negative one: not just the site of social and political problems but also their very cause. Cities, argued critics, fostered rebellious class-consciousness, caused poor health and threatened national power. Though the realities of urban life changed dramatically between the mid- and late nineteenth century and the 1920s and 1930s, the terms of the

---

Progressive Era have tended to date the movement's end to about 1920, as waning public faith in the ability of an activist government to overcome both labour unrest and entrenched business interests, or to inspire greater democratic engagement, was coupled with rising disquiet at higher taxes and suspicion of government intervention. For the orthodox view see Michael Heale, *The United States in the long twentieth century: politics and society since 1900*, London 2015, 45, 63-71.

[36] John R. Griffiths, 'Civic communication in Britain: a study of the *Municipal Journal c.* 1893-1910', *JUH* xxxiv/5 (2008), 17.

[37] Wildman, *Urban redevelopment*; Daniel Amsterdam, *Roaring metropolis: businessmen's campaign for a civic welfare state*, Philadelphia, PA 2016.

debate about the city underworld 'remained strangely static and unaffected'.[38] Untamed sexuality and the improper mixing of the genders, gang culture and youth crime, anonymity and the dangerous speed of modern living, inter-ethnic conflict and weakened social ties: all were still seen to be particularly urban problems. Implicit within this, and sometimes explicit, was a gendered understanding of both cities and the people within them. On the one hand, the city represented masculine might – the home of industry and commerce built by ambitious businessmen. The effects of urban interaction and leisure, however, could also be seen as inherently and negatively 'feminine': trivial and corruptive to the body and soul. The corollary of this was the imagining of the countryside – and untamed wilderness especially – as a space for the performance of a corrective vigorous masculinity. In contrast to the vice of the city, leisure activities in the countryside built character and cured bodily ills. The anxieties of an urban-industrial modernity were thus still refracted through a lionising of the ideal rural life that had supposedly come before.[39]

In Britain, some reformers accordingly wanted to use the regenerative effects of the countryside, whether in movements for recreation or by following Ebenezer Howard's model for new garden cities that melded the best aspects of town and country.[40] Others, however, sought to protect the countryside from the city. Rural preservationists, led by the tireless Clough Williams-Ellis, saw only negative effects in the continuing urbanisation of Britain and the tendency towards unmanaged suburban 'ribbon development'.[41] There was a fear of not just towns but their inhabitants too. Surrounded, as the outspoken critic C. E. M. Joad put it, by 'an environment of ugliness' in their daily lives – dirt, noise and violence – day-trippers could not help but replicate brutality in the countryside.[42] Many of these preservationists simply wanted to keep the urbanite in his city. Critiques were similar in the US. Lewis Mumford, probably America's most inspired, consistent and informed urban commentator, serves as the most famous example. He was, on one level, unequivocal in his damning of the great American cities. In a piece for *Harper's* magazine in 1926, he asked whether: 'The intolerable city: must it keep on growing?' Cities, Mumford argued, had a voracious appetite, swallowing up both resources and people from

---

[38]   Joachin Schlör, *Nights in the big city: Paris, Berlin, London, 1840–1930*, London 1998, 144.

[39]   Kate Murphy, *Fears and fantasies: modernity, gender, and the rural-urban divide*, London 2010, 3. For the complexity of gendered interpretations of the countryside see Melanie Tebbutt, 'Rambling and manly identity in Derbyshire's Dark Peak, 1880s–1920s', *HJ* xlix/4 (2006), 1125-53.

[40]   Abigail A. Van Slyck, *A manufactured wilderness: summer camps and the shaping of American youth, 1890–1960*, Minneapolis, MN 2006; Sian Edwards, *Youth movements, citizenship and the English countryside: creating good citizens, 1930–1960*, London 2018. For Garden Cities see Ward, *The Garden City*.

[41]   See Clough Williams-Ellis, *England and the octopus*, London 1928.

[42]   C. E. M. Joad, 'The people's claim', in Clough Williams-Ellis (ed.), *Britain and the beast*, London 1937, 72.

the country.[43] His opinion on urban living, however, was never as clear-cut as some of his early polemical pieces suggested. Cities, he admitted, also enabled collective living and shared purpose. But mechanisation and haphazard industrial growth had led to ravaged landscapes, ill-health, disorderly districts and ineffectual suburbs. The solution, he believed, was to rebalance the damaging effects of poor planning with opportunities for the 'intellectually stimulating kind of disharmony' that led to a better community. For Mumford, and his contemporaries in the Regional Planning Association of America, this meant building garden cities – lower density, regionally integrated and with buildings where attention was given to the social needs of their occupants. Above all, rationally planned and democratic communities. A growing movement towards decentralisation resulted – an inheritance of planning thought in Britain as well as the Jeffersonian small-town ideal that had inspired many of the reformers of the Progressive Era.[44]

These critiques originated from and sustained a long-standing urban aversion – one that continued to shape the way in which historians in both Britain and the US wrote about the city in the post-war period, too.[45] Success in terms of decentralisation was only ever minor and piecemeal, however, and the growth of cities – though slowing – continued. Behind even the most stubborn urban critiques was a sense that urban problems would have to, and indeed could, be balanced with urban solutions. What is so striking about interwar urban cultural commentary is how a pragmatic perspective replaced the biblical denunciations or unrealistic utopian plans of the late nineteenth and early twentieth centuries. Assessments now contained optimistic notes: the sin of the city, thinkers tentatively posited, contained its own salvation. Critics realised that they were inescapably living in an urban age, with pragmatists accepting that reform was going to have to happen from within the city.[46] A fundamental aspect of urban modernity, then, was the embracing of 'tensions and

---

[43]   Lewis Mumford, 'The intolerable city: must it keep on growing?', *Harper's* (1926), 283-93.

[44]   Idem, *The culture of cities*, London 1938, 6, 1-10, 480-5. David Riesman argues that 'Mumford's work ... cannot be summed up by saying he is "for" or "against" cities': 'Some observations on Lewis Mumford's *The city in history*', *Salmagundi* xlix (1980), 81. For decentralist solutions to the city, such as regional planning or New Towns see Steven Conn, *Americans against the city: anti-urbanism in the twentieth century*, Oxford 2014.

[45]   Urban history in Britain emerged during a moment of urban crisis on both sides of the Atlantic. Briggs surmised that the many conferences on cities taking place pointed to contemporary problems: 'Foreword', to H. J. Dyos (ed.), *The study of urban history: the proceedings of an international round-table conference of the Urban History Group*, London 1968, p. v. Historians in the US focused on tracing antipathy toward the city, ironically recreating an imbalance that goes back to Thomas Jefferson in the eighteenth century: Morton White and Lucia White, *The intellectual versus the city: from Thomas Jefferson to Frank Lloyd Wright*, Cambridge, MA 1962; Paul Boyer, *Urban masses and moral order in America, 1820-1920*, Cambridge, MA 1978.

[46]   See Lees, *Cities perceived*, 258-304.

paradoxes' that were constantly navigated.[47] The rhetoric of the instability that living in 'modern times' encouraged had both creative and destructive understandings of change and innovation. Rather than praising or condemning the present, as had often been the case with the teleological language of progress in the mid-nineteenth century, the language of the modern allowed contemporaries to understand the present in a much more ambivalent fashion.[48] Urban problems could, quite simply, have civic solutions. A few examples from prominent writers and theorists on both sides of the Atlantic display the logic of this interplay.

Writing in 1928, David Lindsay – 27th earl of Crawford, Conservative politician and Chancellor of the University of Manchester – argued that cities had grown too big and were draining both food and people from the countryside. The lives of those who actually lived in a large city were physically damaged by speed, noise and emotional detachment. The continued popularity of cinema, and Hollywood-produced films especially, combined with omnipresent advertising that damaged local character, had led to a 'vulgar', monotonous and corrupting urban environment. Yet he lauded the great extension of municipal control in gas, water, drainage, lighting, transport and policing, and the public spirit of municipal public servants. This 'civic efficiency', he maintained, was 'the starting point for good citizenship'. If closer attention was paid to stimulating the individuality, independence and beauty of the city, individual citizens would increase their service to the wider community and a 'civic revival' of 'collective citizenship' could take place. 'Great cities', he concluded, 'make a great State.'[49]

William Richard Lethaby, an influential architect, historian and educator, came from a similar angle. Drawing on his Arts and Crafts background, and the ideas of the movement's father William Morris, he argued that British society needed to develop a deeper sense of what it meant to be civic. Urbanity and civilisation, he asserted in 1922, were nearly the exact same thing: 'the City' was 'the manifestation of the spirit of its population and the larger body it builds for its soul'. Cities still needed improvement, since dirt and disease did not make for 'the perfect homes of a stout and proud people at the centre of a great commonwealth'. But change had to take place within, in a piecemeal process of building urban pride: streets tidied and cleansed; 'child-citizens' taught to love their home town; and tenants encouraged to attractively maintain their properties. Local associations, study circles and exhibitions were a pragmatic way to reach this urban populace. Leaving the city was not an option: towns had to be made 'delightful homes to live in, rather than delightful to get away from'. 'There is much talk of patriotism', Lethaby acknowledged, but he

---

[47] Tom Crook, 'Accommodating the outcast: common lodging houses and the limits of urban governance in Victorian and Edwardian London', *Urban History* xxxv/3 (2008), 416.

[48] Rieger and Daunton, 'Introduction', 7.

[49] David Lindsay Crawford, *The city and the state*, Birmingham 1928, 10–32.

insisted that 'patriotism requires a ground on which to subsist ... love of home, love of city, and love of country' together.[50]

For some, such as the architect Trystan Edwards, the town planners and housing reformers that sought to decant the population to the countryside were missing the point: the 'whole world' was not 'rural-minded', and there was a danger in letting such a belief frame the response to the city.[51] As well as the tentative optimism of Lethaby and Lindsay, then, there was also outright enthusiasm for city-living. Though interest in the countryside or landscape as a wellspring of leisure and 'Englishness' may have grown in the interwar decades, it was by no means motivated solely by anti-modern or anti-urban ideas. Britons had, in the main, come to terms with the nation's urbanity, and could see the city as a key contributor to national patriotism and power. Most did not wish to return to a rural way of life, but to preserve its opportunities for pleasure and artistic inspiration while developing their modern sense of nation and 'self' – and resolutely remaining a city-dwelling people.[52]

In the US, by the 1920s, a burgeoning field of sociologists had taken the city as the central site of social enquiry for the questions being asked on both sides of the Atlantic. Led by Robert Park, they more systematically took up the mantle of, and often worked alongside, the progressive reformers who had come before. Park traced his understanding of the effects of urban living on society not just to his career of investigative journalism, but also back to the American pragmatist and urban enthusiast William James, and the German thinker Georg Simmel. The former convinced Park of the importance of looking below the surface of people's lives, whereas the latter encouraged him to study the 'mental life' of the city as a whole. Moving to teach at the University of Chicago in 1914, Park embedded himself in Chicago's life and culture, and shaped a new discipline that took the city as its laboratory.[53]

---

[50] W. R. Lethaby, 'Architecture as form in civilization', and 'Towns to live in', in W. R. Lethaby, *Form in civilization: collected papers on art and labour*, London 1922, 1–16.

[51] A. Trystan Edwards, 'The metropolitan idea', *Architecture* (Apr. 1926), 386.

[52] Peter Mandler, 'Against "Englishness": English culture and the limits to rural nostalgia, 1850–1940', *Transactions of the Royal Historical Society* vii (1997), 155–75. Mandler was responding to the influential work of Martin J. Wiener, who argued that the British looked to tradition and the countryside for their values – an anti-modern approach that was to the detriment of economic development: Martin J. Wiener, *English culture and the decline of the industrial spirit, 1850–1980*, Cambridge 1981. More recently, historians have underlined how contemporaries could incorporate aspects of the countryside and tradition (from folk culture to the arts and crafts movement) in ways that were not necessarily backward looking, anti-modern or anti-urban: Jeremy Burchardt, *Paradise lost: rural idyll and social change in England since 1800*, London 2002; David Matless, *Landscape and Englishness*, London 1998; Michael T. Saler, *The avant-garde in interwar England: medieval modernism and the London Underground*, Oxford 2001; Alexandra Harris, *Romantic moderns: English writers, artists and the imagination from Virginia Woolf to John Piper*, London 2010; Paul Readman, *Storied ground: landscape and the shaping of English national identity*, Cambridge 2018.

[53] For Park and his influences, though Park's antipathy toward the modern city is arguably overstated see White and White, *The intellectual versus the city*.

In detailed ethnographic studies, Park and his colleagues came to a similar understanding of this relationship between the city and good citizenship as the British – though admittedly with more nuance.[54]

Urban sociologists recognised what the decentralists and Garden City enthusiasts often downplayed: that the big city could only be mitigated and not dismantled. Both old and new emotionally-driven crusades against the negative effects of city living, they argued, had failed to understand the inherent causes of urban dislocation. Ernest Burgess, one of the Chicago School's most prominent theorists, singled out Mumford's article on 'the intolerable city' and caricatured him and his ilk as wanting to 'abolish' the city, arguing that they had failed to recognise that the continued growth of urban centres suggested that many had already 'decided for better or worse to accept the city'. For Burgess the solution was complex, but clear: understanding the city not as 'a congeries of evils to be corrected' but 'as an organism with functions vital to the life and the welfare of the larger community of which it is a part'. If blind prejudice were replaced with facts, figures and scientific research, he believed, unrealistic urban utopias would give way to new communities based on a clear understanding of 'urban ecology'.[55] Another sociologist, Cecil C. North, effectively summed up the problem in 1926. Because the city was the place where 'the outstanding forces of present-day society are working out their logical consequences', the end result was one of extremes: 'luxury and poverty', 'civic virtue and crime', and 'stable social organisation and appalling disorganization'. For North, the city was beset by problems, but it held within itself an 'essential unity' that was greater than the rural community or even the nation state.[56]

Questions about community only grew in their centrality to disciplines such as sociology and urban planning in the US in the 1930s. As one reviewer wrote in 1938, the previous two years had seen 'wave on wave of big and little books about communal life' as researchers investigated better ways of pragmatically creating, rather than relocating, urban community.[57] The high point of this thinking came with the federal government's Report of the Urbanism Committee to the National Resources Committee, *Our cities: their role in the national economy* (1937). Harold Ickes, Secretary of the Interior and the chair of the committee, acknowledged that much of the focus of the previous four years of federally-led New Deal reform had been on rural America. Now, instead, was

---

[54]   American sociology was, to a large degree, a response to the perceived decline of order resulting from modern urban growth: Philip Kasinitz, *Metropolis: centre and symbol of our times*, New York, NY 1995, 10.

[55]   Ernest W. Burgess, 'The new community and its future', *Annals of the American Academy of Political and Social Science* cxlix (1930), 160–3.

[56]   Cecil C. North, 'The city as a community: an introduction to a research project', in Ernest W. Burgess (ed.), *The urban community: selected papers from the proceedings of the American Sociological Society, 1925*, Chicago, IL 1926, 233–5.

[57]   Lee M. Brooks, 'The urban community', *Social Forces* xvii/1 (1938), 119–28 at p. 120.

the time to focus on the city – 'the focal point of much that is threatening and much that is promising in the life of its people' and 'the great playground and the great battleground of the Nation'. Part of the emphasis was on economic problems, as reflected in the title. But with reformers and sociologists also sitting on the committee, including the important Chicago School author Louis Wirth, the report also acknowledged that urban life had a central role to play in the social citizenship of the US. In the cities, the report argued, were the institutions and conditions through which contemporary cultural activity would flourish and be diffused. But, at the same time, urbanisation had fostered social isolation and, when unchecked, the extremes of poverty. If the greatest national resource was its people, the city was paramount, since 'The prosperity and happiness of the teeming millions who dwell there are closely bound up with that of America, for if the city fails, America fails.' The report's answer to this issue was at only a foundational stage, but one thing was certain: 'the realistic answer to the question of a desirable urban environment lies not in wholesale dispersion, but in the judicious re-shaping of the urban community and region'.[58] Progressive reformers had seen the city as a place with problems that could find solutions, and the social science of the interwar period refined rather than replaced this ideology. The end result of urban reshaping would not just be better cities, but a more secure nation as well.

A complementary approach to balancing the positives and negatives of cities could also be found in the art and literature of the interwar *avant-garde*. Novelists, artists, architects and filmmakers were inspired by the energy of modern metropolitan life yet oppressed by the estrangement and atomi-sation of 'the spectacle of mass society that capitalism staged'.[59] The British documentary movement, for example, highlighted social and economic condi-tions from a social-democratic perspective, and gave considerable attention to slum clearance and rehousing. The movement was heavily influenced by the Scottish filmmaker John Grierson, who developed his understanding of civic education and community formation after studying under Park and other Chicago sociologists and social scientists in the 1920s.[60] In the early 1940s British documentary makers, supported by central government and a cross-party political consensus on the need to tackle housing, moved on to depicting and supporting the planning of Garden Cities and New Towns in the future.[61] Though these films portrayed what was wrong with British cities,

---

[58]   Report of the Urbanism Committee to the National Resources Committee, *Our cities: their role in the national economy*, Washington, DC 1937, pp. v, viii, xiii.

[59]   Gyan Prakash, 'Introduction: imaging the modern city, darkly', in Gyan Prakash (ed.), *Noir urbanisms: dystopic images of the modern city*, Princeton, NJ 2010, 3.

[60]   Zoë Druick, *Projecting Canada: government policy and documentary film at the National Film Board of Canada*, Montreal 2007, 49–54.

[61]   John R. Gold and Stephen V. Ward, 'Of plans and planners: documentary film and the challenge of the urban future, 1935–52', in David B. Clarke (ed.), *The cinematic city*, London 1997, 62, 69. See, particularly, *New towns for old* (1942) and *Proud city* (1945).

they also attempted to promote interest and respect for public services, and the ongoing achievements of local government in furthering social reform. Alongside this, some city councils in the interwar period also commissioned films which showed how the city worked for the citizen.[62] In the US, New Deal-sponsored documentary film, through the United States Film Service, mostly focused on rural issues. In 1939 this changed with *The city*: a hit film produced for the American Institute of Planners for the New York World's Fair. Written by Mumford, it portrayed the loss of eighteenth-century style New England rural communities to industrial, congested and isolating cities. The 'Green City', based on several locations – most obviously the Regional Planning Association's Radburn and the New Deal's Greenbelt – was posited as the solution. Yet, as Grierson recognised when he saw *The city*, the excitement and humour of a scene filmed in New York was much more attractive and engaging than the blandness of the quiet utopian Garden City sequence.[63] Even in art and media that was meant to be critical of modern urban life, then, there was a certain amount of ambiguity.

Urban life clearly still had a role to play in the question of citizenship in these interwar decades. Despite its many problems, the city also offered a solution: communities based on the ideal of civic cohesion and loyalty. To live in the city was to experience 'modern life's possibilities and perils', and to participate in the struggle between modernisation and the preservation of older idealised understandings of society.[64] Wider tensions, however, from political radicalism to economic uncertainty, were also being felt across Britain and the US. To bring these out into clear view, and to untangle how they related to urban life in particular, we can return to the story of the old 'shock cities' that had so long been the cause of urban critique.

Manchester, Chicago and the challenges of changing societies

At the national level, in both Britain and the US, the social and political context of the post-war period combined with old and new criticisms of the city to create a renewed emphasis on citizenship. Manchester and Chicago, as large cities with a reputation for conflict and urban degeneration, strongly experienced this shift. Though no longer 'shock cities', acknowledging their own history was central to the way that the city was tackled and reimagined as a site of community in the interwar years. The unresolved problems of urban conflict, poverty and disorganisation, and the physical and emotional

---

[62]   Thomas Baird, 'Films and the public services in Great Britain', *Public Opinion Quarterly* ii (1938), 98; Toby Haggith, "Castles in the air": British film and the reconstruction of the built environment, 1939–51', unpubl. PhD diss. Warwick 1998, 17–18.

[63]   Jack C. Ellis and Betsy A. McLane, *A new history of documentary film*, London 2006, 96–7.

[64]   Shane Ewen, *What is urban history?*, Cambridge 2016, 95.

memories of their shocking nineteenth-century ascent, had a great bearing on the question of citizenship.

Chicago had undeniably lost some of its power to awe by the 1920s. Los Angeles, then experiencing rapid growth, took over the mantle as most shocking city in the US. Many of the authors who had attempted to find symbolic meaning in Chicago's burgeoning modernity had left for New York in the 1910s and 1920s. By the 1930s a new generation in Chicago looked more to the microcosm of the neighbourhood than the city as a totality – partially a reflection of the sociological investigation that was taking place around them.[65] Some visitors, though, were still attracted to Chicago, keen to understand the further evolution of the industrial and commercial giant. Sensationalist books, such as *Chicago: a history of its reputation* (1925), written by two journalists, were still selling the shock city narrative to a large and titillated audience. Immersed in Chicago, they insisted, the visitor would still find 'a force both thrilling and terrifying'.[66] Bessie Louise Pierce, however, a historian at the University of Chicago, collated a more balanced selection of writings on Chicago for a 'civic soul-searching' book published during the city's World's Fair of 1933.[67] The authors chosen for inclusion showed all sides of Chicago after its birth in the mid-nineteenth century, emphasising an extended understanding of urban development. These essays often had a dualistic and complementary understanding of the city. For Walter Lionel George, a British author and newspaper special correspondent who had visited the city in 1920, Chicago was 'a city of terror and light, untamed and unwearied' and a 'savage animal that plunges and rears'. Yet, at the same time, he saw how the city's 'psychology' was 'deeply colored with self-love', harbouring 'blinding pride'. 'Almost every educated person in Chicago will call his city crude, perhaps even vulgar', he admitted, but would also show 'love and pride'. Waldo Frank, writing a year earlier, also saw Chicago as brutal and savage, but still 'the city of Hope': 'Despair' had 'simply not yet altogether won.' For Mary Borden, a novelist born in Chicago and returning in 1931 after an absence of twelve years, her home city was both 'gorgeous' and 'awful', combining scenes of skyscrapers and the lake in a way 'too beautiful to be credible' with neighbourhoods that were 'a vast scene of desolate ugliness, impossible to match in any slum in Europe'. Above all, Chicago combined desperation and degradation with excitement and promise. Morris Market, a novelist, told how the inhabitants of Chicago viewed their city as 'genuinely a part of their religion, their fundamental belief ... It was an

[65] Frederik Byrn Køhlert, *The Chicago literary experience: writing the city, 1893–1953*, Copenhagen 2011, 131–2.

[66] Lloyd Downs Lewis and Henry Justin Smith, *Chicago: the history of its reputation*, New York, NY 1929, p. vi.

[67] Perry R. Duis, 'Foreword to the 2004 edition', in Bessie Louise Pierce (ed.), *As others see Chicago: impressions of visitors, 1673–1933* (1933), Chicago, IL 2004, p. xxv.

intimate and satisfying experience for them, simply to be a citizen of such a place'.[68]

This ambivalence about modern Chicago had a long trajectory. As Lisa Krissoff Boehm has argued, it was the response to the Great Chicago Fire in 1871 that made the city a national 'anti-model' for urban growth. A story that had elements of disaster, class conflict, wanton sexuality and immorality – and comparisons to biblical visions of other fallen cities, not to mention hell itself – had pointed towards the fate of America if urbanisation continued unchecked. Yet, at the same time, the Fire was an opportunity for rebirth: a phoenix rising from the ashes.[69] Just over twenty years later a similar outpouring of outrage and optimism was stirred up by the muckraking English journalist W. T. Stead when he visited the city during its great World's Fair of 1893.[70] New associations, such as the Civic Federation, were born in response and began to revitalise civic life by reforming corrupt government and tackling vice and crime in order to create a better citizenry. A new civic culture of progressive reformers, charitable volunteers and the city council used local identity and social engagement to transcend boundaries of ethnicity, race, religion and class.[71] By becoming such a centre of investigation and reform, however, Chicago was ironically cemented in the national consciousness as the site of America's urban problems.

Into the early part of the twentieth century immigration and urbanisation continued, and Chicago remained socially fragmented. Between 1880 and 1920 the proportion of foreign-born inhabitants from central, eastern and southern Europe grew from 10.5 per cent to 55.6 per cent and, in 1910, 80 per cent of the city's population was made up of the foreign born and their children.[72] Neighbourhoods were, for the most part, socially segregated, and local life was centred on the complex interplay of communal affiliations such as family, ethnicity, religion and class. The parish church, especially, gave a cohesiveness to community that could be both simultaneously welcoming to incomers from Europe yet exclusionary to other groups – most notably African Americans. White Catholics, for example, could live alongside each other yet attend separate parish churches based on specific ethnicities, such as Polish

[68]   See excerpts from Walter Lionel George, Waldo Frank, Mary Borden and Morris Market in Pierce, *As others see Chicago*.

[69]   Lisa Krissoff Boehm, *Popular culture and the enduring myth of Chicago, 1871–1968*, London 2004, 1-26.

[70]   Stead, *If Christ came to Chicago!*

[71]   Robin Bachin, *Building the South Side: urban space and civic culture in Chicago, 1890–1919*, Chicago, IL 2004, 7.

[72]   Not including the substantial German community. Michael P. McCarthy, 'The new metropolis: Chicago, the annexation movement and progressive reform', in Michael H. Ebner and Eugene M. Tobin (eds), *The age of urban reform: new perspectives on the Progressive Era*, London 1977, 183.

or Irish.[73] To middle-class reformers and outsiders these neighbourhoods may have seemed chaotic and disorganised but, to the residents, they formed the basis for a strong sense of ethnic and religious belonging.[74] The further development of mass consumerism only strengthened these ties, for white immigrants at least, as new forms and sites of mass culture – stores, theatres, radio programmes and music records – were integrated into neighbourhoods and daily life and actually provided a way to celebrate and keep 'traditional culture' alive.[75] Communities thus felt an increased awareness of their own heritage and European nationalism, especially following the First World War, which could frequently lead to conflict between different urban communities.

Tension was most clearly evident, however, in the white reaction to the growing black population. Back in the 1890s the 'old settler' black elites had, to a degree, relied on powerful whites to advance a relatively egalitarian racial agenda at the state and local level. As African Americans were a small minority, politically and economically disempowered, whites did not feel so threatened. Blacks were mostly relegated to unwanted positions (such as domestic and personal services), were isolated from labour conflicts and did not have enough votes to effect change. White overtures to integration, then, were not that contentious, and pragmatically maintained 'relative racial harmony'.[76] Demographic change, however, seriously weakened this stability. More and more African Americans made their way to Chicago during the Great Migration from the south, seeking the economic promise of northern cities.[77] A wartime boom in the economy catalysed this growth. The black population increased from around 6,500 in 1880 to almost 110,000 in 1920 and doubled again in the next decade. Even before the outbreak of the First World War a virtually all-black ghetto on the South Side of the city had taken shape, violently enforced on each side by hostile whites who were supported by the discriminatory Chicago Real Estate Board. Conflict, tainted with racial hate, centred on access to and ownership of economic, private and public space. With economic contraction in the immediate post-war years, competition over

[73]   John McGreevy, *Parish boundaries: the Catholic encounter with race in the twentieth-century urban north*, Chicago, IL 1996, chs i, ii.

[74]   See Dominic A Pacyga, *Chicago: a biography*, Chicago, IL 2009, at pp. 190–201 for the ramifications of war on national identities during the 1910s, and pp. 112–21, 152–3 for local community organising.

[75]   Lizabeth Cohen, *Making a new deal: industrial workers in Chicago, 1919–1939*, Cambridge 1992, 99–159, quotation at p. 156.

[76]   Michelle R. Boyd, *Jim Crow nostalgia: reconstructing race in Bronzeville*, Minneapolis, MN 2008, 3–7. For the classic account see Allan Spear, *Black Chicago: the making of a negro ghetto, 1890–1920*, Chicago, IL 1967, and, more recently, Margaret Garb, *Freedom's ballot: African American political struggles in Chicago from abolition to the Great Migration*, Chicago, IL 2014.

[77]   James R. Grossman, *Land of hope: Chicago, black southerners, and the Great Migration*, Chicago, IL 1989.

employment and housing especially turned neighbourhoods and workplaces into racialised battlegrounds.[78]

The *Chicago Defender*, a newspaper primarily for black readers, kept track of the aggression. Founded in 1905 by Robert S. Abbott, a son of former slaves, the *Defender* encouraged its readers to become involved in the life of their city and country, tracked legal and societal racism, and was at the forefront of forging black consciousness.[79] One report from the summer of 1921 demonstrates the complexity of the problems of racism in the city. A 'free-for-all-fight' on Clarendon Beach, with over 500 combatants, ostensibly began when a Jewish woman made a racist remark to a 'sunburned guard whom she evidently took to be coloured'. According to the *Defender*, the resulting battle was actually between many ethnic groups. 'Think of it!' the newspaper said, 'A beach fight and not a Colored person in sight to fasten the blame on. Wonder if the chronic agitators will petition the city council to set apart separate bathing beaches for the Jews?'[80] The *Defender's* sardonic tone was understandable in light of the vicious race riot that had taken place just two summers before. Eugene Williams, an African American teenager, had been visiting the 29th Street beach and bathing in Lake Michigan on a hot July day. When he drifted into the unofficially 'whites-only' waters of the 25th Street beach, one man on the shore responded by throwing rocks. Williams was struck and drowned. Failure by the police to arrest the white aggressor led to angry recriminations from blacks, which was responded to with more violence from whites. Rioting, arson and murders followed, concentrated especially in the black neighbourhoods of the South Side. In the five days following Williams's death, thirty-eight people lost their lives, 500 more were injured and over 1,000 homes were razed to the ground. The riot only ended after the calling in of the state militia.

A 'commission on race relations' was set up in response, publishing their findings in 1922. Demanded by both progressive reformers and politicians, the report actually sanctioned and embedded racial categorisation in modern citizenship and was consequently resisted by many of Chicago's African American population.[81] A growing black consciousness had already begun to take shape over the previous two decades. The emergence of a physical 'ghetto'

---

[78]   Thomas L. Philpott, *The slum and the ghetto: immigrants, blacks, and reformers in Chicago, 1890–1930*, Belmont, CA 1978, 162–80; Timothy B. Neary, 'Black-belt Catholic space: African-American parishes in interwar Chicago', *US Catholic Historian* xviii/4 (2000), 76–91; Roger Biles, 'Race and housing in Chicago', *Journal of the Illinois State Historical Society* xciv/1 (2001), 31–8.

[79]   Mary E. Stovall, 'The *Chicago Defender* in the Progressive Era', *Illinois Historical Journal* lxxxiii/3 (1990), 159–72.

[80]   'Insulting a Jew', *CT*, 2 July 1921, 1.

[81]   Chicago Commission on Race Relations, *The negro in Chicago: a study of race relations and a race riot*, Chicago, IL 1922. See Cheryl Hudson, '"The negro in Chicago": harmony in conflict, 1919–22', *European Journal of American Culture* xxix/1 (2010), 53–67 and, for the classic analysis, William M. Tuttle Jr, *Race riot: Chicago in the red summer of 1919*, New York, NY 1970.

and widening racial discrimination had opened up opportunities for new middle-class African American social, political and economic leaders. Adapting Booker T. Washington's call for racial solidarity and self-help, the fight for integration was now deemphasised in favour of an associational culture that provided a protective space from discrimination – though essentially by acquiescing to white power. Professional black leaders, rather than directly challenging segregation, now sought to shape their own city on the South Side. Dubbed the Black Metropolis or Bronzeville, they filled it with black institutions – religious, charitable, cultural, economic and political.[82] Organisations such as the Chicago Urban League, established in 1916, provided services and education that helped rural southerners settle into Chicago and, more tellingly, adapt to what they saw as middle-class values of respectability and behaviour.[83] That being said, there was no clear or cohesive idea of 'black community', and black Chicagoans were divided by education, political ideology, class and many other things besides. As Sam Mitrani has put it, 'What ultimately drove them together was less race than racism, and the struggle against it.'[84] Because that struggle was not won in the 1920s and 1930s, African Americans organised, in different ways, to defend themselves from the racism that hemmed their community into dilapidated and poorly serviced neighbourhoods.

Chicago's ethnic and racial tensions, at least in the early part of the period, were also compounded by industrial unrest, and the breakdown of wartime coalitions between unions, reformers, government and industry. In the summer of 1919, 250,000 workers in Chicago went on strike, threatened to do so, or were locked out.[85] In the early part of the 1920s there was a pervasive sense of a radicalised city. Military Intelligence reported that the city was filled with 'disaffected foreigners, blacks, and union members, the kind who gathered in meeting halls to sing: BOLSHEVIK! BOLSHEVIK!'[86] Labour disputes and racial tension became symbols of disloyalty and anti-Americanism as the 'Red Scare' penetrated great swathes of the US.[87] The Russian Revolution may have been geographically distant, but the demographics of cities such as Chicago made it seem worryingly close. The Chicago Community Trust, in a 1919 report on Americanisation, hinted at the effect of foreign politics when it remarked that 'wholesome community consciousness' was being undermined

---

[82]   Grossman, *Land of hope*, 129–31.

[83]   Arvarh E. Strickland, *History of the Chicago Urban League*, Urbana, IL 1966.

[84]   Sam Mitrani, 'Diversity, conflict, empowerment? The politics of black Chicago from abolition to Harold Washington', *JUH* xlii/5 (2016), 959.

[85]   Pacyga, *Chicago*, 209.

[86]   Douglas Bukowski, *Big Bill Thompson, Chicago, and the politics of image*, Urbana, IL 1998, 104.

[87]   Robin Bachin, 'At the nexus of labor and leisure: baseball, nativism, and the 1919 Black Sox scandal', *Journal of Social History* xxxvi/ (2003), 941–62. See also Ann Hagedorn, *Savage peace: hope and fear in America, 1919*, New York, NY 2007.

by a 'sinister class consciousness'.[88] The head resident of the Association House settlement also reported, in the same year, that 'Our Russian friends are talking in seriously anarchistic ways and make us feel that the making of Americans is no easy task unless we "catch 'em young".'[89] For organised labour, however, this proved to be a false dawn. Repressive employers, supported by the government and police, were successful in breaking strikes. Just as important, though, were the divisions within a working class that was fragmented and isolated in neighbourhoods defined by ethnicity and race; it would take a shift in attitudes over the next decade before a revitalised labour movement could emerge in the context of the Great Depression.[90]

In the meantime, the growing criminality of Chicago in the 1920s ascended to the front of public consciousness. The city's reputation as the centre of the illegal alcohol distribution industry during Prohibition, and the open influence of organised crime, was epitomised by the rise to power of gangsters like Al Capone. Gangland killings, bombings and police corruption led to a sense that the city was increasingly lawless.[91] Chicago, in the eyes of civic elites, needed a new form of urban citizenship for the post-First World War period – one that could bracket differences in race, ethnicity and class to create a more civically responsible whole. An enormous number of associations were already working with newcomers in Chicago to encourage belonging and good citizenship. In 1923 a large conference was organised to bring these associations into communication, hosted by the Chicago Historical Society in collaboration with the Americanization Council and the Illinois Society of the Colonial Dames of America. Representatives from a range of organisations, from the Daughters of the American Revolution to the Chicago Council of Social Agencies, gave papers that described their response to the citizenship problem. On one level the significant number of business and industry representatives on the Americanization Council was an example of how value was given to ensuring economic efficiency through education and socialisation. Into the 1920s, now fearful of working-class militancy and aware of the difficulties of maintaining the workforce during periods of labour shortage, more progressive business leaders hoped to unite management and workers through a new sense of 'welfare capitalism'. By giving better wages, promotions and welfare, and experimenting with indus-trial democracy and responsibilities in the community, Chicago's largest employers attempted to create a new harmonious workplace.[92] Citizenship education was arguably one part of this desire.

---

[88] The Chicago Community Trust, *Americanization in Chicago*, Chicago, IL 1919, 3.

[89] 'Report of head resident' (8 Apr. 1919), 2, in *Secretary's report* (Jan. 1919-Dec. 1920), Association House of Chicago records, 1899-1972, CHM, box 2, MSS lot A.

[90] The authority for organised labour in this period is Cohen, *Making a new deal* at pp. 11-51 for the 1919 moment, and chs vi–viii especially for the revitalisation.

[91] Pacyga, *Chicago*, 240-8.

[92] Cohen, *Making a new deal*, 159-213.

But there was also more to the conference: a solemn recognition, across the organisations that made up civic culture, that the demographics of Chicago had changed so rapidly that the potential for instability had grown. Though the president of the Colonial Dames, Frances L. Blatchford, was keen to stress that the word 'Americanization' had been avoided lest it invoke images of people 'forcing our American ideals upon the foreigner', the question of immigration dominated the proceedings.[93] The suggested solutions were multifarious, from English classes and communal demonstrations of patriotism to employment exchanges and music festivals. The range of clubs that offered social services to immigrants, and organisations formed by immigrants themselves, was testament to the multi-layered understanding of the citizenship problem. Associations from backgrounds as diverse as government, business, church and industry worked both alone and together. Chicago's civic culture, a survival but also evolution from the original reform fervour of the late nineteenth century, continued to unite around building good citizenship in spite of the different motivations of individual organisations or institutions.

If Chicago had been surpassed by Los Angeles as a symbol of 'the new' only relatively recently in the 1920s, Manchester's reputation as Britain's shock city was a more distant memory by the twentieth century. London, instead, had become the prime site for ruminations on crime, vice, ill-health and the potential decline of empire.[94] Some aspects of Manchester's Victorian reputation, however, were slow to fade. Slum clearance and council rehousing was never completed in the interwar years, and pockets of terrible deprivation remained. Popular local authors, such as Howard Spring in *Shabby tiger* (1934), still described a dreary and grey Victorian city with awful slums – such as 'the black misery' of the Hulme district.[95] In the 1930s, as depression deepened, other authors were sent by their publishers, or went of their own volition, to 'discover' such problems of the North and to ponder on the state of Britain by proxy. The popular writer J. B. Priestley, who visited Manchester while on his tour of Britain in 1933, found a city scarred by the previous century. Its Victorian legacy, he wrote, was proving hard to shake off, 'the vast, greedy, slovenly, dirty process of industrialism for quick profits' having left behind a sprawling 'Amazonian jungle of blackened bricks'.[96] George Orwell, partially inspired by Priestley, took his own *Road to Wigan Pier* the next year, and noted in passing how 'When you walk through the smoke-dim slums of Manchester

---

[93] 'Conference of those interested in developing a more intelligent and efficient citizenship' (1923), 3, CHM, F38AS.C4co.

[94] See, for example, Andrew Mearns, *The bitter cry of outcast London*, London 1883, and Charles F. G. Masterman, *The heart of the empire: discussions of problems of modern city life in England*, London 1907.

[95] Howard Spring, *Shabby tiger* (1934), London 1973, 96.

[96] J. B. Priestley, *English journey*, London 1934, 252.

you think that nothing is needed except to tear down these abominations and build decent houses in their place.'[97]

Poverty and economic depression, and the hope of political action, coloured the work of these writers, and encouraged them to ignore the more positive aspects of urban culture in the north.[98] Local publications, however, were more optimistic. The soul of Manchester (1929), for example, tried to capture a balanced overview of 'Cottonopolis'. The title was an appropriate reflection of many of the essays within. Written by local characters associated with Manchester's civic and industrial life, it gave an impression that the city was at a juncture where it was under threat but could still be saved. Henry A. Miers, vice-chancellor of the Victoria University of Manchester, was open about the 'sordid inheritance of the too rapid industrial growth' of the previous century, and what he saw as the city's lack of an attractive civic centre. But, at the same time he celebrated the 'intense civic pride' of Mancunians, and the educational, social and religious organisations which were effectively fighting against apathy and indifference to create a new city out of the old. Similarly, for Charles Reilly, an influential architect and teacher, Manchester had 'a very dirty face, scarred with a lot of ugly things and with great patches that are expressionless and dull' but it was also 'full of character', having a 'great tenacity of purpose'.[99] These sorts of observations in the 1920s and 1930s built on a century or more of connecting Manchester's physical landscape to its local and national cultural role. In the early to mid-nineteenth century, this had been one of patriotic wonder and awe, with the new factories and bustling streets demonstrating the growing power and progress of an industrialising country, while civic improvements attested to the city's enterprising middle classes. In the second half of the nineteenth century the development of an ornate and monumental architecture of commerce and civic pride – first, in the Renaissance style, and later in Gothic – caught the attention of tourists. If there was a recognition of the lasting environmental problems of industrialisation, then, it was balanced with an appreciation for the wealth and prestige that it had brought to Manchester – and Britain, too.[100]

In terms of its social context, there was ethnic diversity, and the city was home to some of the largest communities of Italians, Irish and Jews outside London. Conflict did occur; many Britons harboured anti-semitic or racist views, and neighbourhood tensions were apparent between Jewish and white neighbourhoods in Manchester or between colonial black Britons in the nearby

[97] George Orwell, The road to Wigan Pier (1937), New York, NY 1958, 71.

[98] According to Robert Colls, Orwell seemed unaware of working-class networks and mutual support: George Orwell: English rebel, Oxford 2013, 56.

[99] Henry A. Miers, 'Some characteristics of Manchester men', and Charles Reilly, 'The face of Manchester', in W. H. Brindley (ed.), The soul of Manchester, Manchester 1929, 34, 100.

[100] Readman, Storied ground, 195–249.

docks of Salford.[101] Irish nationalism, after the Easter Rising in 1916 and the Irish Civil War (1919–21), was also a feature of the early post-war years. Riots planned in 1920 in Manchester were suppressed without public disturbance, but minor outbreaks continued, and several Sinn Fein leaders were tried at the Manchester Summer Assizes in 1921.[102] At the end of the period, the city was again the site of disturbance following an IRA bombing campaign across Britain – though it was 'no popular mobilization of a minority community' and decidedly less disruptive than in the early 1920s.[103] In general, though, the city avoided the sort of large-scale conflict between communities that characterised Chicago, and its civic culture did not organise around the incorporation of ethnic minorities or newcomers into urban notions of belonging. There was, however, a growing challenge to a stable society coming from other areas. As an industrial city, Manchester felt the rising power of labour that had swept Britain since the start of the century and in the war years especially. Workers fought to maintain wartime gains in the face of rising unemployment and employer pressure for wage reductions, and there were numerous strikes: by industrial workers employed by the city council; a bitter (and unsuccessful) thirteen-week dispute in the engineering sector in 1922; disputes in the cotton mills over the introduction of more machines per operative; and, in 1926, the crowning project of the city's new municipally-led publicity, the Manchester Civic Week, was put back from July to October because of the General Strike.[104]

Suspected disloyalty to the nation could also come from much further afield, with the *Manchester Guardian*, like many others in Britain, looking warily to events in Russia. The prominent Liberal thinker J. L. Hammond, for example, insisted in an article that 'no student of history can fail to see in [the Russian revolution] a danger of the most serious character to constitutional government in this country' and argued that only democracy could secure peace and national stability.[105] Into the 1930s, as the effects of the Great Depression became pronounced, tensions rose further. Unemployed men protesting against the Means Test, organised by the National Unemployed Workers Movement, were met fiercely by mounted and foot police, turning the streets of the city into a battleground. Lurking behind the riots, sometimes in reality but more commonly in the minds of anxious observers, were fears of radical political agitation and foreign influence. When Communists and Jews united to fight the British Union of Fascists following an Oswald Mosley-led meeting at Manchester's Free Trade Hall in 1934, it had seemed like a revolution:

[101] See Bill Williams, 'The Jewish immigrant in Manchester: the contribution of oral history', *Oral History* vii/1 (1979), 50–1, and Jacqueline Jenkinson, *Black 1919: riots, racism and resistance in imperial Britain*, Liverpool 2009, 134–5, 210–11.

[102] Redford, *The history of local government in Manchester*, 22.

[103] Mo Moulton, *Ireland and the Irish in interwar England*, Cambridge 2014, 307–9.

[104] Kidd, *Manchester*, 200–4.

[105] J. L. Hammond, 'A century of Liberalism', MG, 5 May 1921, 53.

'the wildest night Manchester has known for some time'.[106] Ernest Simon, a major industrialist, Liberal (and later Labour) politician and civic figure in Manchester, reacted to this real fear of political extremism by forming the Association for Education in Citizenship, arguing that a failure to appreciate the growth of Fascism abroad would be the downfall of democracy at home.[107]

Each city, then, was experiencing both national- and locally-specific instability in the tumultuous interwar years. Of course, as places, there were significant differences between the two. Chicago, as a defined area, was around three times bigger than Manchester, though the latter often blended into a much larger urban hinterland. Just as obvious was how the issue of new immigration, which dominated Chicago socially, economically and politically, was not really apparent in Manchester. The difference in corruption was also palpable: Chicago was a hotbed of political vice. Frequent cases of municipal 'boodling', the acceptance of bribes for work contracts, hindered those advocating a fair and democratic system of utility ownership. Successes in tackling political corruption, spearheaded by the Municipal Voters League in the 1910s, did not last into the interwar period.[108] Throughout the 1920s local reform enthusiasts lamented the state of municipal politics, and the 'orgy of misrule' of the buffoonish but successful demagogue Republican mayor, William Hale Thompson (in office 1915–23 and 1927–31).[109]

The scale of municipalisation in each city reflected the trust given to urban government. In Chicago, this was very little. Despite a groundswell of support for public ownership in the first two decades of the century as part of an international movement of local government expertise, supported by the Public Ownership League (formed in 1916 in the city), municipalisation never really took hold.[110] The distrust of the city council, dominance of big business, and institutional and financial barriers limited the ability of progressive forces to take city hall. White middle-class flight to the suburbs exacerbated the situation, leaving the inner wards open to politicians happy to exploit ethnic difference to win office, and encouraging the proliferation of 'machine politics'.[111] Manchester, on the other hand, could claim in 1927

---

[106] Joe Carley, *Old friends, old times, 1908–1938: Manchester memories from the diaries of Joe Carley*, n.p. 1990, 42–3.

[107] For more on Simon and the Association see chapter 2 below.

[108] Municipal Voter's League, *Annual preliminary report*, Chicago, IL 1916.

[109] For Thompson's antics – from searching for tree-climbing frogs in Borneo to threatening to punch King George V 'on the snoot' – see George Schottenhamel, 'How Big Bill Thompson won control of Chicago', *Journal of the Illinois State Historical Society* xlv (1952), 30–49.

[110] Public Ownership League of America, *Proceedings of Public Ownership Conference* (bulletin no. 14, 1919).

[111] Gräser, 'A Jeffersonian skepticism'. See Harold F. Gosnell, *Machine politics: Chicago model*, Chicago, IL 1937. Immigrants supported openly corrupt ward bosses as a necessary evil; reformers could not provide an economic support network, so voters turned towards those that could promise jobs or help: Pacyga, *Chicago*, 130–1.

that its annual budget exceeded that of some of the smaller European states, and that one-tenth of the population were dependent on waged employees of the city council. Challenges to municipal ownership in Manchester were only occasionally successful in the interwar period, though debates about governmental reach – such as the siting of reservoirs or airports – did take place.[112] Shena Simon, a councillor, educational reformer, active member of voluntary associations and wife of Ernest Simon, could claim in 1938 that there were 'few echoes of municipal corruption' in a hundred years of city government.[113] Even if this was optimistic, and reflected the desire of the Simons' to create enthusiasm for local service, Manchester was certainly politically honest if compared to Chicago.

The two cities did, however, have some similarities in terms of civic identity. Both occupied a central role economically and culturally in the nation – though Chicago's 'second city' claim was more realistic than Manchester's, which had to contend with both Birmingham and Glasgow. At any rate, the feeling of being a city of importance contributed to how civic elites understood the city's broader contribution to the national community. The rhetoric of the 'Manchester Man', introduced by Isabella Banks in her novel of the same name in 1876 in reference to the self-made entrepreneur of the city's industrial boom, was still worn as a badge of pride by interwar businessmen. In a way this chimed with the similarly masculine 'City of Big Shoulders' adage given to Chicago in 1914 by the poet Carl Sandburg.[114] Gordon Phillips, a drama critic and satirist for the *Manchester Guardian*, even saw a reflection of Manchester's 'inferiority complex' in relation to London in Chicago's own to New York.[115] Each city was a regional *entrepôt* and mercantile powerhouse in its own right, an identity that was carefully shaped between the two wars by their city council, business fraternity and voluntary associations. These two former 'shock cities' serve as archetypes of the modern industrial city – an epitome of a certain form of urban modernity that continued to shape the citizenship narrative of the 1920s and 1930s.

By the interwar period there had been, in both countries, a general shift in understandings of citizenship. Individualist ideas of liberty had been overtaken and replaced with broader collective ideas, both in theory and in civic action – even if this was not always reflected in the reality of local or national party politics. The role of the state and of the association differed between ideologues and reformers, but the success of the nation could no longer be separated from how its inhabitants worked together towards a notion of the greater good. The city played a key role in the formulation of these collective

---

[112] Ernest D. Simon, *A city council from within*, London 1926, 1.

[113] Shena D. Simon, *A century of city government: Manchester, 1838–1938*, London 1938, 404.

[114] Isabella Banks, *Manchester man*, London 1876; Carl Sandburg, *Poetry* 3, no. 6 (1914), 191.

[115] Gordon Phillips, 'Manchester and its critics', in Brindley, *The soul of Manchester*, 262.

citizenship identities. Ideas about urban citizenship left philosophical and political discourse, and were apparent, implicitly but often explicitly, in a range of different spheres of life. The following chapters dig below the surface of urban culture to find this ideology of urban citizenship, despite some key differences, in similar operation in the first half of the twentieth century. By doing so, it will be shown that theories that had developed over the previous three or four decades continued to hold currency but were also adapted to the circumstances of the 1920s and 1930s.

The next chapter begins with civics education, which would have been most people's first explicit introduction to urban citizenship. This was a relatively new discipline in which government, and increasingly the local council in charge of the city, was used as the basis of study. In Britain, this took the form of a commitment inspired by Thomas Hill Green to local civic responsibility and cultural understanding, while, in the US, the new subfield of the social studies emerged from the work of settlements and the philosophy of John Dewey. Enthusiastic teachers now focused on teaching the urban inhabitant the rights and responsibilities that were bestowed upon them as the consequence of living under the benevolent rule of municipal power. This form of citizenship education will first be traced across Britain and the US, and then specifically in Manchester and Chicago. In the former, there was an enthusiasm among the civic elite – led by Ernest Simon, the *Manchester Guardian* and the city council – to provide civics-inflected materials that reflected the power of and support for municipal government in that city. Because of the national limitations of Britain's educational system though – from a weak enthusiasm for secondary education and even outright hostility to direct 'politicised' education – civics in Manchester's educational culture was a relatively small affair, limited to workers' education, private study groups and an inconsistent selection of schools. In Chicago, on the other hand, and somewhat ironically, the superior system of secondary education and broader interest in citizenship education meant that civics penetrated education at all levels – even if the reality of municipal corruption made a mockery of the narrative that it told.

2

Urban Utopias and Education

Civics was a form of education that aimed to induct pupils into an imagined public, based on political engagement, civic responsibility and social belonging. Textbooks, lessons and study groups in the interwar period give the most explicit examples of how the idea of the city was used as an educational tool of citizenship promotion. In a variety of settings and publications, cities were portrayed as interlocking, responsible and responsive communities, whose inhabitants were loyal not just to the nation or the empire but to their neighbours and home town as well. Urban government, for its part, was romanticised as the benevolent father of the citizenry: the source of egalitarian social provision and forward-thinking leadership. Utilities and services managed by the government's (supposedly) non-political bureaucracy, such as gas and water or parks and libraries, were the benefits of belonging to the locality. Municipal government, civic educators insisted, allowed citizens to live the lives they deserved. Such rights, of course, came with a string of responsibilities: civic pride, good urban behaviour and democratic engagement. Widespread civic education was not a new phenomenon and the lessons taught had their basis in late nineteenth-century movements for improving working-class education. Questions about how to create citizenship had, after all, been circulating in the decades before the First World War. The local focus for civics textbooks, though, was more novel. As commentators across Britain and the US questioned how problems of racial or class conflict could be overcome, it was to ideas of urban belonging that they looked.

The flood of new textbooks, on both sides of the Atlantic, demonstrated the currency of the topic.[1] In many cases these texts were not focused on any one place. When civic education discourse filtered down to the city, however, it was adapted to local government and culture. Textbooks for citizenship, as with textbooks in general, varied in style and complexity, depending on the audience that the author had in mind. All had the same central goal, though: to deliver an authoritative overview of an area of knowledge. There are difficulties in knowing exactly how textbooks were actually used, either by teachers constructing their lessons or by students in class. But they are a useful source because they reflect the social conditions in which they were produced – acting not as a site of new knowledge, but as an indication of the state of the field at

---

[1] William E. Marsden, *The school textbook: geography, history and social studies*, London 2001, 16.

the time of publication.[2] In the interwar period, authors in both the US and Britain were clear about their aim: education to create citizens loyal to the city, state and nation.

The first section of this chapter traces the emergence of local civics back to the debates about urban degeneration that were occurring in Britain and the US at the turn of the twentieth century. It investigates how philosophers, and the progressive reformers whom they inspired, questioned what the role of the state, and the local government in particular, should be. Their answer was a reformed municipal body that commanded control over the city – not just in terms of the management of the city and its public institutions, but in the loyalty that it engendered from its ratepayers too. In the second section I trace how this ideology of civics was expressed at the local level in Manchester and Chicago by looking at the activities of the various governmental and associational groups that made up civic culture. In the final section I turn to how this municipal model of civics intermeshed with broader ideas. Though it was a local understanding of citizenship, civics was not in conflict with the other levels of belonging. It worked as a form of 'nested citizenship', from individual to empire, with the neighbourhood, town, region and country in-between. I also, however, investigate how civics could falter or be challenged. Urban government in great American cities failed to live up to the Progressive Era dream of accountable and reformed government. Unequal service provision, and the realities of racial segregation – a feature of civics classrooms and cities more generally – made the egalitarian message of civics sound hollow. In Britain, the experience of faltering economies and widespread poverty in the 1930s also weakened the idea of the city council as capable of caring for its citizens. In contrast to the US, however, the reach of civics in Britain was limited more by the general shortcomings of the educational system and the wariness of the central Board of Education about the 'political implications' of citizenship education.

Idealising the municipal: origins, theory and expression

There was a degree of crossover in civics discourse in Britain and the US due to their similar experience of urbanisation and the transnational communication about problems and solutions that followed. Intellectually, each country embraced the late nineteenth-century shift towards an understanding of the city as an organic social entity. This was readily apparent in urban planning, and in the enthusiasm for zoning – whether through ordinances or Garden Cities. Emphasising the 'social city' was to begin to understand the relationship between inhabitants and their environment, both physical and inter-personal,

---

[2] Chris Stray, 'Paradigms regained: towards a historical sociology of the textbook', *Journal of Curriculum Studies* xxvi/1 (1994), 1–29.

rather than concentrating on individual failings of 'habit' as had previously been dominant in earlier Victorian understandings of poverty and morality. Contemporaries now overcame their unease at trying to comprehend the industrial city and, equipped with new statistical information, instead began to formulate new public policies of intervention.[3]

On both sides of the Atlantic there were particular ways in which this new understanding was expressed. In Britain, the Scottish biologist, planner and geographer Patrick Geddes pioneered an 'applied sociology' of civics that sought to understand urbanisation and its effects on society. He delivered these ideas to social reformers attending the first meetings of the British Sociological Society in 1904 and 1905. Central to his approach was the use of local geographic social surveys to understand urban problems. Civic action and social service, he argued, could only be effective when environmental context, alongside historical and cultural traditions, was fully grasped. Improving the city, in a piecemeal process he dubbed 'conservative surgery', would inspire and train new generations of local citizens.[4] Geddes, however, eventually became more absorbed in actual town planning than education. His disdain for social reform through state intervention, and his insistence on a highly-selective group of acolytes, also meant that his version of civics never became a full movement.[5] His ideas, though, did seep into textbooks in Britain.[6] His legacy to civics education was threefold: firstly, in providing civics enthusiasts with a new conception of how the city shaped community; secondly, placing education for citizenship within the purview of sociology; and finally, encouraging geographers and sociologists to think of the city in relationship to its region – an ideal that transferred to planning practice in the US as well.[7] Before and after the First World War, his version of civics was taken up by the Civic Education League in Britain. Though the League had limited success and was not long-lived, with its influence declining from the mid-1920s, Ebe M. White, one of the League's most consistent supporters, published several civics books in the interwar period that owed a great deal to Geddes.[8]

---

[3] Patrick Joyce, *The rule of freedom: liberalism and the modern city*, London 2003, 171–3; Lees and Lees, *Cities and the making of modern Europe*, 7.

[4] Alex Law, 'The ghost of Patrick Geddes: civics as applied sociology', *Sociological Research Online* x/2 (2005), 5.

[5] Helen Meller, *Patrick Geddes: social evolutionist and city planner*, London 1990, 12, 90, 143–5, 149.

[6] See, for example, Ebe M. White, *Civics in progress: suggestions to teachers of the subject*, London 1929.

[7] Geddes, along with Ebenezer Howard, influenced Lewis Mumford and Clarence Stein, who founded the Regional Planning Association of America: Edward K. Spann, *Designing modern America: the Regional Planning Association of America and its members*, Columbus, OH 1996.

[8] See Peter Brett, 'Citizenship education in Britain in the shadow of the Great War', *Citizenship Teaching and Learning* viii/1 (2013), 62–3.

Like many of his contemporaries who were contemplating citizenship and the city, Geddes also drew on the philosophy of idealism. For Thomas Hill Green, arguably the most influential of the idealists, it was not the business of the state to enforce morality but to maintain the material conditions in which goodness and liberty could thrive. He enthusiastically served as a city councillor while teaching in Oxford and believed that it was through municipal administration and the local community that civic engagement most fruitfully took place. He provided ideas that could justify benevolent state intervention, and a method of bridging seemingly conflicting attitudes of individualism and communitarianism.[9] Green died in 1882, but his ideas continued to influence educational thought and practice in the first half of the twentieth century through social critics such as L. T. Hobhouse, R. H. Tawney and Graham Wallas.[10] This influence also spread into the burgeoning growth of local civics after the First World War. Green's thought gave civics educators a way to think about a common purpose and fellowship that could overcome interwar class politics and social strife, and a language that articulated the role of the local state in terms of its social provision. He was also enthusiastic about the city-states of ancient Greece as a model for civic pride and engagement, reflecting a common attitude in both university social science and educated public culture.[11] Geddes and Green thus represented the shaping of civics in Britain during a wider cultural moment in which the social basis of citizenship was linked with urban conditions.

In the US a similar shift toward a distinctively community- and urban-based notion of civics was taking place. The work of Arthur W. Dunn in the early years of the twentieth century, drawing on ideas that had been circulating in the previous two decades, was a clear point of departure. His book *The community and the citizen* (1907) was a foundational text of 'social studies' in secondary schools in the late 1910s.[12] He emphasised that pupils should participate in the life of their community, living citizenship instead of merely memorising and reciting facts, and specified teaching the services that government performed

---

9   Green, 'Liberal legislation'. See Sandra D. Otter, '"Thinking in communities": late nineteenth-century Liberals, Idealists and the retrieval of community', *Parliamentary History* xvi/1 (1997), 67-4. For a fuller treatment of Green's philosophy and influence see Denys Leighton, *The Greenian moment: T. H. Green, religion and political argument in Victorian Britain*, Exeter 2004.

10   Peter Gordon and John White, *Philosophers as educational reformers: the influence of Idealism on British educational thought and practice*, London 1979, and José Harris, 'Political thought and the welfare state, 1870-1940: an intellectual framework for British social policy', *Past & Present* 135 (May 1992), 116-41.

11   Matthew Grimley, *Citizenship, community and the Church of England: Liberal Anglican theories of the state between the wars*, Oxford 2004, 59-63.

12   Arthur W. Dunn, *The community and the citizen*, Boston, MA 1907. Social studies was defined loosely as the study of the 'those subject matter [that] relates directly to the organization and development of human society, and to man as a member of social groups': Bureau of Education, *The social studies in secondary education* (bulletin no. 28, 1916), 9.

rather than its legal structures or statutes. Dunn believed that it was through government that a community of citizens cooperated, and consequently argued that this relationship should be the focus of civics.[13] The version of civics that Dunn proposed reflected more generally the ideals of many progressive reformers. If the state were responsible for the conditions that determined the health and welfare of society, as they argued, individual liberty would paradoxically arise from the regulation of the urban environment. The relationship between liberty and regulation, of course, was a volatile one. At one end of the scale, the work of reformers can be seen as genuine concern for social justice and democracy; at the other, an attempt at social control from business elites who wished to preserve the power structures of capitalist society. Dunn and his contemporaries in social studies reflected this complexity, though if there was a key figure to whom they looked for guidance, it was the great educational philosopher John Dewey.[14]

Like many of his Progressive Era contemporaries, Dewey looked back to his small-town upbringing for his values.[15] He encouraged the re-creation of the small-town civic community in the city and emphasised the importance of educating children to think of themselves in a communal rather than individual context.[16] That being said, the more radical 'democratic' suggestions of Dewey's civic education philosophy – notably the empowering of parents, students, teachers or community representatives – were side-lined in favour of an 'administrative' perspective that conceived of good citizenship in terms of 'sensible support for modern specialists'.[17] Dewey's pragmatism, if watered down, still encouraged a viewpoint of the American state that went beyond abstract or ideal theories to look at the 'real world' of policies and practices: how officials operated, how policy was formulated and how government worked.[18] The crossover between the ideology of Green and Dewey in this sense, and more broadly British idealism and American Progressivism, is striking. Dewey was aware of and wrote about Green's theories, and he

[13]   Arthur W. Dunn, *Community civics for city schools*, Boston, MA 1921. For context see Julie A. Reuben, 'Beyond politics: community civics and the redefinition of citizenship in the Progressive Era', *History of Education Quarterly* xxxvii/4 (1997), 401–4.

[14]   Thomas Fallace, 'John Dewey's influence on the origins of the social studies: an analysis of the historiography and new interpretation', *Review of Educational Research* lxxix/2 (2009), 604; Ruth A. Nieboer, 'Arthur Dunn: civic visionary from the heartland', conference paper, Annual Meeting of the National Council for the Social Studies, San Antonio, Tx, 16–19 November 2000, <https://catalogue.nla.gov.au/Record/5676049>.

[15]   Quandt, *From the small town to the great community*.

[16]   John Dewey, 'The school and social progress', in Dewey, *The school and society*, 19–46, and *The public and its problems: an essay in political enquiry* (1927), Philadelphia, PA 2012. See James J. Carpenter, '"The development of a more intelligent citizenship": John Dewey and the social studies', *Education and Culture* xxii/2 (2006), 31–42.

[17]   Smith, *Civic ideals*, 464.

[18]   William J. Novak, 'The myth of the "weak" American state', *American Historical Review* cxiii/3 (2008), 764–5.

arguably owed a debt to the philosopher.[19] Idealism thus 'offered a shared language and a shared set of interests' that shaped the 'intellectual playing field' between Britain and the US.[20] Like their European counterparts, Dewey and other educational reformers such as Dunn were seeking practical responses to modern problems.[21] The social studies thus emerged from debates about the effects of urban living on society, and offered a resolution to the conflicting impulses of its leaders through the movement's attack on individualism's supposedly divisive impact on the locality and nation.

The ideas of community civics spread rapidly. In 1913, at a meeting of an association of history teachers, two of the three resolutions passed echoed the tenets of community civics. The report emphasised that the focus of citizenship teaching should be on the functions of government and not just the machinery, and that pupils should be encouraged to work on topics related to their experience of their immediate surroundings.[22] The United States Bureau of Education, the National Education Association and the American Political Science Association also made civics education the core of their policy.[23] In 1929 the historian Armand J. Gerson could summarise that 'In none of the social studies have the changes of the last twenty years been so marked as in the field of civics.'[24] Gone was the simple study of government that had taken the form of a verbatim memorisation of the Constitution. Titles now referred to a new form of instruction, and textbooks argued that the civics movement was distinctly different from that of the previous generation.[25] This may sound like rhetoric, designed to sell new copies of old ideas. But authors actually demonstrated how the discipline had evolved. Rather than simply detailing government and its machinery in order to inform voters, citizenship was now portrayed as 'social': citizens were shown how they lived within, and benefitted from, the existing hierarchy. To achieve this, society was conceptualised as a web of connections between individuals and the governments that maintained their lives. Readers were asked to consider two simple questions:

[19]   See, for example, John Dewey, 'The philosophy of Thomas Hill Green', *Andover Review* xi (1889), 337–55.

[20]   Stears, *Pluralists, and the problems of the state*, 27.

[21]   See Pierre-Yves Saunier, 'Introduction' to Pierre-Yves Saunier and Shane Ewen (eds), *Another global city: historical explorations into the transnational municipal moment, 1850–2000*, Basingstoke 2008, 1–18.

[22]   Rolla M. Tryon, *The social sciences as school subjects: report of the Commission on the Social Studies*, New York, NY 1935.

[23]   See United States Bureau of Education, *Report on the teaching of community civics* (bulletin no. 23, 1915), and S. H. Ziegler and H. J. Wilds, *Our community: good citizenship in towns and cities*, Philadelphia, PA 1918, iii, in which the authors made reference to preparing their book in the style of the Bureau's bulletin. For further discussion see Reuben, 'Beyond politics', 401.

[24]   A. J. Gerson, 'The social studies in the grades, 1909–1929', *Historical Outlook* xx (1929), 272.

[25]   R. L. Ashley, *The new civics: a textbook for secondary schools*, New York, NY 1921, p. v.

what was the community doing for the citizen, and what did the citizen owe the community?[26]

The similar experience of the late nineteenth-century city in Britain and the US, and to an extent a transnational intellectual and progressive municipal culture, had led to a parallel sense of civics in the opening decades of the twentieth century. Textbooks attempted to accessibly depict a complex and vibrant picture of localities transformed by their municipal authority. To be safe, vigorous and happy was to fully receive the benefits of a benevolent city council – one that was less concerned with administration and politics than it was with improving the lives of urban dwellers. Effective government, as one interwar British text put it, created the social conditions that made it 'easy for people to be good'.[27] One text, adapted for the syllabus of the British Association Committee on Training in Citizenship, described the 'State' as 'really a great family': it told citizens 'to do certain things and to avoid others' so that they may become 'good members of this great family'. To achieve this, however, meant avoiding 'the wrong actions' and keeping 'the wishes of the State'.[28] Civics celebrated this vision of the state as 'family' from the perspective of the municipal city especially. Readers were asked to consider what they owed to their home town: clean paved streets, fresh water, protection from crime, schools and opportunities for fun and leisure. Municipal employees were now the heroes of the story: dustmen, health officers, tram drivers, firemen and road menders celebrated as the protectors of the modern city.

In both countries civics texts described the fabric and municipal infrastructure of the city. Readers were invited to imagine what they would see if the top portion of a street was taken off. Water mains, sewers, electric cables: these were technologies mastered by benevolent local governments with the sole purpose of ensuring the life and health of the citizen. Authors stressed how elaborate and complex such systems were and tried to convey just how engrained municipal provision was in the everyday life of the urban inhabitant. Vital to this approach was the use of comparison. Readers were encouraged to imagine what it would be like to live in the dirty, dangerous and unhealthy city of the nineteenth century. In these idealistic narratives of progress, local government had conquered the shock city of the nineteenth century, and, in doing so, enabled those who lived in places with an urban government to attain a full and healthy citizenship.[29] Civics texts carefully informed the

---

[26]   Ziegler and Wilds, *Our community*, p. xi; Edgar W. Ames and Arvie Eldred, *Community civics*, New York, NY 1922, p. v.

[27]   Conrad Gill, *Government and people: an introduction to the study of citizenship*, London 1921, 2.

[28]   C. H. Blakiston, *Elementary civics*, London 1920, 2.

[29]   For Britain see J. R. Peddie, *The British citizen: a book for young readers*, Glasgow 1920, 3; Gill, *Government and people*, 5; and Charles S. S. Higham, *The good citizen: an introduction to civics*, London 1934, pp. ii, 13, 18. For the US see Charles McCarthy, Flora Swan and Jennie McMullin, *Elementary civics: the new civics*, Chicago, IL 1918, 22–4; Peter Roberts, *Civics for*

reader that government would not make individuals live in a certain way; instead, this was deemed to be an inherent and obvious civic responsibility. Showing citizens what was 'being done for them' would implicitly highlight 'what they are expected to do for themselves and for their fellows'.[30] In Britain this was expressed in two ways. Firstly, in Greenian terms, as a 'contract' of citizenship between individuals and the state. Freedom and liberty were the reward for democratic engagement and active citizenship.[31] Secondly, and as Green himself had also liked to invoke, as an inheritance of ancient Greece and its republican practices, Athenian democracy and civic pride.[32] In the US, enthusiasm for the rationalised municipal administration of the Progressive Era, traced through Dewey and Dunn, was similarly used to inspire local people into pride and civic action.

The triumphalism of civics texts demonstrated the centrality of urban ambivalence to interwar citizenship in several ways. Firstly, there was a heavy emphasis on the question of health and the body. Politicians and reformers increasingly stressed the importance of individual physical fitness to ensure national competitiveness in both the economic and military arenas. Education that pointed the citizen towards the health provisions of local government had an obvious relevance in achieving this goal. Secondly, the extensive focus on city government inadvertently betrayed a widespread feeling in administrative circles that municipal work was too much taken for granted, as was especially the case in Britain, or in desperate need of reform, as was painfully apparent in many American cities. Civics education, its promoters hoped, would awaken a new enthusiasm for supporting or holding office in local government. Civics tried, then, to stimulate a common response across urban society: a more intelligent and committed community that saw the city as the site wherein to both receive and enact one's individual citizenship.

Most textbooks were written without a particular city in mind. But local governments and associations also produced their own civics materials, using the city that they knew best as a case study of civic pride and its corresponding responsibility. Political and governmental culture in Manchester and Chicago was, of course, very different. Chicago was plagued by corruption and epitomised dysfunctional government and machine politics. Municipal ownership was limited, and faith was usually greater in private enterprise than in the city council (if only as a lesser of two evils). Manchester's council, in contrast to Chicago's, looked like a much safer body to be entrusted with the life and

---

coming Americans, New York, NY 1917, 53-4; Edwin W. Adams, A community civics: a textbook in loyal citizenship, Chicago, IL 1920, 55; Ames and Eldred, Community civics, 26, 96; and Ashley, The new civics, 13.

30   Mabel Hill and Philip Davis, Civics for new Americans, New York, NY 1916, p. iii.

31   Frederick R. Worts, Citizenship: its meaning, privileges and duties, London 1919, 202, 276; Arthur T. Phythian, The ethics of citizenship: a universal basis from which to determine progressively the rights and duties of citizenship, Manchester 1923.

32   Higham, The good citizen, 184.

health of the city. Despite these differences in framework, however, the ideal of civics in both cities was similar. Thinkers in each drew on the wider trend towards community civics, and the enthusiasm for urban community. At the same time, local associations and government in both cities built their lessons around what they saw as their civic identity and story of progress. The disorganised and degenerative city of the past was now presented as the antipathy of the fruits of good government and urban regulation in the present – from shock city to citizenship city.

Civics in Chicago and Manchester

The rise of machine politics in the 1920s should not obscure how the previous decades of Progressivism had gifted Chicago a public culture where many groups could propose urban reform, and work in broad-based coalitions, with local government as a meeting point or vehicle for change. A kind of politics that joined the state with organisations of reform, labour, women and mass culture survived into the 1920s.[33] The Chicago Board of Education played a central role. In 1921, recognising a lack of central guidance in the city for citizenship and language instructors, it produced a pamphlet for those who worked with classes of adult citizenship applicants. The structure and content of this manual was based on existing naturalisation forms and textbooks, but, as the authors put it, was adapted to Chicago's standpoint. Four simple and linked concepts were central: firstly, that government (city, county, state and nation) was planned, effective and a 'good' system; secondly, that government was both indispensable and convenient, and the only way for objectives to be attained; thirdly, that the people were a 'silent partner' that benefitted from the products of government; and finally, that living in an American city, and America more generally, was a partnership of all people.[34]

Because this publication was meant for instructors rather than their students, the authors were candid in explaining their approach. Civics, they said, had to begin with city government before it proceeded to the level of county, state and federal government. Those being taught were supposedly not accustomed to learning about abstract ideas. 'Products', they emphasised, were to be prioritised over detailed explanations of the mechanics of government.[35] By this they meant utilities and social services rather than the supporting administrative systems. This was a clear inheritance from the ideas of Dunn. Students were encouraged to understand their citizenship in relation to the city where they received benefits such as water or leisure facilities such as parks

---

[33]   Bachin, *Building the South Side*, 306.

[34]   Chicago Board of Education, *Suggestions to instructors on a course in citizenship*, Chicago, IL 1921, 5.

[35]   Ibid. 8.

and baths. Starting with recognisable areas of north, south, east and west, the lesson then moved to neighbourhoods, and finally to streets. One lesson had students repeat a mantra: 'Chicago is my home city. What is home? "There's no place like home."'[36] This home was one, the course insisted, created by local government and its representative officials. To illustrate this, the guide encouraged instructors to use the example of water provision – a popular story of municipal progress since 1909, when the Sanitary District had finished the twenty-eight mile Sanitary and Ship Canal. This was a story of triumph over both the unhealthy shock city and nature, too: the canal improved water quality by enabling the District to reverse the flow of the Chicago River away from Lake Michigan.[37] To make students understand the effort required for something as simple as a glass of water, one lesson traced the flow of water in reverse order from the faucet, water pipe, street water mains, pumping and purification stations, concrete water tunnels that went from the city into the lake, and the source: cribs which stood up in the Lake around four miles offshore. Through municipal technology, the citizens benefitted, both mentally and physically, from baths, clean clothes, tidy streets, watered lawns and parks. Private companies, the text suggested, had failed in the past to deliver enough water. By contrast, Chicago's government had provided 'millions of streams for every emergency'.[38]

The civics focus also went far beyond the official classes organised by bodies such as the Chicago Board of Education, and was directly enabled by the extensive associational network of the city. In 1929, in a period of just nine weeks, fifty-four outdoor Americanisation meetings were held in playgrounds of the South Park System, and forty-five indoor meetings were held in community social centres that were mostly organised on a religious or ethnic community basis. The programme was under the direction of the Stock Yards Community Council, an organisation set up earlier that decade to cover an area of about sixteen square miles.[39] Working with the University of Chicago Settlement, it aimed to give a helping hand to the unprivileged, and to clear away the worst features of the infamous 'Back of the Yards' neighbourhood.[40] According to a report in the Chicago Tribune, thirty-five different nationalities were in attendance at over ninety-eight lectures delivered by the Young Men's Christian

---

[36]   Ibid. 27.

[37]   Louis P. Cain, Sanitation strategy for a lakefront metropolis: the case of Chicago, DeKalb, IL 1978; Bureau of Engineering, Department of Public Works, City of Chicago, A century of progress in water works, Chicago, IL 1933.

[38]   Chicago Board of Education, Suggestions to instructors, 28.

[39]   The Young Citizen i/1 (Dec. 1929), 7.

[40]   The 'Back of the Yards' area of Chicago was immortalised in Upton Sinclair, The jungle, New York, NY 1906. Into the interwar period the area continued to be lamented for its deterioration, disease and delinquency. For a microhistory of this area see Dominic A. Pacyga, Slaughterhouse: Chicago's Union Stock Yard and the world it made, Chicago, IL 2015.

Association (YMCA), with a total attendance of 400,000.[41] Community singing and films were used to make the meetings entertaining, but the main feature was nine stereopticon meetings on the topic of 'The Question of Chicago's Government'.[42]

By the start of the 1930s community civics was entrenched in American educational culture. At this point a new manual was drafted by the Commission on Citizenship Education, a local body appointed by the superintendent of schools, William J. Bogan, and led by the political scientists Augustus R. Hatton and Charles E. Merriam and the educational psychologist Charles H. Judd.[43] *Local government in Chicago* painted a picture of a modern and municipally managed city: clean, paved and brightly lit streets; new and carefully cared-for public buildings; and an efficient system of bridges. Celebrated particularly was the city's sewerage system – the largest publicly owned utility in Chicago, valued at 4.5 billion dollars. Utilities and services were given to the urban inhabitant as a right provided by government: 'not a matter for dispute, but an accepted commonplace'.[44] City dwellers had the right to expect that government would ensure the effective regulation of public health: clean and chemically tested water, the management of smoke pollution and the provision of parks and playgrounds. Financed with a $5,000 grant from the Union League Club of Chicago to undertake an investigation of civic training in the public schools, the manual does not seem to have been used directly in Chicago's classrooms. At any rate, though, the accompanying report was clear: for the city's schools to have an effective programme of citizenship instruction, it had to be based on materials about Chicago. The manual would, they suggested, be an accurate and up-to-date example of how to achieve that goal.[45]

The seeming failure of this large manual to make it into print at the start of the decade was by no means a sign that enthusiasm for civics in Chicago had ended with the onset of the Great Depression in the late 1920s. In 1933 the local historian Bessie Louise Pierce published a study of citizens' organisations in Chicago and their civic training of youth that demonstrated the spread of citizenship education. Not all these organisations were solely concerned with municipal or community civics, of course; a lot fitted more into a nativist or patriotic approach, reflecting the clamour for '100 percent Americanism'. Many, however, shared a direct lineage to the community civics movement.[46] By this point, though, many of the agencies that were providing

[41] 'YMCA says 386,398 persons attended talk on Americanization', CT, 11 Oct. 1929, 42.

[42] *The Young Citizen* i/1 (Dec. 1929), 7.

[43] Chicago Commission on Citizenship Education, 'Local government in Chicago' (1932), CHM, F38E .C421.

[44] Ibid. 3.

[45] 'News and notes', *American Political Science Review* xxv/1 (1931), 161. For the report see Committee on Civic Education of the Superintendent's Advisory Council of the Chicago Public Schools, *Education for citizenship*, Chicago, IL 1933.

[46] Bessie Louise Pierce, *Citizens' organizations and the civic training of youth*, Chicago, IL 1933.

citizenship classes were struggling, as their finances dwindled during the Great Depression. Government expansion at the federal level under the New Deal fortuitously gave the networks of associations a huge boost. Ideals of the federal state and the city were now aligned. Before this unprecedented intervention, the federal government had not often sought to fashion the social aspects of citizenship, concentrating instead on immigration and naturalisation policy.[47] Now, however, there was a fear that democracy was cracking under the pressure of unemployment, and that radical left-wing ideologies were taking root. Millions of dollars now poured into the city, relieving social agencies of financial burdens that had accumulated during the previous few years. From 1933 until after the Second World War, federal funding for adult education, first through the Civil Works Education Service and then the Works Progress Administration, ran into many millions of dollars for Chicago.[48] Federal money consequently led to a widespread rise in citizenship education. By 1937 the Citizenship Department of Chicago's Adult Education Program had grown to 147 centres, 194 classes and 63 teachers, with a weekly attendance of 4,654 in 1937. Three years later there were classes and study-groups in 500 locations throughout the city (*see* Figure 1).[49] By the mid-1930s, 91 per cent of schools also reported that civics texts were used in assemblies and English classes.[50]

The New Deal agencies kept some administrative oversight but depended on cooperation with well-established networks in Chicago. Organisers and supervisors were appointed by local government officials, who retained curricular control, and the classes were organised with churches, YMCAs and settlements, each of which provided classroom space.[51] By the mid-1930s there was already a wide network and choice of neighbourhood for potential students, and the Works Progress Administration was well aware that the success of the New Deal programme depended on its use.[52] Classroom material was given to teachers in these schemes, many of whom were new to the field and had previously been unemployed. As with the earlier guidelines produced by the

[47] Suzanne Mettler, 'Social citizens of separate sovereignties: governance in the New Deal welfare state', in Sidney M. Milkis and Jerome M. Mileur (eds), *The New Deal and the triumph of Liberalism*, Amherst, MA 2002, 231.

[48] Chicago Board of Education, *Adult Education Annual Report for 1937*, Chicago, IL 1938, 3.

[49] Ibid. 13; 'You are invited to visit projects of the professional and service division of the Work Projects Administration' (1940), 2, in Miscellaneous pamphlets on the Adult Education Program of the Work Projects Administration, CHM, F38QF.C4A3z.

[50] Committee on Civic Education, *Education for citizenship*, 29–30.

[51] Vernon Bowyer, 'Some new tendencies in adult education' (1 Oct. 1940), 2, Vernon Bowyer papers, CHM, folder 14, box 2, M1970; 'Introducing Association House' (1935), Association House of Chicago records, box 1, MSS lot A; 'Special committee appointed to study the authority, responsibilities and duties of the persons employed on the Adult Education project' (Jan. 1939), Miscellaneous pamphlets on the Adult Education Program.

[52] 'Have you leisure time?' (11 Mar. 1937), 1, Vernon Bowyer papers, folder 17, box 2, M1970.

Figure 1. A civics class in progress at Association House in Chicago (c. 1930s)

Board of Education, and the aborted *Local government in Chicago*, it was themes of local community and service provision that were stressed. Lessons focused on everyday interaction between city inhabitants and their government; the municipal employees, from firemen and policemen to street cleaners and garbage men, who ensured a safe and clean city; and the schools, libraries and parks where citizens could learn and relax. In turn, they had to pay their taxes, obey laws, protect public property and do their own bit to keep their city clean. Above all, the emphasis was on community and responsibility, and connecting the success of the city to the future of the nation. As one lesson put it: 'we can only have a good country when everyone helps'.[53]

Civics in Britain, in practice, was not as central to school education as it was in the US. Manchester was consequently not atypical in failing to house a movement as cohesive or large as Chicago's – and was, even then, probably still outstanding relative to other British cities. But municipal and community civics ideology still informed civic culture in areas beyond schooling. Taking the lead was the *Manchester Guardian*, with the publication of a civic *Yearbook* in 1925.[54] By encouraging civic engagement and intelligent citizenship in relation to the governance of the city, the *Guardian* reflected its continuing stewardship

[53] Reference was made to the fact that 'community civics' texts were to be used in the adult education classes. See 'Social studies conference conducted by the Chicago Board of Education with the Works Progress Administration' (20-22 Dec. 1937), in Miscellaneous pamphlets on the Adult Education Program.

[54] *Manchester Guardian year book*, Manchester 1925. For the antecedents of this genre of

under C. P. Scott, a Liberal figure of considerable influence. For Scott, the role of the *Guardian* was to be 'more than a business' and to reflect and influence 'the life of a whole community'. As an 'instrument of government' it could 'educate, stimulate, [and] assist' or it could 'do the opposite'.[55] The newspaper's *Yearbook* thus contained information about the city council that it hoped would 'inspire a prouder and more intelligent citizenship' among those living in the 'great community' of Manchester. The council, it insisted, was the best bulwark against the 'dirt, darkness, disease and lawlessness [that] would turn Manchester into a city of Horrible Night'.[56] The *Yearbook* also encouraged the city council to take a more active role in its own promotion. In a section detailing what Manchester citizens received in return for the payment of their rates, it argued that the Corporation had to publicise its activities in a cheap and popular format, reflecting the turn towards more demotic conceptions of citizenship.[57]

This encouragement came at a time when the city council was already beginning to develop a more ambitious approach to civic publicity. In 1925 it also published a new annual handbook: *How Manchester is managed*.[58] It was edited by Matthew Anderson, a young Scottish journalist who was in the process of branding himself as a 'publicity expert' – local government being one key employer in these early years of the 'public relations' profession.[59] The handbook told a story of 'cradle to the grave' care through the services and utilities provided by the council. Municipal administration was the epitome of modernity, since 'As soon as you get beyond the sweep of the scavenger's broom you are outside the machinery of civilisation.'[60] Each year the handbook became more popular, with updated versions getting 'fatter and more informative'; by the 1930s 10,000 copies were printed annually, and were either sold or given to schools, libraries and local conferences.[61] *How Manchester is managed* provided a foundation for citizenship education in a variety of settings, such as the New Lecture Series at the Byrom School in 1934-5, aimed at working men,

---

publication see the discussion of town histories and almanacs in Patrick Joyce, *Visions of the people: industrial England and the question of class, c. 1848–1914*, Cambridge 1991, 180–2.

[55] See *The political diaries of C. P. Scott, 1911–1928*, ed. Trevor Wilson, Cambridge 1970, which demonstrate Scott's importance in Liberal political circles long after he retired from parliament in 1906. For quotation see C. P. Scott, 'A hundred years' in 'The *Manchester Guardian* centenary number', MG, 5 May 1921, 35.

[56] *Manchester Guardian year book* (1925), 12.

[57] Ibid. 13.

[58] Matthew Anderson (ed.), *How Manchester is managed*, Manchester 1925.

[59] 'Publicity expert', *Southern Reporter*, 11 Nov. 1926, 4.

[60] Anderson, *How Manchester is managed*, 50.

[61] 'In Manchester', MG, 2 Nov. 1929, 15, and 'Classified ad 102', MG, 23 Apr. 1938, 5; George Montagu Harris, *Municipal government in Britain: a study of the practice of local government in ten of the larger British cities*, London 1939, 270; 'In Manchester', MG, 12 Nov. 1930, 11.

and the selective Manchester Grammar, which worked with the city council to provide civics lessons for its pupils in the 1930s.[62] Engaged amateurs, such as the rector of Withington and former city councillor Ronald Allen, also used the handbook as a teaching resource. In 1937, concerned by the apathy of the electorate, he started a weekly course of study on civic affairs, attended by thirty young men, taking the theme of 'What the city does for me and what I can do for it'.[63]

As well as *How Manchester is managed*, Allen's civics class used *A city council from within* (1927), written by Ernest Simon – one of Manchester's most important civic figures.[64] Simon was intensely interested in the question of citizenship, which he often articulated as the cooperative relationship of citizens with their municipal authority (he was a councillor from 1912). In tune with popular sociological currents, he also stressed ancient models of citizenship, declaring that 'Every Athenian citizen profoundly believed in and loved his city, and was prepared to work and, if necessary, die for her.'[65] Simon traced his political 'coming of age' to the Liberal social reforms of 1906-14, when he was looking for a framework within which to realise his 'religious' civic duty and had been drawn into the world of the Fabians through Sidney and Beatrice Webb. Linked to the idealism of Green, though with a much stronger commitment to collectivism, the Fabians also gave Simon a connection to other Green-influenced thinkers, such as Graham Wallas and J. A. Hobson. Simon, through his links with C. P. Scott, was also closely affiliated with the New Liberal *Manchester Guardian*. In the interwar period these various connections were cemented through the Liberal Summer School, which Simon was instrumental in forming in 1921.[66]

Simon's thoughts on civics in Manchester were expressed in his detailed exposition of *A city council from within*. The preface was provided by Wallas, who foreshadowed the main points of Simon's text by arguing that 'for the average English citizen the possibility of health, of happiness, of progress towards the old Greek ideal of "beautiful goodness," depends on his local government'.[67] For Wallas this was an important compliment; his only notable criticism of the 'golden period' of Ancient Athens was its neglect of the material infrastructure that gave convenience to the lives of citizens.[68] It was these benefits – such as gas, electricity, water, policing and transport - that Simon described.

[62]   Manchester Education Committee, *A survey of the facilities for adult education available in Manchester*, Manchester 1935, 6-7; Levi Hill, 'School children and local government', *The Citizen* i/3 (1937), 16.

[63]   'The municipal life of Manchester', MG, 14 Oct. 1937, 13.

[64]   Simon, *A city council from within*.

[65]   Ibid. 234-5.

[66]   Mary D. Stocks, *Ernest Simon of Manchester*, Manchester 1963, 23-4.

[67]   Graham Wallas, 'Preface', to Simon, *A city council from within*, p. vii.

[68]   Julia Stapleton, *Political intellectuals and public identities in Britain since 1850*, Manchester 2001, 39.

Municipal provision, he believed, could inspire an Athenian civic dedication. His book sold 'pretty well', shifting just under 2,000 copies by 1937.[69] Though not directly involved in its work, Simon was also linked to the Workers' Educational Association (WEA), subscribing generously to the association's finances and frequently communicating with R. H. Tawney, a key figure in the Association. Tawney derived and expanded his notion of ethical socialism from Green and gave the state a key role in maintaining true equality for individuals to be free and self-improve.[70] As the leading secular provider of voluntary adult education in this period, the WEA absorbed the civic culture of towns and districts where activity took place, as well as expressing the Greenian nature of its leaders such as Tawney and Albert Mansbridge.[71]

One of the WEAs goals was to inspire a working-class enthusiasm for public service.[72] In the educational programme of the Manchester and District Branch of the Working Men's Club and Institute Union Ltd, provided by the WEA, this was clear. The series of talks for 1928 emphasised the relationship between the individual and the state and explained how government directly affected daily life. The first lecture asked 'What would happen if all Government suddenly stopped?', and encouraged students to discuss the benefits of services such as schools, policing and recreational provision. The second lecture went further, detailing how safety and health were 'the first and most important fruits of good government'. Benevolent state intervention gave citizens the freedom to use their energies to their own advantage and also to the benefit 'of the nation as a whole'. Subsequent lectures covered education and government, the citizen's part in making laws and the corresponding duty of ensuring that those laws worked. The final lecture summarised these aspects of government and the nature of its relationship with the individual, the text of which read as a primer of Green-inspired thought: the state's role was in the maintenance of freedom and the ability of the individual to improve him- or herself, for the benefit of the common good – which started within the city.[73]

Civics books in Manchester reached their climax in 1938 with *Your city: Manchester, 1838–1938*, of which 4,000 copies were published to celebrate the centenary of the charter of governmental incorporation.[74] Created by

[69]   Simon, *A city council from within*, 229, 234–5. For sales see E. D. Simon to B. Simon, 22 Dec. 1937, Ernest Emil Darwin Simon papers, MCA, GB127.M14/306.

[70]   Simon to R. H. Tawney, 13 Dec. 1935, ibid. See also Stocks, *Ernest Simon*, 53, and Carter, *T. H. Green and the development of ethical socialism*, 181.

[71]   See Stephen K. Roberts, 'The evolution of the WEA in the West Midlands, 1905–26', and Bernard Jennings, 'The friends and enemies of the WEA', in Stephen K. Roberts (ed.), *A ministry of enthusiasm: centenary essays on the Workers' Educational Association*, London 2003.

[72]   Jonathan Rose, *The intellectual life of the British working classes*, Reading 2001, 292.

[73]   'Educational programme and list of lectures' (29 Feb.–4 Apr. 1928), Records of the Manchester and Direct Branch of the Working Men's Club and Institute Limited, MCA, GB124.G20.13.

[74]   Barker, *Your city*, 14, 20. See also Simon, *A century of city government*. Charlotte Wildman

the Manchester Municipal Officers' Guild, a local branch of the National Association of Local Government Officers, it reflected the priorities of that organisation as well as the wider civic narrative of progress propagated by Simon, the *Manchester Guardian*, the city council and the Workers' Educational Association. In *Your city* the council was concerned with 'making the lives of its citizens happier and healthier', 'from cradle to the grave', so that they could 'become ... useful citizen[s] in the community'.[75] The services that municipal government provided were positioned as part of this narrative, which was richly illustrated with photos of infrastructure such as public housing, sewers and power stations, as well as shots of local government employees (such as nurses, policemen and administrators) who safeguarded life and health. The longer and happier life that the citizen could achieve in modern Manchester was compared with the dire conditions that existed before the incorporation of the city, creating a linear narrative of progress. In the concluding chapter, 'The city of the future: our civic heritage', the reader was asked: 'What, then, is Citizenship? What is freedom? What are the rights and duties of the citizen?' According to the Municipal Officers Guild, it was a simple question of the obligatory responsibilities required due to the rights of municipal government:

> In return for our right to vote for the representative of our choice, for a host of public services, and for freedom, we should pay our rates without protest (but not without criticism), exercise our right to vote, and respect the laws which our representatives make for us.[76]

Municipal pride: complements, limits and challenges

Given the pervasiveness of national identity in the interwar period, the local focus of civics raises an important question. How were distinct loyalties – local, national, imperial or international – reconciled? At the simplest level, and more often than not, different allegiances could be held simultaneously. National citizenship and patriotism, rather than entailing a superseding of local citizenship, were actually an important counterpart. Citizenship was not a zero-sum game, and even though civics celebrated the city as the arena through which individuals were turned into citizens, civics also acknowledged national achievements, the extent of the empire, spoke of the English or American spirit, and detailed voting, politics, the national state, taxation and the justice system.[77] There was no conflict between urban and other forms of

---

gives the figure for 4,000: 'A *city speaks*: the projection of civic identity in Manchester', *Twentieth Century British History* xxiii/1 (2012), 85.

[75] Barker, *Your city*, 14, 16, 20.

[76] Ibid. 54.

[77] For national-focused civics texts see, for example, Charles F. G. Masterman, *How*

geographically-bounded loyalty; civics nested local community in a series of citizenship 'belongings' that went from the local to the imperial.

J. R. Peddie – in *The British citizen* (1920) – argued that the First World War had helped every soldier in Britain realise 'how dear to him was his native village, or town, or city'. Describing troop relationships on the front, he saw the mutual love of one's city as the bond between men fighting for the nation – a tendency encouraged by local groups enlisting as 'Pals Battalions' at the start of the war.[78] For Florence West, writer of the self-study guide *Stepping stones to citizenship* (1923), citizenship was split across three tiers: the town or district of residence, the kingdom and the empire.[79] This method of placing citizens in a set of 'expanding addresses' was common, originating in Geography teaching at the beginning of the century.[80] Though there was no conflict between these 'addresses' or parts, for Richard Wilson, as with many other civics authors, it was in the local and as part of a body of citizens 'acting as a unity' that the interests of the 'community' were best realised.[81] As Worts also explained, echoing Green, governing the modern state was 'so immense a task', and local conditions so varied, that welfare was 'best safeguarded by its authoritative control being in the hands of men who know and live in it'. Local Government was 'thus a natural development as well as a social, governmental and State necessity'.[82]

Civics accordingly balanced national needs with the autonomy of municipal government and the local community. A similar ethos informed the documentary film movement which, rather than creating a 'fixed, homogeneous and central "Britishness"', instead 'presented the nation as the sum total of its many parts'.[83] Imperial identities, more generally, could be filtered and expressed through the lens of the locality. Empire Day, for example, was a national celebration but, in its local staging, was refracted through the relationship of each place to different aspects of imperial power – such as, in Portsmouth, the Navy.[84] Narratives of civic identity and the nation were mutually reinforcing in the Victorian and Edwardian periods.[85] Into the 1920s and 1930s this was arguably still the case, as the local was positioned as the site through which

---

England is governed, London 1921, and Charles F. Dole, *The new American citizen*, Boston, MA 1918.

[78]   Peddie, *The British citizen*, 1.

[79]   Florence E. West, *Stepping stones to citizenship*, Exeter 1923, 9.

[80]   John Ahier, *Industry, children and the nation: an analysis of national identity in school textbooks*, London 1988, 125; Richard Wilson, *The complete citizen: an introduction to the study of civics*, London 1920, 12.

[81]   Wilson, *The complete citizen*, 149.

[82]   Worts, *Citizenship*, 101.

[83]   Scott Anthony and James G. Mansell, 'Introduction: the documentary film movement and the spaces of British identity', *Twentieth Century British History* xxiii/1 (2012), 5.

[84]   Brad Beaven, *Patriotism, popular culture and the city, 1870–1939*, Manchester 2012.

[85]   William Whyte, 'Building the nation in the town: architecture and identity in Britain',

people could become better citizens of both city and nation. In the movement for regional surveys, for example, another legacy of Patrick Geddes's influence, geographical knowledge allowed for the 'orientation' of citizenship; for some, such as H. C. Barnard, this meant the ability to cultivate love of the nation through the 'microcosm' of the locality.[86]

In the US, local citizenship could also contribute to national feeling.[87] Walter Moody, for example, argued in 1911 that national patriotism was supported by the 'companion sentiment' of 'community patriotism', which arose from the pride taken in one's home city.[88] Moody was the managing director of the Chicago Plan Commission, a civic body appointed by the city council in 1909 to implement Daniel Burnham's *Plan of Chicago*. Using modern technologies and techniques – advertising, public relations and filmmaking – the *Plan* was one of the first attempts to 'propagandize' Americans into civic unity. As Moody put it, citizen-making and city-building went 'hand in hand'.[89] Moody's 'sentiments' became located in publications like *Wacker's manual of the Plan of Chicago* (1911), a popular civics book used throughout the interwar period in elementary school classes.[90] Understanding the importance of the local to the national also went beyond civics textbooks and into other popular mediums. As *The Young Citizen*, a magazine published from the late 1920s explained, chaos began in the city and spread throughout the nation. This meant that those who lived in the cities were 'in the front line trenches'. Youth was the city's only hope, and could only be reached, the magazine argued, through a constant programme of civic education that showed youth what they owed to their urban lifestyle.[91] In both countries, most educators were pragmatic: they realised that a type of patriotism that combined love of both city and nation was more powerful than either one on its own.

Even though there was no conflict between local and national, in Britain the municipally-based idea of civics had a tough task in penetrating centrally-led

---

in Whyte and Zimmer, *Nationalism*; Paul Readman, 'The place of the past in English culture *c.* 1890–1914', *Past & Present*, no. 186 (Feb. 2005), 147–99.

[86] David Matless, 'Regional surveys and local knowledges: the geographical imagination in Britain, 1918–39', *Transactions of the Institute of British Geographers* xvii (1992), 475.

[87] See, for example, Bodnar, *Remaking America: public memory*, chs iv, vii.

[88] Walter D. Moody, 'Public schools: teaching the child city building', in Chicago Association of Commerce, *First International Municipal Congress and Exposition*, Chicago, IL 1911, 91.

[89] Ibid. See also Laura E. Baker, 'Civic ideals, mass culture, and the public: reconsidering the 1909 plan of Chicago', *JUH* xxxvi/6 (2010), 748, 751–2, and Boyer, *Urban masses*, 267–76.

[90] Walter Moody, *Wacker's manual of the Plan of Chicago*, Chicago, IL 1920. See also Robert B. Fairbanks, 'Advocating city planning in the public schools: the Chicago and Dallas experiences, 1911–1928', in Robert B. Fairbanks, Patricia Mooney-Melvin and Zane L. Miller (eds), *Making sense of the city: local government, civic culture, and community life in urban America*, Columbus, OH 2007, 57–76.

[91] *The Young Citizen* i/1 (Dec. 1929), 6.

education. Most historians have thus played down the success of citizenship movements in this period.[92] The central Board of Education, which was fairly limited in terms of its powers anyway, was cautious about embracing direct citizenship education in schools. Reports in 1926 and 1938 acknowledged the importance of civics, but thought it was better for the subject to arise implicitly through the teaching of history – reflecting a wider interest in the usefulness of history education for citizenship.[93] According to Peter Brett, this distrust was also due to: a conservative mindset in the higher circles of policy-making; a distrust of politically biased education; dependence upon older notions of 'muscular Christianity' emerging from sport and games; and opposition to secular political education from powerful religious interests.[94] The ability of school education to reach large parts of the population was, at any rate, fairly limited. The Education Act of 1918 built on the social reform concern of the earlier 'New Liberalism', and, in the context of ambitious plans for post-war reconstruction, made secondary education compulsory up to the age of fourteen. But more radical suggestions for education past that age in 'day continuation schools' were included only in principle, with the discretionary nature of the act and its delegating of responsibility to local administration meaning that the take-up, in practice, was very low. Post-war austerity drives and public cuts only further damaged the cause. By 1938 only around 15 per cent of fourteen to eighteen-year olds were attending school.[95] The school experience more generally was limited in the 1920s and 1930s, with a reliance on often outdated textbooks and old-fashioned teaching methods, and the Board of Education only sporadically communicating with Local Education Authorities.[96]

Despite this lack of central support, and the limits of the education system more broadly, civics programmes still took place in towns and cities across Britain.[97] Even those who disliked urbanity, and preferred rural living or the construction of Garden Cities, believed that civics could mitigate some of the harm. Clough Williams-Ellis, in his 1928 rural preservation bestseller, *England and the octopus*, described how teachers could educate by 'stealth', putting on talks about housing, town planning, neighbourliness, local government and

[92] Derek Heater, A *history of education for citizenship*, London 2004, 94–5; Patrick Brindle and Madeleine Arnot, '"England expects every man to do his duty": the gendering of the citizenship textbook, 1940–1966', *Oxford Review of Education* xxv/1 (1999), 104–6.

[93] Laura Carter, 'The Quennells and the "history of everyday life" in England, *c.* 1918–69', *History Workshop Journal* lxxxi/1 (2016), 107–34. For the reports see Board of Education, *Report of the consultative committee on the education of the adolescent*, London 1926, 196, and *Report of the consultative committee on secondary education*, London 1938, p. xxxvii.

[94] Brett, 'Citizenship education', 64–70.

[95] G. E. Sherington, 'The 1918 education act: origins, aims and development', *British Journal of Educational Studies* xxiv/1 (1976), 66–85.

[96] Laura Joyce Carter, 'The "history of everyday life" and democratic culture in Britain, 1918–1968', unpubl. PhD diss. Cambridge 2017, 77.

[97] Tom Hulme, 'Putting the city back into citizenship: civics education and local government in Britain, 1918–1945', *Twentieth Century British History* xxvi/1 (2015), 41–2.

tidiness: an approach that would lead to civilised children and thus civilised citizens.[98] Such a perspective was mostly new – as the American educator John M. Gaus could attest. Visiting Britain in the mid-1920s as part of an ambitious project to chart civic education around the world, led by the University of Chicago political scientist Charles E. Merriam, Gaus had been dismayed by the lack of enthusiasm that he found for direct citizenship education. Returning in the mid-1930s, however, he was encouraged to find the older indirect emphasis 'increasingly supplemented by a more direct and conscious inclusion in the content of the course of study of material relating to public questions and civic life in general'.[99]

Local civics educators, even if they had managed to create a network of civics classes, were still facing a challenge if they were to convince citizens that they should engage with their locality and government. In 1926 Ernest Simon regretted that a cynical attitude towards municipal service was 'unfortunately common amongst all classes'.[100] His Association for Education in Citizenship, founded in 1934 with Eva Hubback to 'advance the study of and training in citizenship', was a direct response to the lack of citizenship education, the indifference of voters or, conversely, the potential radicalism of the working classes.[101] Reacting against the rise of Fascism on the continent, the Association argued that the decline of educated interest in the affairs of the state paved the way for political extremism, with the working classes being particularly susceptible. As well as campaigning for curriculum change and publishing civics texts, the Association brought together a variety of agencies that were working towards instilling local patriotism and civic duty, as well as linking up with other broader citizenship movements, such as the League of Nations Union, with which the Association shared many personnel.[102] But, by the end of the decade, there was still a good deal of cynicism; one study of local government in 1939, for example, remarked that 'almost everywhere ... the apathy of the electors is alarmingly general'.[103]

Citizenship education in the US was more wholeheartedly embraced at all levels of schooling. The US led the world in the expansion of universal

---

[98] Williams-Ellis, *England and the octopus*, 74.

[99] John M. Gaus, *Great Britain: a study of civic loyalty*, Chicago, IL 1929, and 'Civic education in the English schools', *Annals of the American Academy of Political and Social Science* clxxxii (1935), 170.

[100] Simon, *A city council from within*, 235.

[101] Association for Education in Citizenship, *Education for citizenship in secondary schools*, Oxford 1936, 236. See also Association for Education in Citizenship, *Experiments in practical training for citizenship*, Letchworth 1937, and Ernest D. Simon and E. M. Hubback, *Training for citizenship*, London 1935.

[102] For an overview see Guy Whitmarsh, 'The politics of political education: an episode', *Journal of Curriculum Studies* vi/2 (1974), 133–42, and for the Association's links see Helen McCarthy, *The British people and the League of Nations: democracy, citizenship and internationalism, c.1918–45*, Manchester 2011, 116.

[103] Harris, *Municipal government in Britain*, 263.

publicly-funded secondary school education in the first half of the twentieth century. In 1910 just 19 per cent of American youths (between fifteen and eighteen) were enrolled in a high school, whereas, by 1940, that figure had climbed to 73 per cent.[104] Though the 'high school movement' was weaker in the industrial cities, especially those that were experiencing rapid growth and demographic change, it represented a significant financial commitment to the idea that education served an important social role both locally and nationally.[105] The particularly municipal basis that this education could take, though, was not welcomed in all circles. Most of those who designed community civics did so from a progressive political perspective, believing that industrial-urban society was incompatible with older political ideas of minimal government and maximum individual liberty. Community civics therefore aimed to 'wean students from individualistic philosophies and build support for government activism'.[106] Proponents of private ownership, who made their living from selling utilities to urban dwellers, were often angered, complaining that textbooks were written by 'socialists and advocates of public ownership'.[107] Publicity campaigns that encouraged Americans to be 'staunch friends of the public utilities' were organised in response. In Chicago, and Illinois more widely, the response was vociferous. Commanded by the utilities magnate Samuel Insull, his company executives formed the Illinois Committee on Public Utility Information in 1919. This organisation gave talks to schools and published its own civics text: *Chicago's genii, the public utilities* in 1921.[108] In a counter-response, a Save-Our-Schools Committee was organised in 1928 to challenge the propaganda of private utility companies.[109] In cities such as Chicago, where civics texts were less a reflection of governmental reality and more an idealised vision for the future, there was a constant battle between private and public interests to define what the results of municipal ownership would be.

Civics educators in the interwar period held a distinctive conception of the city and its government, drawing on well-established debates about the nature of liberty, state intervention and civic responsibility. They targeted especially those groups that they saw as potential challengers to democracy and stability: the working classes, immigrants and the unemployed. It is likely that civics

---

[104] Claudia Goldin, *The race between education and technology*, Cambridge, MA 2008, 195.

[105] Ibid.

[106] Reuben, 'Beyond politics', 416.

[107] Pierce, *Citizens' organizations and the civic training of youth*, 251.

[108] Illinois Committee on Public Utility Information, *Chicago's genii, the public utilities*, Chicago, IL 1921.

[109] Pierce, *Citizens' organizations and the civic training of youth*, 272. Ernest Gruening detailed the investigation by the Federal trade commission into the propaganda of the public utilities: *The public pays: a study of power propaganda*, New York, NY 1931, 18. His book was published by the Vanguard Press, which was funded by the left-wing American Fund for Public Service.

had its allure dampened, however, by the often–bleak realities of interwar urban living. Civics texts proclaimed egalitarian provision, but day-to-day life showed this to be a hopeless dream. Slums, though increasingly under attack, were a stark reminder of the substantial pockets of poverty in both Chicago and Manchester. Chicago was also a racially stratified city with unequal service provision between neighbourhoods. Bronzeville, on the South Side, was crowded, expensive and dilapidated, with higher rates of mortality, morbidity, juvenile delinquency and crime.[110] As one letter-writer to the *Chicago Defender* noted simply in 1934: 'I would like to know why it is that in the Race districts the alleys are not kept clean as they are in the "white".' Two weeks later the superintendent for the ward wrote back to insist that provision between white and black neighbourhoods was the same, but dogmatically blamed people for throwing their rubbish in the alley rather than in bins.[111] Civics similarly did not try to engage with or even acknowledge inequality or bias. On the contrary, citizenship education often created racial hierarchies by implicitly identifying legitimacy with 'whiteness and middle-class and elite status' in both teaching materials and the background of teachers.[112] Cultural homogeneity in both topics and delivery prevailed over radical suggestions for different religious or ethnic groups to structure their own education.[113] When talking of 'community' and 'the people', civics ignored ethnic ghettoisation – a hypocrisy that cannot have escaped African American adult education students studying civics in classes where 'white and blacks', as one late 1930s report stated, had to 'be kept separate'.[114]

The final chapter of this book will return to the important consequences of these failures in the urban citizenship narrative. What can be said at this juncture, however, is that whether in Britain or America, or from an idealist or pragmatist perspective, the city was an important part of citizenship education in the 1920s and 1930s. Civics was an attempt to create a collective image of the city and its governance: an active response to the difficulties of understanding the nature of urban experience and belonging. In Britain, this emerged in particular from the movement to improve the city and its government in the late nineteenth century and was expressed through an understanding of the social role of the municipal state. Into the 1920s and 1930s this logic was

---

[110] St Clair Drake, 'Profiles: Chicago', *Journal of Educational Sociology* xvii/5 (Jan. 1944), 265.

[111] 'Our streets and alleys', CD, 20 Oct. 1934, 14; 'What the people say', CD, 3 Nov. 1934, 14.

[112] Gidlow, *The big vote*, 143; Colin Greer, *The great school legend: a revisionist interpretation of American public education*, New York, NY 1972, 80; Michael R. Olneck, 'Americanization and the education of immigrants, 1900–1925: an analysis of symbolic action', *American Journal of Education* xcvii/4 (1989), 399.

[113] Smith, *Civic ideals*, 465–6.

[114] 'Monthly report' (Feb. 1939), Association House of Chicago records, folder 5, box 3, MSS lot A.

embedded in the various bodies that sought to create citizens, such as the city council, the local press, workers' education movements and new organisations that were dedicated to maintaining democracy as other countries succumbed to totalitarian regimes. In the US John Dewey-inspired social studies educators, most notably Arthur Dunn in the Progressive Era, oversaw the transition to a study of government that emphasised the products rather than the machinery of local government. This narrative was apparent in the citizenship classes of both the Board of Education and local voluntary associations, and lasted into the 1930s as civic culture was reenergised by federal money during the New Deal.

The form of citizenship embodied in municipal government and urban belonging did not, however, replace all other forms of identity. Local citizenship was articulated as a complementary characteristic of a broader set of affiliations – especially regional, national and imperial. Disseminating such urban-based narratives, as Alev Çınar and Thomas Bender have put it, directed 'the collective imagination into the conjuring up of a city in certain ways so as to fulfil particular goals of the modernizing state'.[115] Judging the reception of this particular 'imagining' through direct education is difficult, and it must be acknowledged that civics never reached a majority of the population in this form. If we look beyond the classroom, however, we can see how the ideals of civics education were socially reproduced in much larger ways. The next chapter turns to look at how local citizenship was performed and ritualised by individuals, associations and local government in great public festivals. These events celebrated the city, and its government, as a fundamental source of citizenship identity. In contrast to civics, however, festivals also had to take note of the ways in which race and ethnicity interacted with the identity, practice and rights of citizenship – an issue that became increasingly recognised as the 1930s drew to a close.

---

[115] Alev Çınar and Thomas Bender, 'The city: experience, imagination, and place', in Çınar and Bender, *Urban imaginaries*, p. xv.

3

Celebrating the City

Civics classes were a formal classroom approach to creating urban citizenship. Teaching the city, however, could also be a much more spectacular affair. Festivals allowed whole places to become an advertisement for municipal government and big business, while also acting as an embellished backdrop for a 'performance' of urban community.[1] Stories about the city, its history and its leaders were told in ways that encouraged loyalty and civic responsibility. Grand civic buildings, symbols of the cultural life provided by the city council, were emphasised through floodlighting and decoration. Mundane local infrastructure, such as power stations and gasworks, were opened to the public and promoted as the height of municipal modernity. The benefits of the modern city were made clear: a decent life provided by a professional local government. Celebrations of the city, though, also went beyond messages of municipal might. Parades, competitions and pageantry provided opportunities for the performance of a more inclusive civic identity. Public rituals that delineated governors and the governed were reinvented to suit the context of modern urban democracy. Not just the civic elite, but a broader urban public too, could make claims to importance in the city's future. Festival-organisers hoped that local people would absorb this message of commonality and faith in local government – and many seemingly did. But festival-goers could promote their own alternative visions of the purpose of the modern city and who it was for – visions that did not always tally with those propagated by official publicity. It was at these points that racial, class and gender inequality became most visible, calling into question the very notion of a cohesive urban community.

Most interwar civic festivals included an entertainment programme. Crowds were invited to watch and take part in sporting competitions, from swimming to boxing, or to simply enjoy public singing, dancing and music. There was more to this festive atmosphere than just enticing visitors, however. Firstly, strong footfall could equate to publicity and business for commercial operators, from the large-scale industrialist to the individual souvenir seller. Secondly, organisers realised that to bring city-dwellers into an arena where they would receive civic education, which even the most serious enthusiast would acknowledge could be a bit dry, required the pull of other attractions. By the 1920s there was a vibrant popular culture – mass sports, the cinema, dancehalls

---

[1]   For an overview of how 'performance' interacts with people, places and identities see Peter Burke, 'Performing history: the importance of occasions', *Rethinking History* ix/1 (2005), 35-52.

– vying for the attention of urbanites who had rising real wages and more leisure time. For civic elites it was a case of competing by embracing consumerism.[2] Thirdly, festivals could relax the normal structures of urban society at times of strain, allowing the city to become momentarily unified. A common mood and experience was fashioned, and differences of social status could be erased – or at least blurred. Groups that were usually barred from high society, elite civic culture or even simply public space, became aware, if only for a short time, of their role alongside local government and big business in the everyday life of the city.[3] Festivals, then, were a balancing act between different interest groups and goals: civic educators and the communication of good citizenship; businessmen and the boosting of the local economy; politicians and municipal officials and the legitimisation of the existing governmental power structure; and festival attendees looking for fun.

This chapter begins by tracing the evolution of civic festivals in the US and Britain into the 1920s, exploring their local and municipal basis especially. In Britain, at the beginning of the interwar period, putting on festivals was viewed, at first, with some caution and suspicion. Urban festivals, and many 'invented traditions' of the nineteenth century, predated these experiments.[4] But the new focus on overt municipal promotion seemed more novel. In the US, city councils turned more quickly to festivals that promoted local products, reflecting both the power of big business in the governance of the city and that country's leading status in the development of mass advertising. In both countries, though, a central place was given to showing how local government was in charge of urban life. The second section demonstrates how this narrative also increasingly depended on the performance of an urban community where distinctive neighbourhood identities were acknowledged. Festival participants could contribute to the civic image while maintaining their own ethnic, racial or religious identities. The final section turns to the festivals of the 1930s and demonstrates the maturing of the narrative that festivals told. In Britain, by the end of the decade, a vibrant publicity industry was cemented in civic culture. Almost all medium or large cities were involved in planning significant 'boosterish' celebrations that celebrated local government, in much the same way as had been the case in the 1920s. In the US, however, festivals were qualitatively different. If 1920s festivals had made overtures to a pluralistic understanding of urban society, in the latter part of the following decade this became more central as a more inclusive sense of an 'American Way' developed.

---

[2]   Ben Roberts, 'Entertaining the community: the evolution of civic ritual and public celebration, 1860-1953', *Urban History* xliv/3 (2017), 459.

[3]   For a historiographical intervention in ritual see Dion Georgiou, 'Redefining the carnivalesque: the construction of ritual, revelry and spectacle in British leisure practices through the idea and model of "carnival", 1870-1939', *Sport in History* xxxv/3 (2015), 335-63.

[4]   Eric Hobsbawn, 'Introduction: inventing traditions', in Eric Hobsbawn and Terrence Ranger (eds), *The invention of tradition*, Cambridge 1984, 1-14.

Civic festivals in the 1920s

Public festivals have a long history and, of course, pre-date the modern period.[5] But with industrialisation and urbanisation, from the mid-nineteenth century especially, their size and importance increased. Huge international fairs now became a prominent part of Western urban culture. The first Great Exhibition was held in London in 1851, organised by a coalition of royals, inventors, manufacturers and artists.[6] Philadelphia held the first World's Fair on the other side of the Atlantic, with its Centennial International Exhibition in 1876. The second in the US, Chicago's World's Columbian Exposition in 1893, holds a special place in the history of the movement. With almost three times as many visitors as Philadelphia's own effort, it marked the arrival of America on the world stage. Taking place in a gleaming new classical-style 'White City' that stood in stark contrast to the reality of 'shocking' Chicago, the Exposition was a moment to ponder the direction of the nation's urban future.[7] In 1933 the city's Century of Progress, now in a distinctly more modern style of architecture, made a bold statement about the American leadership of Western nations.[8] These grand exhibitions of progress and strength sought to portray technological and social progress, and were inseparable from projects of nation-building, imperialism and economic (re)structuring. Urban festivals in the twentieth century, and even those that had their origins in much older and smaller traditions, drew inspiration from these international expositions and replicated many of their aims and techniques. They also had specific local goals, however, targeted at the urban economy and resident citizens especially. Exhibitions, education and entertainment were shaped by the need to promote a sense of urban belonging. Despite increasing centralisation or federalisation, and a possible loss of municipal control, it was local governments that took the lead.

Local public celebrations had been a part of American culture from the early eighteenth century. As David Glassberg has outlined, they had diverse roots: ethnic holiday customs transferred from overseas; partisan, political and often violent protest marches; and commemorations of important dates and events in local, state and national history. Two characteristics defined these events in the mid-nineteenth century: firstly, their lack of general engagement across the city, and limitation at different times to specific sections of society; and secondly, their absence of symbolic imagery of the city. By the turn of the twentieth

---

[5]   Helen Watanabe-O'Kelly and Anne Simon, *Festivals and ceremonies: bibliography of works relating to court, civic and religious festivals in Europe, 1500–1800*, London 2000.

[6]   Jeffrey A. Auerbach, *The Great Exhibition of 1851: a nation on display*, New Haven, CT 1999.

[7]   See, as an introduction, Norman Bolotin and Christine Laing, *The World's Columbian Exposition: the Chicago World's Fair of 1893*, Urbana, IL 2002.

[8]   Lisa D. Schrenk, *Building a Century of Progress: the architecture of the 1933–34 Chicago World's Fair*, Minneapolis, MN 2007.

century, however, this had changed. Organisers now more frequently tried to incorporate all parts of the urban community into a single celebration, and the history of the nation was often replaced with a more specific history of the city. Municipal extravaganzas did not displace older forms of public display or loyalty but added another level of specifically urban allegiance.[9] City Beautiful advocates, and promoters of civic idealism more broadly in the Progressive Era, pushed these ideas. For Newton M. Hall, the city had an essence or soul that could find expression in collective pride; for Percy MacKaye, an influential dramatist and poet, large-scale civic drama would awaken a communal spirit and drive urban masses to a common sense of citizenship.[10] Contemporaries in the 1920s continued to understand the value of these events.

Chicago's Pageant of Progress, which took place in 1921 and 1922, is now a footnote to the great Century of Progress that came twelve years later.[11] Yet, at the time, the pageant was a notable event in the social calendar. Over the course of a two-week programme hundreds of thousands of people enjoyed the entertainments on show on the Municipal Pier (see Figures 2, 3), and also the attractions staged in the surrounding large public boulevards and the smaller streets of neighbourhoods. The festival demonstrated both Chicago's civic culture in action and the logic of urban citizenship, as the city and its inhabitants turned their gaze inwards. The pageant was organised by a coalition of business leaders and the city council, with prominent lawyers, academics and journalists providing support.[12] The festival was partially a commercial exercise. Business leaders used their stalls on the pier to sell both goods and confidence in their ability to provide leadership, stability and prosperity in a turbulent post-war world – the Secretary of Labour James Davis, for example, hoped that the pageant would mark a new era of cordiality between labour and employers.[13] A narrative of technological and industrial advancement was thus emphasised through the display of new goods alongside obsolete historical antecedents. The Chicago Retail Lumber Dealers Association, for example, contrasted a reconstruction of a seventeenth-century primitive log cabin (described as a possible reproduction of the type that the young Abraham Lincoln may have inhabited) with a new bungalow of the industrial age. An

[9]   See David Glassberg, *Sense of history: the place of the past in American life*, Amherst, MA 2001, 62–8, and Mary Ryan, *Civic wars: democracy and public life in the American city during the nineteenth century*, Berkeley, CA 1997, chs ii, vi.

[10] Newton M. Hall, *Civic righteousness and civic pride*, Boston, MA 1914; Percy MacKaye, *The civic theatre in relation to the redemption of leisure*, New York, NY 1912, and *Community drama: its motive and method of neighborliness*, Boston, MA 1917. See also Boyer, *Urban masses*, 254–61.

[11] Robert W. Rydell, *World of fairs: the Century-of-Progress Expositions*, Chicago, IL 1993, 36.

[12] Calculated from 'Description of the sections and section chairmen of the organization of the pageant' (1921), in Pageant of Progress Exposition miscellaneous pamphlets.

[13] 'Davis predicts better industrial relations', *New York Times*, 31 July 1921, 9. For context see Colin Gordon, *New deals: business, labor, and politics in America, 1920–1935*, Cambridge 1994.

Figure 2. The Pageant of Progress under construction on Chicago's Municipal Pier (1921)

Figure 3. Entertainment during the Pageant of Progress (1921)

accompanying brochure explained how the change marked 'the progress of man, brains and machine'.[14] Presenting the past alongside the present allowed the latter to be anchored in the former – to give a sense of progress, but also security, familiarity and cultural alignment.[15] Some visitors implicitly recognised this: as one young woman told a reporter, 'To see the various things as they were in times gone by and contrasting them with the present was well worth the trip to the pier.'[16]

Local and regional government also understood the importance of advertising, and so produced their own exhibition booths that showed visitors what government did for them – and how exactly they did it. The state departments of public welfare, health and agriculture, along with the city's health department, Board of Education and Board of Local Improvements, all provided multiple exhibits. Their displays celebrated government intervention and showed thousands of visitors how to live better and healthier lives. Like the industrial displays, government exhibits also depended on a narrative of progress. The Department of Public Works, for example, juxtaposed an old water pipe that had been used in the early days of the city's expansion with a forty-eight-inch water pipe of the present, and a selection of the modern equipment used in cribs and pumping stations. Health exhibits were accompanied by colourful posters that taught American boys and girls how to increase their physical and mental powers. As the boosterish *Greater Chicago* magazine declared, 'If the Pageant of Progress accomplishes nothing else than the quickening of public sentiment toward personal, civic and national health maintenance and conservation, the holding of this Exposition will prove to be a great asset.'[17] Exhibits were also provided by the Chicago Plan Commission, such as a miniature scale model of the Michigan Boulevard Bridge and the remaining work of the Plan. In the event, the Plan was never completely realised, but selling the fantasy was often as important as the reality.

In Britain, civic exhibitions were being organised for similar ideological and economic purposes. Patrick Geddes, for example, had long stressed the importance of civic exhibitions for encouraging active citizenship. From 1892 he put this idea into action through the 'Outlook Tower' in Edinburgh, using exhibits and a 'camera obscura' to teach locals and visitors about the city.[18] In 1934 Franklin Harold Hayward, an Inspector of Schools for the London County Council, similarly reflected on 'Lessons in Citizenship' and the 'Celebration of the City', and argued that the efficacy of the first increased with

---

[14]   Retail Lumber Dealers Association, 'Progress in Building' (1921), in Pageant of Progress Exposition miscellaneous pamphlets.

[15]   David Lowenthal, 'Past time, present place: landscape and memory', *Geographical Review* lxv/1 (1975), 5.

[16]   'The inquiring reporter', *CT*, 15 Aug. 1922, 17.

[17]   'The exhibitors' story of the Pageant of Progress Exposition', *Greater Chicago* i/12 (Aug.–Sept. 1921).

[18]   Law, 'The ghost of Patrick Geddes'.

the establishment of the second. Local civic celebration, he believed, created a rallying point for civic instruction.[19] The interwar period was a golden era for such local exhibitions in Britain. This blossoming can be traced to the British Empire Exhibition in 1924, a moment when elites in Britain portrayed the nation's global power, superiority and industrial and technological promise for the future. The novelty of the 1924 exhibition for provincial cities, however, was in its acknowledgement of the part of the local in this national and imperial story. Alongside the main Wembley stadium was a smaller building, Civic Hall, where municipal authorities could hold their own 'Civic Week' and display their strides forward in municipal enterprise. After the exhibition had ended, Civic Weeks spread out from Wembley to the rest of the country.[20]

Manchester did not take up the original opportunity at Wembley because its city councillors were suspicious of the cost and potential for failure.[21] It was also not the first city to hold a local Civic Week. After seeing Liverpool's successful attempt in 1925, however, the councillors recognised the benefits that a local exhibition could bring, and a Manchester Civic Week was proposed for 1926.[22] This event holds an important place in the development of the civic week movement; monumental and successful, many other provincial cities followed suit. The organisers saw it as having a distinctive educational purpose. Internal planning reports determined that civic weeks could foster civic spirit by demonstrating how the municipality benevolently governed the city, and would thus be 'the best kind of practical supplement' to *How Manchester is managed*.[23] The total attendance was over 1,000,000: a spectacular if only momentary extension of civic education.

Selling faith in the capability of the industrial and mercantile city to survive and prosper in uncertain economic times was also a part of the Manchester Civic Week. A textile exhibition, which took place at the newly built Belle Vue stadium, was billed as the largest of its kind in Britain's history. A floor space of 70,000 square feet was taken over by demonstrations of the modern industrial techniques pioneered by Manchester and its region – such as cotton spinning and wool dyeing – and a 'mannequin theatre' where the latest textile fashions were displayed.[24] The opening of the exhibition was a major civic event, and an opportunity to reflect on Manchester's industrial status and future. The earl of Derby officiated, accompanied by the mayor, Miles E. Mitchell, and the president of the Manchester Chamber of Commerce, Sir Percy Woodhouse. In a series of speeches, the three men revelled in the foresight and confidence

---

[19]   Frank Herbert Hayward, *Reflections on civics in schools*, London 1934, 10–16, 39–40.

[20]   Tom Hulme, '"A nation of town criers": civic publicity and historical pageantry in interwar Britain', *Urban History* xliv/2 (2017), 276–7.

[21]   'Manchester abandons Wembley', MG, 3 Apr. 1924, 11.

[22]   For Liverpool's week see Wildman, *Urban redevelopment and modernity*, 55–66.

[23]   'Report of committee on Civic Week' (1926), 2, MCA, GB127.M740/2/8/3/2.

[24]   'Opening of the textile exhibition', MG, 1 Oct. 1926, 13.

of Manchester's civic leaders, and the city's wider spirit of cooperation and unity. At a time when the economy was in a precarious state, the exhibition functioned as an advertisement for 'Manchester goods' and a rallying point for Lancashire's courage and faith in its products and future.[25] A Pageant of Industries parade, organised by the Federation of British Industries, visually made the same point: eighty firms, some with as many as seven floats, processed through the city streets to 'demonstrate the fundamental soundness and energy of the city's great organisations'.[26]

Faith in the future of Manchester also went beyond its commercial prestige. Manchester's city council worked hard to present an image of modern service provision, from new public housing and civic airports to older gas and electricity concerns. Transport, for example, provided an example of investment and progressive thinking, and was also depicted through a vehicle parade in the centre of the city. Aiming to show how the 'modern industrial system' was dependent upon 'the modern system of transport', it demonstrated both old and new methods for carrying merchandise and people – from packhorses to 'petrol wagons'. Onlookers were supposedly shocked by how 'so out of date' and 'so utterly useless for the purposes of our modern world' the old forms were.[27] Other exhibits during Manchester's Civic Week showed the more direct work of the city council, with health given a strong emphasis. Modern methods of milk supply, maternity and child welfare were displayed alongside general hospital work. Models, graphs and statistics illustrated the decline of disease due to municipal intervention. The city engineer and city surveyor provided drawings of sewage works and town planning, while the housing committee displayed large-scale photographs of newly built estates. Large diagrams of the Thirlmere and Haweswater aqueducts proved that the bold and adventurous spirit of municipal schemes, which had begun in the nineteenth century in response to the shock city, would continue in the mid-twentieth century.[28] People could also visit the actual departments of the city council to see in action the workers and technologies that they had read about in civics texts.[29] In these exhibitions, past municipal investment was used as a way of encouraging loyalty to a vision of the future.[30]

Festivities and rituals that accompanied exhibitions implicitly celebrated the fabric of the city and its institutions. In Manchester, public buildings and spaces were illuminated. The grey gloom of the industrial city was now given a bright and spectacular hue. Some of the buildings that were chosen,

---

[25] 'Manchester exhibition', ibid. 9 Nov. 1926, 4; 'Lord Derby opens textile exhibition', ibid. 2 Oct. 1926, 17.

[26] 'Civic Week', *Manchester Daily News*, 4 Aug. 1926, 6.

[27] 'The launching of Civic Week', MG, 4 Oct. 1926, 80.

[28] For Thirlmere in Manchester's civic and environmental history see Harriet Ritvo, *The dawn of green: Manchester, Thirlmere, and modern environmentalism*, Chicago, IL 2009.

[29] *Manchester Civic Week: official handbook*, 43; 'Report of committee on Civic Week', 4.

[30] Wildman, *Urban redevelopment and modernity*, 61.

as Charlotte Wildman has rightly argued, symbolised the city's diverse and modern emergent economy – such as the Ship Canal building, the emblem of Manchester's ability to face economic depression, and the 1910 tower of the Refuge Insurance building.[31] But alongside Manchester's pride in its recent achievements was a continued recognition of the city's Victorian municipal heritage. The town hall, a grand and imposing neo-Gothic structure completed in 1877, provided a centre point for the celebration. As the tallest building in the city, the tower secured visual dominance in the overall landscape. All parts of Manchester could be seen, and, in turn, the citizen could almost always see this proud emblem of the city.[32] During Civic Week six powerful electric lights floodlit the town hall's exterior and were also fixed inside and on the roof of the tower. The effect was striking. The *Sunday Chronicle* described the tower as a 'civic beacon', its 'powerful searchlights sending beams to all points of the compass', while the *Liverpool Post* remarked that 'the great, pressing crowd whose heads were turned up by the thousand to see the tower must have all felt in their honest Lancashire hearts some stirring of that pride of city'.[33]

Albert Square, studded with statues of Liberal politicians such as William Gladstone and John Bright, as well as the eponymous memorial to the Prince Consort and a fountain celebrating Queen Victoria's Diamond Jubilee, consequently became a place of public gathering late into the night. One reporter described how 'the ghostly effect of the flood lights' coming from the town hall revealed the 'soul' of the huge building, and brought thousands flocking.[34] One year later the architect Emanuel Vincent Harris won a competition to design the town hall's extension (eventually built between 1934 and 1938). Rather than eschewing the city's symbol of Victorian power, the extension mimicked its neo-Gothic shape with a contemporary accent, thus acknowledging the city's heritage while looking beyond to something distinctly more modern (see Figure 4). Manchester's original town hall had been decorated with symbolic and historical imagery that linked the city to a broader Whiggish story of the nation: the ever-increasing march of constitutional development and self-government.[35] Harris's extension subtly anchored the progress of Manchester in a particularly modern continuation of this spirit.

Public spaces also played a key role in the wider civic ritual. Civic elites, drawing on nineteenth-century traditions, choreographed a symbolic display of leadership. Through this public drama a unified urban community was imagined, with civic leaders making a figurative claim to authority over that

[31]   Ibid. 83.

[32]   Joyce, *The rule of freedom*, 167.

[33]   'Brighter city of Manchester', *Manchester Dispatch*, 30 Aug. 1926, 39; 'Civic Week in Manchester', *Liverpool Post*, 4 Oct. 1926, 30; 'Cotton city's day of pageantry', *Sunday Chronicle*, 3 Oct. 1926, 20.

[34]   'That Civic Week feeling', *Manchester Evening News*, 6 Oct. 1926, 19.

[35]   Whyte, 'Building the nation in the town', 222; Joyce, *Visions of the people*, 182. See also Readman, *Storied ground*, 231–2.

Figure 4. Manchester's gothic Town Hall (1877) and contemporary extension (1938)

community.[36] The opening ceremony of Civic Week, which took place in front of the town hall, demonstrates this. The mayor and his wife stood with other dignitaries of the city on a raised platform: a part of the celebration yet literally and figuratively above the urban crowds (*see* Figure 5). After being presented with an addition to the city's regalia, the mayor proclaimed the beginning of the festival. A sense of theatrical drama moved through the crowd, which seemed awed by the event. Electrically amplifying the speeches, 'the thunder of the spoken word, echoing and re-echoing from the cliff-like buildings' apparently had 'a dramatic effect which kept the crowd strangely hushed'.[37] Manchester's mayor continued to play a leading role in the opening parade, which consisted solely of him driving through the decorated streets of the

---

[36]   Gunn, *The public culture*, 163.
[37]   'The launching of Civic Week'.

city with his wife, alone apart from a mounted police guard (*see* Figure 6).[38] In Chicago, home to Big Bill the Booster, this was also the case. His face and name were prominent on the advertising and souvenirs, and the whole event was often described as being his own personal project. He led the opening parade throwing roses before, at the final destination, all other participants passed before him in review.[39] The importance of civic leaders being seen by the local population to control the public spaces of the city was not a new phenomenon. The greater use of technologies, however, such as electricity and amplification, meant that civic boundaries could now be audibly as well as visibly demarcated and reinforced. Civic elites, and the mayor in particular, were now projected larger-than-life: symbolic leaders that personified municipal government and its authority over the urban population.[40] These festivals, and the images that they crafted, revived and reinvented older rituals of power in urban space.

Not everything about interwar ritual represented continuity, however. Cities did certainly remain 'civic', their identity partially based on their leading institutions and figures. But they had also become more 'municipal', dependent on the machinery and expertise of local government administration. A key part of civic festivals was the attempt to celebrate how the city depended on this more mundane municipal governing. Various city employees were given a chance to process in public. In Manchester a 'Ceremonial Review', consisting of the police force, fire brigade and St John's Ambulance, passed through Albert Square in front of the mayor's podium and cheering crowds.[41] In Chicago, after Thompson made his way to the podium, there followed the police chief, and then fifty motorcycle policemen, 300 mounted policemen, 'thousands' of patrolmen on foot, 1,000 firemen on foot, 1,000 postal employees and 2,000 nurses. The employees of the street department, dubbed the 'white wings', were apparently 'drilled and marched like soldiers, the effect being enhanced by their being in uniform'.[42] On the one hand, this was an opportunity for municipal employees, who by this point often had their own professional associational organisations and unions, to demonstrate the power of their labour. This display, however, was also encouraged by city councils because it reminded onlookers, through the sheer number of uniformed participants, of the freedom and services that they received because of local government.

Like civics more broadly, this performance idealised service provision and masked the disparities between neighbourhoods – rich and poor, white and

38   *Manchester Civic Week: official handbook*, 30.

39   'Parade opens Pageant of Progress', *CT*, 30 July 1922, 3.

40   John Garrard, 'English mayors: what are they for?', in John Garrard (ed.), *Heads of the local state: mayors, provosts and burgomasters since 1800*, Aldershot 2007, 23.

41   *Manchester Civic Week: official handbook*, 30.

42   'Blaze of glory opens Chicago progress show', *CT*, 31 July 1922, 1; 'Parade opens Pageant of Progress', *CT*, 30 July 1922, 3.

Figure 5. Mayor Miles Ewart Mitchell and civic dignitaries opening
Manchester Civic Week (1926)

black – that clearly existed. Parades thus marked out where was important in
this civic vision.[43] Processional routes went through the urban areas of which
civic elites were proudest. The opening parade of the Pageant of Progress took
in both old and new expressions of civic idealism. First, south of the river:
along the east side of Grant Park, a landscaped green space that had been
developed and expanded in the previous twenty years; past Orchestra Hall,
a centre of cultural life designed by Daniel Burnham and built in 1904; and
through the hub of downtown, around two sides of the city hall and to the city
library. So far, the marchers had seen the financial, governmental and cultural
hub of Chicago. Next, across the river on the Michigan Avenue Bridge – a key
part of the Chicago Plan – and east through the Near North, a rapidly developing area of skyscrapers and warehouses. The parade ended by going through
the historic district surrounding the 1869 water tower, one of the few areas left
relatively unscathed by the Great Fire of 1871. Passing through commercial,
cultural and historic areas the parade highlighted an environment that the
pageant's organisers believed would inspire civic pride.[44] Parades accompanying

---

[43] Dennis, *Cities in modernity*, 166.

[44] 'Pageant of Progress Exposition organizations formed in every district of Chicago',
Greater Chicago i/10 (July 1921), 19.

Figure 6. Mayor Miles Ewart Mitchell beginning the opening parade of Manchester Civic Week (1926)

Manchester Civic Week also focused on the streets around the civic centre of the town hall and passed alongside Victorian educational and cultural institutions of national importance, such as the University of Manchester, the School of Art and the Royal Infirmary. In the Civic Week handbook, which sold 70,000 copies, these sites were also marked out and described.[45] Another map, accompanying the *Manchester Guardian* Civic Week supplement, was dominated by thick red lines showing the public tram routes – a visual expression of municipal power.[46] As with the illumination of old and new buildings, parade routes and maps highlighted both the historic institutions of the city as well as the promise of the urban future. By doing so, especially at a point when outside visitors were also in attendance, civic festivals made claims about the relative importance of their institutions and locale to the power and progress of the nation.

In both cities the parades did not enter residential areas or neighbourhoods that failed to fit the image that the authorities wanted to promote. At a women's political meeting a few months after the Pageant of Progress,

---

[45] *Manchester Civic Week: official handbook*, 48–9; 'Another Civic Week invasion', *Manchester Evening News*, 4 Oct. 1926, 75.

[46] 'Civic week number', MG, 2 Aug. 1926, 32–3.

Louise DeKoven Bowen, a notable philanthropist, civic leader and social reformer, voiced a particularly telling critique. Invoking wider fears about race and instability in Chicago, and criticisms of Thompson's alleged patronage of underground culture in Bronzeville, she pithily observed how 'Dirty alleys ... refuse filled streets in the Second ward, black and tan cabarets operating in violation of the 1 o'clock closing law ... these are a few of the forgotten exhibits in Mayor Thompson's Pageant of Progress.'[47] In Manchester, too, there were areas avoided, such as the back-to-back houses and badly paved streets of Ancoats that were a physical reminder of the effects of industrialisation and unplanned urbanisation. Working-class periodicals, such as the *Northern Voice* and the *Co-operative News*, were quick to critically point out how these areas were ignored during Civic Week.[48] Some parts of the city were meant to be seen and celebrated, and other parts were not.

Race, gender and civic participation

The projected identity of the city was thus synonymous with its leading institutions and public spaces, and the visible links between the historic environment, local government and the progress of the future.[49] It is tempting therefore to see civic festivals as a method of control. Spectating was, beyond its entertainment value, consciously about making the existing social order seem natural: a responsible urban government and business elite in full control of society, public space and the economy in times of difficulty and strife. Combining older civic rituals with a new municipal emphasis presented this new social order. But festivals in the twentieth century, as in the nineteenth, also encouraged the gathering of hundreds of thousands of people in public space. Celebrations also motivated the spirit of civil society and drew attention to communities and groups within the city. If people were encouraged to share the same ethos as the organisers, this often happened of its own accord and separate groups could have similar motivations. Notions of respectability or urban pride were by no means confined to the middle class or civic elites, and the working classes could share in the construction of community rather than simply being passive receivers of the ideology of their supposed betters.[50]

---

[47] 'Chicago women hear Thompson regime flayed', *CT*, 28 Oct. 1921, 12. See Chad Heap, *Slumming: sexual and racial encounters in American nightlife, 1885–1940*, Chicago, IL 2009, 78-9.

[48] Wildman, *Urban redevelopment*, 73; *Co-operative News*, 9 Oct. 1926, 4.

[49] Gunn, *The public culture*, 169.

[50] This argument has been persuasively made in relation to the Victorian period, but it was just as apparent in the 1920s and 1930s: F. M. L. Thompson, 'Social control in Victorian Britain', *Economic History Review* xxxiv/2 (1981), 189-208.

Civic festivals were consequently an example of 'social steering': a relationship more of bargaining than control.[51] Such free use of public space, however, could also lead to contestation. Groups were able to use their visibility in the city to shape political identities that could either support or challenge the *status quo* through the power of association and difference – in short, still exercising what Mary Ryan has dubbed 'ceremonial citizenship' – despite the controlled nature of the interwar city.[52] Streets and public spaces thus became an 'ideological battleground', where people from different backgrounds jostled – sometimes violently – for recognition.[53] This was especially the case for the downtown or central area of the city that, because of increasing residential segregation, offered notable opportunities for the 'interaction and negotiation of difference' that could enable both 'community' and 'conflict'.[54]

The opening parade of the Pageant of Progress in 1921 provides a good example of how civic cohesion could work in the ways that organisers intended. The initial part of the parade consisted mostly of the mayor and the municipal departments. The rest of the parade, however, was accessible to other social groups, with as many as 75,000 people taking part. Participants could offer their own agendas: 2,000 women, for example, staged an anti-war display.[55] Twenty-five of the outlying districts of Chicago also had their own section of floats, and, as the parade progressed, spectators joined on to its end, creating a composite ceremony from the symbols of many different associations and groups.[56] Authority was still identified, not least when the marchers went past Thompson on his podium, but there was plenty of opportunity for participation: a cooperating urban community in action. The main parade concentrated on the central 'civic' fabric of the city and its leading institutions and ignored what were seen as less salubrious neighbourhoods. But there were also localised parades that allowed peripheral communities (both physically and ideologically) to show their support. The city was split into twenty-six areas, based on notions of community identity, and a local queen was elected for each. Individual 'community parades' were viewed by between 50,000 and 500,000 people, and the *Greater Chicago* magazine speculated that the overall attendance was as high as 3,000,000.[57] Now that immigration was being reduced, there was the beginning of a sense that communities could concentrate less on assimilating newcomers and more on setting down 'roots'

[51] R. J. Morris, 'Governance: two centuries of urban growth', in R. J. Morris and R. H. Trainor, *Urban governance: Britain and beyond since 1750*, Farnham 2000, 10.

[52] Ryan, *Civic wars*, 59–60.

[53] Ewen, *What is urban history?*, 102.

[54] Alison Isenberg, *Downtown America: a history of the place and the people who made it*, Chicago, IL 2005, 5–6.

[55] 'Coolidge opens Pageant of Progress today', CT, 30 July 1921, 1.

[56] Mary Ryan, 'The American parade: representations of the nineteenth-century social order', in Lynne Hunt (ed.), *The new cultural history*, London 1989, 131–53.

[57] 'The Pageant of Progress Exposition: a typical Chicago exhibition', 4.

in American society.[58] Community parades thus allowed different districts of Chicago to maintain individual and self-perpetuated conceptions of identity, while celebrating under a wider banner of civic unity in Chicago.

Narratives of urban community only went so far, however, and there were complex systems of inclusion and exclusion in operation. Some groups with a less established or emerging political power did try to use urban festivals to stake a claim to social citizenship – asserting inclusion in ways that worked outside the official 'script' of public representations.[59] For civic leaders representing minority groups this was a delicate balancing act of acknowledging ethnic or cultural difference while encouraging loyalty to both city and nation. Festivals were partially inclusive, since they allowed the mixing of men and women, and races and ethnicities. The catalyst of Chicago's race riot two years previously had been access to the segregated public beach; by imagining the Municipal Pier as an inclusive public space, the Pageant of Progress created a site and focal point of community interaction and a perceived local identity that attempted to absorb racial tensions. 'Savage' model foreign villages that promoted the idea of Anglo-Saxon racial supremacy and used black skin for entertainment, a popular feature of world expositions, were absent.[60] For one woman, as she told a press reporter, the most interesting thing about the pageant was 'The people' that she saw there, because 'there were a few of every type represented'.[61] Though this observer did not explicitly mention race, it seems possible that seeing people from different cultural backgrounds socially mixing together was a rarer experience – a telling indictment of the everyday segregation of Chicago.

The leisure and entertainment programme in Chicago also allowed for some displays of ethnic identity. Public singing, in particular, provided a non-threatening expression of civic participation, and was probably the most overt display of racial and ethnic identity at the pageant. Music had already been a key aspect of Progressive Era activism, utilised to encourage better civic engagement and social links between communities.[62] Each day at the pageant featured a different section of Chicago society, such as the Italians or the Poles.[63] Choirs had hundreds or even thousands of members, and enabled minorities to stake a non-aggressive claim to public recognition. Distinctive contributions beyond music, however, were more complicated. A whole day was dedicated to the Chinese, a very small community of around 2,300 people. The central

[58] Pacyga, *Chicago*, 218–19.

[59] Burke, 'Performing history', 42.

[60] Robert Rydell, '"Darkest Africa": African shows at America's world's fairs, 1893–1940', in Bernth Lindfors (ed.), *Africans on stage: studies in ethnological show business*, Bloomington, IN 1999, 135–50.

[61] 'The inquiring reporter', *CT*, 8 Aug. 1922, 19.

[62] Derek Vaillant, *Sounds of reform: progressivism and music in Chicago, 1873–1935*, Chapel Hill, NC 2003.

[63] 'Special musical program', *Greater Chicago* i/10 (July 1921), 17.

event was a parade organised by the Chinese Merchants Association, with floats depicting Chinese industries alongside dragons and other 'oriental idols', and a Chinese Pageant Queen and others who wore striking costumes representing important eras in Chinese history. The joss sticks and oriental lanterns of the Chinese supposedly 'cast a glamour of the Far East' upon the 'occidental' Municipal Pier, in reality commodifying Chinese culture for an American audience. But there was no acknowledgement of the second-class status, socially and legally, that Asians suffered in the 1920s. This disparity was symbolically and forcefully revealed when a confrontation between a gang of white teenage boys and a teenage Chinese boy after the parade ended with one of the youngsters being shot.[64]

In contrast to the Chinese, the black population of over 100,000 was not given a similar celebratory day of floats and historical re-enactment. Their largest public display came in the form of the Metropolitan Community Church Choir, which consisted of 1,000 young black singers – a form of racial demonstration more palatable to white Americans because of its concentration on Christianity rather than protest.[65] Instead of parades, African Americans used the pageant as an opportunity to reflect on the nature of urban and national citizenship. Just two years after the city's brutal race riot, new black leaders returned to the question of progress – or lack thereof. At an event inside the amphitheatre on the Pier, celebrating the abolitionist and reformer Frederick Douglass, Adelbert Roberts, an attorney and budding politician who would go on to be elected as the state's first African American state senator in 1924, chaired a reflective meeting. In his opening remarks he connected African American progress to the pageant, and demanded that whites who were sceptical of African American worth should cast their minds back to the sacrifices made by 'the boys of the Race who have fought in all the wars of our country'. Following Roberts, Bishop Archibald J. Carey Sr told the packed auditorium that the pageant was an example of 'his Race and of the white race [getting] together for their common betterment'. Chicago's physical progress – in its buildings and expansion – mattered little, he said, unless there was 'that spiritual advancement which would raise all men to a plane of common brotherhood'.[66] Such statements had a pragmatic basis. Black advancement and claiming a right to American citizenship, at this point, prioritised assimilation into society through respectability, patriotism and local civic pride.[67] Douglass Day was an event that spoke to these themes – an opportunity to display non-contentious citizenship. But, as the *Defender* noted towards the end of the festival, African Americans had 'little to display in the booths on

---

[64] 'Throng at pier sees 2,000 foot leap into lake', *CT*, 4 Aug. 1921, 23.

[65] 'Mayor seeks 1,000 negroes for chorus at pier show', *CT*, 20 June 1921, 11.

[66] 'Pageant talks featured by Douglass spirit', *CD*, 13 Aug. 1921, 2.

[67] Dennis C. Dickerson, *African American preachers and politics: the Careys of Chicago*, Jackson, Ms 2010, 26–44; Grossman, *Land of hope*, 144–6.

the pier', the main focus of the exposition – despite the community's 'contribution to the prosperity of Chicago' and 'the whole country' having 'more than measured up to that of any other group'.[68]

Recognising the limitations of public African American involvement in 1921, for the second Pageant of Progress in 1922 there was more concerted activity in the South Side. Business men came together to support the organisation of a local parade, made up of the neighbourhood's leading business, religious and civic organisations, and also coordinated the election of a 'district queen' who was locally 'crowned' in the South Side by Thompson after a parade witnessed by 200,000.[69] Organisations from Bronzeville, after seemingly being absent from the 1921 parade, also provided floats for the main parade in 1922. The *Chicago Defender* predictably declared that its own was 'the best in the procession' but also noted the reaction of their 'pale and unknowing fellow-citizens' as copies of the newspaper were thrown their way: 'A goodly number of these were later observed to go where anti-Volstead flasks are wont to be' – the bin, presumably.[70] Even these non-assertive and accommodationist approaches to claiming civic inclusion, then, were optimistic.

The swearing in of 4,650 new Ku Klux Klan members in the south-west suburb of Oak Lawn on the penultimate night of the 1922 Pageant of Progress demonstrated how ignorance was accompanied by outright hostility. In 1921 eighteen Klan organisations in Chicago and another twelve in suburban Cook County had emerged, with a combined membership of between 40,000 and 80,000.[71] The Klan was revived in 1915 after nearly fifty years of being defunct, and rapidly grew in the immediate post-war years as a recession combined with continued white Protestant anxieties about immigration, Communism and the perceived relaxing of sexual and social mores. By 1925 the Klan claimed to have several million members, and was violently active in trying to impose or maintain segregation and oppression.[72] Exposed to pressure from city hall, and from other factors, the Klan gradually faded away in the later 1920s – but the spirit that it represented remained.[73] African Americans in Chicago were subjected to rampant discrimination in jobs, housing and leisure by a large proportion of the surrounding population. Public apathy, antipathy or violent antagonism during civic festivals were merely moments that magnified the obstacles that blacks faced in trying to claim citizenship.

---

[68] 'The Pageant of Progress', CD, 13 Aug. 1921, 16.

[69] 'Mrs. Ernestine Lyles tops girls in popularity test', CD, 22 July 1922, 4; 'South Side represented at Pageant of Progress', CD, 24 June 1922, 4; 'Church entrant is the winner in popularity test', CD, 29 July 1922, 2.

[70] 'Pageant parade shines despite absence of sun', CD, 5 Aug. 1922, 8.

[71] Bukowski, *Big Bill*, 135.

[72] Thomas R. Pegram, *One hundred percent American: the rebirth and decline of the Ku Klux Klan in the 1920s*, Chicago, IL 2011, 3–20.

[73] Teaford, *The twentieth-century American city*, 61–2.

Manchester was not facing racial or ethnic tensions to anything like the same degree when it held its Civic Week. The official handbook did, however, describe the small Italian, Jewish and Greek communities as an interesting tourist sight of the city.[74] Any actual involvement of these communities in Civic Week, though, was minor. The Irish, the largest minority grouping, were at least symbolically recognised: several streets around Deansgate were decorated in green, orange and white by the council's 'Decorations Committee'.[75] This tricolour had only recently become official after the establishment of the Irish Free State in 1922, and it was only a few years since Irish unrest in the city. After the Irish Civil War of 1922–3, however, Irish rates of immigration had drastically slowed and most Irish in Manchester, according to Steven Fielding, 'seemed to want to forget Ireland' – though this may have been a coping mechanism in response to anti-Irish and anti-Catholic discourses.[76] The Irish flag, at least, was not as contentious as it would have been just a few years previously, and could now be 'safely reinterpreted' as a nod to Irishness as a 'heritage' that fitted into civil society rather than appearing as 'a political or even militant threat'.[77] Religious leaders in the city also promoted an inclusive celebration, positioning civic solidarity and service as the outcome of faith. A 'Civic Sunday' in Albert Square was billed as a 'United Undenominational Service' and was conducted by both Christian clerics and rabbis. Delivering the main sermon, the Congregationalist minister Alexander James Grieve asked God to 'Grant unto us a vision of Manchester as she might be', a city without vice and ignorance and where peace was achieved through 'love of all for the city, the great mother of our common life'.[78]

Actual mothers, however, were less visible. 'Where have the women been in the tableaux and processions?', asked the *Co-operative News*, reminding their readers that 'one could never think of Cottonopolis without being reminded of women and girls'.[79] Inequality was demonstrated at the organisational level, too, with men dominating the organising committees. Women could put up bunting or sell souvenirs – demonstrating their citizenship through responsible civic action.[80] But the dominant image of the exposition was municipal and industrial power. Rather than acknowledging women's new democratically won status as citizens, the organisers, purposefully or ignorantly, crafted a narrow, simple and less politically inclusive narrative. The Manchester and Salford

74   *Manchester Civic Week: official handbook*, 15.

75   'Civic week street decorations', MG, 17 Sept. 1926, 11.

76   Steven Fielding, 'A separate culture?' Irish Catholics in working-class Manchester and Salford, c. 1890–1939', in Davies, Fielding and Wyke, *Workers' worlds*, 41–2. See also David Fitzpatrick, 'A curious middle place: the Irish in Britain, 1871–1921', in Roger Swift and Sheridan Gilley, *The Irish in Britain, 1815–1939*, London 1989, 13.

77   Moulton, *Ireland and the Irish*, 4–9.

78   'The launching of Civic Week'.

79   *Co-operative News*, 9 Oct. 1926, 4.

80   *Historical Pageant of Manchester: Heaton Park*, Manchester 1926, 6–7.

Women Citizens' Association (formed in 1914), none the less, still attached their own ethos to that which was being celebrated in the Civic Week. Through activism and education the Association sought to construct an active place for women and gendered social issues in Manchester's civic culture.[81] During Civic Week the Association published a special issue of its magazine, *The Woman Citizen*, which highlighted the importance of local government – and the role of women within its work.[82] In tune with wider conceptions in the 1920s and 1930s, the Association displayed a secular and non-partisan form of citizenship across classes, political affiliations and religions that stressed active citizenship for women.[83] In Chicago, women played a more public role in the 1921 Pageant of Progress. A comprehensive programme of events, lasting eight days, was created both by and for women. Each day showed a different aspect of women in public life, with speeches from prominent female academics and presidents of local and regional Women's Clubs, as well as entertainment.[84] Public festivals, then, could encourage a 'counter-civil society', and give women alternative access to political life that did not just centre on voting.[85]

More generally there were opportunities for the associations and clubs that made up civic culture to take part in festivities. The *Greater Chicago* magazine was enthusiastic about the new life that the Pageant of Progress had given to many nearly defunct organisations, and described how clubs joined together to make the event a success. The Loyal Order of the Moose, a fraternal business club in Chicago, staged its own pageant and 'initiated' 3,000 new members at Congress Hall on the Pier.[86] A section in the official handbook of Manchester Civic Week listed the societies, institutions and charities of the city that kept 'a watchful eye on all in want', listing their meeting points, times and activities. Visitors were encouraged go and see these associations in action, with the idea that they could then get involved.[87] Public festivals continued the late nineteenth- and early twentieth-century attempts to ideologically bond the different groups of urban society together.[88] The surviving primary sources of

[81]   J. Smith, 'The Manchester and Salford Women Citizens' Association: a study of women's citizenship, 1913–1948', unpubl. PhD diss. Manchester 2007, 2.

[82]   '"The woman citizen": a Civic Week number', MG, 27 Sept. 1926, 4.

[83]   Helen McCarthy, 'Parties, voluntary associations, and democratic politics in interwar Britain', *HJ* l/4 (2007), 892.

[84]   'Pageant of Women's committee', *Greater Chicago* i/10 (July 1921), 12–14.

[85]   See Nancy Fraser 'Rethinking the public sphere: a contribution to the critique of actually existing democracy', *Social Text*, no. 25/26 (1990), 56–80. This article is a reformulation of Jürgen Habermas, *The structural transformation of the public sphere: an inquiry into a category of bourgeois society*, Cambridge, MA 1989.

[86]   'Pageant of Progress Exposition organizations formed in every district of Chicago', 18; 'Moosehearts great chorus to sing at pageant', CT, 12 Aug. 1922, 5.

[87]   *Manchester Civic Week: official handbook*, 25–6.

[88]   Mike Goldsmith and John Garrard, 'Urban governance: some reflections', in Morris and Trainor, *Urban governance*, 16.

these events thus reflect the rhetoric of the hopes and beliefs of the organisers. The fears and challenges of those on the urban social, economic and political margins – the targets of this bonding – are much harder to discern. Examples of agency can be found, such as activists distributing their own political pamphlets, but these voices were in the minority.[89]

It was possible, however, for marginalised groups in the city to utilise the format and discourse of these civic festivals to organise their own events. In 1925, for example, the Republican Woman's Club in Chicago staged a Woman's World's Fair. Taking place in the American Exposition Palace, and supported by President Coolidge amongst others, around 150 exhibitors displayed the strides that women had made in arts, science and industry. A success, attracting 200,000 visitors and making $50,000, it was subsequently repeated in 1926, 1927 and 1928. African American women, to an extent, were included, distributing a 'folder of facts' about important black women in art, literature, politics, law and social service – such as Edmonia Lewis and Violette Anderson – and presenting a musical and theatrical programme.[90] An artistic booth also exhibited the African-inspired sculptures of the soon-to-be-famous Richmond Barthe.[91] As Tracey Jean Boisseau has argued, the fair was a demonstration of how women maintained an interest in female-centred activism well beyond the achieving of suffrage by uniting across class and race to shape public opinion about their importance, both in the world of work and the domestic sphere, to modern society. This serious engagement contrasted with the World's Fairs of the 1930s, where women were marginalised by men and either sexualised or targeted as consumers.[92] Women may not have succeeded in changing the course of politics in the US after the achievement of suffrage, but they were still an active and important part of civic culture.

Chicago and Manchester's 1920s festivals were, in general, a success. In Manchester, nearly 100,000 people visited the city's institutions and municipal departments, over 80,000 paid for admission to the textile exhibition at Belle Vue (which also resulted in orders for more than £250,000 worth of goods) and many hundreds of thousands more saw some aspect of the festivities.[93] In Chicago, the 1921 exposition attracted daily crowds of 55,000, and the

[89]   The Quaker Society of Friends distributed Women's International League leaflets in Manchester, for example. See 'Civic Week at Manchester', *The Friend*, 9 Oct. 1926, 1.

[90]   'Close Woman's World's Fair', *CD*, 2 June 1928, 8.

[91]   'Artistic booth at women's world fair', *CD*, 2 June 1928, 3.

[92]   Tracey Jean Boisseau, 'Once again in Chicago: revisioning women as workers at the Chicago Woman's World's Fairs of 1925–1928', *Women's History Review* xviii/2 (2009), 265–91.

[93]   'Civic Week's meaning to Manchester', *MG*, 16 Oct. 1926, 113; 'Civic pride: what Manchester is doing this week', *Walsall Observer*, 9 Oct. 1926, 152. Figure from *Manchester Guardian Yearbook*, Manchester 1927, 230.

Tribune estimated that 2,000,000 people saw the closing firework display.[94] Profits from sales and admission tickets totalled $300,000.[95] The pageant also boosted the spirit and future orders of manufacturers; a banquet given to honour the mayor following the exposition noted that it had 'brought more wholesale buyers to Chicago during the Pageant of Progress than ever before' generating 'numbers of new customers and many millions of dollars' worth of additional business'.[96] It is trickier to measure whether the exhibitions cemented local citizenship, though some certainly believed that it had. The *Municipal Journal and Public Works Engineer* argued that Manchester's Civic Week had shown that 'the citizen is not the apathetic creature which disgruntled candidates and parties habitually declare him to be', noting that 'For the elector to waken it was only necessary that the Council should awake.'[97] The Anglican bishop of Manchester wrote to the mayor and congratulated him on the development of 'the sense of corporate life', noting how individuals now felt 'that they belong to something greater than themselves'.[98] In Chicago, the city was proclaimed to be 'a pageant of progress in itself' by the *Tribune*, with its factories, warehouses, shops, stores, streets, homes, parks and playgrounds telling 'the whole story of America and America's progress'.[99] All 'went home agreeing that Chicago is being made civically wealthier every day the show runs', apparently – though some, such as businessmen, clearly benefitted more than others.[100] At a meeting of the Chicago Federation of Labour, in 1921, the chairman of the committee on Russian affairs instead lamented the now cold reaction to Soviet policies, observing that 'There is no longer any handclapping when Russia is mentioned in our meetings.' He directly attributed this to the 'superficial glamour' of the pageant, arguing that it prevented 'the people from functioning properly mentally' instead of giving 'earnest consideration of the problems of industrialism' – though it probably reflected, more generally, the waning of the labour movement in the US.[101] No more festivals on the scale of the Pageant of Progress or Civic Week were held in the 1920s, but, when the enthusiasm for boosterism again grew in the 1930s, it was in these original events that civic elites found a workable model.

---

[94] 'Pageant ends in doubled blaze of fireworks', *CT*, 15 Aug. 1921, 3. Attendance figures from Lloyd Wendt and Herman Kogan, *Big Bill of Chicago* (1953), Evanston, IL 2005, 202.

[95] Wendt and Kogan, *Big Bill*, 202.

[96] 'The Pageant of Progress Exposition: a typical Chicago exhibition', 4.

[97] 'Manchester's Civic Week', *Municipal Journal and Public Works Engineer* xxxv/1758 (1926), 1516.

[98] 'Civic Week of Triumph', *Daily Dispatch*, 16 Oct. 1926, 15.

[99] 'City pageant puts new heart in nation', *CT*, 31 July 1921, 1.

[100] '100,000 make it breathing room only at pageant', *CT*, 8 Aug. 1921, 3.

[101] 'Labor now cold to Russ Soviet, Fraenckel says', ibid.

Festivals for the 'thirties

Before moving on to local festivals in the later 1930s in particular, it is worth looking briefly at the gigantic Chicago World's Fair (or Century of Progress) in 1933, to make a few observations about its relationship to local citizenship. A central element of the Pageant of Progress was its industrial and commercial promotion: a hopeful response to the post-war depression. The Century of Progress, controlled by local business elites who were trying to overcome both the Great Depression and the negative portrayals of the city after a decade of gangsterism, continued this approach – albeit by placing the city in a much larger frame of reference. The exposition's success in raising consumer spending led President Roosevelt to suggest to the organisers that the fair should open again the following year; despite the work involved, they happily assented. By the time that it finally closed 50,000 temporary or permanent jobs had been created; it had led to $50,000,000 worth of construction and maintenance work; and the 36,500,000 paying visitors had left $700,000,000 in the pockets of the Chicagoan business community.[102] Whatever the political ideology of festivals, they had to have a solid economic foundation as well.

Yet part of the 1933 World's Fair was still about the idea of the city. Henry Justin Smith, a writer of both fiction and history and managing editor of the *Chicago Daily News*, was commissioned by the organisers to write *Chicago's great century* – a lively portrayal of the city's history that did not shy away from dealing with crime, conflict and corruption. For Smith, it was the tumultuous nature of Chicago's past that meant that it was prepared for the present and the future:

> Just as the scandal of Chicago's 'Sands,' the railroad riots of the '70s, the anarchist bomb, the graft and vice of the '90s, not to speak of numerous other black pages, subside into material sought only by historians, so the 'reign of crime' in the puerperal 1920s sinks gradually into dust-laden oblivion in newspaper libraries. And just as Chicago's pioneer endeavours, its emergence from mud and confusion, its grand rally from the disaster of '71, its Columbian Exposition, and its triumph over one crisis after another, constitute its predominant story, so also its demonstrations of a noble spirit at a time when the world could think of nothing but insulting adjectives for it, represent the actual theme of its present-day phase.[103]

Smith ended his book with the triumph of the Century of Progress – the city overcoming its latest obstacle: the Great Depression. Rufus C. Dawes – a local businessman who served as president of the World's Fair organisation – explained in the foreword how the drama of the city's history could only

---

[102]   John E. Findling, *Chicago's great World's Fairs*, Manchester 1994, 143.

[103]   Henry Justin Smith, *Chicago's great century: 1833–1933*, Chicago, IL 1933, 180.

'increase the civic patriotism of Chicagoans'.[104] The *Official guide* to the fair also told the familiar civic story of Chicago's success over the previous hundred years: from a 'huddle of huts, hewn of logs, clinging to the shadows of Fort Dearborn for safety from the Indians' to the second largest city in America, fourth in the world and an economic and cultural hub.[105]

Like the Pageant of Progress, many of the exhibits further used the comparative method of 'before and after' – the benefits of a modern city apartment juxtaposed with the hard lifestyle of a Colonial family, for example. But now, however, it was a generic 'American family', and portrayed more as the result of general scientific advancement than municipal ambition.[106] Other publicity and souvenirs were also distinctly national. James Weber Linn, a teacher at the University of Chicago, eulogised the fair in the souvenir *Official pictures* booklet as an experience that did the 'valuable work of demonstrating to the nation that it is a unified nation, a high-hearted nation, [and] a nation undiscouraged and unafraid'.[107] In general, exhibits went far beyond demonstrating the vitality of Chicago. Like the 1893 Exposition, the Fair also took place in an environment outside the downtown of the city. Belgian villages, exhibits of Chrysler Motors and federal displays had more to say about entertainment, industry and national pride than the city in which they were housed. The World's Fair in 1933 eschewed the classic architectural vision of 1893, which now seemed old-fashioned and even anachronistic, in favour of architectural modernism and visions of the future.[108] Its design had little to say about Chicago's historical or even recent physical growth and development. Despite its name, the Pageant of Progress had sold continuity. This was less apparent in the planning and execution of the World's Fair in 1933, which was more of a conscious break. Dawes, indeed, realised that a successful fair needed a broader theme than the past, present and future of Chicago. Instead, working with the National Research Council, he positioned the fair as an appreciation of science and industry: the foundation of modern America, and a clarion call to move beyond the Great Depression.[109] Unlike the civic parades of the Pageant of Progress, the inaugural day opening ceremony of the World's Fair was also more outward looking – consisting of a parade of 500 people in various national costumes carrying their country's flags.[110]

The city's next large festival, the Chicago Jubilee in 1937, was much narrower in its purview. Organised by a broad civic coalition, it had more in common

[104] Rufus C. Dawes, 'Foreword', ibid.

[105] *Official guide: book of the Fair, 1933*, Chicago, Il 1933, 8.

[106] Ibid. 60–1.

[107] James Weber Linn, 'A Century of Progress Exposition', in *The official pictures of A Century of Progress Exposition*, Chicago, Il 1933.

[108] Findling, *Chicago's great World's Fairs*.

[109] Ibid. 36–9, 92. See also Robert Rydell, 'The fan dance of science: American World's Fairs in the Great Depression', *Isis: A Journal of the History of Science* lxxvi (1985), 525–42.

[110] Findling, *Chicago's great World's Fairs*, 57.

Figure 7. Commemorative brochure of municipal government published for Chicago's Jubilee (1937)

with the Pageant of Progress than the World's Fair. The commemorative date was, ostensibly, the granting of the city's charter by the state legislature in 1837. The city itself was once more the subject of the celebration, and no new site was built. Publications again drew attention to the physical and commercial progress that was being supported by municipal provision (*see* Figure 7). Parades, such as a 'Summer Comes to Chicago' procession in June, with over 25,000 taking part and 250,000 watching, refocused on the civic centre of the city.[111] The language of the event, which concentrated on projecting the city into the future, was again an evocation of civic pride. But there were also some points of departure. In 1921, and even to a certain degree in 1933, the shock city of the past had often been used as a demonstration or temporal marker of what had been overcome in following periods. In 1937 there was instead a sense that the city had matured, its historical disasters now part of a heritage that could be combined into a broader modern outlook. The Chicago Historical Society, for example, organised a 'Historic Chicago Week', when neighbourhoods held their own lectures, exhibitions and tours. There were also seventy-eight bronze plaques affixed to sites of historical notability – such as crossroads, taverns and pioneer settlements or the spot where Mrs O'Leary's cow (allegedly) kicked over the lantern that started the Great Fire in 1871.[112]

Celebrating Chicago's unity in the present, while acknowledging its divergent ethnic heritage, was also a key part of the Jubilee. Urban ethnic festivals had become more common from the mid-1920s onwards, promoted by liberal commentators who believed that only through appreciation and respect for the 'cultural gifts' of immigrants would newcomers bond with their adopted country.[113] The homogenising aspects of the 'melting pot' were now rejected, with considerable practical success, by educationalists responding to the poisonous atmosphere of the early post-war years. There was now a more pluralist multiracial and multi-faith understanding of society at work.[114] Into the decade of depression this ethos developed even further. Businessmen, interfaith activists, government officials and cultural elites from across the political spectrum consciously attempted to forge the idea of an 'American Way'. In the context of economic chaos, the rise of political extremism abroad and a growing defensiveness about the ability of corporate leaders to lead the nation, such an ethos stressed individual freedom, cultural pluralism and

---

[111] *Chicago's Charter Jubilee bulletin of progress* i/12 (22 Apr. 1937), CHM, qF38CD.1937. C4.W7, 3.

[112] Ibid. 4–5; 'Southwest side historic sites to be marked', *CT*, 12 Sept. 1937, 1. See Chicago Charter Jubilee Committee, 'List of historical markers placed at various sites throughout the city' (1937), CHM, qF38.HN.C3.

[113] Victor Greene, 'Dealing with diversity: Milwaukee's multiethnic festivals and urban identity, 1840–1940', *JUH* xxxi/6 (2005), 837. See Allen Eaton, *Immigrant gifts to American life: some experiments in appreciation of the contributions of our foreign-born citizens to American culture*, New York, NY 1932.

[114] Diana Selig, *Americans all: the cultural gifts movement*, London 2008.

the ability of 'diverse individuals to live together harmoniously'. Some of the promoters of this consensus defined 'diversity' in terms of ethnicity, whereas others emphasised religion and the idea of America as a 'Protestant-Catholic-Jewish' nation – though virulent anti-Catholicism and anti-semitism certainly continued.[115] Roosevelt's New Deal also contributed to the revitalisation of civic nationalism. Because the previous decade of anti-immigration legislation had reduced the number of immigrants and increased pressure on others to Americanise, 'a kinder and gentler' nation building could now take place – one that embraced the achievements of European immigrants and 'welcomed them into the American family'.[116]

Urban religion had for centuries been providing the resources that enabled migrants and immigrants to anchor themselves in the USA. As cities were rapidly transformed in the modern age, the social practices of minority faiths were even more heavily mapped onto the geography of city and neighbourhood. In the late nineteenth century this had caused consternation, with 'native-born Protestants' linking the growth of Catholic and Jewish neighbourhoods with a supposed weakening of their own moral and cultural authority.[117] But, in the 1930s, there was now a degree of acceptance for the religious facets of urban affiliation. If unity in diversity had partly been rhetoric in 1921, then, the 1937 Jubilee reflected broader shifts in the acceptance of different ethnicities and religions and was more successful in giving weight to the words. Business and industrial interests were still involved in the celebration, and there was definitely a boosterish motive, but it was a celebration of the city and its people that concentrated more on communality than commercialism. As the mayor, Edward Kelly, explained after the Jubilee had finished, an effort had been made to create 'some event, some spectacle to interest and enchant every racial group, every nationality, every section of the city'. [118] The organising committee of the Jubilee actively targeted their press releases to ethnic newspapers, tailoring each with a 'distinct community slant'.[119] All of the city's largest

---

[115] Wendy L. Wall, *Inventing the 'American way': the politics of consensus from the New Deal to the civil rights movement*, Oxford 2008, 5–7.

[116] Gerstle, *American crucible*, 128–38, quotation at p. 139.

[117] See Josiah Strong, *The twentieth century city*, New York, NY 1898. Excellent recent overviews of religion and the city in this period, and the topic's historiography, can be found in Christopher D. Cantwell, 'Religion in the American city, 1900–2000', in *American history: Oxford research encyclopaedia*, Oxford 2016, <http://americanhistory.oxfordre.com/view/10.1093/acrefore/9780199329175.001.0001/acrefore-9780199329175-e-355>, and Katie Day, 'Urban space and religion in the United States', *Religion: Oxford research encyclopaedia*, Oxford 2017, <http://religion.oxfordre.com/view/10.1093/acrefore/9780199340378.001.0001/acrefore-9780199340378-e-470>.

[118] Edward J. Kelly, 'Report concerning Chicago's Charter Jubilee', *Journal of the Proceedings of the City Council of the City of Chicago, Illinois* (10 Nov. 1937), 4722 (hereinafter cited as 'Kelly's report').

[119] *Chicago's Charter Jubilee Bulletin of Progress* 1, no. 7 (22 Apr. 1937), 3, qF38CD 1937 C4 W7.

communities were involved, with most given a celebratory day. Attendances for these were impressive: 50,000 people saw a Polish play that portrayed the city's rise; 30,000 attended an Irish Day picnic; and 20,000 were present for singing and historical re-enactment from the Croatian, Serbian and Slovene communities.[120] Across the course of the summer, according to the city council, 1,394,250 spectators attended 166 major events and many more 'lesser affairs' across the city.[121] Communities could still try to come together under the larger unity of Chicago, then – despite the city's ongoing fractures and inequalities.

African American involvement was also greater than it had been in the expositions of the early 1920s. The *Defender*, still reflecting an accommodationist approach, encouraged its readers to support the jubilee and 'fall in line and march forward', and noted that 'Chicago's Race citizens' were 'doing their bit'.[122] A South Central District Charter Jubilee Committee was set up, supported by local civic leaders and businessmen. Quartets sang on the streets of Bronzeville, a 'gigantic' music festival took place in Washington Park, 20,000 men, women and children marched through the neighbourhood representing various social and civic clubs, and a book that sketched 'the history of the Race in Chicago and the invaluable contribution it has made' was proposed.[123] Perhaps most important symbolically, however, was the recognition given to the community by the Chicago Historical Society during the Jubilee. It set aside a week to 'commemorate' the district's 'contribution to the city's cultural-industrial growth', working with black civic leaders such as Joanna Snowden Porter to put together an exhibition of documents, pictures and articles that celebrated the history of African Americans in the city.[124] Given that it was just a year since the society had been forced, following protests, to cancel the screening of the virulently racist film *Birth of a nation* (1915), the inclusion of African Americans in the Jubilee represented progress.[125] It was, however, in many ways too little and too late: a much more expressive and bold black consciousness was beginning to challenge segregation and racism – one that sought the material benefits of rights and protection rather than the limited progress of civic representation.

In many large industrial cities in Britain there also continued to be local exhibitions, held to coincide with a variety of commemorations such as Royal jubilees, the granting of municipal borough status or the celebration of centenaries of past city charters. Local government publicity had grown to

[120] 'Erin's children dance hornpipe at Irish picnic', CT, 16 Aug. 937, 11; '50,000 watch Polish pageant of city's rise', CT, 9 Aug. 1937, 3.

[121] 'Kelly's report', 4724.

[122] 'Run down prejudice', CD, 20 Nov. 1937, 16.

[123] 'Race to play major role in city jubilee', CD (no date) in '1936–1938 scrapbook', 8-93, YMCA Wabash Records, University of Illinois at Chicago Special Collections and University Archives (hereinafter cited as UIC); 'Get ready for our big parade', CD, 17 July 1937, 12.

[124] 'Chicago honors outstanding race pioneers', CD, 12 June 1937, 19.

[125] 'Halt "Birth of Nation" exhibition', CD, 8 Feb. 1936, 1.

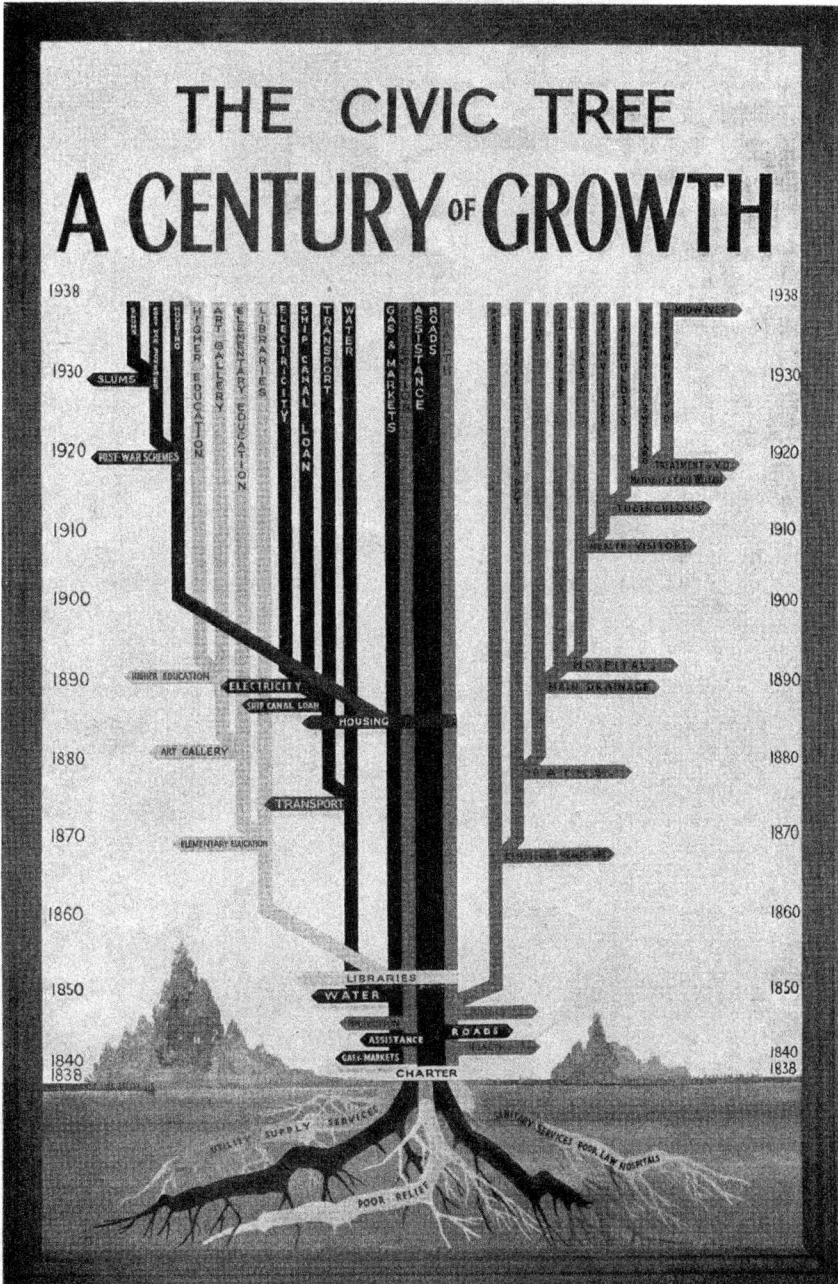

Figure 8. The 'Civic Tree' that grew from Manchester's 1838 incorporation (1938)

be a prominent part of British culture by the 1930s. With the centenary of the Municipal Reform Act in 1935, city councils became part of a celebration of the achievements of municipal government in welfare, civic pride and urban intervention. This upturn in municipal government publicity, however, also acknowledged that it was a response to general and growing problems. Administrators and politicians alike worried about what they saw as a decline in local intelligence and commitment when it came to matters of municipal politics. Glowing accounts of municipal achievements over the previous hundred years were also tinged with a recognition that central government was growing and replacing local government functions. Municipal publicity, then, was as reactive as it was progressive.[126]

It was in this context of insecurity, yet acknowledgement of long-term municipal success, that Manchester's city council staged a celebration of the centenary of the city's 1838 charter of governmental incorporation.[127] Building on and expanding ideas and formats that had been tested twelve years previously in Civic Week, this was an event almost entirely focused on the city. A municipal exhibition in a purpose-built City Exhibition Hall on Deansgate cemented a narrative of progress, using exhibits of both historical and contemporary Manchester to tell the story of the development of municipal provision from incorporation to the present.[128] As one poster, 'The Civic Tree', ideologically claimed, it was the early nineteenth-century roots of municipal action – from poor relief and utility service provision – that formed the impetus for the 1838 Charter. Over the next hundred years, branches grew from this tree into all spheres of life, from transport and education to housing and hospitals (see Figure 8). Another model unpacked the financial detail of the Council's provision to visually explain how the citizen's taxes went towards ensuring a healthy and supportive environment for them and their children (see Figure 9).

Even beyond the exhibition the council made sure that citizens would be reminded, at least for the course of the centenary, of the investment that came from local government. A striking 'streamline moderne' bus for example, decorated in lights and text that proclaimed '100 Years Progress', drove around the city to hammer home the point (see Figure 10). Other exhibits included models and pictures of the before, after and future of municipal intervention: sewers, bridges, canals, roads, electric lighting and transport. The centenary, however, was not just about celebrating and justifying the council's schemes, but also encouraging further use of the city's services – a pamphlet accompanying the exhibition, for example, described the health and happiness benefits of municipal services such as public baths, but drew attention to the campaigns of the National Council for Physical Fitness and finished by asking: 'are you

---

126 Hulme, 'Putting the city back into citizenship'.

127 For an overview see Wildman, *Urban redevelopment*, 74–9.

128 'Draft: City of Manchester charter centenary celebrations' (1938), 1, in Charter centenary celebrations, MCA, GB127.M68/21/3/11.

Figure 9. Model showing ratepayers 'where the money goes' during Manchester's centenary celebrations (1938)

Figure 10. Illuminated bus during Manchester's centenary celebrations (1938)

not convinced that you are the loser by not utilising the many and varied facilities provided for your use by the Baths Committee?'[129] National narratives of the importance of national fitness, a key attribute of citizenship – especially in the context of 1930s military preparedness – filtered into local civic aims.

In the foreword to the exhibition brochure the mayor made the point of the celebration clear: to acknowledge the successes of municipal government and remind citizens of the 'bold ventures' provided by the city council for the benefit and 'happiness of millions of people who reside within the region of which Manchester is the natural metropolis'.[130] Parties of special guests were also shown around important sites of economic and municipal power – such as the new town hall extension, the Trafford Park Estate and the newly built Wythenshawe housing estate. A central part of the programme was three films, two made by the amateur Manchester Film Society and one by the Metro-Vick Amateur Cinematograph Society, shown at the Civic Theatre (seating for 300) in the exhibition hall. These told a civics-style story of municipal inter-vention: 'Sewage' detailed the technical governance of sewage from the city to the sea; 'A Breath of Fresh Air' depicted Manchester's 2,143 acres of parks and gardens – 'one of the City's most valuable assets' and a corrective to 'the idea that Manchester is a city of greys and blacks, typical of the Industrial North Country'; while 'Inward Bound' traced the course of a steamer up the Manchester Ship Canal.[131] These three films combined to create a story about the fruits of municipal government in both social and economic life, with voluntary societies co-opted into producing the vision.

Parades were also again used to convey an image of municipal leadership. On the day that the lord mayor of London (Harry Twyford) visited, a cavalcade of cars took the civic party, in full regalia, from the town hall to the exhibition. Like the opening parade of the Manchester Civic Week, the urban population watched and did not participate – a reason why, perhaps, the response was less than spectacular.[132] There were also opportunities for inclusion, however. Before a Sunday civic service there was a massive procession around the main streets of the civic centre, leaving from the town hall and arriving at Manchester Cathedral. Included were the city police, units of the territorial army, groups of war veterans, youth organisations, wardens from the cathedral, national government officials, international consuls, MPs, the present mayor along with previous incumbents, professors from the Victoria University, a

[129] 'Centenary Exhibition: Baths and Wash-Houses Department' (1938), 30, and 'Centenary celebration of Manchester's incorporation: official handbook' (1938), 33–56, ibid. GB127. M68/21/3/4 and 2.

[130] Joseph Crookes Grime, 'Foreword' in 'Centenary celebration of Manchester's incorpo-ration: official handbook', 7.

[131] 'Programme of entertainments in the Civic Theatre', Charter centenary celebrations, MCA, GB127.M68/21/4.

[132] 'General programme' (1938), 10, MCA, GB127.M68/21/2; 'Lord mayor of London visits Manchester', MG, 4 May 1938, 11.

whole host of literary, scientific and musical societies, professional associations, Co-operative societies, trade associations, hospital and medical charities, women's associations, moral associations and many others. Altogether, around 200 different associations, clubs, societies or institutions were represented – a striking imagining of an integrated civic community, embraced even more wholeheartedly than during Civic Week, and a good example of how middle-class civil society had survived well into the interwar period.[133] In the week after the main exhibition there was a further programme of civil and military displays, including 1,000 members of the Women's League of Health and Beauty, six organisations working with the National Fitness Council, a hundred members of the English Folk Dance Society, the Police and Fire Brigade and a whole host of boys' and girls' clubs.[134] Manchester's commemoration thus contributed to several aims: national citizenship projects of fitness; municipal ideals of engagement; and intra-urban communication between local associations.

A notable development from the 1926 celebration was the more active response from the leaders of religious groups. Manchester's Jewish community, organised by the Council of Manchester and Salford Jews, showed enthusiasm for the centenary by organising a special religious service at the central synagogue. The mayor attended with aldermen and city councillors to show their appreciation and inspected the guards of honour of ex-servicemen and Jewish Lads' Brigade cadets. Dr S. M. Lehrman addressed the congregation and told them that their gathering was a symbol of the cooperation, tolerance and brotherhood of all sections of Manchester society – adding that Jews in Manchester had an 'untarnished record of good citizenship'. He went on to list the educational, social and philanthropic benefits that the community had brought to the city, before ending with a show of gratitude to the *Manchester Guardian* and its opposition to persecution and injustice, so vital in 'days when the lights of civilisation are being extinguished one by one in Europe'.[135] Jewish representatives also added Manchester to the Golden Book of the Jewish National Fund in Jerusalem, planted an extensive grove of trees in the King George V Jubilee Forest on the hills of Nazareth (dubbing it the City of Manchester Grove) and presented an illuminated album (containing the names of all the subscribers to the Grove) to the mayor at a commemorative event.[136] In mainstream Jewish culture, it was possible to be not just a good Jew, but a good Englishman – and a good Mancunian, too. Constructing a narrative of local citizenship was thus one way in which Jewish leaders could demonstrate

---

[133] Civic service at the Manchester Cathedral', 3, Charter centenary celebrations, GB127. M68/21/5.

[134] 'Manchester centenary', MG, 31 Mar. 1938, 13.

[135] 'Jewry's tribute', MG, 16 May 1938, 13.

[136] 'Commemorative volume by Jewish community of the centenary of incorporation', MCA, GB127.MS.f.296.M150.

their assimilation as a minority group and challenge the growing anti-semitism of the 1930s.[137]

The Nonconformist Sunday School Union, along with the Church of England Sunday schools, also signed a special bound roll that the bishop of Manchester then presented to the mayor at a civic reception.[138] Churches in Manchester were happy to attach themselves to the celebration. The Revd Jacob Phillips, for example, told a large congregation that Manchester deserved the title 'City of Churches', and was blessed with liberal-minded citizens who were dedicated to the moral uplift of the general community. The centenary celebration, 'in which all the religions of the city had co-operated', he argued, was an indication of the stability of faith relations.[139] This connecting of Christianity to a non-contentious sense of civic identity was indicative of broader shifts in the place of the Church in British life. The convergence of Christianity, nationalism and imperialism, which had been strongest in the Edwardian period, was dented by the First World War and consequently receded to a limited and more humble patriotism.[140] But, in terms of both local and national life, writers and clergy actively contributed a liberal and Anglican sense of citizenship and community in the interwar period. In the context of dislocation, such as war, the General Strike and the Great Depression, they looked back to Thomas Hill Green, and the philosophy of idealism. Rather than accepting the 'authoritarianism of the Idealist state', however, they instead stressed common social purpose and civic duty; civic festivals were an expression of this ethos.[141]

According to the final internal report, admission to the exhibition was 'moderate' on the first day, but afterwards 'surpassed expectation'. It was extended by another week, which was even better attended than the first. Altogether, around 100,000 adults visited the exhibition, plus 24,000 school children. Public opinion of the event, again according to the report, was seemingly good – with the remark that 'I never thought the Corporation did so many things' apparently being frequently heard. The report concluded that 'it would be difficult to furnish a better introduction to education for citizenship'.[142] Ronald Allen, the rector of Withington, agreed. He wrote in to the *Guardian* to appeal to Manchester citizens to visit the exhibition – which he found 'interesting and inspiring'. Though he lauded the demonstrations of

---

[137] 'Manchester Jewry and the centenary', MG, 18 May 1938, 15. See Sharman Kadish, *A good Jew and a good Englishman: the Jewish Lads' and Girls' Brigade, 1895–1995*, London 1995, pp. xvi–xvii. For how Jewish leaders constructed 'defensive stereotypes' see Williams, 'The Jewish immigrant in Manchester', 43.

[138] 'Autographs for the lord mayor', MG, 12 Sept. 1938, 13.

[139] 'Manchester's progress: the place of the churches', MG, 23 May 1938, 11.

[140] John Wolffe, *God and greater Britain: religion and national life in Britain and Ireland, 1843–1945*, London 1994, 211–12.

[141] See Grimley, *Citizenship, community, and the Church of England*, quotation at p. 102.

[142] 'Draft: City of Manchester charter centenary celebrations', 5–8.

Manchester's municipal progress and the human effort that had led to such public services, he acknowledged that more could still be done by the city council. Smoke, slums, lack of town planning, higher maternal mortality, rising juvenile crime, the failure to provide community life on new estates, general indifference to local politics: all needed the future cooperation of Manchester's citizens.[143] Manchester's 1938 commemoration may not have reached the size of the Civic Week, nor its originality, but it portrayed the consistency of the municipal narrative in the city, which, at its forefront, placed local government as the arbiter of civic ideals and urban citizenship.

During the 1921 Pageant the *Tribune* sent out a roving reporter to ascertain public opinion about Chicago's great exposition. Respondents were enthusiastic about the exhibits, and impressed by the handling of the large crowds, and some even saw the event as indicative of the wider progress that the city was making. Not everyone, however, was so easily convinced: as one man cynically observed: 'I think it was just a huge advertising scheme where the public was soaked for all it was worth.'[144] Despite his misgivings, the message of these events was clear: the contrast of the Chicago of old with the Chicago of new, the future rising out of the 'shock', and a chance to rethink the city and participate in the emergence of its new social order.[145] Even though festivals were short-lived, they continued to exist as a memory in small souvenirs and special eyewitness accounts. Items of memorabilia presented official viewpoints, imbued with the ethos of the celebration, and brought to life the memory of the fair for both those who attended and those that did not.[146]

At points, though, the façade of urban community could slip. A photograph from Manchester's Civic Week, for example, seems to show men in topcoats and tails laughing as they observe street children below (possibly picking up coins which had been thrown down to them: *see* Figure 5). Caught on camera, the scene reminds us that the seemingly honourable intentions of civic celebrations to create any sort of 'classless community' should, in the context of complex class politics and interwar instability, be approached with caution. A civic image dominated these urban festivals because their organisers were mostly elites drawn from local government and business. Ideas about the city and its government, which had been circulating in educational culture following the rise of the civics movement, were brought to the fore. This top-down narrative, however, should be balanced with the real participation in pageants and parades, as well as examples of those who chose not to participate. Chicago was dealing with more newly disparate communities and tensions, and

---

[143] 'The progress of Manchester', MG, 10 May 1938, 22.

[144] 'The inquiring reporter', CT, 15 Aug. 1922, 17.

[145] Warren Susman, 'Ritual fairs', *Chicago History* xii/3 (1983), 6.

[146] See, for example, J. F. Delaney, 'A trip thru Chicago's Pageant of Progress exhibition', Pageant of Progress Exposition miscellaneous pamphlets. See also Susman, 'Ritual fairs', 5.

tried to incorporate these groups delicately, without exacerbating urban strife. Some ethnic communities of the city, or sections of such communities, did respond to this message. They held celebrations that did not subsume their identity into that of the city, but instead made a place for the city within their own. Different types of citizenship, then, could co-exist. At the same time, though, there was a racialised hierarchy that meant that this new social order was defined, usually implicitly but sometimes explicitly, through exclusion. Black Chicagoans, most evidently, were held back from full inclusion despite their attempts to support the civic narrative. The city, then, was not just the site of leisure and entertainment but a 'stage on which identities [were] performed and from which they faced critical evaluation'.[147]

Civic festivals worked by combining things that could seem, at first, to be opposites: history and progress; entertainment and education; local and non-local identities. Nowhere was the fruitful combination of these binaries more visible in interwar culture than in the vogue for historical pageants. Already an important part of the Pageant of Progress and Manchester Civic Week, large-scale historical pageants had, by the time of the Chicago Jubilee and Manchester Centenary, become central to the construction of local ideas of citizenship – both inclusionary and exclusionary. These forms of public theatre articulated a similar ethos of civic belonging, allowing an even more specific and visible narrative of the modern city to be created through the re-enactment of the local past. At the same time, they also depended on participation – and could be challenged or subverted if they failed to follow a story that matched local expectations. Groups that identified in ways beyond the urban could even stage their own pageants: an opportunity to contest dominant narratives of citizenship from the point of view of racial, religious or class identity. In Manchester this meant that the Communist Party could actively recruit new members by challenging the city council's story of the local past, which they thought excluded the radical voice of the working man. In Chicago, groups that found themselves discriminated against, most notably African Americans, turned to re-enactment to demonstrate their importance to American society. In doing so, however, they looked to African heritage and history beyond the US. Historical pageants thus give a further depth of understanding to the crafting of urban images and citizenship from above and below, and the ways in which the urban inhabitants, on which civic governors depended on for success, could respond.

---

[147] Robert Hawkins, 'The city as stage: performance, identity, and cultural democracy', *JUH* xli/1 (2015), 158.

History, Progress and Community Performance

From 1905, and until at least the Second World War in the US and the 1960s in Britain, thousands of villages, towns and cities staged at least one historical pageant. Huge casts of more than 10,000 people could bring in total audiences of over 200,000, and millions of individuals either saw or performed in a pageant in the twentieth century. This form of historical re-enactment allowed civic officials to construct a 'civic image' that made 'place' the 'hero' and joined disparate peoples into a community that shared common purpose through a collective history.[1] Like civics, historical pageants linked the past and present of urban life together to inspire pride and belonging, transferring responsibility for the urban future to the general populace. Pageants did not just show the transition to the municipal city after the problems of the nineteenth century, however. Instead, it was a story of before, during and after the shock city, and a celebration of how local people had responded to dislocation throughout history. Pageants demonstrated how and from where the present city had gained its power: from historic and not just historical beginnings, and through adversity – whether war, depression or conflict.

Pageants often looked to the pre-industrial past, but this did not necessarily mean that they were conservative or rooted in a bucolic and rose-tinted belief in the hierarchical power relations of rural society.[2] In more nuanced theories of modernity, historians have stressed the continuities between pre-modern and modern – a connection that contemporaries were also capable of making.[3] This chapter begins by showing how pageant authors and organisers in Manchester looked to both the distant and recent past to frame the image of the contemporary city. There was no contradiction in finding the soul of the industrial city in the Roman fort, the medieval monastery or the folk traditions of sixteenth-century Merrie Old England.[4] The city council led the creation of

---

[1]   David Glassberg, *American historical pageantry: the uses of tradition in the early twentieth century*, Chapel Hill, NC 1990, 78, 281–3. For a similar overview of pageantry in Britain see Mark Freeman, '"Splendid display; pompous spectacle": historical pageants in twentieth-century Britain', *Social History* xxxviii/(2013), 423–55.

[2]   For a critical example of historical pageantry as reactionary social control see Michael Woods, 'Performing power: local politics and the Taunton pageant of 1928', *Journal of Historical Geography* xxv/1 (1999), 57–74.

[3]   Gunn, *History and cultural theory*, 128.

[4]   Roy Judge, 'May Day and Merrie England', *Folklore* cii/2 (1991), 131. For folk culture in Britain in this period see Katie Palmer Heathman, 'Revival: the transformative potential of English folksong and dance, 1890–1940', unpubl. PhD diss. Leicester 2016.

pageants which told this story to huge crowds in urban parks and stadiums. By the 1930s these narratives foregrounded the inclusivity of urban society. A focus on 'everyday' citizens of the city, and not just institutions and industry, reflected shifts to a more demotic sense of citizenship in Britain. The second section of the chapter outlines Chicago's rather different trajectory of historical pageantry. Chicago claimed less than seventy years of 'recorded' history – that is, tangible evidence of European settlement. But civic elites still attempted to create a civic identity for a population that could not, for the most part, claim long genealogical ties to the US. In the early post-war years, it was a 'melting pot' story, where European immigrants were transformed into American citizens if they emulated a white Protestant archetype.[5] By the 1930s, however, an evolution had taken place, and a more nuanced story was told. Immigrants could now maintain ethnic or religious identities, as well as urban and national belonging, as a growing politics of consensus emerged in response to the fractious experience of the Great Depression.

Civic pageants, despite these progressive evolutions, still relied on a conventional history that actively excluded contentious aspects of history. The final section of the chapter shows how those that were neglected, ignored or stereotyped responded by creating their own pageants that told an alternative story of citizenship. In Chicago, the growing African American population especially was barred from mainstream pageants, unwelcome in the American Pageant Association and rarely depicted in historical narratives that celebrated the 'great white hero'.[6] Black Chicagoans instead created their own events that looked back to Africa for identity and pride while also seeking to demonstrate their importance to the US in the present. In Manchester, some on the left felt that Manchester's pageants had failed to grasp the importance of the working man. The Communist Party staged its own pageant that championed the exploited working class and, in a time of unemployment and 'means tests', located the power of the modern urban community in the radical movements of the past. These alternative pageants showed how urban citizenship was always in dispute, even at the height of expressions of power in municipal and civic pride.

Manchester: from Roman civilisation to municipal modernity

The historical pageantry movement owed its existence to the composer and theatre impresario Louis Napoleon Parker, a bombastic character of English, American and French heritage. He drew on English traditions,

---

[5]   This was introduced in Israel Zangwill's popular play, *The melting pot* (1908). See S. E. Wilmer, *Theatre, society and the nation*, Cambridge 2004, 11, 99.

[6]   Paul A. Shackel, 'Public memory and the search for power in American historical archaeology', *American Anthropologist* ciii/3 (2001), 656. See also Juanita Karpf, 'Get the pageant habit: E. Azalia Hackley's festivals and pageants during the First World War years, 1914–1918', *Popular Music and Society* xxxiv/5 (2011), 429.

from Shakespeare to the Morris revival, and from further afield too, such as Wagnerian opera and Oberammergau's 'passion play'.[7] In Sherborne in 1905, for the 1200th anniversary of the foundation of the town, he recruited 800 local performers from a town of 6,000 for a pageant seen by 30,000 people.[8] The premise was simple: the re-enactment of a series of historical episodes, usually from the Roman period to the reign of Elizabeth I; outdoor performances; folk dancing and singing; amateur voluntary casts; and an educational ethos of inspiring local and national patriotism. Parker's movement rapidly spread but, before 1914, full-scale pageants had only taken place in three of the twenty biggest cities in England: London, Bristol and Liverpool. Small towns in southern rural counties, such as Dorset or Suffolk, were the movement's main home. As modernisation threatened to pass such places by, historical pageants were one way to draw attention to past glories for present commercial and civic purposes.[9]

By 1939, however, fourteen of the top twenty cities – mostly industrial centres – had staged at least one pageant. Northern and Midlands manufacturing cities became the key site for the performance of popular history. For urban boosters this was a conscious attempt to promote local economies and civic stability.[10] Manchester was home to several historical spectaculars, two of which concentrated solely on the story of the city.[11] The first, in 1926, was choreographed by a local theatrical impresario, F. E. Doran, as one of the main events of Civic Week. Its two performances in the Bandstand Amphitheatre in Heaton Park were seen by a total audience of over 100,000. When the city celebrated the centenary of its incorporation in 1938, another pageant was the main event. At least 80,000 saw the production staged by the notable pageant-master Nugent Monck and his cast of 10,000 volunteers. Both pageants told a romantic story of the city's history and industry, and, through the lens of the past, projected success into the future. Civic worthiness and economic heft was at the forefront, but this was also a story of the citizenry itself: a way to put the people alongside the institutions at the heart of civic development.

Manchester's pageants can be traced to Parker's events of the early 1900s, but they had evolved to suit interwar tastes. Parker had focused on dialogue

---

[7]   Ayako Yoshino, *Pageant fever: local history and consumerism in Edwardian England*, Tokyo 2011.

[8]   'The Sherborne Pageant', *The Redress of the Past*, <http://www.historicalpageants.ac.uk/pageants/1193/>.

[9]   Angela Bartie, Linda Fleming, Mark Freeman, Tom Hulme and Paul Readman, 'Performing the past: identity, civic culture and historical pageants in twentieth-century English small towns', in Luda Klusakova (ed.), *Small towns in the 20th and 21st centuries: heritage and development strategies*, Prague 2017, 31–2.

[10] This shift is explained in Hulme, 'A nation of town criers', 278–80.

[11] The third, the Lancashire Cotton Pageant, concentrated on the world of cotton. See 'The Lancashire Cotton Pageant', *The Redress of the Past*, <http://www.historicalpageants.ac.uk/pageants/1111/>.

and spectacle through crowd size, with props and technology playing a relatively minor role. But the vision of another pageant-master, Frank Lascelles, had become more popular by the 1920s: even bigger casts; humour and romance as much as serious historical rumination; the dramatic movement of crowds of people in colourful dances and processions rather than dialogue; and, informed by Lascelles's practice as a painter and interest in the Pre-Raphaelites and the Arts and Crafts movement, the creation of landscaped historical backdrops. Lascelles, as Deborah Ryan has argued, 'embraced modernity' rather than rejecting it, and his pageants were similar to other contemporary events that used the spectacle of thousands of people (such as the plays of Max Reinhardt, industrial and national exhibitions, and the cinema epics of D. W. Griffith).[12] For the Manchester Pageant of 1926, for example, a giant backcloth of towers, steeples and warehouses, illuminated by four floodlights, was created. Episodes and tableaux happened at the same time, creating a constant visual spectacle.[13]

A sweeping episodic narrative, from the origins of the city to its recent past and present, created a progressive urban history: a march towards contemporary power and prestige.[14] This story was, for the 1938 pageant, also told in microcosm through the front cover for the programme – in post-impressionist style – which overlaid generations of key figures associated with Manchester, from Romans and medieval knights to the heralder of the 1838 charter and even Queen Victoria (see Figure 11). Much of the subject material and style of many of the episodes for the Manchester pageants were taken by the producers from the famous murals that the Pre-Raphaelite painter Ford Madox Brown had completed for Manchester town hall in 1893. The subjects of these murals, which went from Roman times to the local work of the scientist John Dalton in the early 1800s, were chosen to represent pride in Manchester's civic and commercial values: Christianity, education, science, mechanical invention and textiles.[15] They linked the city to the nation by telling a Whiggish story of development.[16] This teleological form of history had declined after the First World War disrupted the sense of continual progress, but 'Whig tendencies' remained

---

[12] Deborah Sugg Ryan, '"Pageantitis": Frank Lascelles' 1907 Oxford Historical Pageant, visual spectacle and popular memory', *Visual Culture in Britain* viii/2 (2007), 68–9, and 'Staging the imperial city: the Pageant of London, 1911', in Felix Driver and David Gilbert (eds), *Imperial cities: landscape, display and identity*, Manchester 1999, 118.

[13] 'Memorable spectacle at Heaton Park', MG, 4 Oct. 1926, 11.

[14] The following descriptions of episodes are taken from *Historical Pageant of Manchester: Heaton Park*, Manchester 1926, and *Manchester Historical Pageant*, Manchester 1938.

[15] Julian Treuherz, 'Ford Madox Brown and the Manchester murals', in John G. Archer (ed.), *Art and architecture in Victorian Manchester*, Manchester 1985, 173. Brown also slipped in critical and satirical elements that acknowledged working-class and radical contributions to Manchester's civic history. See Julie F. Codell, 'Ford Madox Brown, Carlyle, Macaulay and Bakhtin: the pratfalls and penultimates of history', *Art History* xxi/3 (1998), 324–66.

[16] Whyte, 'Building the nation in the town', 223.

Figure 11. Post-impressionist style front cover of the Manchester Historical Pageant programme (1938)

in the decades after – especially in the sorts of popular histories that appealed to pageant authors.[17]

The first historical scene in both of Manchester's pageants was the founding of a Roman fort around AD 79. In the Edwardian period the treatment of the Romans had been ambivalent, reflecting a lack of historiographical consensus. Sometimes they were seen in a positive light as a civilising force (and Christian, depending on the point at which the empire was depicted). At other points they were portrayed negatively as brutal and sadistic invaders subjugating native peoples.[18] In Manchester, recent archaeological excavations meant that the Roman past was in the local imagination, and the pageants leaned towards a positive interpretation. Native Britons either aided the legionaries in the building of the fort or performed a gently comedic or villainous role. Other episodes displayed a solid reverence for Christian history. Heathen Danes were defeated by valiant and clever Anglo-Saxons in both pageants, with the tenth-century episode in 1926 subtitled 'Paganism versus Christianity'. Other scenes in 1926 included the baptism of King Edwin by Paulinus in AD 627; the third crusade, which featured Sir Hugh de Byron becoming a piously secluded monk; and the trial of John Wycliffe in 1377 (in reality this took place in London, but the scriptwriters believed its inclusion could 'also call to mind certain landmarks in the general ecclesiastical history of Manchester').

Historical pageants rooted municipal modernity in a pre-modern past – even in Manchester, which lacked a celebrated medieval history. Medieval-era stories provided romance and melodrama – as filmmakers in the 1920s also recognised.[19] But interest in Manchester's more distant past had also steadily increased over the course of the nineteenth century to become entrenched in civic culture, reflecting the antiquarianism that permeated the city's ruling class.[20] Civic elites also understood that the medieval period was important because it could be seen as containing the birthplace of the nation. Before 1914 this had been the Anglo-Saxon period especially but, with the continuing waning of the Norman Yoke interpretation of the Conquest, the later period came to be more appreciated.[21] There was, however, crossover between the two: Manchester's pageants found instructive lessons in both Saxon and

[17] For shifts in historiographical writing in this period see Michael Bentley, *Modernizing England's past: English historiography in the age of modernism, 1870–1970*, Cambridge 2005, 119-193, quotation at p. 131.

[18] Ali Parchami, *Hegemonic peace and empire: the Pax Romana, Britannica and Americana*, London 2009.

[19] Kevin J. Harty, 'Robin Hood on film: moving beyond a swashbuckling stereotype', in Thomas Hahn (ed.), *Robin Hood in popular culture: violence, transgression, and justice*, Cambridge 2000, 91.

[20] Readman, *Storied ground*, 232-3.

[21] Angela Bartie, Linda Fleming, Mark Freeman, Tom Hulme, Alexander Hutton and Paul Readman, 'Historical pageants and the medieval past in twentieth-century England', *EHR* cxxxiii/563 (2018), 866-902.

Norman times, reflecting a historiographical tradition where Britain was seen as being able to combine different invaders into one people.[22] Both pageants placed Manchester firmly in a wider story of the nation, reflecting the continued importance of historical pageantry as a form of local patriotism that contributed to national pride.[23] Important figures visiting and complimenting the city, especially royalty, connected locality to a purpose larger than just its own. In the 1938 pageant, for example, Henry VII was portrayed as coming to the city in 1495 and declaring 'So this is Manchester! A fair town and a lusty race of men as any in my realm of England.'[24] Other important nationally-inflected events included the siege during the Civil War; the contributions of the local astronomer William Crabtree in the early seventeenth century; and Lancashire mustering her men on the approach of the Spanish Armada in 1588. Demonstrating how local people had advanced the nation, whether by fighting enemies or contributing to scientific advances, made the story of Manchester seem more important.

Municipal history, however, became even more important in the 1920s and 1930s. Local autonomy was depicted through the bestowal of special charters for governance and markets, such as the charter in 1301, a weights and measures proclamation in 1556, or the incorporation of the borough in 1838. These episodes were a reminder of the legal recognition of the city's right to self-government. A constitutional narrative of the 'civic Middle Ages', consisting of political liberties and stability, was thus important in historical pageantry in this period.[25] With contemporary fears about the growth of central government and local political apathy, historical re-enactment was the civics textbook come-to-life: a way to educate local people about the rights that they gained through municipal government. Complementing this focus on autonomy were episodes about industrial development. Parker had avoided the modern period, often ending his pageant storylines before the Civil War. His vision of a stable hierarchical society, at a time when labour and politicised women were contesting the establishment, depended on obscuring or ignoring contentious historical events. He also saw pageants as a way to limit the effects of commercial and urban development, his sympathies being firmly with conservative rural visions of England.[26] For historical pageants to make sense in industrial cities, however, narratives had to pay attention to contemporary history. Lascelles, and new pageant-masters such as Monck, understood this well. In both 1926 and 1938 there was a variety of episodes that portrayed the economic and commercial development of Manchester, such as the invention

---

[22]   Asa Briggs, 'Saxons, Normans and Victorians', in *The collected essays of Asa Briggs*, i, Brighton 1985, 215–35.

[23]   Readman, 'The place of the past in English culture', 176.

[24]   *Manchester Historical Pageant*, 52.

[25]   David Matthews, *Medievalism: a critical history*, Woodbridge 2015, 30.

[26]   Louis Napoleon Parker, 'Historical pageants', *Journal of the Society of Arts* (22 Dec. 1905), 142–3.

of the Flying Shuttle by John Kay in 1753, the opening of the Bridgewater Canal in 1761, the scientific achievements of John Dalton in the early 1800s, the opening of the Manchester and Liverpool Railway in 1830 and the Ship Canal in 1894. By tracing the industrial and commercial past of the city, civic elites hoped to both reassure citizens and court consumers in the midst of economic uncertainty.

Parker, unsurprisingly, complained in his late 1920s autobiography that his invention had been grossly commercialised.[27] But pageant authors did not necessarily whitewash the downsides of industrialisation. In the 1938 pageant modern-day children, tired of the noise of the city, were led away by the narrator, Father Time (*see* Figure 12), and entertained by Sir Lancelot. Balancing urban-industrial power with the restorative purity of the countryside was a delicate act, but nostalgia for rural ways of living has often been an important aspect of 'the modern condition'.[28] Industrial problems were also, conversely, an opportunity to show the hardiness of Manchester's citizens – an instructive lesson in the context of variable interwar economic fortunes. In 1938, for example, an episode about the 1864 Cotton Famine portrayed Lancashire grit and spirit rather than dwelling on the hardship of unemployment.[29] The inclusion of these sorts of scenes also signalled an increased acknowledgement of the everyday urban inhabitant in history. This development was already apparent in history teaching from the late nineteenth century, when democratic enfranchisement was starting to be reflected in a 'less censorious attitude to the history of "the people"' in school textbooks.[30] Pageantry, however, was slower to catch on, and Parker's pageants were dominated by the ecclesiastical and monarchist prerogatives of elite authors. But interwar pageants corrected this imbalance. Scenes that featured the usual royal visits were now from the point of view of common town-dwellers, who narrated visits with humorous dialogue – an effective way of making pageants relatable to urban-industrial workers.

For Doran, in 1926, the pageant symbolised 'the growing power of the people through the centuries', indicating 'the part played by Manchester people in moulding the thought, institutions and commerce of the country' and how 'beyond the veil of smoke and the forest of chimneys our civic life is based on heroic and romantic incidents, [and] the endeavours and struggles of the common people'.[31] As Monck similarly argued in 1938, it was how the 'crowd' had influence in 'municipal government' from the Romans to 'universal suffrage and state ownership' that had become 'the central theme of

27 Idem, *Several of my lives*, London 1928, 297–8.

28 Murphy, *Fears and fantasies*, 2.

29 'Manchester's pageant: city's story from pre-Roman days to Ship Canal', MG, 8 Jan. 1938, 14.

30 Joyce, *Visions of the people*, 190.

31 *Historical Pageant of Manchester*, 4.

Figure 12. Father Time leads weary children away from the city in the
Manchester Historical Pageant (1938)

modern pageantry'.[32] Prioritising the history of everyday lives was a response to fears about democracy and the supposed susceptibility of the working classes to political radicalism following political enfranchisement, yet it was also an attempt to demonstrate a less elitist sense of society after the mass participation and sacrifice of the First World War.[33] Parker's Edwardian pageants had reasserted class lines and hierarchy, but there was now room for a more progressive vision. Monck's mention of suffrage is also indicative. Women had a greater role in organising pageants in the 1920s and 1930s and made up a larger proportion of the cast. Both activists and organisations saw pageants as a means whereby women could be shaped into non-contentious active citizenship, following suffrage, by providing opportunities for contributing to the community. Pageants could also legitimise the multifarious roles that women had played in the past, from domestic lives as wives and mothers to active roles in politics.[34]

By demonstrating the importance of the 'common man' throughout the city's history, and increasingly the 'common woman' too, pageant-masters hoped to downplay any idea that society needed to be reorganised. This was also reflected in the actual structures of pageant hierarchy. Positions of power were taken by municipal elites, ecclesiastical figures and industrialists, and the biggest acting roles went to prominent members of local society – as had been the case since the beginning of the movement. But the organisation was also cascaded down through urban society, and better represented the local affiliations of a socially diverse cast. In 1926 the organisers split Manchester into districts, with each responsible for a different episode and mobilised by local church leaders.[35] It was public, popular and participatory, and the press argued that it fashioned a local consensus of civic feeling. As the *Manchester Evening Chronicle* cried: 'You're in it! We're all in it! You may not be acting the part of Sir Lancelot, or defending Manchester from the Roman marauders at Heaton Park, but you're in it!'[36]

Pageantry authors and organisers in Britain thus emphasised a long common history, municipal achievement, industrial resilience and the importance of the people, while smoothing over antagonistic debates, overt class politics or urban conflict. Local historical achievements provided inspiration

---

[32] W. Nugent Monck, 'English fond of pageantry', *Portsmouth Evening News*, 7 June 1938, 6.

[33] Angela Bartie, Linda Fleming, Mark Freeman, Tom Hulme, Paul Readman and Charlotte Tupman, '"And those who live, how shall I tell their fame?": historical pageants, collective remembrance and the First World War, 1919–1939', *Historical Research* xc/249 (2017), 636–61.

[34] See Zoe Thomas, 'Historical pageants, citizenship, and the performance of women's history before second-wave feminism', *Twentieth Century British History* xxviii/3 (2017), 319–43.

[35] 'Manchester world', *Christian World*, 2 Sept. 1926, 77.

[36] 'Sunshine smiles on glorious send-off', *Manchester Evening Chronicle*, 2 Oct. 1926, 69.

for the future and were a way to adapt to change and progress, anchoring the present in history while creating a sense of civic pride and loyalty in modern-day urban inhabitants.[37] American interwar urban pageantry shared many of these attributes, especially in the country's industrial cities. There were some differences, however. In Britain, many towns could make a claim, spurious or not, to millennia of recorded history. In the US, and away from the East coast especially, a long-sweep approach was more problematic. American cities also depended on the labour of recent mass immigration for their commercial power, yet the sort of ancestry that American city boosters usually wanted to trace was, in the main, white and Northern European. To understand how civic elites attempted to bridge this gap demonstrates the nature of urban citizenship – its possibilities and limitations – in microcosm.

Chicago: race, progress and the American metropolis

Even in the early days, when Parker's vision spread across Britain and the press dubbed it a strange new disease called 'pageantitis', historical pageants proved alluring to Americans. They were advertised and commented upon in American newspapers, and visited by tourists – such as Mark Twain, who saw the Oxford Pageant (1907) and told the press that he was attending in order 'to get some ideas for his own funeral'.[38] Americans were sentimentally courted by Parker, who sometimes ended his performances with allegorical imaginings of a mother-daughter relationship between the two nations – a clever appeal to a burgeoning sense of Anglo-Saxon solidarity after decades of animosity.[39] In comparison to Britain, though, the American interest in collective commemoration had come later. Republican values in the early years of independence produced tensions between democracy and tradition, while in the antebellum era, according to Paul Shackel, Americans saw their nation as one with a future rather than a glorious past. By the end of the nineteenth century, however, demographic shifts and a need to heal a nation split apart by civil war encouraged the search for a useable heritage.[40] Historical pageants served this need.

In the US historical re-enactments became tied to Progressive Era interests in civic drama, and a belief that they could achieve several interlinked

---

[37]   Readman, 'The place of the past', 191; Rieger and Daunton, 'Introduction', 5–6.

[38]   'Mark Twain's grim humour', *Yorkshire Evening Post*, 18 June 1907, 4.

[39]   Erik Goldstein, 'Diplomacy in the service of history: Anglo-American relations and the return of the Bradford History of Plymouth Colony, 1898', *Diplomacy and Statecraft* xxv/1 (2014), 26–40. At the end of the Sherborne Pageant a letter from the town council of Sherborn, Massachusetts, was read out as the Star Spangled Banner was played: 'The Sherborne Pageant', *The Redress of the Past*, <http://www.historicalpageants.ac.uk/pageants/1193/>.

[40]   Shackel, 'Public memory and the search for power', 661–2.

goals: 'community betterment, increased civic consciousness, and patriotic education'.[41] Florence Magill Wallace, author of several books about the educational potential of pageantry, described in 1918 how cooperation in staging pageants was particularly important for cities, with 'the factions, the wards, the north sides and the south sides [becoming] less divided against each' as 'the whole community' became 'acquainted with itself'.[42] In practice this was also often an attempt to Americanise immigrant populations. During the First World War, American identity continued to be shaken by continuing waves of immigration and the strain of international conflict. Playwrights, along with many other cultural commentators, asked: 'what America had been, what it could become, and how [could it] achieve these goals'?[43] Associational culture mostly promoted patriotism and voluntarism and saw pageants as a useful ploy – though stripped back from the long and expensive chronological productions of the opening decade of the century to shorter and cheaper allegorical masques.[44] Edwin Greenlaw, a university educator and scholar of Renaissance literature, described in a publication for a War Information Series how the 'Community Pageant' had gained a 'New Significance'. For 'the soul of American democracy' to be 'organized for war' many different groups – such as Russian Jews, Italian New Yorkers or north-west Swedish peasant farmers – had to be fused into one 'national consciousness'. Greenlaw meant more than just the subsuming of ethnic differences into one 'national ideal', however – 'local unities of labor or of capital', 'big business and small' and 'North or South or West' could also be 'merged into a new tradition'.[45] Pageantry took on a spiritual role of inspiring sacrifice both at home and at the front, working in tandem with the national preparedness movement, and also sought to quell rising labour tensions and fears of radical politics.[46]

As the playwright Constance D'Arcy Mackay argued in a manual entitled *Patriotic drama in your town* (1918), foreign citizens had 'not been American enough', so pageants showed what America gave to the immigrant rather than the other way around.[47] Even members of well-established and relatively privileged minority groups could be accused of 'divided national loyalties' in the heightened atmosphere of the post-First World War period.[48] This was, of

[41]   Jessie Palmer Weber, 'Introductory note', in Florence Magill Wallace, *Pageant building*, Springfield, IL 1918, 4.

[42]   Wallace, *Pageant building*, 5–6.

[43]   J. Ellen Gainor, 'Introduction' to Jeffrey D. Mason and J. Ellen Gainor (eds), *Performing America: cultural nationalism in American theater*, Ann Arbor, MI 1999, 8.

[44]   Glassberg, *American historical pageantry*, 213, 218.

[45]   Edwin Greenlaw, 'The new significance of the community pageant', in *The community pageant: an agency for the promotion of democracy* (University of North Carolina extension leaflets, war information series, 16), Chapel Hill, NC 1918.

[46]   Glassberg, *American historical pageantry*, 208–15.

[47]   Constance D'Arcy MacKay, *Patriotic drama in your town*, New York, NY 1918, 8.

[48]   Gainor, 'Introduction', 8.

course, especially the case for German Americans, who suffered widely from anti-German hysteria.[49] In 1918 the State Council of Defense organised a pageant in Chicago to celebrate the centenary of Illinois. Directed by Arthur Hercz – a Hungarian-born but naturalised American citizen – rumours circulated that his pageant was 'pro-German'. The German-born conductor for the pageant, William Boeppler, bore the brunt of the ensuing abuse – despite his insistence that he was a 'loyal American'.[50] He eventually withdrew because of the pressure, and was replaced by Daniel Protheroe, head of the American Choral Society. American national airs now took the place of Handel, Schumann and Schubert as the pageant became 'all straight American'.[51] The resulting patriotic performance ended with war scenes where performers pledged allegiance to democracy, freedom and the nation. As the *Tribune* proudly stated, the pageant had been 'shorn of all suspicion of Teutonic influence', showing how 'All the nations that have been thrown into Illinois' melting pot' pledged 'their devotion to the war purpose'.[52] Before the war, it had been common for pageants to celebrate the contribution of immigrants to American society as a form of 'civic nationalism'. Now, in the early post-war years and in the context of industrial strikes, race riots and Red Scares, pageants prioritised 'ethno-racial nationalism'.[53]

The atmosphere of conflict and hyper-patriotism raised the question of civic identity in the past as well. By the 1920s, according to pageantry expert David Glassberg, a successive story of local development generally receded in American pageants and was replaced with an emphasis on the gulf between the distant and static 'old-fashioned' past and a dynamic and fast-moving present.[54] Chicago, however, lacked a story of 'historic' northern European settlement, and had only a 'shocking' recent history. Two pageants that took place in the early post-First World War years offer some indications of how civic elites dealt with this issue.[55] The first was another pageant staged for the Illinois centenary in 1918, while a second larger event in 1921 observed the semi-centenary of the Great Fire of 1871. There was, on the one hand, an

---

[49]   Erik Kirschbaum, *Burning Beethoven: the eradication of German culture in the United States during World War I*, New York, NY 2015.

[50]   'Debates hold up centennial pageant plans', *CT*, 17 Sept. 1918, 13.

[51]   'Edit German from pageant; Boeppler quits', *CT*, 21 Sept. 1918, 1.

[52]   'Stage pageant ready for dress rehearsal', *CT*, 22 Sept. 1918, 10. For the challenges the German community faced in Chicago see Pacyga, *Chicago*, 199.

[53]   Greene, 'Dealing with diversity', 842.

[54]   Glassberg, *American historical pageantry*, 258, 266–7.

[55]   The description in the following paragraphs, unless otherwise cited, is taken from West Chicago Park Commissioners, *Illinois Centennial Pageant, 1818–1918*, Chicago, IL 1918, and 'Book of the Chicago Festival Play', in Chicago Association of Commerce, *Chicago commerce: Chicago Fire semi-centennial celebration issue* (1 Oct. 1921). Some analysis of this latter pageant is given in Linea Sundstrom, 'The "Pageant of Paha Sapa": an origin myth of white settlement in the American West', *Great Plains Quarterly* xxviii/1 (2008), 17–18.

attempt to join the city and state to a broader national story of development, progress and democracy. In 1918 scenes included the Civil War, and Illinois's most famous son, Abraham Lincoln, preserving the union of the nation; and, in the final scene, staying 'True to her old ideals of liberty and justice for all', Illinois sending 'out her sons "to make the world safe for Democracy"' in the First World War.[56] More prominent, however, was the concentration on Chicago itself, and its development as an industrial metropolis. Both pageants portrayed the late nineteenth-century boom by juxtaposing the Great Fire of 1871 with the World's Columbian Exposition of 1893. In doing so, they demonstrated how the contemporary city owed its power to the overcoming of adversity in the past. The city 'amid her ruins ... [and] overcome with grief' was thus followed by the 'glories' of the Exposition as Chicago 'astonished the world' by rising 'Phoenix-like from her ashes, young, strong, joyous, and triumphant'.[57] In 1921 the pageant also ended by evoking the future through the Chicago Plan – 'a vision of the Chicago of tomorrow, its ideals realized, its hopes come true'.[58] Episodes portrayed destruction or difficulties, yet also the positive response of the city and its governors. In doing so, they encouraged a comparison with contemporary concerns, and reassured the viewer that the city would again triumph.

The common people were also highlighted in Chicago as a 'community that had fought so bravely to establish itself'.[59] Who the 'community' was, though, depended on a specific reading of history. Both pageants began their historical story with the beginnings of European influence, visualised through the explorations of the Chicago area by the French missionaries Jacques Marquette and Louis Jolliet in 1673. The Native Americans who occupied this area before the eventual European settlement in the mid-nineteenth century were depicted unsympathetically. Scenes that showed meetings between Europeans and Native Americans focused on 'red men' and 'hostile Indians' attacking settlers, women and children in incidents such as the Fort Dearborn massacre in 1803.[60] No contextual mention of the United States' conflict with the British Empire during the Napoleonic Wars or the broader relations of settlers with the Native population was given. Instead, a simplistic story legitimised the actions of settlers who were protecting their families from 'hyper-male savages'.[61] Each pageant also had scenes that showed the departure of the Native Americans in the 1830s after they had signed treaties ceding land to the government – the 'Passing of the Red Man', as it was put in 1918 – and ended with 'savage'

---

[56]   West Chicago Park Commissioners, *Illinois Centennial Pageant*, 4.

[57]   Ibid.

[58]   'Festival Play', *Chicago Commerce* (27 Aug. 1921), available at the Great Chicago Fire and the web of memory, <https://www.greatchicagofire.org/commemorating-catastrophe-library/festival-play>.

[59]   Ibid.

[60]   Ibid. and West Chicago Park Commissioners, *Illinois Centennial Pageant*, 2.

[61]   Sundstrom, 'The "Pageant of Paha Sapa"', 18.

Illinois Potawatomie performing a war dance 'for the last time on the ground of their fore-fathers where Chicago now is situated'.[62] With Native Americans gone there was, as the 1921 pageant put it, 'a great change': 'a thriving city' now marking the site.[63]

Native American history was a foil for the progress of 'the white man' – an 'origin myth', as Linea Sundstrom puts it, that portrayed white settlers as the 'rightful heirs' of the modern community, won through 'persistence, struggle, and divinely ordained destiny'.[64] Before the mid-nineteenth century, American theatre could portray Native Americans as romantic 'noble savages' and 'proto-Americans' in a sentimental searching for an alternative to the neoclassicism of the Enlightenment. After this point, however, as frontier settlement increased dramatically, they became figures of savagery or ridicule, providing 'the moral justification' for the depriving of their lands.[65] The impact of European coloni-alism on Native peoples was morally 'minimized if not ignored' or culturally appropriated through white civic elites dressing up and re-enacting the history of the peoples they had displaced.[66] The white director in 1921, for example, took the role of the fictional character of 'Chief Che-ca-gou, the Revealer, the great chieftain of the Illinois', in an example of the practice of 'playing Indian'.[67] In the aftermath of the First World War, these pageants attempted to present a both nostalgic and entertaining image of social order. This meant whitewashing the origins of urban places by creating a 'foundational narrative' that prioritised European settlement over Native history.[68]

By the late 1930s the depiction of race and ethnicity in Chicago's pageantry had changed. Native Americans now mostly disappeared as a fundamental part of the story – though they still featured in some of the 'Wild West' re-enact-ments and the Indian Village of the World's Fair. As belonging remained fractured across racial and ethnic lines though, especially as immigrants were scapegoated during the economic distress, the central question of the period remained how could separate groups, with distinct aims and levels of social capital, be acknowledged yet melded into one cohesive city-wide whole?[69] According to David Glassberg, pageants at this point became more likely to portray history as a stable refuge from the present.[70] Yet, for Chicago, the

---

[62]   West Chicago Park Commissioners, *Illinois Centennial Pageant*, 4; 'Festival play'.

[63]   'Festival play'.

[64]   Sundstrom, 'The "Pageant of Paha Sapa"', 3.

[65]   Wilmer, *Theatre, society and the nation*, 9; Lester G. Moses, *Wild West shows and the images of American Indians, 1883–1933*, Albuquerque, NM 1996, 13.

[66]   Alison Norman, '"A highly favoured people": the planter narrative and the 1928 Grand Historic Pageant of Kentville, Nova Scotia', *Acadiensis* xxxviii/2 (2009), 117.

[67]   'Thousands defy chill winds to view fire play', *CT*, 5 Oct. 1921, 17; Norman, '"A highly favoured people"', 130. See also Philip J. Deloria, *Playing Indian*, New Haven, CT 1998.

[68]   Norman, '"A highly favoured people"', 117.

[69]   Greene, 'Dealing with diversity', 833.

[70]   Glassberg, *American historical pageantry*, 272–4.

dominance of the 'shock city' narrative, and the prioritising of a history that celebrated the city's ability to overcome its problems, meant that this was not an option. The pageants bookmarking the Chicago Jubilee in 1937 offered two alternative approaches.

On 4 March 1937 the exact centenary of the granting of the city's charter by the state legislature, a pageant was held in the Chicago Stadium (built in 1929, three miles west of the Loop). More than 100,000 people saw 1,000 amateurs depict the city's rise from a humble trading post to a major metropolis. The story began with Chicago's first mayor, William Ogden, predicting the city's greatness, in an echo of the early 1920s pageants. A following scene, however, came from a different angle. As the *Chicago Tribune* described it, the pageant allegorically showed the 'molding' of immigrants 'into Chicago citizens' through groups of children, after performing folk dances in national costume, quite literally entering a huge melting pot.[71] As Edward Kelly described it, the 'Melting Pot Pageant' demonstrated the 'drama of all nationalities and races which have united to find a common home on American soil' while also 'stimulating the civic consciousness and giving evidence of the traditional I Will spirit that has made Chicago renowned among the great cities of the world'.[72] Seven months later another pageant, the 'Light of Ages', was held as the climax to the Jubilee. Taking place at the Civic Opera House (built downtown in 1929 by the utilities magnate Samuel Insull), and sponsored chiefly by the city council with other civic dignitaries taking organisational roles, it had a cast of 500 and ran for eight days. This pageant followed earlier examples of the urban development narrative by not avoiding 'former moments of gloom for Chicagoans' and instead demonstrating how 'always the city rose to new sunshine, peace and prosperity'.[73] Scenes included Chicago before European settlement, as a flower-covered sand-dune and swamp; the building of the city's first churches; the Fort Dearborn massacre; the development of transportation from 1848; the devastation of the Great Fire in 1871 before the triumphalist Columbian Exposition in 1893; and the patriotic response to the First World War. 'Chicago's symbolic spirit', as the press reported, 'never fails through decades of struggle, disasters, and victory'.[74] In several ways, then, these pageants continued the approach of the early 1920s.

But the 'Light of Ages', with its clear religious focus, was also a departure from older examples. The name of the pageant came from a popular short hymn written by Samuel Longfellow, a Unitarian minister, in the late nineteenth century, and obviously had strong religious themes. The pageant

---

[71]   'Chicago hails its past; looks to the future', *CT*, 5 Mar. 1937, 2; 'Sirens, bells to sound for city's birthday', *CT*, 4 Mar. 1937, 1; 'West Side areas wind up charter jubilee plans', *CT*, 28 Feb. 1937, 2.

[72]   'Kelly report', 4722.

[73]   'Light of Ages casts reverent spell on crowd', *CT*, 16 Oct. 1937, 16.

[74]   'Pageant a saga of city's growth', *CT*, 14 Oct. 1937, 19.

was written by Marchus Bach, a recent winner of a national playwriting contest and former pastor with academic interests in inter-faith culture. Dr Fred Eastman, the Reverend James Magner and Dr Solomon Goldman advised on religious features from the perspective of Protestantism, Catholicism and Judaism respectively, and brought the inter-faith ideal into practice. The story began with a 'patriarch' standing amid flashes of lightning on a mountain top, as a multitude below chanted 'Sh'ma Yisroel' (Hear, [O] Israel), and, at one point, Catholics, Protestants and Jews all trekked toward their historic sites of worship together. The pageant ended in the present with light again coming from the mountain, as the patriarch re-entered, and the narrator declared that 'the city of the future as not only of steel and stone, but as a dwelling place for every creed, where each man prays his native prayers; and each, with upturned gaze, looks to his God'.[75] According to Judge John P. McGoorty, the theme was how Chicago symbolised the spirit of religious freedom, and how 'here in the most American of American cities men of every creed and race live and worship in a comradeship of faiths'.[76] As Edward Kelly also summarised, the pageant showed 'the role of religious tolerance in the city's life for the last hundred years' and stressed 'tolerance and good will as a permanent policy for all our peoples today and tomorrow'.[77] Spiritual progress, accessible to individuals across religious divides, was now used to unite diverse communities. The city housed and enabled this progress and local and national intertwined and created a dualistic sense of citizenship.

Until this point the agency of religious or ethnic groups in mainstream civic pageants had been mostly absent and there was a pageantry pecking-order: European history was valorised, but the traditions of immigrants (particularly from southern and eastern Europe) were smoothly absorbed into Americanism; Native American history was featured, but caricatured and disregarded; and African American history was avoided altogether, apart from brief references during Civil War scenes.[78] Historical pageants in Chicago tended to cherry-pick more comfortable and comforting narratives. But the pageants in 1937 showed that there had been some progress in acknowledging individuality as well as absorption, and the ability of 'different cultural heritages and their contributions to American life' to remain discernible in the 'melting pot'.[79] Chicago's elites saw the power of this narrative in the 1930s, even if loftier aims of civic uplift and morality had declined in the broader pageantry movement.[80] The 'Light of Ages' pageant thus reflected the turn towards the more inclusionary

---

[75] 'Light of Ages casts reverent spell on crowd'.

[76] Ibid.

[77] 'Kelly report', 4724.

[78] Mary Simonson, *Body knowledge: performance, intermediality, and American entertainment at the turn of the twentieth century*, Oxford 2013, 52.

[79] 'Kelly report', 4724.

[80] Glassberg, *American historical pageantry*, 286-7.

politics of the 'American Way' through its focus on religious difference or the ability of 'old world' folk culture to be at one with Chicago's civic identity.[81] At the same time, however, minority groups did not have to depend on the progressive evolution of civic pageants: they could also challenge the dominant meanings of public memory by creating a new one that much better suited their agenda.[82]

Alternative pageantry: power, identity and conflict

The civic pageants staged in Chicago and Manchester aimed to promote tourism and business, while solidifying local feelings of pride and belonging. Yet, as with the Pageant of Progress and Civic Weeks, there was also an opportunity for less politically powerful groups within the city to use this form of performance to offer their own version of belonging. By creating their own historical pageants, these groups could challenge that presented in official versions, reversing the dominant stereotypical images of theatre and film and creating a more egalitarian citizenship culture.[83] Before 1914 the use of history in this way was already happening on both sides of the Atlantic.[84] After the war this continued, and reached its heights in the 1930s, as tensions in both countries bubbled to the surface during the Great Depression. What could be termed 'alternative pageants' now entered mainstream culture. In Britain, 'far-left' re-enactments challenged orthodox municipal narratives. Working-class people, and their contribution to urban and national progress, was emphasised. In the US, immigrant and minority groups performed pageants that drew attention to both their heritage and new American identity. Race – if obscured, discriminatory or caricatured in civic pageants – moved to the forefront of historical explanation. There were certainly limits to what performance could achieve, but, if only for a short time, it allowed disenfranchised groups to carve out a space for their own vision of belonging. Vitally, this was a sense of identity that did not necessarily match the hopes of those trying to shape a particularly urban sense of citizenship.

The pageants that debuted at Chicago's World's Fair in 1933-4 went far beyond assimilatory narratives. Over twenty separate days were given to immigrant groups to present their own programme, and Irish, Jewish and Polish organisations all staged pageants at Soldier Field (a neo-classical

---

[81] Wall, *Inventing the 'American way'*.

[82] Shackel, 'Public memory and the search for power', 655.

[83] Wilmer, *Theatre, society and the nation*, 13.

[84] See, for example, the Paterson Strike Pageant in New York in 1913 or various women's suffrage pageants on both sides of the Atlantic, especially around 1909-14.

municipal stadium built in the early 1920s and a source of great civic pride).[85] Each pageant sought, to varying degrees, to portray the importance of the immigrant's national culture – both back home and in modern-day America. Governmental authorities supported these sorts of ethnic display because they were acceptable and 'tightly orchestrated' alternatives to 'unpredictable' street meetings or parades.[86] But such pageants were still an opportunity for 'racialised groups' to put across their own 'counterscript' that could challenge dominant cultural representations of their place in American society.[87]

For the 'Pageant of the Celt', staged in 1934, it was a chance to define a respectable 'Irishness' at a time when Irish identity within the Anglo-Protestant American establishment was in question. The perceived immorality of the 'roaring twenties' clashed with the image of the new puritanical Catholic Irish state, and there were fears that Irish folk traditions were being trivialised. Accordingly, an Irish Free State-sponsored exhibition at the Fair was lauded for its respectable portrayal of Ireland, while an entrepreneurial 'Irish Village' was castigated for its vulgar and stereotypical entertainment.[88] In the pageant, wholesome Celtic folk and religious traditions of the past, and their contribution to Christian society and righteousness in the present, sat alongside the modern development of Irish government. A cast of 1,500, in front of a total audience of 20,000, performed episodes such as the arrival of the (almost certainly mythical) Milesians in Ireland, operating as an origin story for Gaelic Ireland; the coming of Christianity and St Patrick lighting the paschal fire; and the 1916 Easter Rising against British governance that led to the Free State.[89] A Polish pageant took a similar approach but with an added focus on the New World. A cast of 5,000 re-enacted scenes from a Polish village with 'rustics in native costume' singing folk songs and dancing, but later scenes showed 'Poland's contribution to the field of arts, sciences and industry, [and] the world war' in modern America.[90]

The 'Romance of a People', staged in 1933 by the Jewish Agency for Palestine in cooperation with national and local organisations, was the first of several Jewish historical pageants in the US from the 1930s to the 1950s. These events demonstrated transnational notions of Jewish identity and solidarity and aroused political consciousness and moral support as the

[85] For an overview of the pageants see Liam T. A. Ford, *Soldier Field: a stadium and its city*, Chicago, IL 2009, 153–65.

[86] Linda J. Lumsden, *Rampant women: suffragists and the right of assembly*, Knoxville, TN 1997, 96.

[87] See Natalia Molina, *How race is made in America: immigration, citizenship, and the historical power of racial scripts*, Berkeley, CA 2014.

[88] Charles Fanning, 'Dueling cultures: Ireland and Irish America at the Chicago World's Fairs of 1933 and 1934', *New Hibernia Review* xv/3 (2011), 94–110.

[89] Irish Historical Productions, *The Pageant of the Celt*, Chicago, IL 1933.

[90] 'Pageant tonight to close Polish week in Chicago', *CT*, 22 July 1933, 5.

horrors of Nazism and the Holocaust unfolded.[91] As Rabbi Solomon Goldman put it in the programme's foreword, '[though] oppressed by the bitter events in Germany' the 'Jewish people remains' and, through pageantry, called up 'all the forces of the past, as well as the promise of the future'.[92] A cast of 3,500 actors accordingly portrayed 'the faith and destiny of the Jewish People from its beginnings to the present time', mostly through biblical episodes: the Creation; the coming of Abraham; Egyptian slavery and 'deliverance'; the wandering of exiles; and a 'new liberation' – which predicted 'Palestine rebuilt'.[93] Though its historical narrative paid no attention to the US, the pageant still spoke to local pride. As the *Chicago Jewish Tribune* noted, 'Meyer Weisgal [the producer] put the Jewish community in Chicago on the map' because so many 'journeyed to this city to be present and participate in the greatest Jewish Day in the history of the Diaspora'.[94] Similarly, in the *Chicago Jewish Chronicle*, Maurice Rosenfeld wrote that the pageant was both 'an outstanding event in Chicago's history and in the advancement of the Jewish race'.[95] In terms of identity, though, the Romance of a People was distinctly about ethnicity rather than the civic.[96]

Perhaps the most provocative pageant was 'O, Sing a New Song' (1934) – or the Afro-American Pageant, as it was also termed. The previous year, a similar pageant (the 'Epic of a Race') had been staged as part of the 'Negro Day' at the World's Fair. But mostly organised without the input of local Chicago community groups and hindered by issues of racism and segregation at the Fair, both the pageant and the day were criticised by the *Defender* and failed to garner much attention from African Americans.[97] 'O, Sing a New Song', in contrast, was strongly based in the civic culture of Bronzeville. The pageant was first suggested by Nahum Daniel Brascher, a *Defender* columnist, editor of the Associated Negro Press and executive director of the not-for-profit artistic organisation National Auditions (which went on to stage the show). Noble Sissle, co-author of the successful black musical *Shuffle along* (1921), took the lead producing role, and recruited a host of musical stars: Harry Lawrence Freeman, W. C. Handy and Major N. Clark Smith, amongst others.[98] Supported by the *Defender*, with Edward Kelly and Rufus C. Dawes,

[91]   Stephen J. Whitfield, 'The politics of pageantry, 1936–1946', *American Jewish History* lxxxiv/3 (1996), 221.

[92]   Solomon Goldman, 'Foreword' to *The romance of a people*, Chicago, IL 1933, 16.

[93]   Ibid.

[94]   'The kaleidoscope', *Chicago Jewish Tribune*, 7 July 1933.

[95]   Maurice Rosenfeld, 'The romance of a people', ibid.

[96]   It is worth noting that this was not always the case. For how Jewish people reinvented themselves as Americans through musical theatre see Andrea Most, *Making Americans: Jews and the Broadway musical*, Cambridge, MA 2004.

[97]   Cheryl R. Ganz, *The 1933 Chicago World's Fair: a century of progress*, Urbana, IL 2012, 113–15.

[98]   Ford, *Soldier Field*, 160.

the promotional buzz of the pageant ensured its success. Over 5,000 actors and 3,500 singers took part, and 60,000 spectators filled Soldier Field stadium on the opening night.[99]

There was a longer history of black activists using re-enactment and performance, drawing on perceptions of the history of Africa, to advance their community's citizenship in the US. For black scholars in the late nineteenth and early twentieth century, such as George Washington Williams, a complex understanding of 'ancient Ethiopia' or Egypt served as examples of a culturally superior black society, disrupting 'white historical hegemony' and establishing a sense of dignity and racial pride for African Americans in the present.[100] Drawing on interpretations of the Bible, African American clergy came to believe that Africans were a 'chosen people'. This 'prophecy' was incorporated into popular culture and thus the storylines of historical pageants. Both the Universal Negro Improvement Association and the National Association for the Advancement of Coloured People furthered their cause by creating pageants that celebrated historical figures and traditions of Africa, often placing them alongside allegorical characters that represented 'America' or 'democracy'.[101]

For W. E. B. Du Bois, a prominent African American scholar and activist, pageants could teach 'the colored people themselves the meaning of their history and their rich, emotional life' while also revealing 'the Negro to the white world as a human, feeling thing'.[102] His spectacular pageants in the 1910s and early 1920s used the African past, from the invention of iron welding in 50,000 BC to the resistance to slavery in 1500, to create a collective consciousness among black people – one that demonstrated the historical 'gifts' of Africa to the US in order to combat mainstream racist stereotypes. If civic pageants looked to Europe for identity and the origins of America, black pageants looked to Africa. In doing so, they created a radical transnational sense of citizenship that celebrated the diversity of blackness and its contribution to civilisation through commerce, science and the arts.[103] As the Harlem Renaissance in New York began to blossom

---

[99]   Ibid. 162.

[100]   Renee Ater, 'Making history: Meta Warrick Fuller's *Ethiopia*', *American Art* xvii/3 (2003), 21–2.

[101]   Colin Grant, *Negro with a hat: the rise and fall of Marcus Garvey*, Oxford 2008, 344; Clare Corbould, *Becoming African Americans: black public life in Harlem, 1919–1939*, Cambridge, MA 2009, 43.

[102]   W. E. B. Du Bois quoted in Ater, 'Making history', 26.

[103]   David Krasner, *A beautiful pageant: African American theatre, drama, and performance in the Harlem Renaissance, 1910–1927*, Basingstoke 2002, at pp. 110–18. Du Bois's pageants included the Star of Ethiopia Pageant (written in 1911 and performed at the National Emancipation Exposition in 1913) and the Seven Gifts of Ethiopia to America (performed at the America's Making Exposition in 1921).

in the 1920s, the imagery and ideology of Ethiopia remained.[104] By the early 1930s Chicago was also beginning to experience a 'Black Renaissance' of its own. Both old settlers and new migrants came together to produce 'a new expressive culture' that gave 'voice and form to their New Negro, urban/ cosmopolitan identities'. Through art, literature, music and performance they fashioned a new sense of pride in 'blackness', drawing on a sense of Pan-Africanism that could challenge the implicit 'whiteness' of American identity and citizenship.[105]

'O, Sing a New Song' drew on these older pageants and reflected the emergence of an ambitious and confident African American identity. The programme art (see Figure 13) depicted a collage of past and present: bare-chested drum-playing tribesmen, harp players next to the pyramids and sphinx of Ancient Egypt and a contemporary young black singer, accompanied by dancers and piano players, wearing a pin of the 'Winged Globe of Ethiopia and Egypt'. Charles Dawson, a leading black artist, explained how the scene suggested 'the vast historical background of present day Negro Music'.[106] The pageant depicted how this vibrant 'Jungle' civilisation had disintegrated following invasion and slavery, yet had begun to find its revitalisation in present-day America through faith, endurance and hope. Music and religion were highlighted as the way in which African culture had expressed its 'rebellion' and scenes were mostly visual and musical, relying on colour and drama rather than dialogue.[107] The final episode, 'Modern America', showed a glimpse of Booker T. Washington's life, accompanied by several musical numbers of spirituals, ragtime and contemporary blues, and a demonstration of African American contributions to the US military from the Civil War to the First World War. At the end, a 'chronicler' described how all had a place in the 'great march' forward of America.[108] The *Defender* hopefully summarised the pageant as 'the story of a people that had its birth in misery and oppression, finding its outlet and partial freedom in a country and a Constitution that in part determines the freedom of its nation'.[109] It was, as Robert S. Abbott, put it, 'to inspire you and all of us to higher and nobler deeds'.[110]

---

[104]   See Ater, 'Making history', and Katharine Capshaw Smith, 'Constructing a shared history: black pageantry for children during the Harlem Renaissance', *Children's Literature* xxvii (1999), 40–63.

[105]   Darlene Clark Hine, 'Introduction', and Samuel A. Floyd, Jr, 'The negro renaissance: Harlem and Chicago flowerings', in Darlene Clark Hine and John McCluskey, Jr (eds), *The black Chicago renaissance*, Urbana, IL 2012, pp. xvi, 21–43.

[106]   Charles C. Dawson, 'The artist's conception of the pageant', in *National Auditions annual: a Century of Progress souvenir edition of the Afro-American Pageant*, Chicago, IL 1934, 1.

[107]   Ibid.

[108]   *National Auditions annual.*

[109]   'Many thanks to all', CD, 1 Sept. 1934, 1.

[110]   'Message from Robert S. Abbott', in *National Auditions annual.*

Figure 13. From ancient Africa to modern America on the cover of O, Sing a New Song (1934)

The pageant's focus was national or transnational: more about African American identity than urban belonging. Other events in Chicago however, such as Bud Billiken Day, celebrated a locally-situated sense of black citizenship. The Bud Billiken Club, formed in 1929 by Abbot and named for an ancient Chinese 'guardian angel of children', was a large network of black youth clubs.[111] The club's annual celebration combined myth and African identity, and connected black culture – past and present – to the streets of Bronzeville. African dignitaries were invited, such as the Crown Prince Allaoumi of Nigeria, and West African music, dance and costumes were incorporated.[112] Reports in the *Defender*, filtering down into the Billiken columns, focused on both historical and contemporary African culture and heightened this sense of connection to Africa.[113] Contemporary black artists and musicians were also invited, such as Sissle and Duke Ellington (*see* Figure 14). The parade functioned as a similar, yet alternative, form of civic culture to the earlier Pageant of Progress: it passed in review in front of Abbott who was the civic leader; black municipal employees, such as policemen, figured prominently; and local community organisations, such as the Wabash YMCA, took part. Narratives of respectability and communal self-governance joined with African expressions of racial identity, forging an alternative notion of citizenship for African Americans in the city – one of solidarity, history and neighbourhood. It evoked, as one young observer remembered, 'a deep sense of race pride, community, and togetherness' in opposition to the realities of poor housing, segregation and racism: 'For one day a year, black children could imagine that the city of Chicago was all theirs.'[114]

Ethnic parades in Manchester were also a feature of the city's civic culture. The Italian community of about 2,000, served by the non-political Italian Society (formed by a local priest in 1889), staged Whit Walks that celebrated Italian cultural heritage and enabled the marchers to stake a claim to inclusion in Manchester's public culture. Yearly on Whit Friday, the first after the Christian holiday of Pentecost, they joined other Roman Catholic communities in parades numbered in the tens of thousands. At the front of the Italian section men carried the Italian Society banner, followed by the priest and his altar boys. Older Italian girls carried the St Peter's banner, followed by the Calvary. The most popular feature of the Walk was the Madonna figure, surrounded by the youngest girls in their prettiest dresses. Finally, at the back, were Italian women in their national costumes.[115] Large crowds gathered to watch the parades in the 1930s, often halting traffic.[116] Marchers celebrated their Italian and Catholic heritage, while making a legitimate claim to civic

---

[111] Peter M. Rutkoff and William B. Scott, 'Pinkster in Chicago: Bud Billiken and the mayor of Bronzeville, 1930–1945', *Journal of African American History* lxxxix/4 (2004), 318.

[112] Ibid. 319, 321.

[113] Hayumi Higuchi, 'The Billiken Club: "race leaders" educating children (1921–1940)', *Transforming Anthology* xiii/2 (2005), 154–9.

[114] Allyson Hobbs, *A chosen exile: a history of racial passing in American life*, Cambridge, MA 2014, 3.

[115] Anthony Rea, *Manchester's Little Italy: memories of the Italian colony of Ancoats*, Manchester 1988.

[116] 'Roman Catholic procession marred by rain', MG, 11 June 1938, 13.

Figure 14. Group associated with early Bud Billiken Parade: (from left) Noble Sissle, David Kellum, Duke Ellington, Nathan McGill, unidentified, Earl Father Hines, and unidentified (c. 1930s)

inclusion through their temporary ownership of Manchester's public space.[117] Though this did not directly challenge the municipal identity of the city, it at least provided a *caveat* of diversity.

Lacking the sheer size of ethnic communities of Chicago, though, there were no pageants in Manchester that could compare with the World's Fair events. But the city council's own re-enactments were not safe from ideological challenge, especially in terms of class politics – as a controversy surrounding the question of including Peterloo in the centenary pageant in 1938 demonstrates. This bloody incident in Manchester's history happened in 1819 when the military charged into a crowd of 60,000 or more that had gathered in St Peter's Fields, in a time of unemployment and famine, to demand parliamentary reform. Several hundred were injured, and fifteen killed. Radical and left-wing groups, from the Chartists to the Independent Labour Party, perpetuated the memory of these martyrs at moments of class conflict in the following century. During the 1919 centenary the social context of Peterloo was compared with

[117] Charlotte Wildman, 'Religious selfhoods and the city in inter-war Manchester', *Urban History* xxxviii/1 (2011), 103–23.

the experiences of the demobilised unemployed working classes of the present and, throughout the 1920s and 1930s, the Communist Party used Peterloo as an instructive example of the struggle between capital and labour.[118] For the ruling classes of Manchester, this raised an issue: how could the difficult memory of Peterloo be integrated into the city's public culture? Already there had been moments when this tension had arisen – such as in 1877, when Ford Madox Brown was banned from depicting the scene in the Manchester Town Hall murals.[119]

When the committee charged with suggesting historical episodes for the 1938 pageant considered Peterloo, they did so using a longer understanding of its place in Manchester's history.[120] Led by a local academic historian, they first suggested an apologetic yet reactionary approach: the Riot Act was read but 'not heard' before the charge of the Yeomanry, and the scene ended with the organisers of the crowd being 'severely punished'.[121] This scene fell out of favour, however. A few months before the pageant one member of the executive committee tried to pass the motion 'That no reference whatever be made in the pageant to Peterloo.' An amendment, passed by thirteen votes to eight, instead suggested Peterloo be only briefly mentioned, with 'some representation' of characters from the event being included without it taking up 'a whole episode'.[122] As the *Guardian* admitted the following day, Peterloo was too recent to be retold without causing ill-feeling.[123] In the actual event, the incident was portrayed as part of a longer processional historical tableau preceding the eighth episode, so short and indistinct that the *Manchester Guardian* could not even tell if it had happened at all.[124]

Trade Unions raised their concerns about this lacklustre portrayal, but the most angered was the local branch of the Communist Party. In a penny-pamphlet, *100 years of struggle: Manchester's centenary, the real story*, an alternative history of working-class protest in Manchester was laid out: eighteenth-century food riots, Chartism, the Blanketeers in 1817, trade unionism, the Co-op movement, women's suffrage, the establishment of the Labour Party and the foundation of the Communist Party after the war. Like the main centenary

[118] Joseph Cozens, 'The making of the Peterloo martyrs, 1819 to the present', in Keith Laybourn and Quentin Outram (eds), *Secular martyrdom in Britain and Ireland: from Peterloo to the present*, Basingstoke 2018, 31–58.

[119] Ibid.

[120] For such 'historical culture' see Martha Vandrei, 'A Victorian invention? Thomas Thornycroft's "Boadicea group" and the idea of historical culture in Britain', *HJ* lvii/2 (2014), 485–508.

[121] 'Suggested episodes' (1937–8), Centenary Pageant, MCA, GB127.M740/2/8/2/39.

[122] 'Pageant Committee and Executive Committee minutes' (12 Apr. 1938), MCA, GB127. M467/4/3.

[123] 'Peterloo for Manchester Pageant', MG, 13 Apr. 1938, 11.

[124] *Manchester Historical Pageant*, Manchester 1938, 85; 'Manchester Pageant', MG, 24 June 1938, 13.

celebrations, the pamphlet looked back to the 1838 Charter, but as the culmi-nation of local ratepayer struggles against the landowner of the time (Sir Oswald Mosley). Incorporation, however, had not brought the results that the working classes deserved: the city council was still controlled by the wealthy and 'the most reactionary elements in society'. Ordinary contemporary Mancunians had to organise to 'take up the liberal traditions of Manchester's past' and 'carry them forward' towards a collectivist future. Unlike the main celebrations, the pamphlet drew attention to recent struggles and protest, such as the General Strike in 1926 and the use of batons and horses against a 50,000-strong crowd that protested against the Means Test in 1931. It was the 'shameful' represen-tation of class struggle in the centenary pageant, the pamphlet argued, that meant that the working class had to 'rescue Manchester's centenary from this mockery of its history'.[125] After the pamphlet was published the party also staged its own historical re-enactment. Short and simple, it focused on working-class struggle in the previous hundred years, portrayed by hundreds of Communist Party members, young and old, carrying three-sided banners painted with historical scenes and slogans. It began with Peterloo and ended with demands for 'A Manchester with no unemployment', 'A Manchester without the threat of war' and 'A Manchester that belongs to its people'.[126] The pageant rebuked the official history presented by the city council and provided an opportunity for members of the Communist Party to come together and imagine an alternative future.[127]

Mainstream historical pageants in both Chicago and Manchester presented a linear narrative of progress that saw the modern city as the culmination of historic urban events and experiences. A troubled past – war, economic hardship and disasters – made present achievements worthier of acknowl-edgement. Historical pageants promoted place and community and shaped urban belonging by encouraging cast and audience to internalise 'their local story' and be aware of 'their town's role in the march of progress'.[128] By the 1930s, in both cities, this was a broadly inclusive vision. In the case of Chicago, references to ethnicity and religion in pageants were more inclusionary, while, in Manchester, pageant-masters realised that their narratives had to pay heed to working-class lives and wants – even if they did not depict the most important historical episodes of conflict. Local identity was 'reformulated, revised and reasserted' in this attempt to maintain a hegemonic notion of

---

[125]   Communist Party of Manchester, *100 years of struggle: Manchester's centenary, the real story*, Salford 1938.

[126]   'Manchester's centenary: a Marxist pageant', MG, 20 June 1938, 13.

[127]   Alan Burton, *The British consumer co-operative movement and film, 1890s–1960s*, Manchester 2005, 34; Mick Wallis, 'Pageantry and the Popular Front: ideological production in the thirties', *New Theatre Quarterly* x/38 (1994), 134.

[128]   Sundstrom, 'The "Pageant of Paha Sapa"', 4.

community.[129] Evaluating the success of pageants is difficult, though. One-off events could not combat structural economic change any more than they could permanently quieten dissent that emanated from the disenfranchisement of institutionalised racism and segregation. That alternative pageants drew such strong crowds suggests that civic pageants did not even begin to overcome the problems of urban conflict. Neither, of course, could alternative pageants effect any such solution. As Stephen Whitfield puts it, 'while art can enhance and illumine and expose power, only countervailing force can effectively confront it'.[130] Pageantry was probably not that countervailing force, but the varied nature of its storylines demonstrates, at least, that public memory was 'more a reflection of present political and social relations than a true reconstruction of the past'.[131]

Through their role as performers, volunteers and spectators, urban inhabitants did give a certain degree of complicit support to the narratives portrayed. How often these episodes were understood by the performers and spectators, though, is debatable. By focusing on the published text of the pageant, we can miss the conditions of performance that constrained the spectacle's ability to transmit often complex ideas.[132] In Manchester's 1926 pageant, for example, a scene depicting the launch and capsizing of a local cargo ship on the River Irwell in 1828 was met with laughter from the audience rather than reverence for the dead. With a ship and waves created from cardboard, spectators believed that 'something had gone amiss, not in history but in their pageant'. As the *Manchester Guardian* asked, 'How many ... not having studied the programme, will treasure this moment in years to come as the most memorable in all Saturday's performance – and all in the mistaken belief that it was one of those comic fiascos which ought not to have happened?'[133] As reports collected by the British anthropological organisation Mass Observation concluded, the reception of pageants could be mixed: spectators turned up to see celebrities in the cast rather than the history on show; struggled to hear the dialogue; and did not join in with the patriotic songs either out of apathy or because they did not know the words.[134]

Newspaper reports, though, also lauded the enthusiasm of the crowds and their respectful solemnity during episodes portraying funerals or war. The cynic might respond that the press, a mouthpiece for the local and national establishment, would predictably do so. But their willingness also to lambast pageants if they did not reach expectations suggests that they treated pageants

---

[129] Wilmer, *Theatre, society and the nation*, 3.

[130] Whitfield, 'The politics of pageantry', 241.

[131] Shackel, 'Public memory and the search for power', 656.

[132] S. Michael Halloran, 'Text and experience in a historical pageant: toward a rhetoric of spectacle', *Rhetoric Society Quarterly* xxxi/4 (2001), 12.

[133] 'Memorable spectacle at Heaton Park', MG, 4 Oct. 1926, 11.

[134] 'St Paul's Steps', *The Redress of the Past*, <http://www.historicalpageants.ac.uk/pageants/1318/>.

as art forms which were open to criticism. Evidence from scrap books, diaries and oral histories also suggests that pageants could be enjoyable and formative experiences – for young people especially. This was partly personal: meeting new romantic partners; escaping family and school; or the enjoyment of performing in front of loud appreciative crowds. For the audience, too, it was their own atmosphere and spectacle – noise, colour and motion – that formed the main event. The pageant itself, then, was often just a 'side-show'.[135] Recent interviews with British pageanteers of the 1950s, however, have hinted that the process of re-enacting the local past did stir feelings of civic pride – if details of historical achievement could be hazy, the idea of representing ones home town was not.[136]

Attendance records certainly suggest that the pageantry movement – despite, in the US, having declined and splintered from its pre-1914 heyday – struck a chord at some level. Performing was a huge commitment, and pageants depended on the willingness of participants to go the extra mile. By bringing together a diverse audience, then, pageants began to create or at least reflect a 'public' – not 'an assemblage of isolated individuals' but an 'enactment of their social order'.[137] This was again social steering: an attempt to co-opt urbanites in the creation of their own civic responsibility and citizenship through negotiation rather than control. At other points, however, the machinery of civic culture – local associations, the city council, the national state – could be much more interventionist. Civic pageants sought to draw attention to the entitlements and responsibilities of citizenship that were due to the inheritance of the past. At the same time, a coalition of local associations and city councils was ideologically shaping the meaning of urban citizenship by directly drawing close attention to the nature of the modern city. The next chapter will concentrate on how civic culture negotiated the realities of modern urban life in a time of social and economic instability by looking specifically at the associational culture of youth.

[135] Halloran, 'Text and experience', 6–8. Roberts, 'Entertaining the community', 449. For scrapbooks see 'Sister's Pageant Memories', *The Redress of the Past*, <http://historicalpageants. ac.uk/publications/blog/sisters–pageant–memories/>.

[136] Oral histories recorded by the author in 2014–15 in Bury St Edmunds. See 'Historical Pageants', *SoundCloud*, <https://soundcloud.com/tom-hulme-9>.

[137] Halloran, 'Text and experience', 6.

5

The Citizen of Tomorrow

For many reformers and associations, the central question of citizenship was how society should guide the lives of the young. They were the next generation: the clay from which workers, soldiers and mothers of the nation would be sculpted. Youth citizenship was conceptualised, in many ways, as an urban problem that had a civic solution. Changing the city and its public culture, reformers believed, would transform both health and behaviour. Fears about the condition of city children were nothing new, and by the late Victorian years there was already an established network of voluntary and charitable organisations that endeavoured to provide direction, welfare and citizenship training. But the problem had evolved by the 1920s. Older debates about urban degeneration and 'national efficiency' were now combined with extensive sociological investigation and criticism of how modern youths spent their leisure time. A renewed sense of urgency emerged in the 1930s with the Great Depression, the rise of extreme political regimes in continental Europe and the looming prospect of another global war. Mass unemployment sparked contradictory fears: on the one hand, of possible revolutionary behaviour; and, on the other, of political apathy.[1] Stopping youths from being seduced by crime, malaise or radical ideologies were all of paramount importance.

A new type of citizen, equipped for these competitive challenges, was shaped by the state and voluntary associations. Individual fitness was still emphasised – an element of continuity from the late nineteenth century. But there was also a shift towards foregrounding community and cohesion in the fragmented modern city, reflecting the importance of the ideals promoted by civics education and urban festivals. Youth citizens needed good personal health and morality, but also an enthusiasm for teamwork and social conformity under the umbrella of a collective civic identity. These attributes fitted them into future roles in the local and national economy, urban society and even possible warfare. Young people and their bodies, then, were the problem, but 'youth' was a catch-all term for a large group that had many differences in gender, class, race and ethnicity, as well as simply in terms of age. It could, following the

---

[1]   For Britain see David Fowler, *Youth culture in modern Britain, c. 1920–c. 1970*, Basingstoke 2008, 89, and Melanie Tebbutt, *Being boys: youth, leisure and identity in the inter-war years*, Manchester 2012, 24. For the US see Richard A. Reiman, *The New Deal and American youth: ideas and ideals in a depression decade*, Athens, GA 1992. For both countries see Jon Savage, *Teenage: the creation of youth, 1875–1945*, London 2007, chs xix, xx.

growth of scientific and biological understandings of adolescence as a stage of life, be associated with the developmental phase of puberty – itself difficult to pin down in terms of an age range.[2] More commonly in civic culture, however, was a looser social understanding that saw youth as a period of life from the early teens to early twenties and, more importantly, a 'state of mind or set of attitudes' that were not solidly fixed by age.[3] In this chapter the emphasis will be on the cultural imagining of youth, and the ways in which it interacted with concerns about behaviour and citizenship; its analysis will not necessarily be limited by age.

Late nineteenth-century press coverage and crime figures had already confirmed to moralisers that young males were most at risk. In Chicago's Juvenile Court, established in 1899, they represented 92 per cent of cases.[4] In Manchester, the urban gangs of boy hooligans or 'scuttlers' fascinated and appalled the British courts and public in the 1880s and 1890s.[5] Citizenship instruction began in schools, but reached intensity for boys in the difficult years of adolescence, and was present throughout the transition from school-child to economic worker and community member. Into the interwar years, the attendance rate of young females at organised recreational activities was lower because associations focused their energy on boys or young men. In the Lower North Side of Chicago between April 1938 and March 1939, for example, only 28.6 per cent of girls were reported as participants in supervised recreation, compared to 84.6 per cent of boys, reflecting the network of boys' clubs and their specific initiatives. Tellingly, only 1.3 per cent of women had delinquency records, compared to 17.6 per cent of men.[6] In Manchester, there were many clubs for 'lads', but those for girls were often limited to friendly societies or the Guides. The place of adolescent females was mostly seen as being domestic, helping mother with chores. Girls and young women had scant time for relaxation or 'leisure' – at least in comparison to boys. Yet they were still citizens – particularly as future wives and mothers who would guarantee the power of nation and empire.[7] Gendered youth citizenship was varied and complex in the interwar period. New leisure habits, such as Jazz Age dancing or 'flapper' fashion, continued to feed fears about purity and untamed sexuality. Magazines such as *Vogue*, which had both a British and an American issue, courted a modern femininity of consumeristic desirability and freedom, yet

[2]   For the origins see Richard M. Lerner and Laurence Steinberg, 'The scientific study of adolescent development', in Richard M. Lerner and Laurence Steinberg (eds), *Handbook of adolescent psychology*, I: *Individual bases of adolescent development*, Hoboken, NJ 2009.

[3]   Tebbutt, *Being boys*, 17.

[4]   Savage, *Teenage*, 65.

[5]   Geoffrey Pearson, *Hooligan: a history of respectable fears*, London 1983, 95.

[6]   Chicago Recreation Commission, *Recreation and delinquency: a study of five selected Chicago communities*, Chicago, IL 1942, 63.

[7]   Alice Jane Mackay and Pat Thane, 'The Englishwoman', in Colls and Dodds, *Englishness*, 217–54.

also sought to control. Youth was pivotal to this feminine modernity either way, and consequently both girls and young women did not escape scrutiny from voluntary associations or the state.[8]

Hundreds of bodies, from voluntary clubs to governmental departments, were especially involved with citizenship training.[9] This chapter focuses on local organisations, and the 'urban lower classes' in particular – a loose group defined as the problem most distinctive to the modern city. Looking at the relationship between young people and civic culture, and the experience of the working classes especially, shows the ambivalence of urban citizenship in microcosm. The first section will trace how the modern city in the interwar period was still seen as enabling the wrong sort of leisure and mixing between genders, classes and races. This was a perceived sense of urban problems that was developed through the interplay of reformers, sociologists, the state and local associations. Section two turns to the result of this interaction: the reshaping and reconceptualising of the city as a potential site of cohesive civic community. Though this stressed inclusivity it was also coded by class, gender and race. In Chicago, black youths especially were designated as being particularly susceptible to modern urban life yet were barred from many of the mainstream citizenship initiatives. The final section demonstrates the increasing power of the state to shape society. By the mid-point of the interwar period, it was becoming clear that local and national government had the power to enrich but also surpass associational initiatives – an important shift in the shaping of citizenship discourse that is further picked up in the final thematic chapter of this book.

Health, behaviour and the modern urban community

To understand interwar associational culture and youth citizenship it is necessary to look back to the debates that came with urbanisation, industrialisation and armament in the late nineteenth century. Concerns about economic and military power in both countries were articulated in similar debates about urban degeneration and declining morality. In Britain there were fears about 'hooliganism' and the lack of law and order. Working-class boys especially, empowered by a resilient juvenile labour market and growing consumer opportunities for popular leisure, were seen as potentially deviant and susceptible

---

[8] Penny Tinkler and Cheryl Krasnick Warsh, 'Feminine modernity in interwar Britain and North America: corsets, cars, and cigarettes', *Journal of Women's History* xx/3 (2008), 113–43.

[9] This was especially true of Chicago. There is a survey of a range of associations in Pierce, *Citizens' organizations*, and, for a statistical breakdown of clubs see Boys' Club Federation, 'A special study of the boy situation in Chicago' (1929), Chicago Boys and Girls Club Records, 1901–69, CHM, folder 12, box 1, MSS lot C.

to the broader emergence of working-class political movements.[10] Manchester, with neighbourhood-specific gang dress and language, was seen as a hotbed of problems.[11] City-living was, more generally, blamed for the poor health of workers and soldiers. A 'degenerationist' mode of thought crossed national boundaries in nineteenth-century Europe even before, and often separate from, Charles Darwin's *Origin of species* (1859) that provided justifications for those who sought to develop pseudo-scientific eugenicist or 'Social Darwinist' policies. By the last two decades of the century, these concerns had reached fever pitch, as environmental and evolutionary thought worked together to provide a widely held sense that the urban-industrial order was in crisis.[12] The high proportion of men discovered to be unfit for service during the Boer War in 1899 brought these issues into stark relief in Britain. In Manchester, for example, out of 11,000 volunteers 8,000 were rejected and only 1,200 were accepted as fit in all respects.[13]

A cry for 'national efficiency' gathered steam as commentators questioned how the nation could compete globally when its citizens were physically inferior. This debate and discourse crossed conventional lines of 'left' and 'right', 'liberals' and 'conservatives', 'socialists' and 'capitalists', and was found in policies as diverse as tariff reform, compulsory military service and eugenics. The Interdepartmental Committee on Physical Deterioration of 1904 added to the climate, while associations such as the National League for Physical Education and Improvement, the Health and Strength League and the Boy Scouts grew in this context.[14] A biologically-based rhetoric was adopted by many medical professionals and the policy-makers whom they informed, even though eugenics had only a limited influence in British policy-making; the power of an entrenched public health structure, the propagators of which were more interested in environmental than biological determinations of health and behaviour, limited the practical use of eugenics.[15] Government social legislation, however, made youth fitness one of its primary goals, through acts such as the Education (Provision of Meals) Act in 1906 and the Education (Administrative Provisions) Act in 1907, which established free school meals

---

[10] Tebbutt, *Being boys*, 20. For the classic analysis see Pearson, *Hooligan*.

[11] Andrew Davies, *The gangs of Manchester: the story of the Scuttlers, Britain's first youth cult*, Preston 2008.

[12] Daniel Pick, *Faces of degeneration: a European disorder, c.1848–c.1918*, Cambridge 1989. See also Bill Luckin, 'Revisiting the idea of degeneration in urban Britain, 1830–1900', *Urban History* xxxiii/2 (2006), 234–52.

[13] Joanna Bourke, *Working class cultures in Britain, 1890–1960: gender, class and ethnicity*, London 1997, 172.

[14] Searle, *The quest for national efficiency*.

[15] Ina Zweiniger-Bargielowska, 'Raising a nation of "good animals": the new health society and health education campaigns in interwar Britain', *Social History of Medicine* xx/1 (2007), 75; Dorothy Porter, '"Enemies of the race": biologism, environmentalism, and public health in Edwardian England', *Victorian Studies* xxxiv/2 (1991), 173.

and medical inspection respectively. The youth of Britain found themselves with a new identity: 'Children of the Nation'.[16]

Comparable concerns were evident in the US. Between 1880 and 1920 'child saving' – rescuing working-class children from social and economic hazards such as economic exploitation, unrestricted immigration and unsupervised street culture – was the country's most widely supported reform cause.[17] The pioneer of the American settlement movement, Jane Addams, argued in 1912 that many of America's young people had no positive outlet for their energies.[18] Her settlement, Hull House, founded in 1889 following a visit to Toynbee Hall in East London and staffed mainly by highly religious college-educated women, aimed to integrate the immigrant into the city – whether through moral example or coercion – and had a special interest in youths. By 1909 eighteen settlement houses had been opened in Chicago, part of a wider flowering of settlements in the US – from six in 1891 to more than 400 by 1910.[19] There was also a broader concern with health and fitness, heavily tinged with fears of 'race suicide'. In the 1880s the birth-rate of Americans with supposedly superior 'Anglo-Saxon' heritage was revealed to be in decline. Immigration continued to grow as it had throughout the century, but now increasingly came from southern and eastern Europe, leading a *New York Times* editorial to describe an invasion of 'the physical, moral and mental wreck … which we are better without'.[20] Emphasising heredity focused American concerns for the vitality of the nation directly on physical health.[21]

Organised sports and bodily activity was one way in which contemporaries thought that the decline could be halted. Progressive reformers connected intellect and physical fitness, believing that urban living had damaged both.[22] Voluntary organisations responded accordingly. Originally, the Chicago YMCA in the 1870s had tried to lead boys and men into active Christian lifestyles but, by the 1880s, it was instead developing a programme of exercise to 'build bodies rather than save souls'.[23] In the 'play movement', organisers left behind traditional distinctions of mind and body, instead arguing that

---

[16]   Beaven and Griffiths, 'Creating the exemplary citizen', 209.

[17]   See Dominick Cavallo, *Muscles and morals: organized playgrounds and urban reform, 1880–1920*, Philadelphia, PA 1981.

[18]   Jane Addams, *Twenty years at Hull House*, New York, NY 1912, 48.

[19]   Peter Hall, *Cities of tomorrow: an intellectual history of urban planning and design since 1880*, Chichester 2014, 46.

[20]   *New York Times* quoted ibid. 37. See also Charles Beresford, 'The future of the Anglo-Saxon race', *North American Review* clxxi (Dec. 1900), 802–10.

[21]   Harvey Green, *Fit for America: fitness, sport, and American society*, Baltimore, MD 1986, 225.

[22]   Roberta J. Park, 'Healthy, moral, and strong: educational views of exercise and athletics in nineteenth-century America', in Kathryn Grover (ed.), *Fitness in American culture: images of health, sport, and the body, 1830–1940*, New York, NY 1989, 123–68.

[23]   David S. Churchill, 'Making broad shoulders: body-building and physical culture in Chicago, 1890–1920', *History of Education Quarterly* xlviii/3 (2008), 346, 348, 353.

muscular conditioning influenced the content and quality of both mental and moral attributes. When ideas of the body and the corrupting influence of the city were taken alongside the scientific child study movement of educators and psychologists such as G. Stanley Hall, James Mark Baldwin and Dewey, all whom argued for a distinctive adolescent stage of life, the body and health of the urban youths became vital.[24]

By 1900 there was thus a perception on both sides of the Atlantic that the large city was 'the source of multiple social evils, possible biological decline, and potential political insurrection'.[25] Poverty, and its societal effects, had of course existed before. But the industrialised 'shock city' – which had both geographically and mentally separated middle-class populations from the working class and poor by concentrating population in different areas – heightened the fears. The idea of the degenerate city, or more specifically a segregated underworld filled with a 'residuum' out of reach of reform, was mapped and sold to an anxious 'bourgeois readership' through novels, newspapers and the *exposés* of 'slummers'.[26] Despite the slowing down of a sense of a specifically urban crisis in the years before 1914, these themes persisted into the interwar period.

Social commentators and researchers in Britain continued to show that bodily defects hindered the creation of good youth citizens, as the First World War brought a renewed sense of urgency in raising the standard of fitness of men in Britain. Again, as with the Boer conflict, high rates of army recruit rejection made physical inadequacy all too obvious. Only 36 per cent in Britain were graded fully fit (A1), and 31 per cent were found completely unfit for combat (C3). These categories entered the popular imagination and public debates, with the desire to become an 'A1 population' being a rallying call.[27] The ideal 'good citizen' in this context was still, then, a physically fit, muscular and male body, combining strength, restraint and endurance.[28] In the 1920s new social hygiene health movements, such as the Sunlight League or the New Health Society, emerged to improve national health. For girls and young women, organisations such as the Girl Guides and the YWCA (Young Woman's Christian Association) sought to regulate adolescent sexual knowledge and behaviour, and to train girls for a family and societal role.[29] In the 1930s these ideas of national fitness for both genders were revived with renewed urgency,

[24]   Cavallo, *Muscles and morals*, 51, 54–77.

[25]   Hall, *Cities of tomorrow*, 47.

[26]   Thomas Heise, *Urban underworlds: a geography of twentieth-century American literature and culture*, New Brunswick, NJ 2011, 33; Luckin, 'Revisiting the idea of degeneration', 250. See also Lees and Lees, *Cities and the making of modern Europe*, 146–51.

[27]   Ina Zweiniger-Bargielowska, 'Building a British superman: physical culture in interwar Britain', *Journal of Contemporary History* xli/4 (2006), 601.

[28]   Sonya Rose, *Which people's war? National identity and citizenship in Britain, 1939–1945*, Oxford 2003, 153–7.

[29]   Zweiniger-Bargielowska, 'Raising a nation of "good animals"'. See also Carolyn Oldfield, 'Growing up good? Medical, social hygiene and youth perspectives on young women,

especially following the launching of the National Government's National Fitness Campaign. Concerns about the decline of health, then, continued to shape 'social, medical and environmental ideas and policies' – and especially in relation to cities.[30]

George Newman was a particularly influential figure in this obsession with physical fitness. He was appointed as the first Chief Medical Officer to the Ministry of Health in 1919 and retained the same role for the Board of Education. Newman has been described, by the historian of health Bernard Harris, as the 'most important single figure in the history of the British public health administration' in the first half of the twentieth century.[31] Having absorbed the ideals of national efficiency, Newman consistently made links between physical health and citizenship. His chosen framework in response was 'preventive medicine'. For Newman, cultivating human health and capacity was the fundamental task of state-building, with health and illness tied to the relationship between individuals and their environment. More medical powers to schools, and concurrent health campaigns, underlined his belief in these ideals.[32] On a more local stage, Health Centres emerged in the 1920s to educate youths in personal wellbeing – part of the wider concern with 'positive health' and unfulfilled potential. Environmental determinism was still a key part of physical fitness, then, and depended largely on public health authorities.[33] The cumulative effect of health movements and state ideology was an emphasis on personal health and habits of restraint – whether in cleanliness or leisure – and, linking the two together, the goal of good citizenship.

Enthusiasm for health and fitness also blossomed in the US. The push for personal health and cleanliness, a cornerstone of late nineteenth-century respectability, intensified: consumer products, such as electronic devices that promised to renew vigour, flooded the market after the War; the science of nutrition, and popular consciousness of diet, reached new heights; and the expansion of modern advertising by large pharmaceutical companies led to a 'vitamin-crazy' nation.[34] In some ways this health focus was detached from its earlier emphasis on national or racial health, since Social Darwinism as

---

1918-1939', unpubl. PhD diss. Warwick 2001, 8, 10. For the Sunlight League see Simon Carter, *Rise and shine: sunlight, technology and health*, Oxford 2007, 77.

[30]   Luckin, 'Revisiting the idea of degeneration', 237.

[31]   Bernard Harris, *The health of the schoolchild: a history of the School Medical Service in England and Wales*, Buckingham 1995, 50.

[32]   George Newman, *The rise of preventive medicine*, Oxford 1932, p. vi. See also Steve Sturdy, 'Hippocrates and state medicine: George Newman outlines the founding policy of the Ministry of Health', in Christopher Lawrence and George Weisz (eds), *Greater than the parts: holism in biomedicine, 1920–1950*, Oxford 1998, 112–34.

[33]   Abigail Beach, 'Potential for participation: health centres and the idea of citizenship c.1920-1940', in Christopher Lawrence and Anna-K. Mayer (eds), *Regenerating England: science, medicine and culture in interwar Britain*, Atlanta, GI 2000, 218.

[34]   Peter N. Stearns, *Battleground of desire: the struggle for self-control in modern America*, New York, NY 1999, 20; Green, *Fit for America*, 263; James C. Wharton, 'Eating to win: popular

a 'conscious philosophy' had, by the end of the war, 'largely disappeared'.[35] Attaining the 'perfect' body was now more about the enjoyment of the process and result than fulfilling any top-down social or political ends. Americans could thus think of play and sport as personal pleasure and fulfilment and required little external social justification from the state or associations. Health, fitness and sporting competition had its own reward. Bodily behaviour and training certainly remained important to societal relations – activities that were 'fun' could also create a happy and well-adjusted personality – but, for adults at least, some of the moralising edge had been lost to be replaced by a subtler sense of 'morale'.[36]

If a focus on sport in terms of its moral attributes had diminished for adults, using sport and physical culture to promote health and community remained a key pillar of youth citizenship. The perceived loosening of behaviour in preceding decades also provoked new forms of self-control for new indulgences, and a renewed intensity in the laments of moralists.[37] Beyond the continued physical aspect of citizenship, then, was also the social. In the eyes of observers, the problem of youth culture in American society took on new and dramatic forms in the 1920s. Unlike the issue of juvenile offenders and slum children in the Progressive Era, the issue was now less how youths could be drawn away from crime and assimilated into the mainstream of culture, but how cultural changes – the rapid growth of 'hypercommercialised' amusements and a liberating consumer society, especially – had made that mainstream undesirable to 'the guardians of Victorian values'.[38]

In Chicago such changes were evident. The development of commercial leisure areas or 'interzones' in cities, where boundaries of race and class could be breached, caused particular concern. A significant minority of white men and women, both heterosexual and homosexual, went 'slumming' and looking for entertainment and sexual excitement in African American neighbourhoods. Recalling the race riot in 1919, commentators saw racial mixing as not only a danger to female purity but to the very fabric of white political dominance.[39] Athletic clubs and other youth associations structured an everyday environment

concepts of diet, strength, and energy in the early twentieth century', in Grover, *Fitness in American culture*, 87, 91.

[35]   Hofstadter, *Social Darwinism*, 203.

[36]   Reiman, *The New Deal and American youth*, 5; Green, *Fit For America*, 11; Donald Mrozek, 'Sport in American life: from national health to personal fulfilment, 1890-1940', in Grover, *Fitness in American culture*, 18, 20, 23.

[37]   Stearns, *Battleground of desire*, 5, 46, 3-30.

[38]   For quotations, and the meanings of mass culture in this period see Paul V. Murphy, *The new era: American thought and culture in the 1920s*, Lanham, MD 2011, ch. ii. In relation to youth see the classic Paula S. Fass, *The damned and the beautiful: American youth in the 1920s*, Oxford 1977, 6, 14, 18.

[39]   Heap, *Slumming*, 2-3, 79; Kevin Mumford, *Interzones: black/white sex districts in Chicago and New York in the early twentieth century*, New York, NY 1997.

of racial hostility, as young men made sense of what it meant to be masculine and 'white' or 'black'.[40] Urban crime also concerned onlookers, not just for the moral decline that it suggested, but also for its cost. The new American Citizenship Foundation, based in Chicago, made this point continually, determining that an annual taxpayer outlay of an extra $14,000,000 was needed to maintain the police, the court and prisons. It was the youth of Chicago that was painted as the source of crime. Official statistics showed that 85 per cent of offences were committed by those under twenty-one – an age, reminded the foundation, where a negative path of life was correctable.[41]

National debates about 'fitness', physical culture and health provided context, but researchers and voluntary organisations made sense of youth citizenship in relation to cities. Urban 'ecology' and its influence on societal behaviour was rigorously investigated by the Chicago School of Sociologists, whose work was, in essence, an analysis of 'the nature of social bonding in the modern, fragmented, city'.[42] P. G. Cressey's *The taxi-dance hall: a sociological study in commercialized recreation and city life* (1932), for example, explored the new halls where men paid young women for short dances. In the foreword Ernest Burgess, a leading figure in the School, categorised taxi-dance halls as indicative of the modern city. Leisure time was based around a demand for stimulation, commercialised recreation and the pursuit of sex. The 'ordinary devices of social control', such as the church and the family, ceased to work in a 'culturally heterogeneous and anonymous society'.[43] Coupled with these academic understandings of dance halls was a much more mainstream fear about new forms of music and dancing. Jazz, in particular, provoked concern. As a type of music originating and mostly performed by African Americans, though often in clubs that they could not frequent as patrons, it was feared by privileged elites as a conscious attempt by blacks to undermine their supposedly morally superior white lifestyle.[44]

The focus on interactions between young men and women also reflected a general crisis of sexuality, emerging especially from the liberalisation of some aspects of young women's lifestyles during and after the war. Fashionable and skimpy clothing, greater sexual opportunity and the growing availability of sexual images and innuendo, particularly from Hollywood, formed the basis

---

[40] Andrew J. Diamond, *Mean streets: Chicago youths and the everyday struggle for empowerment in the multiracial city, 1908–1969*, Los Angeles, CA 2009, 20

[41] 'Save the boys', *The American Citizen* i/3 (Jan. 1927), 13, CHM, LC251.A5.

[42] Mike Savage, Alan Warde and Kevin Ward, *Urban sociology, capitalism and modernity*, Basingstoke 2003, 13.

[43] Ernest Burgess, 'Introduction', to P. G. Cressey, *The taxi-dance hall: a sociological study in commercialized recreation and city life* (1932), New York, NY, 1968, p. xv.

[44] Mitchell Newton-Matza, *Jazz Age: people and perspectives*, Santa Barbara, CA 2009, p. xiv; Lynne Dumenil, *The modern temper: American culture and society in the 1920s*, New York, NY 1995.

for wild social fears.[45] Trying to make sense of why such urban lifestyles were so attractive, the Chicago sociologists looked to what had been lost. They found that the desire for stimulation had previously been expressed through family, neighbourhood, the varied activities of village life or in the pioneering settlement of the west. With the passing of the frontier and a supposed decline in family and neighbourhood recreation, '"The jungles" of the city' became the site of excitement and experience.[46] Frederick Thrasher's *The gang* (1927) made this point central. Robert Park argued in the preface that the modern American city and its slums or 'city wilderness' gave the city gang its natural habitat.[47] Because of the failure to control customs and institutions – such as the family, school, religion and 'wholesome recreation' – boys tried to recreate a society for themselves, and the result was gangs. Thrasher's 'conservative estimate' of gangs in Chicago was 1,313 with a total of 25,000 members.[48]

E. Franklin Frazier, a notable African American scholar, made the specificity of the urban experience central to his understanding of the past, present and future of African American progress. His book *The negro family in the United States*, based primarily on work carried out in Chicago under Park and Burgess, ambitiously traced the various dislocations that blacks had undergone – from Africa to America, slavery to freedom and finally, from plantation to metropolis. In 'The City of Destruction', he argued, black men may have escaped 'traditional subordination to white overlords' but they were also 'cut loose from the moral support' of relatives, neighbours and church that had characterised southern rural life. Now 'individuated', and lacking 'traditional' values, a high proportion of formerly 'naïve and ignorant peasant folk' succumbed to the 'disorganization' of slum life or temptations of 'the anonymity afforded by the city'. Crime, anti-social behaviour, family desertion and breakdown, illegitimacy and 'loose' sexual behaviour were the results.[49] It was, as Frazier summarised, 'The disorganization of Negro family life in the urban environment, together with the absence of communal controls, [that resulted] in a high delinquency rate among Negro boys and girls.'[50]

Chicago School sociologists, in general, idealised the nature of rural or preindustrial life, gave little attention to the longer history of middle-class and religious fears about urban living, and did not acknowledge their racialised tendency to draw comparisons between (often unidentified) 'savage' lands

---

[45] Stearns, *Battleground of desire*, 194; Mark Haller, 'Urban vice and civic reform: Chicago in the early twentieth century', in Kenneth T. Jackson and Stanley K. Schultz (eds), *Cities in American history*, New York, NY 1972, 299.

[46] Burgess, 'Introduction', p. xv.

[47] Robert Park, 'Editors preface' to Frederick M. Thrasher, *The gang: a study of 1,313 gangs in Chicago* (1927), Chicago, IL 1936, p. xi.

[48] Thrasher, *The gang*, 5, 38, 79.

[49] E. Franklin Frazier, *The negro family in the United States*, Chicago, IL 1939, 271–392.

[50] Ibid. 358.

and urban slums.[51] They also, as was particularly the case with Frazier, under-estimated the ability of urbanites to resist chaos and disorganisation and to build meaningful communities.[52] Perhaps most problematically, they neglected human choice almost entirely in favour of environmental causation.[53] Their 'scientific' articulation of problems, however, gave renewed energy to associational culture. Sociological studies directly called for further voluntary activity to mediate these shifts in behaviour, and sociologists' conclusions moved from academic studies into local consciousness. Thrasher's study of gangs, for example, was cited by the Chicago Council of Social Agencies even before publication.[54] The Local Community Research Committee at the University of Chicago, formed in 1923 and chaired by the heads of five different departments, was central to this cooperative culture. It sought to understand local urban problems, and to attract groups and individuals looking for expert advice.[55] It sponsored one of the most famous of the interwar investigations, The Gold Coast and the slum (1929). Written by Harvey Warren Zorbaugh and based on his PhD thesis completed under Park, it analysed segregation and social disorganisation. Zorbaugh argued that there was 'scarcely an area' that could be called a community. He worked directly with voluntary associations like the United Charities, the social settlement Eli Bates House and the Lower North Community Council to complete his study. Much like Thrasher, Burgess and Cressey, Zorbaugh blamed the anonymity of the slum; isolation and loneliness; the lack of old traditions of social control; and the sheer size of the city. He found a variety of social (mis)types making their home in the slum: opium users, drunkards, the 'queer', criminals, outcasts and people of 'unstable or problematical character'. Standing above all this, representative of the 'topsy-turvy' nature of the city, was 'youth on the social throne'.[56] Both academic studies and popular representations of the urban thus informed and

---

[51] An understanding of the inner-city poor being a 'race apart', often drawing on imperialistic tropes of conquered 'savage' lands, was common in the late nineteenth century in both Britain and the US: Briggs, Victorian cities, 62; Heise, Urban underworlds, 30–76.

[52] Anthony M. Platt, 'The negro family in the United States: E. Franklin Frazier', in Gwendolyn Mink and Alice O'Connor, Poverty in the United States: an encyclopaedia of history, politics and policy, i, Santa Barbara, CA 2004, 495–7. As Platt points out, Frazier's work was significant in showing that Western civilisation, and not inherent racial-biological difference, caused these problems.

[53] Howard P. Chudacoff, 'Introduction to 1976 edition', in Warren Zorbaugh, The Gold Coast and the slum: a sociological study of Chicago's Near North Side (1929), Chicago, IL 1983, p. xii.

[54] Chicago Council of Social Agencies, Preliminary inquiry into boys' work in Chicago, Chicago, IL 1921, 8, 10–11.

[55] T. V. Smith and Leonard White, Chicago: an experiment in social science research, Chicago, IL 1929, 33. Albert Guttenberg positions the committee as one of the continuing fruits of the Progressive Era: The language of planning: essays on the origins and ends of American planning thought, Urbana, IL 1993, 225.

[56] Zorbaugh, The Gold Coast and the slum, 48, 132, 182.

confirmed the beliefs of associational volunteers and reformers. Chicago, as it stood, was not a good place for the making of young citizens.

Local debate in Britain was not directed by academic sociological studies to the same extent. Many of those who worked with urban youths in Manchester, however, had the same criticisms of the city as their Chicago contemporaries. Like Cressey, the local reformer Sydney O'Hanlon believed that the urban environment was dangerous because of the ways in which it allowed the sexes to mix. She came to this conclusion after working with women patrols in Manchester's streets during the First World War. The Manchester Citizens' Association, formed following a National Council of Women meeting in Manchester's town hall in 1918, owed its existence largely to her efforts. Young male and female workers, she believed, needed a wholesome social environment after a hard day's work. For the unemployed especially, downhearted and discouraged, the club would provide a cheery and friendly place to recover a sense of self-worth.[57] As the mayor remarked, in a speech complimenting the association's growth, young men and women who went to the public house for warmth and friendship needed a 'pure and temperate' alternative.[58] At least some of Manchester's youth were amenable to the message: in 1927 a larger home was opened on Grosvenor Street, as the club's membership grew, with as many as 160 paying for entry some nights.[59] The Manchester University Settlement, formed in 1895 in the context of the international debate about urban poverty and morality, made similar arguments. The city, one study group reported in 1928, was still causing 'growing girls and women, as well as men ... to seek comfort in unhealthy excitement'.[60]

The power of the city to corrupt thus reflected wider concerns in Britain about morality during and immediately after the war – a belief that family life, religiosity and sexual morality was on the wane. Robert Roberts, in his memoir of growing up in Salford, remembered how 'folk were scandalized' by the new 'Bold teenage girls, a type never encountered before'. His own sister, who had begun working during the war in a cotton mill, refused to stop wearing make-up – despite threats of eviction by their father.[61] Young people in Britain, increasingly including women, often found employment easily

[57] Manchester Citizen's Association, 'First annual report' (1918), 1, and 'Third annual report' (1921), 4, Hulme Lads' Club, MCA, box 5, GB127.M716. This association was first named the Manchester Comrades' Club and renamed the Manchester Citizens' Association between 1920 and 1921. Margaret Pilkington, an important arts civic figure, singled out O'Hanlon as the key influence behind the Association's forming: 'Social service', in Brindley, *The soul of Manchester*, 233–44.

[58] Manchester Citizen's Association, 'Ninth annual report' (1927).

[59] 'Manchester citizens' club', MG, 24 May 1928, 14.

[60] Manchester and District Regional Survey Society, *Social studies of a Manchester city ward: a study of the health of Ancoats and some suggestions for its improvement*, Manchester 1928, 7.

[61] Robert Roberts, *The classic slum: Salford life in the first quarter of the century* (1971), Bungay 1983, 205.

because their labour was cheap, and without as many responsibilities as their parents they were a ready market for the purveyors of clothes, entertainment and leisure.[62] A new female self-confidence and independence was described in magazines and the press, with women workers being perceived as keen to explore pleasure and experience.[63] In the period that followed the end of the war, there was consequently a desire from many to reassert order on the basis of 'sexual difference'. Importantly, it was girls and women that were often singled out; only by returning to a 'traditional' distinction between the proper roles of men and women could the sexual aggression of men, supposedly awakened by the war, be curbed.[64] Into the 1930s Mass Observation and its army of mostly middle-class 'observers' also attempted to understand the sexual relations of urban youths.[65] The fears of local associations were a part of this shift. As the Girls' Friendly Society of Eccles warned in 1926, a new 'freedom and liberty' had arrived – one that was incompatible with 'purity'.[66] Leaders of clubs for boys were also describing and lamenting leisure habits, and the shift to mass commercial culture that 'feminised' and threatened manly vigour.[67] In 1924 the Jewish Lads' Brigade thus blamed increased disposable income and the rise in cinemas and other forms of cheap undesirable attractions. 'More urgent than ever' was the provision of 'character training' and 'healthy outlets for the spirits and energies of the boys'.[68]

The popularity of the cinema, in both countries, was a particular concern. Thrasher reasoned that movies provided a cheap and easy escape from reality in Chicago while also giving the 'gang boy' exploits to emulate. Of the hundred such gang boys he interviewed, average cinema attendance was three times a week, and thirty boys even went every day.[69] Attendance in Chicago remained high throughout the period and, in 1939, twice as much time was spent by boys in the movies as in supervised recreational activities.[70] Much of the same story was true in Manchester where, in 1937, the city's cinemas could seat around 15

---

[62] Penny Tinkler, *Constructing girlhood: popular magazines for girls growing up in England, 1920–1950*, Abingdon 1995, 4; David Fowler, *The first teenagers: the lifestyle of young wage-earners in interwar Britain*, London 1996, 1. For an overview of both the opportunities for youth yet also the fracturing by class and poverty see Selina Todd, 'Flappers and factory lads: youth and youth culture in interwar Britain', *History Compass* iv/2 (2006), 715–30.

[63] Oldfield, 'Growing up good?', 14, 20–48.

[64] Susan Kingsley Kent, *Making peace: the reconstruction of gender in interwar Britain*, Princeton, NJ 1993, 97–113.

[65] P. J. Gurney, '"Intersex" and "dirty girls": Mass-Observation and working-class sexuality in England in the 1930s', *Journal of the History of Sexuality* viii/3 (1997), 256–90.

[66] Cutting from *St Andrews Parish Magazine*, 'A jubilee' (1926) in 'Log book', Girls' Friendly Society, Eccles, St Andrew, MCA, GB127.L286/5/5.

[67] Tebbutt, *Being boys*, 26.

[68] 'Report for 1924' (1925), 8, Jewish Lads' Brigade, MCA, box 6, GB127.M130.2345.

[69] Thrasher, *The gang*, 102. See also Chicago Bureau of Recreation, *Annual report*, Chicago, IL 1926, 23–8.

[70] Chicago Recreation Commission, *Recreation and delinquency*, 240.

per cent of the population at any one time.[71] It is, of course, debatable whether the cinema actually had a negative effect on youth behaviour. But it remained a real worry to those trying to promote more wholesome forms of recreation. Councillor Will Melland, presiding over a meeting of the Manchester Citizens' Association, stereotyped the cinema as 'rather demoralising' and an inadequate form of leisure, reflecting broader concerns about how Hollywood glamour was blunting the critical faculties of the working classes.[72] In general, modern leisure pursuits outside of the control of moralising reformers blossomed in these two decades. Investigations in Manchester in the late 1930s found a range of 'unwholesome' amusements. In the working-class district of Hulme, for example, there were eight cinemas (with four more on the outskirts), one variety theatre, twelve dance halls, eight billiard halls and 143 public houses.[73]

In the 1920s and 1930s, in summary, there was a consensus across associations and reformers in Manchester and Chicago, and Britain and the US more generally, that the modern city, with its opportunities for the 'wrong' types of leisure, was having a harmful effect on youth citizenship. When political fears combined with social anxieties about gender, and a broader concern for the health and physical efficiency of the nation, the question of how to educate and reform the young citizen was of clear importance. As President Calvin Coolidge told the National Council of the Boy Scouts of America in 1926, 'Towns and cities and industrial life' were 'very recent and modern acquirements', and 'if the usual environment has been very largely changed, it becomes exceedingly necessary that an artificial environment be created to supply the necessary process for a continuation of the development and character of the race'.[74] From a similar perspective, if not quite such a powerful societal position, the British author Sidney Frank Hatton described how 'The streets of our big cities are flowing with this young stream of Life; a stream for good or evil. It must not trickle away into lonely little pools of purposelessness, but must be guided, cleansed and led into deep channels of useful citizenship and service to the state.'[75]

This was a task to which associations were keen to rise. An obvious method was to remove children from the corrupting city into the healthy and educational

---

[71] Calculated from figures in Fowler, *The first teenagers*, 118.

[72] 'The citizens' club: a happy retreat for young men and women', MG, 1 Apr. 1927, 13. See also Fowler, *The first teenagers*, 119–25, and Brad Beaven, *Leisure, citizenship and working-class men, 1850–1945*, Manchester 2005, 105–7.

[73] H. E. O. James and F. T. Moore, 'Adolescent leisure in a working-class district', *Occupational Psychology* xiv (1940), 134.

[74] Calvin Coolidge, 'Address before the National Council of the Boy Scouts of America, Washington, D. C.', 1 May 1926: Gerhard Peters and John T. Woolley, *The American Presidency Project*, <http://www.presidency.ucsb.edu/ws/?pid=395>. For the Boy Scouts of America see David I. Macleod, *Building character in the American boy: the Boy Scouts, YMCA, and their forerunners, 1870–1920*, Madison, WI 1983.

[75] Sidney Frank Hatton, *London's bad boys*, London 1931, 49.

countryside.[76] In Chicago the Boys' Clubs travelled to Lake Winona, Indiana; Hull House boys went to Bowen Country Camp, near Waukegan; and Long Lake, Illinois, was the destination of the Jewish People's Institute. In 1923 nearly every boy's agency provided summer camp opportunities.[77] In Manchester, too, all of the major clubs either owned or rented summer camp retreats, and other organisations such as the Manchester Ramblers' Federation also understood the power of the countryside for the 'social readjustment' of urbanites.[78] But the countryside in both countries remained distant or not immediately available to all children, if only because of cost. A yearly retreat to 'nature' also meant little when most 'negative' interaction occurred every day after school or work, or at the weekend. It was a more pragmatic approach to reform urban culture *in situ* that was necessary.

Creating an alternative urban culture

Shaping an 'artificial environment' for youth culture – one with both anti-urban and pro-urban dimensions – was a process that had begun before the 1920s. Organisations that targeted the 'boy problem' had long – and connected – histories on both sides of the Atlantic, with movements such as the YMCA and the Boy Scouts dating to the late nineteenth and early twentieth century. Now, however, new and old organisations made it their central civic duty to improve youth character and morals. In Chicago, the Union League, chartered in 1879, formed its first Boys' Club in 1919 after feeling that the city's businessmen could do more to help 'boys become good citizens'.[79] For businessmen, training youths stopped crime as well as providing a future workforce. Other new organisations, such as the American Citizenship Foundation (formed in Chicago in 1920), expressed similar desires: citizenship training that would lead to loyalty, patriotism and an intelligent public opinion.[80] Youth associations in Manchester experienced a more tumultuous period. New clubs did form, such as the Manchester Citizens Association in 1918 or the Eccles Girls' Friendly Society in 1926. Some associations, however, such as the Broughton Girls' Friendly Society and Hulme Lads' Club, complained of dwindling attendances – the latter also reporting,

---

[76] See, as an introduction, Van Slyck, *A manufactured wilderness*, and Edwards, *Youth movements, citizenship and the English countryside*.

[77] 'Many summer camps provided for boys', *Chicago Illinois News*, 17 May 1923, in Chicago Boys' Week Federation, Scrapbook of newspaper clippings, photographs, forms, posters [hereinafter cited as CBWF], vol. 1, 53, CHM, F38JV.C4s.

[78] Ben Anderson, 'A liberal countryside? The Manchester Ramblers' Federation and the "social readjustment" of urban citizens, 1929-1936', *Urban History* xxxviii/1 (2011), 84-102.

[79] Bruce Grant, *Fight for a city: the story of the Union League Club of Chicago and its times, 1880-1955*, Chicago IL 1955, 214.

[80] 'The American citizen's pledge', *American Citizen* i/2 (Dec. 1926), 8.

in 1928, that 'other Clubs were in the same unhappy position as ourselves'.[81] Manchester's associations, none the less, did continue to attempt to mould minds, bodies and habits. The 1925 annual report of the Groves Lads' Club (boldly titled 'The youth of a nation are the trustees of posterity') declared that lads' clubs were still one of the most important factors in teaching boys to lead 'honourable and healthy lives' so they could become 'really worthy and useful members of the general community'.[82] More broadly, there was a renewed interest in Britain in understanding how leisure time could be better regulated in order to create a more cohesive social citizenship.[83] Manchester served as an important site in this debate, hosting a national conference on 'The Leisure of the People' in 1919 that brought together many reformers, municipal figures and voluntary associations.[84]

There were several organisations and institutions that were shaping urban culture in Manchester. The Procter Gymnasium and Hulme Lads' Club solution was to provide a pleasant place where young men could 'spend their spare time with profit and pleasure' and 'exert every possible influence for their moral elevation'.[85] The Manchester Citizens' Association similarly aimed to cater for the poorer young men and women, replacing their recreation in the streets, the public house, the cinema and the dance hall. Its rooms offered a respite from the stimulation of the modern city – a place where they would 'receive a welcome and rest and read or find a friend'.[86] Morality and 'wholesomeness' were watchwords for associations such as the Manchester University Settlement when they arranged alternative events, such as Saturday night dances, at their 'Round House' in Ancoats (see Figure 15).[87] Even religious venues, after 'much troubled thought', thought it better to hold their own alternative gatherings than to miss out on the enthusiasm of the dancing boom.[88] Providing forms of regulated leisure was an attempt to satisfy the desire for excitement and adventure, for both boys and girls, while carefully maintaining

---

[81] 'Minutes' (24 Apr. 1928), 55, Hulme Lads' Club, box 2, GB127.M716; 'Minutes' (14 Oct. 1933), Girls Friendly Society of Broughton, Lower Broughton, The Ascension, MCA, GB127.L154/5/1.

[82] 'Annual report 1925' (1926), 4, Jewish Lads' Brigade, Grove House Club correspondence, box 3.

[83] Robert Snape, *Leisure, voluntary action and social change in Britain, 1880–1939*, London 2018, chs vi–xi.

[84] *The leisure of the people*, Manchester 1919.

[85] 'Annual report for the year ended Sep. 29 1918', 3, and 'Annual report for the year ended Sep. 29 1924', 1, both in Hulme Lads' Club, box 5, GB127.M716.

[86] 'A mixed club for young working people', 1, in Manchester Citizen's Association, box 5.

[87] Michael E. Rose and Anne Woods, *Everything went on at the Round House: a hundred years of the Manchester University Settlement*, Manchester 1995, 35.

[88] Roberts, *The classic slum*, 232, 236.

Figure 15. University of Manchester Settlement's 'Round House'

'appropriate' behaviour that emphasised the differences and future societal roles of each gender – whether 'manly' citizen or feminine 'mother'.[89]

Changing urban leisure was also a popular cause in Chicago. The Off-the-Street-Club did what its name suggested, taking the child into a regulated playground or clubroom to guard against 'the moral breakdown of society'. It also trained boys to develop 'strong, healthy bodies' and 'keen, alert minds'.[90] The Chicago Boys' Clubs Federation had a large roster of pursuits to occupy young men, from radio and woodwork to athletics and dramatics. Instead of loafing, or 'bothering' people, youths were now learning and improving. As the Federation insisted, the alternative of 'street play undermines and demoralizes character in a most serious manner'.[91] Organisations such as the YMCA or Association House sited their clubrooms in the city, because that was where the 'gangs' of boys could be found, and aimed to elevate morals and behaviour by providing an alternative to the street (*see* Figures 16, 17). Boys' Week, organised and financed by the Rotary Club in Chicago annually from 1921, encapsulated

[89] For how this tension between mass leisure and desire and maintaining gender roles played out in the Scouting and Guiding movement see Tammy M. Proctor, *On my honour: Guides and Scouts in interwar Britain*, Philadelphia, PA 2002, chs iii, iv.

[90] 'Off-the-Street-Club' (1920), 12, in *Off-the-Street-Club miscellaneous pamphlets*, CHM, F38JW.O3z.

[91] 'Character built in fun of boys' clubs', *Chicago Illinois News*, 9 May 1923, CBWF, vol. 1, 10.

Figure 16. Boys waiting in line to enter the YMCA in Chicago (Dec. 1933)

the attempt to forge a new urban citizenship. Following the lead of the Rotary Club in New York, which first organised a Boys' Week in 1920 through their Americanization Committee, the Chicago chapter hoped that 'more interest' and 'better citizen training' in the city's communities would ward against 'the perils of modern social conditions'.[92] 'American boyhood [w]as the material with which the future of business, industry and government in America' would be 'built', the Rotary Club argued, reinforcing the work of the school, and developing 'the spirit of co-operation'.[93]

Each Boys' Week consisted of different days that targeted separate aspects of boy life. In 1923 the event began with a loyalty parade of boys, numbering more than 50,000, that aimed to instil respect and adherence to the urban community. Different organisations, such as the Reserve Officers Training Corps or the parks and playground department of the city council, provided floats that celebrated key attributes of good citizenship – from respect and discipline to health and teamwork (*see* Figures 18, 19, 20). Other events included 'Athletics Day' in schools, playgrounds and boys' centres; 'Boy's Day

[92]   'Newspaper: to all local papers', 1, and 'The week of the boy', *The Literary Digest*, 21 Mar. 1923, 18, ibid.
[93]   [Chicago Boys' Week leaflet], 68, ibid.

Figure 17. Children in front of Association House (c. 1930s)

in Church'; 'School and Thrift' Day, arranged by local banks; 'Industry and Safety' Day, managed between schools and employers; and 'Boys' Day with Dad', arranged by the YMCA. 'Health Day' was a particularly important part of every Boys' Week. Dr Herman Bundesen, the city Health Commissioner, lectured classes of schoolchildren about diet, exercise, play and sleep. His tips, he stated, would help boys be 'healthy in body, in mind and in morals'. Keeping youth healthy, he argued, was vital for the economic and social stability of the city. How else could boys 'grow up into the kind of men Chicago needs' with 'habits ... that will result in' making them 'a desirable member of [Chicago's] great community'?[94] Personal health habits were joined to diet, and public health education was constructed as the leading way to healthier and happier people – the basis of better communities and a more productive workforce.[95]

For the Boys' Week of 1925 the organisers even attempted to create a taxonomy of citizenship, searching for Chicago's future 'best citizen in 1950'.

[94] Herman N. Bundesen, 'How to keep well and grow strong', 72, ibid.

[95] Elizabeth Toon, 'Selling the public on public health: the Commonwealth and Milbank health demonstrations and the meaning of community health education', in Ellen C. Lagemann (ed.), *Philanthropic foundations: new scholarship, new possibilities*, Bloomington, IN 1999, 125.

Figure 18. Acrobats on a float during the Chicago Boys' Week opening parade (1923)

A hundred of the city's civic and business leaders – including the mayor, university professors, bankers and educators – listed their own opinions of the vital characteristics of citizenship. The call to find this individual was spread throughout the press – from the dominant *Tribune* to smaller titles like the *Englewood Times*. Announced in May 1925, the ideal citizen was seemingly a combination of social and physical attributes: one who fitted into his environment, community and workforce, as well as the nation. As the Superintendent of Schools, William McAndrew, summarised, 'the best citizen must be ready to cooperate in team work; to consider the other fellow's rights; to manifest tolerance toward other people's views; to help increase the resources of the country in the time of peace, and to be ready to protect its interests in time of war; and to temper his natural selfishness with greater civic generosity'.[96] The process did not mention race nor ethnicity, though some casual observers, at least, did see Boys' Week more generally as an indicator of improved race relations. A housewife, Mrs D. F. Dorsett, nostalgically compared the opening parade of Boys' Week to the famous World's Fair of

---

[96] 'Seek Chicago's best citizen of year 1950', *CT*, 12 Apr. 1925, and 'Best Chicago boy to be selected on character', *Chicago Herald and Examiner*, 23 Apr. 1925, *CBWF*, vol. 4, 1.

Figure 19. Reserve officers' training corps procession during Chicago Boys' Week Federation (1923)

Figure 20. Boys playing ping pong at the YMCA in Chicago (c. 1930s)

1893, when she believed it had similarly been the case that 'race mingled with race in harmony' – though African American leaders, such as Frederick Douglass and Ida B. Wells, would not have agreed with Dorsett's interpretation of the Fair.[97] One newspaper also described the 1925 Week as 'a big, hearty, entertaining, instructive display of Chicago boys – white and black, Catholic, Jew and Protestant, ragged and natty, good and not so good – at their best'.[98]

Keeping a more judicious track of race relations, however, was the *Chicago Defender*. During the 1929 Boys' Week, the paper reported on a parade that took place at the Soldier Field stadium, in which many thousands of boys participated. Headlining the article was a photo of a black boy leading a mostly white safety patrol of the Farragut Junior High School. In another article, titled 'Our Boys Form Honor Guard in Big Parade', the *Defender* described the various representatives of the African American community in Chicago marching down Michigan Avenue in 1924, drawn from schools, settlements, parks and cadet corps. The photo by-line of a troop of black cadets sardonically noted: 'If these young men would have attempted to enter such an event in the South they would have been placed under arrest and sentenced to the work farm or shot to death.'[99] These examples of progressive race relations, drawn from the consciously inclusive civic exercise of Boys' Week, should not mask the much deeper issues of structural racism in Chicago, nor how citizenship agencies could actively reinforce the colour line. Controversies surrounding the American Citizenship Foundation in the 1920s give some indication of the problem. The Foundation was explicitly nationalist, defining citizenship as '100 per cent Americanism', and emphasising patriotism and loyalty. It claimed to be open to all regardless of race or religion, yet, in practice, this was not the case. Questions were immediately asked of the Foundation in October 1926, when the *Defender* compared what it said it 'hoped to accomplish', such as teaching children American history and traditions, or counteracting subversive societal movements, with what it 'ought to accomplish': fighting discrimination and 'Jim Crowism in defense of our dark-skinned brothers who are denied full citizenship rights'.[100] When an invitation sent to a Chicago citizen for a Washington birthday dinner was retracted, seemingly after it was discovered that the invitee was black, the *Defender* considered its suspicions confirmed, and declared that the Foundation had 'showed its true colours on the race question'.[101]

Race structured citizenship both explicitly and implicitly. Some groups, most obviously the Ku Klux Klan, were unabashedly nativist and racist, and

---

[97] 'The inquiring reporter', CT, 19 May 1923, CBWF, vol. 1, 6. See Ida B. Wells (ed.), *The reason why the colored American is not in the World's Columbian Exposition*, Chicago, IL 1893.

[98] 'Exposition lets you into heart of Chicago' (1925), CBWF, vol. 4, 62.

[99] See 'Chicago honors her 700,000 boys', CD, 1 June 1929, 10, and 'Our boys form honor guard in big parade', CD, 31 May 1924, 10.

[100] 'American citizenship', CD, 16 Oct. 1926, 3.

[101] 'That citizenship foundation', CD, 19 Mar. 1927, 2.

aggressively against an inclusive citizenship. Others had a more complicated and often contradictory approach. The Chicago Boys' Club was, at first, seemingly happy to accept black members. In 1907, for example, 30 per cent of its boys were Italians, 30 per cent Jews, 15 per cent 'negroes', while only 3 per cent were 'Americans'. The remaining 12 per cent represented 'almost every nation on the earth'.[102] Yet, in 1917, only six years after opening, the Club closed its third location, arguing that the proximity of an African American community made it an 'undesirable' location.[103] The largest settlements mostly operated in white areas and, though their workers sometimes supported new settlements in African American neighbourhoods, they were not enthused about bringing blacks and whites together in the same space. 'All but a handful' in Chicago were for whites only, and the rest were for blacks 'exclusively'.[104] Settlements may have loosely supported the unification of a segmented society ideologically, though without taking a national stance on the issue, but, in practice, they often reinforced the colour line through their reluctance to extend their programmes to African Americans.[105] Little wonder, then, that associational civic leaders in Bronzeville organised their own network – the Chicago Council of Clubs – to try and tackle problems of youth citizenship in the segregated city. The Wabash YMCA was one of the most notable, instituted in 1914 to provide a place for young African American men away from the streets of the Black Metropolis. The YMCA supported a vibrant calendar of sporting events, while trying to sneak in religious study, and encouraged tournaments and competitions with white settlements and church groups. It did not 'hope by itself to solve the race problem', but to 'furnish a common meeting ground where men and boys of all races may meet and work out those principles common to all'.[106]

Manchester's youths were not ghettoised by race to the same extent, though there were specific clubs for Jewish lads and tacit understandings between Jewish and non-Jewish clubs about social and romantic mixing.[107] In their general aims, however, clubs and societies in Manchester still mirrored the attempts of Chicago to create a healthy and stable community. Physical training and sport for junior Co-operative Union members, for example, was 'designed to develop the students physically and mentally, and to encourage the team spirit'.[108] Some historians of youth culture have seen the decline of

---

[102] 'Membership in Chicago Boys' Club' (c. 1907), Chicago Boys and Girls Club records, 1901–69, folder 1, box 1, MSS lot C.

[103] Short history of the Chicago Boys' Club (1917), folder 2, ibid.

[104] Philpott, The slum and the ghetto, 274–5, 346.

[105] See Elisabeth Lasch-Quinn, Black neighbors: race and the limits of reform in the American settlement house movement, 1890–1945, Chapel Hill, NC 1993.

[106] 'Executive secretary report' (22 Jan 1926), 6.CY, YMCA Wabash Records, UIC. For the Chicago Council of Clubs see newspaper clippings in '1936–1938 scrapbook'.

[107] Kadish, A good Jew and a good Englishman.

[108] The Co-operative Union Limited, Continued education for junior Co-operative employees: an account of the classes attended by junior employees in Manchester, Manchester 1929, 7.

moral education and parallel proliferation of games and sports as a sign of both the waning influence of clubs and the lack of importance given to character training and citizenship.[109] On the contrary, this shift actually signified the importance of health as a primary attribute of citizenship, and an evolution of older citizenship ideas that had emphasised the individual to one that emphasised the collective. As Robert Snape has argued, social thinking on voluntarism in the Edwardian and interwar years – influenced by Thomas Hill Green – had shifted away from Victorian ideals. Before, it had been common to see social work as 'helping the deserving individual'; now, such action would be 'for the good of the community as a whole'. Leisure, especially, was a key site through which voluntary associations could achieve this goal with youths.[110] At the same time, the provision of activities that were less clearly 'moralistic' was an implicit recognition that youths were different from before the War – more 'independent' and less susceptible to direct imposed citizenship education.[111]

The combination of these shifts can clearly be seen at work in Manchester. The Jewish Lads' Brigade, for example, still encouraged self-discipline as part of its desire to acculturate young people into mainstream life, but explained in 1926 that it was because that restraint encouraged a general 'harmony' so 'all may march in unison': the 'collective effort alone' mattered.[112] Communal citizenship was also clear in the activities of the Co-operative Society of Manchester, which argued that 'the energy and fire of adolescence' could only find expression in cooperativity, reflecting, more broadly, their belief that cooperation should replace individualism and competition.[113] By employing popular recreations, clubs created an environment where a collective yet competitive spirit, the key to a productive workforce, could be generated under the watchful eyes of association leaders. The Grove House Club, for example, organised dances and concerts for both girls and boys. Chess, draughts, dominoes and other table games were played regularly in local leagues. To gain access to these popular pursuits, new members had to be examined by a medical officer. Each boy had one hour of physical training every week, where he took part in drill, gymnastics or physical games (*see* Figure 21).[114] Access to popular leisure was thus dependent on fulfilling certain responsibilities of health. An ethos of collectivism and community for youths in Britain beyond the boys' and lads' clubs was also apparent in the Band of Hope temperance movement and in popular boys' magazines.[115]

---

[109] Fowler, *The first teenagers*, 159, 141.

[110] Snape, *Leisure, Voluntary action and social change*, 73.

[111] Tebbutt, *Being boys*, 22.

[112] 'What a game' (1927), 6–9, Jewish Lads' Brigade, Grove House Club correspondence.

[113] H. J. Twigg, *Junior co-operators and their organisation*, Manchester 1923, 10; Co-operative Union Ltd, *Ten year plan for Co-operative education*, Manchester 1935, 18.

[114] 'Annual report' (1928), 6–7, Grove House Club correspondence.

[115] Lilian Lewis Shiman, 'The Band of Hope movement: respectable recreation for

Figure 21. Youths in the gym of the Grove House Lads Club (c. 1937)

The usefulness of games, sport and festivals in both cities consisted of such leisure activity's ability to focus on health while moving away from individualist definitions of citizenship. Youths were now the building blocks of a collectively bonded society. In the crowded modern city, individualism was seen as being unsuitable, and cooperation its only possible replacement. A variety of voluntary agencies believed this, as did reformers and sociologists, and all worked towards broadly similar goals, shaping a new urban culture for youths. Yet, regardless of their efforts, by the 1930s they found their power waning. At the same time the state 'caught up', however, and increased its role in youth leisure and citizenship. Voluntary agencies now had the chance to both modify and collaborate with public bodies as the quest to create citizens continued.

The rise of the state and the limits of associations

It was impossible for associations to reach every youth in the city. A 1921 study in Chicago surveyed 297 agencies and calculated that, of the 325,000 boys in Chicago between the ages of ten and twenty, only 52,912 (16.2 per cent) were involved in organised recreation. Even this estimate was generous,

working-class children', *Victorian Studies* xvii/1 (1973), 69; Kelly Boyd, *Manliness and the Boys' Story paper in Britain: a cultural history, 1855–1940*, Basingstoke 2003, 70–101.

since the same boys were probably enrolled in more than one organisation. In general, this survey showed the problem of youth leisure in Chicago. In many neighbourhoods there were as many as 70,000 people to a square mile. Most lots had unsupervised rear buildings, and the usual playground was still the street. When the study concluded that 'no matter how many and how efficient the boys' clubs of the city are, they cannot do the whole job', it was an understatement.[116] Still, associations should be given their due. By the end of the 1930s, their reach was wide. Figures provided by the Chicago Recreation Commission investigation of five areas suggested that youth involvement in supervised recreation was now approximately 80 per cent of the eligible population. But, within Chicago, there were significant differences between neighbourhoods in the extent of supervised recreation. South Chicago, with its large black population, lacked recreational agencies and had the lowest participation, with 62.1 per cent of boys and 41.4 per cent of girls in 1938. Fuller Park, made up of various European ethnicities such as Polish, Italian, Irish and German, reached over 90 per cent of boys and 75 per cent of girls at some point during that year.[117] In general, associations still believed that they were successful in shaping youth culture. The Union League Boys' Clubs in Chicago, for example, noted how there was a 76 per cent decrease in juvenile crime after a year in operation in the district where the Boys' Club No. One was located.[118] Club No. Two had a similar success story, with a decrease of 68.1 per cent in neighbourhood delinquency after twenty months.[119]

Social agencies in Chicago, recognising their limitations, still looked to city government to help fulfil their aims. Playgrounds built during the 'child saving' movement of the late nineteenth and early twentieth century had already been taken over by local government. After campaigning by social settlement leaders such as Jane Addams and Charles Zueblin, the city government ensured its responsibility for urban playgrounds with the construction of the South Park system in 1903 – accommodating approximately 5,000,000 people every year in one of the most congested and impoverished immigrant areas of the city. By 1920 voluntary play organisations were overshadowed by the public school – a result that the play movement actually celebrated.[120] The Chicago Association of Commerce could contrast the situation in 1905, when the city council operated seven playgrounds, with an annual expenditure of $23,000, with that of 1925, when it controlled twenty-two municipal playgrounds, seventy-two small parks, four bathing beaches, four sanatoriums, the Municipal Pier,

---

[116] Chicago Council of Social Agencies, *Preliminary inquiry into boys' work in Chicago*, 8–9, 24.

[117] Chicago Recreation Commission, *Recreation and delinquency*, 154.

[118] Grant, *Fight for a city*, 221.

[119] 'A special study of the boy situation in Chicago', 16.

[120] Cavallo, *Muscles and morals*, 29, 30, 48.

twenty public baths and four public comfort stations, at an annual cost of $700,000.[121]

Parks, stadiums and the new municipal pier were there to convert boys from 'street-and-alley-time', offering enjoyable, safe and wholesome amusements.[122] Municipal parks and playgrounds were regulated, with physical instructors employed to give health information to children, and wardens to make sure that girls and boys did not 'mingle' without supervision.[123] Progressive reform may have stalled in some areas, such as political corruption, but achievements in the creation of a civic welfare state, and one that actively shaped youth culture, arguably continued well into the 1920s and 1930s.[124] Associations did not just abandon the child to local government initiatives, however. Civic groups and municipal authorities treated the welfare of children as a joint concern, and often worked in tandem. When the 1930s depression hit, the Montefiore School, for example, claimed that it was 'impossible to discuss all of the social agencies' that had worked with the school: general organisations such as the United Charities; women's interest groups such as the Chicago Woman's Club; specific youth associations such as the YMCA; and settlements such as the Chicago Commons.[125]

In Manchester, in contrast, attendance at some clubs stagnated. Club officials often blamed the high cost to its members – especially during economic depression. The 1st Broughton Troop of Boy Scouts, for example, conceded in 1926 that the entrance fee was putting boys off and consequently halved it.[126] Despite the broadening of Scouting from its middle-class base before 1914 into a diverse movement, one that attempted to attract working-class boys by embracing elements of mass leisure and culture as a 'conservative modernity', financial considerations were still important.[127] In many respects associations were fighting a losing battle and unregulated leisure in the city continued to grow in popularity. In 1928 the Hulme Lads' Club acknowledged that the club struggled to compete with the cinema and moaned bitterly that 'boys seemed to be able to find enough money for these entertainments but would not keep up their Club subscriptions'.[128] The Ancoats Lads' Club shared their view and lamented that Lads' Clubs 'nowadays must be up-to-date if they

---

[121] 'Survey of public improvements', in Chicago Association of Commerce, *Survey of Chicago*, 17.

[122] W. McAndrew, 'Twenty years progress of the public schools', ibid. 11.

[123] City of Chicago Bureau of Parks, *Playgrounds and bathing beaches, rules and regulations*, Chicago, IL 1926.

[124] See chapter 6 below.

[125] Chicago Board of Education, *5th annual report of Montefiore School, 1933–34*, Chicago, IL 1934, 25.

[126] 'Minutes', 14 Apr. 1926, 1st Broughton troop of boy scouts, Lower Broughton, the Ascension, MCA, GB127.L154/5/5/2.

[127] For the evolution of the Scouts in this period see Proctor, *On my honour*.

[128] 'Minutes', 3 Apr. 1928, 52, Hulme Lads' Club, box 2, GB127.M130.2345.

are in any way to be a counter attraction to the growing and not too elevating influence of the cinema'.[129]

Sunday Schools especially suffered. In the late 1920s the Lancashire Congregational Union all but admitted defeat, describing a loss of hope and initiative. Of particular concern was the fact that, in the county, they had seen a decrease of 20,000 scholars between 1907 and 1926. Religious leaders had not only to compete with the attractions of the modern city, but also with growing, though uneven, secularisation in the interwar period, which limited the power of religious elites to regulate leisure time.[130] Optimistic volunteers in Manchester still believed that their activities were worthwhile, however. The Manchester Citizens' Association in 1928, for example, eagerly reported a comment from the police that the neighbourhood had been 'much quieter' with 'less trouble' since the Club opened.[131] Still, other observers in Manchester continued to have a more damning view of the efforts of associations. In their study of Hulme, the sociologists Moore and James concluded that existing clubs only reached a small proportion of the population, occupied only a small percentage of leisure time and filled that time with too trivial activities for their practical results to be effective.[132] Even when youths did participate in the activities of associations they often did so on their own terms instead of in accord with the 'lofty ideals' of club leaders, making organised leisure work for them rather than any broader societal purpose.[133]

Only a minority of young people thus participated in youth organisations, but far more came into contact with the school, despite the limitations of education provision in Britain. In Manchester, the local government directly took over many of the functions of associational culture.[134] In 1934 the Hulme Lads' Club realised that 'the State, Municipalities, and other bodies for school children' had superseded them, and instead began to focus its energies on the young adult worker.[135] The Evening Play Centres movement – which originated at the Passmore Edwards Settlement in London in 1897 – provides a comprehensive example of the ascension of local government at the expense of voluntary associational culture. In 1904 the London County Council recognised the value of providing an alternative for children who would otherwise

[129]   Fowler, *The first teenagers*, 140.
[130]   'Young People's Committee' (c. late 1920s), Zion United Reformed Church, MCA, GB127.M187/24. See Jeremy Morris, 'The strange death of Christian Britain: another look at the secularization debate', *HJ* xlvi/4 (2003), 963–76.
[131]   Manchester Citizen's Association, 'Report for 1928'.
[132]   James and Moore, 'Adolescent leisure in a working-class district', 145.
[133]   Tebbutt, *Being boys*, 97.
[134]   This reflected the increasing problems of corruption and lack of funding to schools in Chicago, compounded especially by the Depression: M. J. Herrick, *The Chicago schools: a social and political history*, Beverley Hills, CA 1971, 188–215.
[135]   'Annual report for the year ended 30 Jun. 1934', 5, Hulme Lads' Club, box 5.

be tempted by street gangs and formed seven centres across the city. When juvenile crime seemingly rose during the First World War, central government empowered the Board of Education in 1917 to give grants to Local Education Authorities for the formation of more centres.[136] The Education Committee of Manchester's city council, 'regardful of the wider training of future citizens', took full advantage of these grants and created twenty-one centres in congested working-class districts, such as Ancoats and Miles Platting, by 1925.[137] Open four evenings each week from September to March, and three evenings March to June, they replicated the environment of lads' clubs, and concentrated on self-reliance, self-control and the rational use of leisure time. Above all, they provided 'enjoyable physical and mental recreation free from the rough and tumble and aimlessness of play in confined streets': the defining aspect of youth citizenship training in interwar Britain.[138] Centres were a cooperative endeavour of the central state, which provided the funding; the local state, which gave buildings and staff; and associations, which offered volunteers. The movement had some success. In 1916, before the first centre was opened, 889 cases were brought before the juvenile courts; by 1924 this had fallen to 258 cases – though, naturally, wartime conditions were significantly different. In 1918 there were already 6,552 children registered, rising to a peak of 14,142 in 1924. Even so, the proportion of those registered represented only 5.3 per cent of children attending the elementary schools in 1918, and 12.4 per cent in 1924.[139]

Beyond the play centres there were other examples of the city council working with established associations. The Co-operative Union of Manchester, for example, was particularly successful in steering its relationship with schools towards citizenship training. Beginning in 1921, the Co-operative Union organised continuing education for boys and girls aged between fourteen and eighteen who were employed in the wholesale and retail trade, as well as in offices, banks, insurance, factories and elsewhere. The emphasis in the classes was 'not only on intellectual advancement and commercial and indus-trial efficiency, but more especially on the development of character'. Classes provided a 'training for life' where 'all ... faculties are developed – our bodies pure and fit, our minds keen and alert, and our creative spirits fine and firm'. Classes were organised by the Manchester Education Committee, which provided teachers and equipment, and were held in YMCA buildings. The Co-operative societies allowed their employees to attend for one half-day of four hours, or, in a few cases, two half-days of three hours each and paid travelling expenses. For the first course, in autumn 1921, 214 boys and girls were enrolled;

---

[136] Janet Penrose Trevelyan, *Evening play centres for children: the story of their origin and growth*, London 1920, pp. xi, 3.

[137] Manchester Education Committee, *General survey: 1914–24*, Manchester 1926, 71–2.

[138] Manchester Education Committee, 'The programme' (19 May 1919), 290, in *Epitome of Proceedings of Committees* 36 (1918–19), MCA, 352.042.M12.

[139] Manchester Education Committee, *General survey*, 78.

by 1929 this had increased to 750.[140] Through a sharing of civic responsibility between government, industry and associational culture, attempts were made to create a citizen who met the desires of all three: healthy, enterprising and community-orientated.

During the interwar period a wide network of different agencies used similar techniques to encourage good citizenship in youths. At the heart of their activities was a gendered understanding of how boys and girls interacted in the modern city and through the new and old opportunities for leisure and social mixing that urban life provided. In some ways this was simply a continuation of the older desire to maintain or regulate both morality and health: an under-standing that, to secure the future of the nation, youth had to be guarded from temptation. It was also, however, an evolution of those pre-1914 years. Now, categories of masculinity and femininity seemed to be in flux. Young women, with more disposable income and the degree of freedom that could bring, seemed to be challenging conventional social mores. Young men, on the other hand, were in danger of being 'feminised' – whether by the continued rise of mass leisure or the demoralising experience of unemployment. Long-standing concerns with health and morality combined with the changed landscape of gender relations both during and after the First World War to renew the emphasis on pragmatically reforming urban culture. Health and fitness remained important but was joined by a desire for comradely communities that could overcome individualistic mindsets.

Undoubtedly, the creators of youth activities experienced varying degrees of success in this pursuit. In Manchester, some organisations struggled with both financing and declining attendance, as the lure of new forms of leisure proved too strong. But new optimistic associations were still formed, and youth reformers could rightly claim to be an important part of civic culture in the 1930s. In Chicago, the interwar period saw an expansion of youth-orientated organisations, reflecting both the tumultuous reality and public opinion of the city during the 'Jazz Age' of the 1920s and the severe depression decade that followed. The inability of these associations, and the events that they created, to overcome the issues of unequal provision based on racial neighbourhoods, was their biggest failure. And undeniably, in neither Manchester nor Chicago, could civic associations claim to have reached the majority of young people: alternative temptations were simply too strong. In both the US and Britain the 1920s and 1930s saw the continued development of a particularly urban leisure culture – one that encompassed sport, music, dancing and the cinema. Associations could try and adapt, adjusting their programmes to provide similar leisure opportunities, but it was always going to be a difficult competition.

Youth was still on the citizenship agenda at the end of the 1930s. Under the New Deal in the US, agencies such as social settlements and the YMCA

---

[140]   The Co-operative Union Ltd, *Continued education for Junior Co–operatives*, 2–3.

received a boost to their citizenship activities. Local initiative became only one factor in a much larger field of policy as federal government intervened in cities. The growing central state also dealt directly with youth, through initiatives such as the National Youth Administration, which attempted to protect democracy and national security by encouraging the decentralised teaching of citizenship education.[141] In Britain, with the realisation that war was on the horizon, the 1937 Physical Training and Recreation Act created local committees to direct central government funding towards both Local Education Authorities and voluntary associations that supplied recreational facilities. Municipal government was gradually either working alongside associations or taking over their functions, supported by the central state. The next chapter maintains this focus on the interplay of associations and the state but moves away from adolescents towards adults and welfare. As central/federal and local government provision grew, new opportunities for urban voluntary organisations emerged. In Chicago, this process was particularly apparent during the exceptional conditions of the Great Depression and the ensuing New Deal legislation of the 1930s. Old organisations, struggling for money and desperate for volunteers, were rejuvenated and brought further into a cooperative sphere of citizenship creation. Now enabled with federal money and workers, they were the first line of defence in the fight to quell any signs of social or political unrest brought on by the depressed conditions. In Britain, the rise of the state was a long-term and piecemeal process which shifted the responsibilities of local associations. As it did, however, it created new opportunities for the creation of urban citizenship – as Manchester's experience reveals. In both countries, therefore, the distribution of welfare – despite its increasingly centralised administration – was a key area in which urban citizenship was shaped.

---

[141] Reiman, *The New Deal and American youth.*

6

Civic Culture and Welfare

Growing intervention in youth culture reflected wider shifts in how cities and their inhabitants were being governed by the interwar period. In Britain, the early part of the twentieth century saw the consolidation of an increasingly interventionist state with the expansion of government into the 'social sphere'. Liberal reforms set new standards in areas such as pensions (1908), employment insurance (1911) and schools (1906–7). A few years later the demands of 'total war' encouraged more central expansion and socio-economic planning. Interwar legislation grew unevenly, disrupted by economic instability and frequent switches between governing parties, but policy continued to be centralised in new and powerful departments. City councils could consequently find their powers restricted, regulated or taken away entirely – such as with the Unemployment Act in 1934, which created a national system for relief. But the period also saw a last flowering of municipal government. Local councils reached the height of their spending and administrative power, retained most of their municipalised utilities and were encouraged by central aid to enter new areas of social welfare. Signs of the rise of the post-1945 welfare state, then, were apparent – but centralisation was a complex process, and never totally assured.[1]

In the US national myth-making and exceptionalism has often downplayed federal ascendancy. Until relatively recently, according to William Novak, the American past has been seen as one of limited government and an individualist quest for civil, economic and social freedom. The American state however, he argued, has always been 'more powerful, capacious, tenacious, interventionist, and redistributive' than commonly believed.[2] The New Deal moment in the mid-1930s, which saw significant social and economic reform across all areas of life, can mask a longer history of state intervention. In the nineteenth

---

[1] For a long view see Pat Thane, *Foundations of the welfare state* (1982), Harlow 1996, and Bernard Harris, *The origins of the British welfare state: social welfare in England and Wales, 1800–1945*, Basingstoke 2004. For the central/local relationship see John Davis, 'Central government and the towns', in Daunton, *Cambridge urban history of Britain*, iii. 259–86. For urban government see W. Hamish Fraser, 'From civic gospel to municipal socialism', in Derek Fraser (ed.), *Cities, class and communication*, Hemel Hempstead 1990, and Barry M. Doyle, 'The changing functions of urban government: councillors, officials and pressure groups', in *Cambridge urban history of Britain*, iii. 287–314.

[2] Novak, 'The myth of the "weak" American state'. Novak credits historical sociologists, such as Theda Skocpol, and political scientists, such as Stephen Skowronek, for beginning the process in the 1980s and 1990s of bringing the state back into American analysis.

century the federal government had frequently acknowledged responsibility for citizens affected by unforeseen disasters and had distributed emergency relief.[3] The First World War also had an unprecedented impact on the expansion of federal government at the local level, as the need to intervene in areas such as 'enemy alien' registration, war bond raising and food rationing were central to achieving victory. Before the war, annual federal budgets never reached $800,000,000; during the conflict, expenditure averaged $43,000,000 per day.[4] Federal spending in the 1920s was low in comparison to the unprecedented war years, but still higher than what had come before. More important was the continuing shift in attitude: federal policies in the 1920s solidified and extended the principles of intervention that had been catalysed by mobilisation for war.[5] A similar story can be seen for local government. Historians such as Daniel Amsterdam now draw attention to the consolidation of a 'civic welfare state' – led by businessmen and local government – that invested in moral, physical and cultural reform throughout the 1920s.[6]

The growth of local and national government in the early twentieth century raises the question of how voluntary societies and civic associations, the engine of reform activity and citizenship creation in the nineteenth century, responded to these entrants into their sphere of activity. In Britain, earlier histories characterised the welfare state as a gradual triumph of collectivism over individualism, and the negation of the voluntary sector's role as a service provider. In the last few decades, though, this teleological story has been given more nuance. Historians now highlight a 'mixed economy of welfare', where the voluntary sector worked with government in a co-constitutive relationship to deliver services. Charitable or philanthropic bodies could disband when the state replaced their functions, but many evolved while often maintaining their traditions and ideology.[7] In the US, as the voluntary sector moved away from 'moralizing amateurism' and toward scientific 'business models and methods' in the Progressive Era, a range of charitable or philanthropic organisations continued to provide social services. Local, state-level and federal government policy was geared towards promoting cooperation between the state, business

---

[3]   See Michele Landis Dauber, *The sympathetic state: disaster relief and the origins of the American welfare state*, Chicago, IL 2013.

[4]   Adam J. Hodges, *World War I and urban order: the local class politics of national mobilization*, Basingstoke 2016, 1–2.

[5]   Randall G. Holcombe, 'The growth of the federal government in the 1920s', *Cato Journal* xvi/2 (1996), 175–99; Hodges, *World War I and urban order*, 8. See also Marc Allen Eisner, *From warfare state to welfare state: World War I, compensatory state building, and the limits of the modern order*, University Park, PA 2000.

[6]   Amsterdam, *Roaring metropolis*. For examples of the civic welfare state in Chicago see the Chicago Association of Commerce, *Survey of Chicago*.

[7]   Geoffrey Finlayson, 'A moving frontier: voluntarism and the state in British social welfare, 1911–1949', *Twentieth Century British History* 1/2 (1990), 183–206; David Gladstone (ed.), *Before Beveridge: welfare before the welfare state*, London 1999; Matthew Hilton and James McKay (eds), *The ages of voluntarism: how we got to the big society*, Oxford 2011.

and voluntary sectors.[8] After a boom period of new associations in the mid- to late nineteenth century their number remained stable enough to maintain an important place in interwar civic culture and could even grow during times of increased federal government activity as public and private organisation became interdependent.[9]

Previous chapters in this book have demonstrated how widely civic coalitions operated in Manchester and Chicago. This chapter concentrates on how fluctuating relationships of power created new possibilities for shaping urban citizenship through the distribution of welfare. The first section focuses on Manchester, and the local charitable associations that worked with the government to emphasise the moral obligations of locally- or nationally-provided unemployment relief. Older Victorian self-help organisations maintained their purpose of encouraging working-class respectability, but they were joined by new groups in the interwar period that developed a more holistic approach to creating urban communities. The second section moves to Chicago to show how associations utilised new sources of state funding during the New Deal to prolong traditional forms of citizenship education and community creation. Old associations may have struggled to articulate a convincing reform ideology, but their recreational and social work was still a vital part of civic culture. In a period in both countries of unemployment and urban unrest, whether real or perceived, the question of community and citizenship became paramount. The chapter ends with a case study of social working-class housing: a moment when the state and associations collaborated and the quest for better citizenship reached its ultimate expression in welfare architecture. In both the US and Britain the city was not just the site of welfare interactions between the individual and the state, but an important factor that shaped their articulation.

Obligation and citizenship: the evolution of 'the gift' in Manchester

To understand the evolution of civic welfare in Britain in the interwar years, and the citizenship discourse that circulated through it, we must go back to the nineteenth-century shock city. As industrialisation and urbanisation proliferated, urban spaces became physically segregated by class.[10] New statistical

---

[8]   See Peter Dobkin Hall, *Inventing the nonprofit sector and other essays on philanthropy, voluntarism, and nonprofit organizations*, Baltimore, MD 1992, 15, 53–57.

[9]   Theda Skocpol, Marshall Ganz and Ziad Munson, 'A nation of organizers: the institutional origins of civic voluntarism in the United States', *American Political Science Review* xciv/3 (2000), 527–46, and Theda Skocpol, 'The Tocqueville problem: civic engagement in American democracy', *Social Science History* xxi/4 (1997), 455–79.

[10]   Engels, *The condition of the working-class in England*, and other contemporary accounts such as Léon Faucher, *Manchester in 1844: its present position and future prospects* (1844), London 1969, and William Cooke-Taylor, *Notes of a tour in the manufacturing districts of*

approaches flourished as the middle classes tried to understand urban society and provide information that would enable its improvement. Reports shaped analytical categories – crime, ill-health, pauperism, delinquency, degeneracy – and associated them with the city. A fundamental part of this 'social science' movement was judgements made about the lives and behaviour of the working classes. Questions about 'the physical and moral conditions of the people', as the Manchester and Salford Sanitary Association put it in 1855, were articulated through an understanding of how people related to their environment: how they could be corrupted by it, or indeed contribute to its corruption.[11] By the final third of the century, urban conditions became mainstream news – and even entertainment – as muckraking journalists exposed the state of the nation to scandalised readers.[12]

As the level of urban understanding expanded rapidly, so too did the opportunity for civic action. Urban investigators – and the associations that they spawned – created a moral agenda for charitable giving. Civic associations, such as the District Provident and Charity Organisation Society of Manchester and Salford (DPS) (formed 1833), or the Manchester Surgical Aid Society (formed 1897), had a distinctive understanding of the purpose of welfare. Advice on frugality, or the occasional donation of money or medical appliances, was not an acknowledgement of the inherent inequalities of capitalism that found their ultimate expression in the new 'shock cities', but the means through which the poor could be given the tools of self-improvement. Above all, the purpose of charity was to maintain moral responsibility in both donor and recipient. The 'gift' of welfare implied a personal relationship of voluntary sacrifice, prestige and superiority for the giver, and obligation and good behaviour for the receiver. This was a tiered sense of citizenship: a product of the fear that the 'demoralised' poor would claim that which they were not entitled to, thus corrupting them further. The mechanics of this relationship depended on the ability to observe and control, so, with increasing suburbanisation and the separation of the classes towards the end of the century, the 'gift' was 'deformed': the direct relationships of giving became harder to maintain, and charity supposedly lost its power as a form of social control.[13]

Lancashire, London 1844. For context see Alan Kidd, 'Introduction: the middle class in nineteenth-century Manchester', in Alan Kidd and Kenneth Roberts (eds), *City, class and culture: studies of social policy and cultural production in Victorian Manchester*, Manchester 1985, 1-25.

[11] Manchester and Salford Sanitary Association, *Public health considered in reference to the physical and moral condition of the people*, Manchester 1855. See Felix Driver, 'Moral geographies: social science and the urban environment in mid-nineteenth century England', *Transactions of the Institute of British Geographers* xiii/3 (1988), 275-87.

[12] See Lees, *Cities perceived*, ch. v.

[13] Gareth Stedman Jones draws on the sociologist Marcel Mauss: *Outcast London: a study in the relationship between classes in Victorian society* (1971), London 2013, ch. xiii. See also George Campbell Gosling, 'Rethinking the gift relationship in the British history of voluntary action', *Historische Zeitschrift*, forthcoming.

Changes in the ideology of welfare and the role of the state, however, gradually combined to force an evolution of 'the gift'. From the beginning, the relationship between civic associations and local government was one of partnership and guidance, with a clear overlap in membership between the two. By the beginning of the twentieth century the balance in this relationship was beginning to tip. With the rise of 'the social' understanding of the role of government, and pioneering social science research that sought to understand the degree and causes of poverty, the nature of pauperism was reconceptualised. The boundary between 'deserving' and 'undeserving', which had provided the framework for nineteenth-century charity, now blurred. Poverty was beginning to be acknowledged, at least partly, as not totally the fault of the poor but of the environment created by the capitalist systems that governed their lives. Social settlements sought to remake the environment of the poor and working classes through community leisure organisation, but there was a broader acknowledgement that it was the state – both local and central – that had the power to raise living standards.[14] Into the early part of the twentieth century, central reform in pensions, schooling and insurance was articulated as a way not just to combat the misery of poverty, but also to pacify labour tensions and ensure British imperial power. Even before this central reform, results at the local level were impressive. Commentators did not fail to recognise the way that 'municipal socialism' had crept into and cemented itself in political discourse in the late nineteenth and early twentieth centuries, even if it did so under different guises. As the Fabian Sidney Webb had noted in 1889, 'The "practical man", oblivious of any theory of the Social Organism or general principles of social organisation' had been 'forced by the necessities of the time into an ever-deepening collectivist channel' by unwittingly using the many municipally owned and run services.[15]

This expansion of the apparatus of the municipal and central state meant that some of the roles that had formed the field of action for local associations were being taken away. In 1908, for example, Manchester's public health department took over the role of health visitors, depriving the Manchester and Salford Ladies' Health Society (1862) of a long-held purpose.[16] The National Insurance Act (1911) had a similar effect. The legislation provided some protection against sickness and debilitation and distributed its money through private 'approved societies', but Manchester's Provident Dispensaries Association, which had used worker subscriptions to pay for medical care, was not one of these societies. As its members left for other approved societies, the Association lamented the 'disastrous effect' of the act; all of its branches had

[14] See Vernon, *Modern Britain*, 268–91, and David Englander, *Poverty and poor law reform in Britain: from Chadwick to Booth, 1834–1914*, London, 1998, 65–78.

[15] Sidney Webb, *Socialism in England*, London 1890, 116–17.

[16] Anderson, *How Manchester is managed*, 43.

171

shut down by 1917.[17] Further legislation during the Great Depression extended and redefined the statutory benefits rights of the unemployed at the expense of approved societies. Local associations were facing difficult financial circumstances anyway. The DPS, for example, was struggling by the 1920s due to a lack of subscribers and the effects of an unstable economy. 'Month by month', according to the Anglican canon of St Peter's Church (Salford), Peter Green, it sank 'further and further into debt'. Writing in 1922, he blamed a general downturn in societal responsibility for the poor fortunes of societies, arguing that 'there was not the spirit of giving that there used to be a generation ago'.[18] Middle-class flight from the city into the suburbs and countryside over the previous thirty or so years had removed the problems of poverty from sight and often from mind as well.[19]

At any rate, by the 1930s the shift in power was clear at both the local and national level. For some authorities, such as Manchester's, the interwar period was one of consolidation and extension of the autonomous and progressive approach usually attributed to the local council of the second half of the nineteenth century.[20] But this by no means signalled a death of purpose for voluntary associations. Social policy and public health administration did become more institutionalised in government departments and professional groups, but this was a long-term process. Associations were also capable of reformulating their mid-Victorian social-scientific culture for new circumstances. The First World War, for example, created new areas of obligation by spurring 'the philanthropic conscience' and bringing volunteers into closer cooperation with national and local authorities. [21] The DPS found itself distributing funds from another charity, the Royal Patriotic Fund Corporation, to widows and children of injured or killed servicemen. The Soldiers' and Sailors' Families' Association also turned to the DPS to register their names and addresses as applicants for assistance, encouraging a new wave of volunteers. The city council even provided sixty of its own clerks to undertake work for the Society during the war, intensifying the existing relationship between the association and the local government.[22] This cooperation between charities and statutory authorities was apparent across Britain, and grew throughout the interwar period.[23]

[17]   'Annual report of the Manchester and Salford Provident Dispensaries Association' (1913), The Family Welfare Association of Manchester Ltd, MCA, GB127.M294/1/7; 'Annual report of the Manchester and Salford District Provident Society', The Family Welfare Association of Manchester Ltd, [hereinafter cited as 'DPS annual report'] (1917), MCA, GB127.M294/1/7.

[18]   'DPS annual report' (1920), 9; (1922), 3.

[19]   Katharine Chorley, *Manchester made them*, London 1950, 137–9.

[20]   Doyle, 'The changing functions of urban government', 289; Charlotte Wildman, 'Urban transformation in Liverpool and Manchester, 1918-1939', *HJ* lv/1 (2012), 143.

[21]   Harris, 'Political thought and the welfare state', 121; Finlayson, 'A moving frontier', 194.

[22]   'DPS annual report' (1914), 9–11; (1915), 8–11.

[23]   Thane, *Foundations of the welfare state*, 161.

For reformers interested in citizenship, the shift in conceptualising poverty and the role of the state also raised new questions. Firstly, how could the middle-class volunteers of civic organisations survive the diminishing of their own responsibility as the state increased its purview in almost every area of urban life? As one member of the Surgical Aid Society worried in the early 1930s, if the state assumed 'responsibility for all forms of medical treatment' it could 'result in a lessening of the individual's moral responsibility for helping his fellow man'.[24] The importance given to participation in voluntary action as a duty in a democratic society thus lasted until at least the 1940s.[25] Secondly, how could good citizenship be maintained in the beneficiaries of the proto-welfare state when the giving of benefits or relief was now so centralised and impersonal? In 1922 the DPS committee argued that 'one longs to be assured that character, self-reliance, and the sense of individual responsibility, have not been materially sapped by State control'.[26] This seemed to confirm Sidney Webb's prognosis that, as public authorities acquired extensive powers, there would be a simple two-way relationship between the state and the individual, leaving no role for voluntary associations.[27] As one member responded to the report at the Annual Meeting of the DPS, it was not 'a healthy stage of things to contemplate' for the DPS and its 'kindred organisations'. So, a new tack had to be taken: they had to 'do their best to develop a better feeling in those among whom they worked'.[28]

Voluntarist citizenship for the middle classes now partly became bound up with a responsibility to ward off the excesses of welfare relief: a reawakening and reimagining of the moralising of the Victorian 'gift', but where the state was the main giver rather than charitable individuals or bodies. This could be seen in the ideology of the National Council of Social Service, which believed that the relationship between the state and associations gave opportunities to enact 'the public good' and encourage participatory citizenship in the beneficiaries of welfare.[29] The Manchester University Settlement welcomed the rise of the state, but similarly still saw its own role as working with urban inhabitants to 'instil a belief in health, beauty and cleanliness'.[30] In this way

[24]   'Annual report' (1934), 3, Surgical Aid Society, Manchester Branch, Family Welfare Association of Manchester LTD, MCA, GB127.M294/7/2.

[25]   Jane Lewis, 'The voluntary sector in the mixed economy of welfare', in Gladstone, *Before Beveridge*, 14.

[26]   'DPS annual report' (1922), 6.

[27]   Richard Rodger and Robert Colls, 'Civil society and British cities', in Robert Colls and Richard Rodger (eds), *Cities of ideas: civil society and urban governance in Britain, 1800–2000*, Farnham 2004, 16.

[28]   'DPS annual report' (1922), 5.

[29]   S. D. Adderley, 'Bureaucratic conceptions of citizenship in the voluntary sector (1919–1939): the case of the National Council of Social Service', unpubl. PhD diss. Cardiff 2002, 4.

[30]   Manchester and District Regional Survey Society, *Social Studies of a Manchester City Ward*, No., 14. The Society was affiliated to the Manchester University Settlement.

a growing social democratic notion of citizenship, understood as the social rights of government, was mixed with older liberal notions of obligation and improvement. For urban associational culture this meant local intervention in the 'clientelist relationship between the citizen and the state'.[31] Instead of giving 'merely his money', the responsibility of the social worker, as the DPS recognised in 1926, was to provide 'more and more of himself, his time and his sympathy'. In the annual report for 1929 this theme was elaborated further. 'The State', argued the committee, 'can only be an impersonal and rigid kind of helper ... the voluntary organisation must and does continue to render indispensable service because of its elasticity and, what is of paramount importance, in a human way.' Voluntary societies, then, could suggest 'to the mind of many an applicant the ways he can best help himself: and to do this involves much more than filling up an application form, however complete the details'.[32] A further depersonalising of 'the gift' would be the result without this relationship – and good citizenship the victim.

The onset of depression in the late 1920s and early 1930s brought this approach to local citizenship into stark relief. While recognising that the State had 'stepped in to relieve the individual of many of his responsibilities', the DPS report for 1931 stated that 'many of the fundamental causes of distress are still existent'. At first, then, 'the work done by voluntary organisations' was 'proved to have been abundantly justified and would appear to-day to be more than ever necessary'.[33] The DPS consequently gave convalescent treatment to workers, arranged the provision of tools for men starting new jobs, gave short-term loans to those awaiting wages and distributed increasing amounts of private charity from forty-four different organisations.[34] But the appointment of the government's Unemployment Assistance Board in 1934, responsible for giving means-tested unemployment relief to those not qualified for benefit-based contributions, was a further cementing of state responsibility for the unemployed. This test disqualified certain categories of individuals, using old charitable distinctions of deserving and undeserving. As Geoffrey Finlayson has argued: 'the frontier of the state moved, but took voluntarist convictions with it'.[35] The DPS 'welcomed' the formation of the new Board, noting that 'the Society has always held that it is not primarily a "relief society"'. Instead, it wanted to 'encourage others to give wisely and constructively and to act for them; and also, to encourage applications to become self–supporting and independent'. With the 'huge relief-giving machinery conducted by the state and the local Corporations' the DPS could instead 'concentrate intensively

[31]   John Harris, 'State social work and social citizenship in Britain: from clientalism to consumerism', *British Journal of Social Work* **xxix**/1 (1999), 917.

[32]   'DPS annual report' (1926), 6; (1930), 7.

[33]   'DPS annual report' (1931), 6, 9.

[34]   'DPS annual report' (1933), 8–9

[35]   Finlayson, 'A moving frontier', 192.

upon constructive case-work': the key point of contact between the benefactor and recipient, and process through which citizenship values of obligation were received.[36] The annual report of the Pilgrim Trust in 1936 could thus claim that unemployment had led to 'unparalleled activity' of a social kind to the extent that 'the state's efforts were dwarfed by those of a voluntary character'.[37]

Civic welfare retained its nineteenth-century basis as a partnership between local association and government, but was now increasingly national as well as urban. Indeed, it was the growth of central government that necessitated the role of the local association. If the state acted as the impersonal financial backer, it also provided new opportunities for voluntary associations to thrive and to continue to set the agenda for moral guidance. The Manchester and Salford Council of Social Service (MSCSS) epitomised this shift in the first half of the century and provides a useful example of the new reality of voluntarism, governmental cooperation and citizenship. It was formed in 1919 following communication between the National Council of Social Services and local government in Manchester and Salford, with the primary remit of ensuring the 'local organisation of social work' in the context of a 'complex modern life'. Specifically, it tried to ensure a minimal overlap in voluntary work, and strong communication between public and private agencies, to make the social welfare system of Manchester an integrated whole. It also helped to 'foster developments likely to raise the standard and promote the welfare of the community, and to receive and administer funds for the general well-being'.[38] Its purview was wide, with eighty-seven member organisations in 1920 covering a whole range of purposes and viewpoints. From its inception the MSCSS had strong ties with municipal government, and positions on the committee were filled by the mayor, other councillors and municipal administrators, as well as representatives from Manchester's churches and associations.

The practical relationship between government and association reflected what the social welfare theorist Elizabeth Macadam termed in 1934 the 'New Philanthropy'.[39] Rather than being the primary provider of welfare, the voluntary sector moved towards a role that complemented and supplemented the local and central state by being active in research and experimentation, identifying areas of concern, creating propaganda and articulating responses to problems. Associations now focused on specialised issues, while being organised through a coordinated body like the National Council of Social Service on the national level, or the MSCSS at the local. This relationship benefitted central government, because charitable organisations were cheaper than sole state

[36]   'DPS annual report' (1934), 5–6.

[37]   Finlayson, 'A moving frontier', 195.

[38]   'Annual report of Manchester and Salford Council of Social Service' (1920), 7–11, The Family Welfare Association of Manchester LTD, GB127.M294/15.

[39]   Elizabeth Macadam, *The new philanthropy: a study in the relations between the statutory and voluntary social services*, London 1934.

responsibility, yet it also enabled charities to maintain their own interests when costs were increasing.[40] Voluntary associations, in the nineteenth century, had led the way in developing an understanding of the nature of welfare and voluntarism and its relationship with citizenship. Though government began to take over some of these functions in the early twentieth century, a role still existed for these stakeholders to ensure what they saw as the ideological underpinnings of welfare distribution. As the DPS argued in 1929, 'State help can never possess that elasticity which is so essential in dealing effectively with human troubles, and it is just here where our Society, unencumbered by red tape, can step in to give just the right form of assistance at just the right moment.'[41] Undoubtedly the balance in the welfare mix had changed, and the state had taken on a larger role. But voluntary associations responded positively to new state initiatives and developed new functions when their own were taken over. At the end of the interwar period, therefore, while not as financially sound as before the First World War, voluntarism had adapted to the rise of the state and its welfare policies, expanding in the areas of character and citizenship building, and still played a vital role in the life of the city.

Urban welfare reform, especially in the opening decades of the twentieth century, did not take place in a vacuum. Government officials, technicians, engineers, scholars and reformers travelled extensively, and contributed to an international science of progressivism. The 'shock' problems that were so easily identifiable with cities such as Manchester became part of a wider discourse of urban intervention. Coalitions of reformers and municipal officials sought to implement socioeconomic change, and in some ways cemented a key role for local government – though without necessarily challenging the political or legal system of the country involved. Though an exchange of ideas, the direction of knowledge was more towards the US in the early twentieth century. In this period, American politics became 'peculiarly open to foreign models and imported ideas' and a progressive kind of social politics gathered steam.[42] Chicago, as a 'shock city' in need of reform, became a key site for this development.

New Deal – new citizens? Associational culture and the federal state in Chicago

As was the case with Manchester in Britain, it was the response during periods of rapid urbanisation that shaped the reform agenda in Chicago as it continued to evolve in the period after. As the city grew in size and stature in the final

---

[40]   Ibid. See Elizabeth Darling, '"Enriching and enlarging the whole sphere of human activities": the work of the voluntary sector in housing reform in inter-war Britain', in Lawrence and Mayer, *Regenerating England*, 149–78.

[41]   'DPS annual report' (1929), 6.

[42]   Rodgers, *Atlantic crossings*, 4.

third of the nineteenth century, two moments stood out. The Great Fire in 1871 was a point at which the whole nation reflected on the ramifications of urban growth. Widespread and sensationalised newspaper accounts, as Lisa Krissoff Boehm has described, presented Chicago as a place of both physical disaster and moral malaise. As a city seemingly without humility, where drunkenness, crime, class-mixing and sexual licentiousness could not be controlled, Chicago became a focal point for anti-urban feeling. At the same time, however, the disaster awoke a spirit of charity across the country, with local relief efforts combining into support that totalled millions of dollars. Back in Chicago, a narrative began to emerge of the city as a 'phoenix': ready to rise from the ashes to face and overcome all challenges.[43] Just over twenty years later the city faced its second major test – and at a time of self-celebration. In an example of how discourses of urban degeneration could travel across the West, W. T. Stead visited the city during the World's Columbian Exposition in 1893 and wrote about what he found. His *exposé* of vice and corruption, published the following year, accelerated a longer tradition of mid nineteenth-century associational culture reform movements, such as temperance and the abolition of slavery. In sensational terms he 'berated the city' and 'condemned it as a center of evil', reflecting, in a populist form, wider currents of anti-urban feeling in the final decades of the nineteenth century.[44] In the ten years after the Exposition, a variety of civic associations were formed, such as the Civic Federation (1894), the Municipal Voters League (1896) and the City Club of Chicago (1903). All aimed to improve the social, economic and political conditions of the city in some way and to energise the public conscience.

Chicago's experience reflected the central place of the city in Progressive Era debates about how best to secure the health and progress of the nation.[45] Movements for reform action had a divergent set of aims. Activist women saw Chicago as a 'city of homes' in which to rear children, with government responsible for social welfare and justice for all urban residents: a municipal and maternalistic welfare state instead of untrustworthy private enterprise.[46] Desires for a city that worked for its less well-off citizens, however, contrasted and conflicted with prominent business-oriented ideas of good government, which instead espoused a 'gospel of efficiency' where experts imposed scientific order on what they saw as a chaotic urban environment.[47] Local government was to be reclaimed from corrupt forces and transformed into a professional

---

[43] Boehm, *Popular culture and the enduring myth of Chicago*, 1–26.

[44] Ibid. 67–8; Stead, *If Christ came to Chicago!* See Conn, *Americans against the city*, 13–17.

[45] For a recent overview see Michael B. Kahan, 'Urban America' in Christopher M. Nichols and Nancy C. Unger, *A companion to the Gilded Age and Progressive Era*, Chichester 2017, 31–43.

[46] Maureen A. Flanagan, *Seeing with their hearts: Chicago women and the vision of the good city, 1871–1933*, Princeton, NJ 2002, at pp. 85–122.

[47] Robert G. Spinney, *City of big shoulders: a history of Chicago*, DeKalb, IL 2000, 147; Jaher, *The urban establishment*, 505–6.

corporation run by committed businessmen rather than extended as a welfare provider. Schemes such as the Chicago Plan, published in 1909 by the Commercial Club of Chicago, dominated the planning discourse in Chicago and reflected this divergence. Instead of improving access to recreational facilities, as female activists hoped, it was 'ultimately deficient in the human element' because it instead aimed for 'unequalled facilities for the easy, quick, and economic transaction of business'.[48]

Settlement houses, of which there were thirty-two by 1911, worked on a more local citizen-based level, most famously represented by Addams and Hull House. Voluntary settlement workers tried to improve the lives of urban inhabitants and immigrants through art, drama, music, public baths, baby care, job training and English classes. Though the national cultures of immigrants were sometimes recognised, reformers still hoped to 'liberate' communities, which they saw as helpless and transitory, from their inefficient and backward-looking 'ethnic religious and secular leadership'.[49] Settlement workers also investigated urban conditions and urged the abandonment of voluntarism in favour of using governmental power to correct injustice and create social democracy. Gradually the maelstrom of activity that defined the Progressive Era began to wane, however. Addams and other social settlement workers remained notable civic figures in Chicago but, as the scientific management model of professional social provision gained credence, amateur volunteerism became a less important part of direct services.[50] Proponents of municipal intervention viewed this positively because it suggested that city government had taken on responsibility for improved conditions: associations essentially existed 'for their own annihilation'.[51] But it also reflected other issues that civic reform organisations were facing. By the 1920s they had lost 'well-born' leadership, were struggling with nativist hostility towards ethnic minorities and organised labour and were considerably weaker than in previous periods. Many social settlements consequently transitioned to social work rather than active reform.[52]

Progressive political forces, however, failed to capture city hall and Chicago's council remained corrupt and inefficient – in spite of the steady growth of its

[48] Metzger, What would Jane say?, 1. For the continued business articulation of the plan in the 1920s see C. H. Wacker, An appeal to business men: provide work now for the unemployed, relation of national prosperity to city planning, business and the Chicago plan, Chicago, IL 1921, 4.

[49] Pacyga, Chicago, 129.

[50] Jean B. Elshtain, 'A return to Hull-House', in Elshtain, The Jane Addams reader, p. xxxvi.

[51] M. Fessler, 'Relation of voluntary to municipal bodies', in Chicago Association of Commerce, First International Municipal Congress and Exposition, 58.

[52] Jaher, The urban establishment, 546. See also Robert Mors Lovett and Oscar Ludmann, 'Hull-House, 1921–1937', in Allen F. Davis and Mary Lynn McCree (eds), Eighty years at Hull-House, Chicago, IL 1969; and Mark Wukas, The worn doorstep: informal history of Northwestern University Settlement Association, 1891–1991, Chicago, IL 1991, 39.

administration throughout the 1920s and 1930s.[53] The civic welfare state was thus one still partly created by private institutions and associations, from labour leaders and women's groups to churches and businessmen, who continued their attempt to shape society.[54] Despite the shifts towards professionalism, and the decline of a reform impulse in some of the stalwart associations of the Progressive Era, just over half the expenditure on social work in 1922 still came from voluntary or charitable private agencies. A huge rise in money spent in the first two decades of the century, in areas such as unemployment relief (tripled), child care (quadrupled), homes for the aged (ten-fold) or 'character building' (five-fold), had thus been paid for by both public and private bodies. The Great Depression transformed this situation. When the returns of the Federal Census of April 1930 became available in the summer of 1930 the seriousness of the economic situation was forced into the public's consciousness. Out of 1,558,949 workers in Chicago, 167,934 – or 10.8 per cent – were unemployed. The situation continued to worsen. By January 1931, 448,739 were out of work, and in March 1931 the number of families in Chicago receiving relief was more than four times that of the previous March. That year, Chicago's overall unemployment rate stood at 30 per cent – far greater than the national rate – with black unemployment not far off twice as high.[55] By the end of 1933 about $75,000,000 had been spent on social work, with public expenditure now accounting for nearly 70 per cent of the total. [56] By the end of the second winter of the depression the funds of many of the private relief agencies in the city were exhausted, and President Hoover's commitment to individualism, self-help and private charity – though already beginning to shift in the early 1930s – was exposed as incapable of responding quickly enough to the scale of the crisis. The welfare and social benefit functions of private organisations were the first to feel the squeeze due to their reliance on the support of increasingly hard-hit businesses. The ability of the local 'associative state' to provide a welfare system was thus severely weakened.[57]

[53]   F. Rex, *General outline of the municipal government of the city of Chicago*, Chicago, IL 1937, 7.

[54]   Gräser, 'A Jeffersonian skepticism'; Bachin, *Building the South Side*, 306.

[55]   Pacyga, *Chicago*, 251–3. For statistics see J. D. Hunter, 'Family relief and service', in Chicago Council of Social Agencies, *Social service year book 1932*, Chicago, IL 1933, 9. The Depression hit African Americans harder because they already occupied the lowest occupational level, faced discrimination in hiring procedures, were excluded from a number of unions and were confined to areas with disproportionately high rents. See Lionel Kimble, Jr, *A New Deal for Bronzeville: housing, employment and civil rights in black Chicago, 1935–1955*, Carbondale, IL 2015, 10.

[56]   Expenditure calculated from A. J. Todd, 'Financing of social work in Chicago', in Chicago Council of Social Agencies, *Social service year book, 1933*, Chicago, IL 1934, 72–80.

[57]   See James N. Giglio, 'Voluntarism and public policy between World War I and the New Deal: Herbert Hoover and the American Child Health Association', *Presidential Studies Quarterly* xiii/3 (1983), 430–52; Vincent H. Gaddis, *Herbert Hoover, unemployment, and the public sphere: a conceptual history, 1919–1933*, Oxford 2005; and Ellis W. Hawley, 'Herbert

After a period of flux, when obligation was still laid partly at the door of private charitable agencies, both networks of associations and the newly-elected Democrat mayor, Anton Cermak, began to look openly toward state and federal sources of money to ensure that their activities could continue. As the Chicago Workers' Committee on Unemployment put it, on behalf of its 12,000 members, there was an 'urgency of some immediate provision' that required state intervention.[58] In making this demand, they built upon a longer history of local public-private attempts to mitigate unemployment in times of panic and depression.[59] The Illinois Emergency Relief Commission in February 1932 answered the call of the private charities. A fundamental shift in responsibility for unemployment now occurred: money for the Commission first came from Illinois taxes, and then, from July 1932, the federal government. Funds were distributed primarily by public, but also by private agencies. With the combination of older Cook County relief structures and new state and federal funds, the proportion of unemployment relief between 1934 and 1939 accounted for by public funds never dropped below 97 per cent.[60] In the ten years after the economic crash of 1929 federal government was thus significantly enlarged by Roosevelt's New Deal legislation. As government expanded in many directions in an attempt to provide relief to the unemployed, it also promoted economic recovery and the reform of the financial system. With the establishment of the Works Progress Administration in 1935, the federal government became the largest employer in the country.[61] If the New Deal programme was not unprecedented in terms of the acknowledgement of welfare responsibility by the state, it was a clear departure in scale and operation.

A shift toward central power did not necessarily herald a decline in local associational activity, however. The New Deal did concentrate power in some respects, especially in terms of policy, but it also continued existing American statist approaches of distributing public goods and powers through the locality and the private sector.[62] Furthermore, higher levels of government intervention did not secure the ascendancy of national citizenship over local. On the contrary, local associations responded positively and used this stratospheric rise

Hoover, the commerce secretariat, and the vision of an "associative state", 1921-1928', *JAH* lxi/1 (1974), 116-40.

[58] 'An urban famine: suffering communities of Chicago speak for themselves' (1932), 3, Frank W. McCulloch papers, 1931-88, CHM, folder 1, box 4, MSS lot M.

[59] Daniel Amsterdam, 'Before the roar: US unemployment relief after World War I and the long history of a paternalist welfare policy', *JAH* ci/4 (2015), 1124-6. See also David C. Hammack, 'Failure and resilience: pushing the limits in depression and wartime', in Lawrence J. Friedman and Mark D. McGarvie (eds), *Charity, philanthropy, and civility in American history*, Cambridge 2003, 263-80.

[60] Frank Ziegler Glick, *The Illinois Emergency Relief Commission: a study of administrative and financial aspects of emergency relief*, Chicago, IL 1940.

[61] Alonzo Hamby, *For the survival of democracy: Franklin Roosevelt and the world crisis of the 1930s*, New York, NY 2004, 418.

[62] Novak, 'The myth of the "weak" American state', 769.

in public funding to rejuvenate their own citizenship-creating activities. Many associations were now supported by public funds to set up new initiatives. In 1932, for example, twenty-four homeless shelters serving 13,000 people in Chicago were supported by either the governmental Joint Emergency Fund or the Illinois Emergency Relief Commission, but they were operated by agencies such as the Salvation Army, the Chicago Christian Industrial League and the Chicago Urban League. Other agencies, such as the Pacific Garden Mission and the Jewish Shelter, administratively cooperated with public authorities while supporting themselves financially. New initiatives thus offered opportunities to build up healthier, intelligent and loyal urban citizens. As the *Social service year book* for 1932 boasted, Chicago had recognised 'the need for character, morale-building and other recreational activities for men housed in shelters'. These entertainments and other activities included talent productions, team sports and games, and inter-shelter athletics competitions. Using teachers from the Board of Education, education was also provided. The 'fruits of these activities', it was hoped, would be 'manifest in terms of well-adjusted personalities and employable men when the depression has become history'.[63] The entry of public agencies into unemployment relief, according to the United Charities organisation, meant that voluntary agencies 'could devote more of their time and resources working with those basic problems of family and individual maladjustment' – key pursuits in ensuring urban stability.[64]

Following the First World War many social settlements had inwardly wondered if their methods had become outdated: 'perhaps the settlement should slip quietly out, ready as it had always been to adapt itself to changing circumstances', suggested one report of Association House.[65] Settlements were certainly facing a wide range of problems: competition from a multitude of other neighbourhood organisations in the 1920s; a lack of financial support and leadership as the richer classes moved out of the cities; the growing professionalisation of social work; a stifling of innovation due to war-induced nationalism and the post-war Red Scare; and an inability to attract the young reformers that had been so vital earlier in the century.[66] In times of distress and unemployment, however, associations that provided activities that encouraged good citizenship found a new social purpose: maintaining urban stability. As another report of Association House put it, 'seething unrest' needed to 'be tempered before it erupts into forceful demonstration'; men who came to the House were not necessarily 'Communistic in either thought or demonstration',

---

[63] R. Beasley, 'Care of non-family men and women', in Chicago Council of Social Agencies, *Social service year book, 1932*, 25-8.

[64] United Charities of Chicago, *Yesterday, today, 1857–1957*, Chicago, IL 1957, 11.

[65] 'Yesterday, today and tomorrow at Association House' (*c.* mid 1930s), 1, Association House of Chicago records, box 1, MSS lot A.

[66] Walter I. Trattner, *From poor law to welfare state: a history of social welfare in America* (1974), New York, NY 1979, 153-4; P. H. Stuart, *Philanthropy, voluntarism, and innovation: settlement houses in twentieth-century America*, Indianapolis, IN 1992.

but the unchecked socioeconomic impact of the depression might just push them over the edge.[67] Contemporary observers did indeed worry that mass unemployment would lead to instability and community breakdown, with violent strikes and militant rallies leading many middle-class Americans to fear that the depression was nurturing working-class radicalism. An atmosphere of suspicion began to envelop the city, as revitalised Communist organisations began to organise mass marches and open-air events. When men could not find work, and families lived under the constant threat of eviction, destitution and starvation, it was 'only natural', as the Chicago Workers' Committee on Unemployment put it, 'that community standards should break'.[68]

It was in the context of these fears that local associations reacted to changes in urban culture and began to articulate a renewed sense of purpose. Millions, 'through no fault of their own' according to the Jewish People's Institute, were facing 'leisure without purpose'. It was the job of the welfare agencies, then, to 'take care' of this recreation time. Not doing so would result in a loss of balance in community life, broken families, defective health and the growth of bad habits. This was particularly important for the young who, 'unless protected', would be left with 'permanent scars'. The local programme of welfare organisations, then, was 'Not icing for the cake, but leaven for the dough of the national bread-loaf ... a measure of prevention for social sickness.'[69] For Association House, the 'confusion and chaos' of the depression created 'new, overwhelming, astounding needs'. Now that most of the unemployment relief load was carried by public agencies, the settlement's priorities had to be helping Chicagoans 'to live through these trying days, and to take their part in making better days with more equal opportunities for them and for all'.[70] The House's services included providing sympathetic listeners for the unemployed; help and tips for mothers seeking to economise on cooking; group meetings to study potential solutions for the economic situation; recreation in the form of athletics, games, music and entertainment; and clubs and classes for boys and girls to watch for physical and mental 'signs of breakdown'. People took advantage of this programme: the attendance in 1931 was an 'enormous' 148,910.[71] According to the *Chicago Daily News*, the work of Association House

---

[67] 'A dark winter – seeing people through' (c. 1930s), Association House of Chicago records, box 3, MSS lot A. See also G. Taylor, *Chicago Commons through forty years*, Chicago, IL 1936, 191.

[68] 'Chicago Workers' Committee on unemployment: it's purpose and platform' (1931), and 'An urban famine: suffering communities of Chicago speak for themselves' (1932), Frank W. McCulloch papers, 1931–88, folder 1, box 4, MSS lot M. More broadly see David M. Kennedy, *Freedom from fear: the American people in depression and war, 1929–1945*, New York, NY 1999, 218–48.

[69] Jewish People's Institute, *Community culture in an era of depression*, Chicago, IL 1932, 5. See also Jewish People's Institute, *The development of a social force in Chicago*, Chicago, IL 1934.

[70] 'Yesterday, today and tomorrow at Association House'.

[71] 'Program of family work' (1931–2), Association House of Chicago records, box 3, MSS lot A.

was 'more or less typical of what is going on in each of Chicago's thirty-four settlements, neighborhood houses and centers'.[72]

It is debatable whether settlements remained innovative forces in reform terms, with one historian describing Hull House as 'little more than a relief agency during the dark years after 1929'.[73] But the Great Depression had increased demand for existing services, led to a large rise in volunteering and indirectly led to associations being given new funds for citizenship training. Group work agencies were mostly operating to capacity, and many associations reported increases in membership – such as a 37 per cent gain for the Chicago Boys' Clubs, and an all-time record for the Boy Scouts.[74] In 1939 the Chicago Boys' Club continued to open new locations, and the YWCA opened a new centre in the Stockyards district.[75] Attendance at the House of Happiness settlement remained strong throughout the 1930s and, in its thirtieth anniversary year, 1938, 1,585 different individuals participated in a total attendance of 83,183. In the winter session of 1928 there had been eight boys clubs; six evening gym classes; and two Saturday gym classes. By 1937 this had grown to: eighteen senior boys groups; six junior groups; twenty-eight evening gym classes; and nine Saturday classes.[76] Associations in Chicago, while experiencing problems in the interwar period, continued to be qualitatively important, especially in the domain of encouraging citizenship. The spirit of association and tendency of 'Americans of all ages, of all conditions, of all minds, [to] constantly unite', that Alexis de Tocqueville so famously described in 1835, was still evident in Chicago a hundred years later.[77] The expansion of government, whether local, regional or national, had not diminished the public role of organisations – especially when economic instability made their social services so vital.

Citizenship house: building solutions for the city

The evolution of voluntary societies in the first half of the twentieth century underpinned a form of citizenship with several key characteristics: civic

[72] 'How a leader copes with distress in settlement', *Chicago Daily News*, 21 Apr. 1932, in 'Miscellaneous historical notes and clippings before 1940', ibid. box 1.

[73] Edmund Wilson, 'Hull House in 1932', *New Republic* lxxiii (25 Jan 1933); Hall, *Inventing the nonprofit sector*, 10. For more on the decline of reformism see Judith Ann Trolander, *Settlement houses and the Great Depression*, Detroit, MI 1975, 15-16, 29-31.

[74] E. Eels, 'Group work agencies', in Chicago Council of Social Agencies, *Social service year book*, 1933, 56-60.

[75] Chicago Council of Social Agencies, *Social service year book, 1939*, Chicago, IL 1940, 65-6.

[76] 'House of Happiness', 1, Benton House Records 1892-1980, CHM, folder 13, box 3, MSS lot B.

[77] Alexis de Tocqueville, *Democracy in America* (1835), trans. Harvey C. Mansfield and Delba Winthrop, Chicago, IL 2000, 489.

responsibility on the part of middle-class associational workers; good social behaviour and gratitude on the part of those in receipt of welfare; and cross-class community for all urbanites. The growth of large-scale professional government intervention in welfare, however, brought even bigger possibilities. Nowhere was this clearer than in the provision of public housing. The ethos that had animated many urban reformers since the nineteenth century now took built form. Governmental bodies, working alongside pioneering investigative associations, sought finally to mitigate the effects of the degenerative city through direct intervention in the lives of the working classes. Results in Britain were dramatic: after a Housing Act in 1919 estates the size of small towns sprang up on the outer reaches of cities, and over 1,500,000 houses were built by local authorities by the end of the 1930s – including 23,000 in Manchester.[78] In the US the growth of public housing was slower and less comprehensive, only starting after the government began formally to take on the responsibility of a housing programme during the New Deal. By 1943, however, 161,000 units had been completed, 8,483 of which were in Chicago.[79] Public housing in Britain and the US also looked very different in architectural terms, with the preference for low-density cottage-style dwellings in the former contrasting with the higher-density low-rise flats of the latter. But, in both countries the function of the house and the management of the tenants within was a direct attempt to shape health, local community and a sense of good citizenship.

By the turn of the twentieth century there had been a wave of criticism about the failure of both philanthropic and commercial developers to provide adequate living conditions for poorer members of society. Dwellings designed for renters left behind by the private market were a rarity, and subsidised or public housing was experimental and left to large paternalistic employers or particularly progressive local authorities. Pressure for better housing came from a range of radical and progressive sources, such as the labour movement and settlement houses. Underlying most campaigns however, especially in governmental terms, were politicised fears about the implications for national strength if the slums were not cleared. In line with the broader debates on urban degeneration, observers worried that the slum provided a seedbed for radicalism, created an unhealthy workforce, spread crime and undermined citizenship. If the slums could be removed, argued commentators from both 'left' and 'right', the nation could potentially be saved.[80]

---

[78] Stevenson, *British society*, 221.

[79] John F. McDonald, *Urban America: growth, crisis, and rebirth*, London 2008, 25.

[80] Hall, *Cities of tomorrow*, 13–48. See also David Ward, *Poverty, ethnicity and the American city, 1840–1925: changing conceptions of the slum and the ghetto*, Cambridge 1989, ch. iii; Luckin, 'Revisiting the idea of degeneration in urban Britain'; Jo Ann E. Argersinger, 'Contested visions of American democracy: citizenship, public housing, and the international arena', *JUH* xxxvi/6 (2010), 792–813; and Daniel Freund, *American sunshine: diseases of darkness and the quest for natural light*, Chicago IL 2012.

The ascendancy of this mindset was the result of a process of urban investigation and understanding that had started in the previous century. Volunteers, usually representing associations that made up a vibrant civic culture of progressive reformers, businessmen, ecclesiastical figures, academics and politicians, journeyed into the poorer neighbourhoods of the city.[81] Once there they met families and entered their homes to describe the awful conditions in which they lived: a lack of clean water that made it difficult for tenants to clean their houses and themselves; flimsy walls and antiquated heating systems that led to cold draughty rooms or, consequently, encouraged tenants to block up all sources of ventilation; and a lack of sanitary conveniences that led to the accumulation of filth. Staged photographs (*see* Figures 22, 23) drew attention to the darkness of houses, unsuitable or shared utilities, crowded conditions and the need for repair and created the sense of a need for reform. Key figures in these images were curious children: the most vulnerable victims of urban degeneration.[82]

Written reports, and the photographs with which they were illustrated, allowed social reformers to 'imagine' the slum for a much broader audience. Slums may have been 'objectively' recordable in terms of their physical conditions, but the social and moral facets of being a 'slum-dweller' that made up this imagining was an outside subjective imposition rather than necessarily a lived or accepted identity.[83] Despite a general sympathy at the level of degradation, there was an often explicitly critical assumption made about the behaviour of slum-dwellers. A 1904 Manchester report led by Thomas Hill Marr, a key civic figure and progressive former student of Patrick Geddes, could acknowledge the hopelessness of housing conditions while still arguing that many houses 'would have been wholesome dwellings but for the carelessness and dirtiness of the tenants' – a longstanding critique of the slums that blamed the poor rather than industrialisation and a lack of utilities.[84] The Chicago Woman's Club, authoring a report in 1912, similarly described the horrific conditions of the city's poorest districts yet apportioned some of the blame to the laziness and 'apathetic slovenliness' of female immigrants.[85] Entrenched Victorian

---

[81]   See Peter Shapely, *The politics of housing: power, consumers and urban culture*, Manchester 2007, and Nick Hayes, 'Civic perceptions: housing and local decision-making in English cities in the 1920s', *Urban History* xxvii/2 (2000), 211–33. Motives for such journeying into the slums could, however, be darker than a genuine desire to help the poor: Seth Koven, *Slumming: sexual and social politics in Victorian London*, Princeton, NJ 2004.

[82]   See, in particular, Jacob Riis, *Children of the tenements*, New York, NY 1903. See also Maren Stange, *Symbols of ideal life: social documentary photography in America, 1890–1915*, Cambridge 1989.

[83]   Alan Mayne, *The imagined slum: newspaper representation in three cities, 1870–1914*, Leicester 1993.

[84]   Thomas H. Marr, *Housing conditions in Manchester and Salford: a report prepared for the Citizens' Association for the Improvement of the Unwholesome Dwellings and Surroundings of the People*, Manchester 1904, 102.

[85]   Chicago Woman's Club, *Tenement housing conditions in the twentieth ward*, Chicago, IL

Figure 22. Typical 'slum property' in Miles Platting area of Manchester (c. 1930s)

ideologies about the deserving and undeserving poor in Britain, and racialised understandings of deprived immigrants in the US, meant that tenants were essentially blamed for their surroundings.

Gradually, however, this sort of criticism softened. Broader shifts in the understanding of poverty also began to position slum housing as an unavoidable outcome of an unregulated capitalist market.[86] In the 1920s and 1930s Edith Abbott, a leading educationalist and advocate of social reform, drew attention to the 'almost inexhaustible patience' of women in Chicago who tried to maintain cleanliness in dilapidated houses.[87] From the same perspective, reports by the Manchester and Salford Better Housing Council in the early 1930s expressed surprise that 'so many do grow up to be good, healthy citizens' when conditions were so deficient – to the 'ever-lasting shame to all those other Manchester citizens who are reputed to be so able to tackle the job

1912, 4. See also *Hull-House maps and papers: a presentation of nationalities and wages in a congested district of Chicago*, New York, NY 1895, and Robert Hunter, *Tenement conditions in Chicago: report by the investigating committee of the City Homes Association*, Chicago, IL 1901. For context see Pacyga, *Chicago*, 176–8.

[86]   Dennis, *Cities in modernity*, 29; Alison Ravetz, *Council housing and culture: the history of a social experiment*, London 2001, 14–17.

[87]   Edith Abbott, *The tenements of Chicago, 1908–1935* (1936), New York, NY 1970, 223.

A - 16 2

Figure 23. Substandard housing in Chicago's Near North Side, proposed site of Frances Cabrini homes

that needs doing, and to have such loyalty for their city'.[88] An understanding of the relationship between poverty and living conditions was not only apparent in written social investigation. The British documentary film *Housing problems*

[88] See, for example, Manchester and Salford Better Housing Council, *Some housing conditions in Chorlton-on-Medlock*, Manchester 1931, 15.

for example, released in 1935, was novel in its recording of interviews with both slum-dwellers and the rehoused. Portraying the process of despair to hope demonstrated a willingness to move away from the uncertainty about whether it was the house or the inhabitant that produced unhealthy living conditions.[89]

Regardless of the apportioning of blame, the openly stated goal of housing investigations – 'scientific, thorough, and exhaustive' – was to agitate for governmental intervention.[90] Understandings of housing need followed a similar trajectory in Britain and the US, reflecting not just the shared experiences of urban poverty but also the vibrancy of intra-European and transnational exchange in social ideas and planning. Governmental responses, however, diverged greatly. In Britain, there had been some notable model housing schemes at the local level, created by paternalistic employers or progressive governmental bodies such as the London County Council. Yet providing alternative environments wholesale to reshape individual behaviour – and society as a consequence – had not materialised by the outbreak of the First World War.[91] It took intervention in the unstable housing market, ostensibly to ensure workforce productivity in a time of 'total war', to open up the possibility of a more comprehensive public housing programme following the cessation of hostilities.[92] In American cities the quest to make housing a municipal priority was hampered by apathy – and even downright hostility – from powerful businessmen who shaped the city from their economic and political vantage-point and with their own real estate interests in mind.[93] The reformist atmosphere of the New Deal helped to change this. The established rhetoric of the evils of the slum, propagated by progressive reformers, now merged with the failure of the housing market and the social instability of the Great Depression to present a new call for state-provided housing. New Dealers, who were mostly hoping to secure rather than replace capitalism, were buoyed by Britain's economic recovery – noting its correlation with investment in public housing.[94] The Housing Division of the Public Works Administration, formed in 1933 as the first of the New Deal housing agencies, was the result.

---

[89] Gold and Ward, 'Of plans and planners', 67.

[90] Hunter, *Tenement conditions*, 14. See Philpott, *The slum and the ghetto*, 27–41.

[91] Driver, 'Moral geographies', 284.

[92] Historians differ on their interpretation of the timing of this intervention, with positions on the relationship of the labour movement, party politics and economic policy framing the possible motivations of the government. For this debate see Tom Hulme, 'Urban materialities: state housing and the governing of the body', in Simon Gunn and Tom Hulme, *New approaches to governance and rule in urban Europe since 1500*, London forthcoming.

[93] Abbott, *The tenements of Chicago*, 174, and Philpott, *The slum and the ghetto*, 251–4. See also Margaret Garb, 'Health, morality, and housing: the "tenement problem" in Chicago', *American Journal of Public Health* xciii/9 (2003), 1420–30.

[94] Gail Radford, *Modern housing for America: policy struggles in the New Deal era*, Chicago, IL 1996, 59–83; Rodgers, *Atlantic crossings*, 473–7; D. Bradford Hunt, *Blueprint for disaster: the unravelling of Chicago public housing*, Chicago, IL 2009, 17–20.

The actual practical results of public housing schemes, both in construction and tenant management, reflected the discourse of 'positive environmentalism' that had been steadily developed by urban investigators over the previous fifty years. In Britain, the government's Tudor Walters Committee (1918) set the agenda.[95] Christopher Addison, Minister of Reconstruction (1917–19) and Health (1919–21), appointed the committee and was the key figure behind the ensuing Housing, Town Planning, &c. Act 1919. Addison pushed local authorities to work with local medical and sanitary officials to ensure that housing was efficient, healthy and met the physiological and biological needs of the individual. Addison, as a proponent of the ideas of 'national efficiency', argued that national health was the central foundation of a 'sane and well-ordered political future'.[96] The Tudor Walters Committee also drew heavily on established housing experts from the voluntary sector – and particularly those who made up its Women's Housing Sub-Committee. Design stipulations sought to create a living environment that stressed health and a traditionally gendered understanding of stable working-class family life. The 'new feminists' accepted the housewife's prerogative of keeping a clean, tidy and moral home, and also argued that labour-saving designs would provide more time and space for women to develop their own identities as active citizens.[97] Housing legislation was a political football in the 1920s and 1930s, kicked back and forth by Labour and Conservative governments, but the central ethos of the Tudor Walters Committee remained in place. By the end of the 1930s the Ministry of Health maintained that good housing was 'of fundamental importance to the nation's health' – a statement that reflected both the initial ethos of public housing as well as a renewed enthusiasm for physical health movements as the spectre of war on the continent grew.[98]

In the US Catherine Bauer's 1934 *Modern housing*, a description of British and continental European housing programmes, had considerable impact

[95] Local Government Board, *Report of the Committee appointed by the president of the local government board and the secretary for Scotland to consider questions of building construction in connection with the provision of dwellings for the working classes in England and Wales and Scotland and report upon methods of securing economy and despatch in the provision of such dwellings* [hereinafter cited as 'Tudor Walters Report'], London 1918.

[96] Matthew Hollow, 'Housing needs: power, subjectivity and public housing in England, 1920–1970', unpubl. DPhil. diss. Oxford 2011, 49–52.

[97] Barbara McFarlane, 'Homes fit for heroines: housing in the twenties', in Matrix (ed.), *Making space: women and the man-made environment*, London 1984, 26–36; Elizabeth Darling, 'A citizen as well as a housewife: new spaces of femininity in 1930s London', in Hilde Heynen and Gülsüm Baydar (eds), *Negotiating domesticity: spatial productions of gender*, London 2005, 49–64; Krista Cowman, '"From the housewife's point of view": female citizenship and the gendered domestic interior in post-First World War Britain, 1918–1928', *EHR* cxxx/543 (2015), 352–830.

[98] Walter Elliot, 'Foreword' to Ministry of Health, *About housing*, London 1939, 5. For physical health movements see John Welshman, 'Physical education and the School Medical Service in England and Wales, 1907–1939', *Social History of Medicine* ix/1 (April 1996), 31–48.

on the beliefs of the federal Housing Division. The key, in her opinion, was a simple change: housing constructed for use instead of profit. Providing sunlight, effective ventilation and privacy was central. If Bauer's work came from a progressive position of improving conditions for the less well-off members of society, the Division also saw housing as an opportunity to engineer society, arguing for the public benefits of replacing crime and disease-breeding social environments.[99] As G. H. Gray, an American architect and city planner, noted in his 1946 *Housing and citizenship*, 'Because a wholesome sunlit home environment is fundamental to clean, efficient living and loyal citizenship, good housing is a matter of national concern.'[100] This was also an inherently gendered vision of 'the good society', with federal government information pamphlets, for example, highlighting homemaking as the citizenship responsibility of the housewife.[101]

As with other American cities, the first three housing projects in Chicago were constructed by federal government agencies. Local authorities had little impact on the decisions made, and local architectural firms and building contractors were closely supervised by the Public Works Administration.[102] The new Chicago Housing Authority (CHA), however, was clearly in tune with the Administration, reflecting the power that local urban studies had had on creating a national reform mentality. Elizabeth Wood, the CHA's first executive director, was a former caseworker for the Chicago United Charities who had personally witnessed the human costs of the slums during the Depression.[103] In a lecture to the Illinois Committee of the Chicago Association of Commerce in 1941, she told the audience that slums affected inhabitants physically and socially, so the CHA consequently took 'the poor family from the slum, puts it in decent housing, and attempts to make an asset out of the family and out of the neighbourhood'. It was, she argued, the provision of better standards of living that would enable Chicagoans to become 'healthy citizens'.[104] When the CHA turned to constructing its own projects in the late 1930s and early 1940s, it thus continued to follow the pattern set by the central Housing Division.

In Manchester, ideas about the material environment and its relationship to citizenship creation also shaped how the city council promoted, built and

---

[99] Radford, *Modern housing for America*, 59–83; Rodgers, *Atlantic crossings*, 473–7.

[100] G. H. Gray, *Housing and citizenship: a study of low cost housing*, New York, NY 1946, 1–2.

[101] A. W. Satterfield, 'Publications disseminated by the US government during the early 20th century for the American housewife: a selected bibliography', unpubl. MSc diss, Chapel Hill, NC 2005.

[102] Radford, *Modern housing for America*, 99, 105. For plans of Chicago's schemes see 'Illinois projects', Maps and plans of housing projects, PWA (1933–6), RG 196, 330\20\1\3–5, National Archives, Washington, DC. The first three projects were the Jane Addams Houses on the Near West Side, the Julia C. Lathrop Homes on the North Side and the Trumbull Park Homes on the far South Side.

[103] Bradford Hunt, *Blueprint for disaster*, 36.

[104] *Chicago Housing Authority Bulletins* i/6 (1 May 1941), 2–3, CHM, HD7288.78.U62.

managed its housing. In case they considered reneging on their new commitments, or were tempted to provide inferior housing, voluntary associations – and local women especially – were keeping a close watch. In 1921, for example, the Manchester and Salford Women Citizens' Association were successful in pressing for the installation of a central hot-water supply on all the large estates.[105] A flurry of reports from voluntary associations in the early 1930s, carried out under the umbrella organisation of the Manchester and Salford Better Housing Council, also continued to make links between poor conditions and the formation of bad citizens, pressuring municipal authorities to continue their schemes.[106] The Housing Committee of the city council, throughout the 1920s and 1930s, worked carefully with the city architect, the medical officer of health, a Women's Advisory Sub-Committee and the housing commissioner of central government to ensure that housing met the material needs of the new tenants. Maintaining this environment, in 1934, called for over a hundred painters, twenty-two joiners, eighteen plumbers, twenty-nine bricklayers, four electricians and three plasterers to service fifty-one estates.[107]

Though the new estates built by the Manchester council and the federal government in the US had teething issues, they were visually a clear and startling improvement on previous working-class housing (*see* Figures 24, 25). Building better housing, however, was only the first stage in creating good citizenship: the second was the art of tenant management. Teaching tenants how to use their new home correctly, a management tradition that had been influentially emphasised by Octavia Hill in London in the late nineteenth century, was seen as essential by both governmental and non-governmental bodies.[108] It was widely assumed that former slum-dwellers would not know how to live in their houses, due to its great difference from their previous accommodation. Hill's ethos thus remained, but her amateur middle-class managers were increasingly replaced by trained educated specialists. In Britain, the Association of Women House Property Managers was formed in 1916 (by women who had trained under Hill), followed by the Institute of Housing in 1931 (by local government officers) and the Association of Women Housing Estate Managers in 1932. Annual conferences and a housing magazine in

---

[105] 'Keeping a watch on housing', MG, 18 Mar. 1921, 12.

[106] Such as Manchester and Salford Better Housing Council, *Angel Meadow and Red Bank: report of a survey undertaken in part of St Michael's and collegiate wards of the city of Manchester by the Red Bank Survey Group*, Manchester 1931.

[107] See Housing Committee minutes vol. 16: 'Maintenance staff' (11 June 1934), 142; vol. 17: 'Maintenance staff' (12 Nov. 1934), 3, Housing Committee, MCA, GB127.Council Minutes/Housing Committee.

[108] For the latest work on Hill see Elizabeth Baigent and Ben Cowell (eds), *'Nobler imaginings and mightier struggles': Octavia Hill, social activism, and the remaking of British society*, London 2016.

Figure 24. Blackley Housing Estate in Manchester (c. 1920s)

the 1930s cemented a profession that was also supported by the Ministry of Health.[109] In the US there was a similar enthusiasm for housing management, again influenced by Hill. The National Association of Housing Officials (NAHO), based in Chicago, printed a periodic publication, *NAHO News*, as well as a *Housing Management Bulletin*. It also worked with local authorities and the United States Housing Authority to organise demonstrations and training in housing management.[110]

Housing managers were keen to impress upon tenants the importance of properly maintaining their new homes and articulated it as a key part of loyal citizenship. Tenant manuals drew attention to how the houses had been constructed to purposefully encourage better upkeep. The 'white, hard, smooth, glazed surfaces' of the bathroom fittings in Chicago's 1940s Altgeld Gardens, for example, were 'not only for appearance sake' but to make cleaning 'easier'.[111] In Manchester there were seventeen basic rules and conditions of

---

[109] Ravetz, *Council housing and culture*, 112; Ministry of Health, *The management of municipal housing estates*, London 1939.

[110] National Association of Housing Officials, *Housing yearbook*, Chicago, IL 1939, 222.

[111] 'Handbook for residents of Altgeld Gardens' (1944), 7, Harold Washington Library Centre Municipal Research Collection (hereinafter cited as HWLCMRC), Chicago Housing Authority, Cx.H84.1944xa,

Figure 25. Trumbull Park Homes in Chicago (opened 1938)

tenancy that governed how private and communal spaces should be used and looked after.[112] The process of tenant education began on the day that they moved in. Manchester City Council trained its own property managers for seven years, and empowered rent collectors, dressed in a uniform complete with the city coat of arms, to use 'notices to quit' to discipline tenants into improving their behaviour.[113] In Chicago, the housing manager explained the rules of tenancy, showed the family how to use domestic equipment and informed the tenant that 'the public housing program is to enable him to better himself both economically and socially'.[114]

---

[112] Shapely, *The politics of housing*, 119. Similar advice was given in generic tenant manuals across Britain and used by countless local authorities. See, for example, Tyldesley Urban District Council, *The municipal tenants' handbook*, Gloucester 1939.

[113] See Housing Committee minutes vol. 14: 'Special sub committee re clothing of rent collections' (14 Mar. 1932), 39; 'Rent collectors and investigators' (12 Sept. 1932), 189; 'Staff-uniform clothing' (14 Nov. 1932), 231; vol. 20:'Tenancy section – uniform clothing' (13 Dec. 1937), 219.

[114] 'Annual report to the Mayor' (1941), 24-5, Chicago Housing Authority, Cx.H84r, HWLCMRC.

Management processes such as these raise the spectre of 'social control' and 'social engineering' – an understandable charge.[115] Debates on urban degeneration at the turn of the century, which continued to inform policy into the 1920s and 1930s, had encouraged welfare with a social-engineering objective. In their own words, reformers and politicians believed that good housing and successful management would achieve national goals of good health, productive workers and better citizenship. But working-class tenants could appreciate the ideals of housing planners and managers, linking beliefs in environmental uplift to their own sense of respectability and pride in exacting standards.[116] There has been a tendency, especially following the break-up of social housing estates later in the twentieth century, to focus on a 'discourse of disaster' and 'social pathologies'.[117] Tenants, however, could challenge 'externally imposed, stigmatized identities' to create meaningful communities.[118] Whether through (limited) decoration or personalisation of their homes and gardens, or by taking part in estate-wide social activities and competitions, tenants could actively subscribe to the vision of a new society that housing schemes tried to present. Even with the support of tenants, though, the carefully curated utopia of public housing could break down, with even the most innovative designs still suffering from familiar problems of damp, noise and lax maintenance.[119] Tenants could also resist the disciplinary logic of housing by using their properties in ways that were not envisioned – and certainly not encouraged. In Manchester in the mid-1920s, for example, the Housing Committee worried that more than double the original estimate of hot water was being used on the estates: many now revelled in the ability to have deep hot baths.[120] More frustrating for the Women's Advisory Sub-Committee was how their carefully thought-out system of windows – key to ensuring good ventilation and thus health – were being used: windows were opened too wide and at times that they deemed illogical.[121]

Housing problems in Britain also created opportunities for tenants to articulate a growing understanding of themselves as deserving citizens in the

---

[115]   Sean Damer, '"Engineers of the human machine': the social practice of council housing management in Glasgow, 1895–1939', *Urban Studies* xxxvii/11 (2000), 2007–26.

[116]   Anne Hughes and Karen Hunt, 'A culture transformed? Women's lives in Wythenshawe in the 1930s', in Davies, Fielding and Wyke, *Workers' worlds*, 74–101; J. S. Fuerst, *When public housing was paradise: building community in Chicago*, Westport, CT 2003, 4.

[117]   Edward G. Goetz, *New Deal ruins: race, economic justice, and public housing policy*, Ithaca, NY 2013, 2. For Chicago see Bradford Hunt, *Blueprint for disaster*, and Sue J. Popkin, *The hidden war: crime and the tragedy of public housing in Chicago*, New Brunswick, NJ 2000.

[118]   Kevin Fox Gotham and Krisa Brumley, 'Using space: agency and identity in a public-housing development', *City and Community* i/3 (2002), 268–9.

[119]   Elizabeth Darling, 'What the tenants think of Kensal House: experts' assumptions versus inhabitants' realities in the modern home', *Journal of Architectural Education* liii/3 (2000), 172.

[120]   Housing Committee minutes vol. 5: 'Central hot water supply, Blackley Estate' (11 May 1925), 205.

[121]   Ibid. vol. 6: 'Building types sub committee' (10 May 1926), 199.

'gift' relationship between the individual and the state. Now that they were the beneficiaries of public provision, they understood themselves as having not just responsibilities but also an entitlement to certain services. The accountability of municipal landlords, or at least the ability to challenge them in public ways, provided an opportunity for tenants to shape a new form of citizenship identity. When the gas fires used by tenants to supplement the inefficient heating systems installed by the Manchester council began to emit toxic fumes, tenants were quick to write directly to the Housing Director. Adopting the language of civic responsibility, they argued that their good tenancy 'entitled' them to a better service.[122] Tenants, then, could behave as 'angry customers of a service' rather than 'recipients of municipal benevolence' or 'charity'.[123] Working-class urbanites could manage the managers, utilising emerging consumerist discourses, as well as older ideas of respectability, to their own gain. This could often begin before tenancy had even taken place, with prospective tenants writing to city councils or even visiting councillors at home to ask for special consideration of their case – using 'a story' which appealed 'to the sensibilities of the member concerned' who then could not help but 'promise to use influence to further the interests of the applicant'.[124]

Public housing in the 1920s and 1930s illustrates, in microcosm, the ways in which the state collaborated with local associations to intervene in urban society. Longstanding debates about the relationship between environment and good citizenship were embedded in a new understanding of welfare and its architecture. State-built houses came ready-made with a set of presumptions about the habits and behaviour of their working-class tenants, and were designed to create better health, reinforce gender norms and build a sense of citizenship. Many public housing tenants, though certainly not all, actually welcomed close management because of the respectability that it brought – a way to replace the stigmatisation of the slums.[125] Others turned it to their advantage and articulated new demands for social provision based on their changed relationship with the state. Working-class tenants were thus brought into a sort of 'material politics' – exercising their rights and engaging directly with the powerful apparatus of the local and national state.[126]

The process of designing, building and managing public housing shows how local associations, city councils and the central or federal state shaped citizenship through the physicality of the city. But it also begins to demonstrate

---

[122] See, for example, ibid. vol. 3: 'Presence of rats on Gorton Estate' (26 Aug. 1921), 91.

[123] Shapely, *The politics of housing*, 126.

[124] Central Housing Advisory Committee, *Management of municipal housing estates*, London 1945, 8; Ravetz, *Council housing and culture*, 26.

[125] See oral histories in Fuerst, *When public housing was paradise*, and Ravetz, *Council housing and culture*, 117.

[126] Frank Trentmann, 'Materiality in the future of history: things, practices, and politics', *JBS* xlviii/2 (2009), 283–307.

the limitations of urban- and local-based ideals of citizenship by pointing towards the emergence of competing forms of identity, contestation and belonging. In Britain, the neighbourhoods that tenants had left, denigrated as 'slums' by earnest middle-class reformers and council planners, could also be romanticised as working-class communities. Manchester memoirs recall the sadness that slum clearances caused, and the feeling that thriving communities had been destroyed – a conclusion that some contemporary surveys, but certainly not all, also supported.[127] The attempt to construct a new civic community, then, could be hampered by a failure of feeling as well of environment. In the longer term, the treatment of tenants also points towards other shifts in how citizenship was articulated in British welfare discourse. The active egalitarianism that characterised the expansion of the welfare state in the 1940s saw communities of social housing tenants as a necessary expression of a better society – and one that was national rather than necessarily local. The emphasis on urban degeneracy, and its effects on health and citizenship, was gradually lost. Instead, the British government became more concerned with consumer opinion as it turned towards post-war reconstruction. Potential tenants were active contributors to this shift, increasingly expecting the state to help them to achieve the ideal home and life that had been marketed to consumers throughout the interwar period.[128] By the 1950s and 1960s council housing tenants were treated by government less as 'unitary subjects with universal needs' and rather as individuals with 'preferences and desires'. Consumerist ideals had turned the 'recipient' of welfare into a 'client' or 'customer' of the national state. Social democratic rights further became entangled with consumer rights as Britain began the transition to market-orientated forms of government.[129]

Different issues were at play in American cities. African Americans, despite the public statements of the CHA, received less than their 'quota' and projects remained officially segregated in the 1930s.[130] Robert R. Taylor, the housing commissioner and consultant on Defense Housing, had been agitating for housing in the South Side since the early part of the decade, hoping that new

[127] See, for example, Neil Scott, *People of Hulme: some Manchester memories*, Hulme 2003, 15, 21, 82. For the range of opinion about both old housing areas and new estates see Bourke, *Working class cultures in Britain*, 155-9.

[128] Sandra Trudgen Dawson, 'Designing consumer society: citizens and housing plans during World War II', in Erika Rappaport, Mark J. Crowley and Sandra Trudgen Dawson (eds), *Consuming behaviours: identity, politics and pleasure in twentieth-century Britain*, London 2015.

[129] Ravetz, *Council housing and culture*, 90, and Matthew Hollow, 'The age of affluence revisited: council estates and consumer society in Britain, 1950-1970', *Journal of Consumer Culture* xvi/1 (2016), 286-7. See also Alistair Kefford, 'Housing the citizen-consumer in post-war Britain: the Parker Morris Report, affluence and the even briefer life of social democracy', *Twentieth Century British History* xxix/2 (2018), 225-58.

[130] T. A. Guglielmo, *White on arrival: Italians, race, color, and power in Chicago, 1890-1945*, New York, NY 2003, 153-4.

housing could help to improve the societal position of African Americans through an appeal to 'Race pride'.[131] Governmental policies, however, only exacerbated problems. New 'public housing monoliths' gave old racial enclaves a new and visual permanence. Forty-nine out of fifty-one of the public housing sites approved by the city council between 1955 and 1966 were in 'ghetto' areas, as Chicago was designated the nation's most residentially segregated city.[132] By the 1970s the Robert Taylor Homes (opened in 1962 with almost all its 27,000 residents being African American) was beset by maintenance problems and wracked by escalating violence, and had become a 'national symbol of public housing failure'.[133] Even before this catastrophe became apparent, public housing was incapable of overcoming the racism that structured everyday experiences of hostility in the interwar city. If anything, it brought it into focus. As one black former resident of the Ida B. Wells project poignantly lamented, public housing was merely an 'experimental biosphere ... Then they opened the door and said, "Well, go ahead out!" And they didn't tell us there was no oxygen out there'.[134] It was at this point, frustrated by the discrimination and lack of progress that was apparent at the local level, that African Americans increasingly began to turn towards federal government for their rights.

[131] 'Better housing makes better citizens', CD, 20 June 1942.

[132] Biles, 'Race and housing in Chicago', 34–7. See also Arnold Hirsch, *Making the second ghetto: race and housing in Chicago, 1940–1960*, New York, NY 1983.

[133] D. Bradford Hunt, 'What went wrong with public housing in Chicago? A history of the Robert Taylor Homes', *Journal of the Illinois State Historical Society* xciv/1 (2001), 96–123.

[134] Fuerst, *When public housing was paradise*, 57.

Conclusion: After the Citizenship City

For those residing in the industrial city in the early twentieth century, day-to-day interactions were still affected by the fragmentation of society heralded by nineteenth-century urbanisation. To live, work and socialise in Manchester or Chicago was to be brought into contact with a diverse range of people who did not necessarily share beliefs or values.[1] This experience, sometimes dislocating yet often exciting, shaped both the theory and reality of modern citizenship. Foregrounding the importance of the city in this way encourages an appreciation of the urban as an independent factor or 'variable' – the idea that towns and cities were not just sites that reflected the wider societies that sustained them, but that those societies were themselves, in part, constituted through urban place, experience and identity.[2] This study has, in common with those of other historians, acknowledged that this was especially the case in the nineteenth century: the zenith of the 'shock of the new'. Cities both housed and catalysed rapid change, and so were in the front line when it came to rethinking society. In this assessment of the following decades however, and the 1920s and 1930s especially, it has been shown how the city continued to shape ideas about community and belonging long 'after the shock'. Urban life and government was comparatively stable by the early twentieth century but cities continued to grow, and civic leaders did not consider urban problems to have been solved. In responding to new forms of leisure, conflict and social fragmentation they none the less still stressed the suitability of the city as the basis for good citizenship. Municipal councils, supported by a network of voluntary associations, public-minded businessmen and increasingly the central state, demonstrated considerable ambition in their attempts to build urban community. Their goal was to transcend 'traditional politics' by 'steering' urban-dwellers towards a shared identity – one where small inter-locking communities created a larger civic whole.[3]

Investing in the future of the city, both materially and emotionally, these leaders entwined intervention with a language of local belonging. Looking back to the shocking city from where they had come, they celebrated a narrative of resilience, progress and determination. Urban-dwellers were told, whether in festivals, pageants or civics classes, that they belonged to an important

---

[1] Kasinitz, *Metropolis*, 3.

[2] Iain S. Black, 'Modernity and the search for the urban variable', *JUH* xxxii/3 (2006), 466–7; Martin J. Daunton, 'Introduction', to *Cambridge urban history of Britain*, iii. 1–56; Ewen, *What is urban history?*, 20–6; Michael B. Katz, 'From urban as site to urban as place: reflections on (almost) a half-century of US urban history', *JUH* xli/4 (2015), 560–6.

[3] Shapely, *The politics of housing*, 11; Morris, 'Governance', 10.

community with a distinctive history as well as a promising future. Moulding this civic pride across the different groups that made up urban society happened in many areas of life. Tracing the similarities and differences between Manchester and Chicago, and Britain and the US more broadly, the role that the city and its culture could have in shaping the identity, policies and practices of citizenship in the first half of the twentieth century has been emphasised. In this concluding chapter, I first summarise the conceptualising of this urban citizenship. In the following two sections I offer an epilogic explanation of the unravelling of urban importance, in citizenship terms at least, in the post-Second World War period.

Urban citizenship in the twentieth century: key characteristics

There were clear differences between Britain and the US in the period studied by this book, and divergent experiences between Manchester and Chicago. Urbanisation took place later in the US, and at a more rapid pace. As the 'New World' absorbed the emigrating population of the 'Old World', the explicit concentration in the US on the changing demography of urban places led to a more racially-inflected sense of citizenship. Chicago's relative youth, and its political culture of corruption and lower level of government inter-vention, also meant that it experienced urban problems at a higher intensity than Manchester. There was still, however, an overlap in experience between the two nations. Both shared a common belief in technological progress and were shaped by the 'common power of mass production, mass media and mass consumption' that accompanied the transition to predominately urban societies.[4] From the late nineteenth century into at least the 1930s Britain and the US also shared a specifically urban sense of citizenship.

Part of this similarity was due to an ideological link between the two nations. In the late nineteenth century industrial development and environ-mental degeneration incited a common response. Urban critiques circulated across the Atlantic, and the two nations were brought together through their similar understanding of how to create a better city. British idealists, American pragmatists and reformers – despite their clear differences – were ideologically conjoined by how they understood the negative effects of the modern city on the minds and bodies of its inhabitants. Egalitarian government, and its counterpart of active local citizens, was formulated as a response – whether through the language of Green and Geddes or Dewey and Dunn – that could provide the basis for a new and particularly local sense of citizenship. Philosophers thus joined with educators and administrators to encourage the belief that the municipalised city was the site of both rights and responsibilities. This late nineteenth-century progressive ideology also influenced educational

---

[4]   Dennis, *Cities in modernity*, 349.

understandings of citizenship after the First World War and until at least the 1930s. In the words of educators can be traced an enthusiasm for happy and cooperative communities that were, at least in theory, equal under the service provision of their benevolent city government. Civics education attempted to put this discourse of local belonging into action as a key contributor to national identity and power as one tier of a 'nested citizenship'.

Visual and performative practices of civic identity were also shaped by the response to the modern city. Older forms of spectacle and ritual were adapted and reinvented for the contemporary urban context. Municipal figures continued to play principal roles in the performance of hierarchy, demonstrating their leadership through visibility and dominance in public space. Civic identity, too, was still heavily linked to the institutions – governmental, cultural and commercial – that lined the streets of central or downtown areas and represented the national importance of the city. The ability to emphasise certain aspects of the urban and its governors, however, was augmented by the utilisation of new visual and communication technologies. During civic festivals, electric lighting, amplification and motor transport made the key characteristics of urban identity even clearer. Floodlighting the most important buildings, drawing visual and audible attention to the mayor, and parading the departments of the city council could each mark out civic identity for the watching local population. Historical comparison was also a key method of portraying municipal modernity. Exhibitions and tours of city council departments demonstrated how the 'shock city' had been overcome through technological and scientific ingenuity.

Demonstrating urban progression, though, was not a simplistic or binary understanding of 'past' and 'present': history was neither rejected by the 'new moderns' nor nostalgically and conservatively embraced. The storylines of historical pageants demonstrate this. These events encouraged spectators to think about the city's history in a longer perspective, and to trace contemporary power to the past – whether mere decades for Chicago, or millennia for Manchester. Historical re-enactment responded to the difficulties of modern urban life by remembering the endurance or triumphs of the city and its people throughout history, and connecting those events to a broader national story of progress. To tell such a tale, however, civic organisers had to acknowledge how modern society – and its evolution through mass entertainment, enfranchisement and working-class political power – necessitated a broader sense of civic inclusion. Elites could not just shape a narrative of middle-class municipal progress and expect 'the people' to listen, so 'the people' were given their own starring role. Urban citizenship, then, depended on a degree of democratisation of both identity and practice. Festivals and pageants thus adapted the enthusiasm for mass spectacle, from costumed drama to giant demonstrations, to romanticise the contribution of the 'normal' inhabitant to urban cohesion and national glory.

Such celebratory and reflective events also allowed different urban groups – whether based on ethnicity, race, class, religion or gender – to contribute their pride to the larger civic whole and thus stake a claim to public impor-tance. Citizenship in the interwar period was articulated, in part, through a rhetoric of inclusion. By pledging allegiance to the locality and performing 'good citizenship' through the accumulation of civic knowledge or celebration of place, individuals and communities could claim membership of the city and the nation by extension. In the event, though, groups with low cultural and political capital experienced varying degrees of acceptance, and there were important distinctions within local and national hierarchies of power, identity and belonging. Urban citizenship, despite the celebration of the 'civic banner' under which all could supposedly gather, was still implicitly classed, gendered and racialised. This reflected the societal role for which the 'ideal' citizen was being groomed. Urban intervention continued the late nineteenth-century enthusiasm for 'national efficiency' and the production of efficient workers and soldiers to safeguard national power in an increasingly competitive world. As fears about political radicalism grew in both countries, especially at points of economic depression or international political upheaval, shaping a workforce that was less susceptible to revolutionary beliefs also became of paramount importance.

The working classes, and immigrants in the case of the US, were conse-quently disproportionately targeted by those that sought to create citizenship. Public housing, for example, was partly a response to fears about urban living and the physical deterioration of the nation's greatest resource: its people. New forms of architectural welfare enabled the state to directly regulate the life and behaviour of the working classes to make them better workers and soldiers. Building homes for the less well-off also explicitly depended on gendered stereotypes and expectations. Women, despite advances in suffrage, were still predominately envisioned as wives and mothers rather than as political citizens, while men were conceptualised in terms of strength and economic productivity. Homes were designed and managed in a way that confirmed the gendered division of labour and engrained these different notions of citizenship. Youth citizenship was similarly classed and gendered. It was the specific nature of the modern urban environment, argued sociologists and the voluntary associations that they informed, that caused problems of youth citizenship – from fears of miscegenation and the sexual opportunities of dancehall life to the streets of the 'jungle' that encouraged gangs. Boys and girls, as proto-citizens, were to be led away from the sins of the city and towards more wholesome activities that provided well-rounded cooperative individuals for the nation. Gendered ideas of 'correct' behaviour, and the relationship between the sexes especially, encouraged – where associations had the resources – the clear regulation of leisure time.

In Chicago it was newcomers or minorities that were seen as most in need of civic training. The solutions that most associations or settlements proposed in the early 1920s, however, were more about assimilation into a white patriotic mainstream than celebrating national, ethnic or racial difference. The discourse of local citizenship worked alongside, and often supported, broader ideas of how best to Americanise immigrants, by envisioning the city as a contributing tier of belonging within the nation. But there were also distinctions within the hierarchy. African Americans, especially, found themselves constantly confined to a third rank of citizenship, with white Anglo-Saxon Protestants at the top and other European ethnicities and religions jostling for importance somewhere in the middle. Even when black leaders encouraged the inhabitants of Bronzeville to support local and national patriotic events and causes, they found that – whether in youth culture or public exhibitions – the notion of civic inclusion was mostly rhetoric. Beyond the limited representation or even erasing of black contributions and identity in civics and celebrations was the poisonous reality of segregation. By the 1930s a new consensus of an 'American Way' had emerged that allowed white immigrant communities to find a place for their ethnic identity within Chicago's civic culture, but African Americans consistently had their social citizenship blocked by structural racism.

The nature of urban life, nevertheless, meant that the dominant exclusionary discourses of urban citizenship were open to challenge, contestation and re-definition. Civic outsiders, ignored or marginalised, still had a degree of agency in their response to moments of explicit top-down intervention from governments or local associations. It was at these points that we can see the inherent fragility in urban conceptions of belonging or citizenship. Women, in both Manchester and Chicago, worked to construct a version of the public sphere that melded political, economic and social demands. From World's Fairs to new Citizen's Associations, they shaped their own form of civic action in the post-suffrage landscape. Communities based on race, ethnicity or religion could also challenge the dominant paradigms of urban citizenship by expressing their own ideas about history, community and identity. In Manchester, this meant that Italian Catholics could process through the city streets carrying the symbols of their faith while, in Chicago, African Americans could celebrate their own Bud Billiken Day or look back to African history in great historical re-enactments.

Urban citizenship, then, was an ideological form of 'steering' that sought to create a more harmonious – and pliable – population. But the reality of the modern city – a space in which different groups could articulate their own identity or demands – meant that the dominant civic narrative could be met with direct challenges. Just as likely as contestation, though, was apathy: the plans, policies and schemes of local councils and voluntary associations could simply be ignored. Civics classes, for example, never reached anything like the majority of urban inhabitants. In Britain especially there was a wariness of including citizenship education in the curriculum and, in both countries, the unrealistic idealism of civics would have been apparent to those who lived in poorly serviced or segregated areas. Schoolchildren were a more captive audience, but adults had the demands of work, as well as leisure options, which meant that formal education could only reach so far. Fun festivals and entertaining pageants were a more successful way of spreading the civic message further, but performers and spectators decided their level of involvement, taking part for reasons that may have had more to do with entertainment and self-realisation than 'active citizenship'.

Much the same could be said for youth culture. Urban reformers were led by a moral agenda of improving morals and behaviour, but the games and sports that they provided were always more popular than classes or study groups. Even if associations had some success in taking adolescents off the streets, they certainly never captured the attention of all as the modern city continued to stimulate the senses of pleasure-seekers. Evidently, throughout the 1920s and 1930s, the quest to provide civic solutions to urban problems was never fully achieved. This was partially due to the failure of cultural responses – whether in philosophy, representation or reality – to overcome underlying socio-economic problems. It was also, however, the nature of a dialectical civic culture: new understandings of urban problems and behaviour led to the evolution of citizenship-creating policies.

By the 1940s, nevertheless, alternative and fundamentally non-urban models of citizenship were in the ascendancy and the city was beginning to lose its power to shape the identity, practices and rights of citizenship. It was also at this point that the differences between the urban contexts in the two countries became more important than the similarities, and the solutions consequently began to diverge. In Britain, the new contract between the individual and the state, articulated mainly through welfare programmes, began to demonstrate how social democratic understandings of citizenship were growing. As the provision of services became mostly controlled by national government after 1945, the emphasis on the special relationship between local government and the citizen became less tenable. Compounding this distance between the urban-dweller and their government was an increasingly private-focused suburban culture that eschewed the centre of the city in terms of both leisure and identity. In the US, on the other hand, the experiment of public housing exposed the limitations of governmental welfare – especially in the 1950s when riots rocked the city following attempts to racially integrate housing projects. Urban-based narratives of belonging seemed outmoded and were patently unable to solve the engrained problems of segregation and racism. A move toward a battle for legal civil rights through the justice system thus began to gather steam.

From urban citizenship to social democracy in post-war Britain

Supporters of local government in Britain had ended the interwar period with a positive mindset. In 1935 the centenary of the Municipal Corporations Act was widely acknowledged, as local councils celebrated the benefits that they had brought to the country in health, services and culture. The future of local government was bright; looking to the next centenary, the authors of one commemorative volume predicted an 'unlimited vista of future usefulness and expansion'.[5] But there were also signs that this success was laid on shaky foundations: central government committees on local and national expenditure in the 1930s had begun to make recommendations that constrained municipal government; there were concerns about the imbalances of municipal energy across the country; and conservative fears about regions where 'socialism' was the only option. And finally, government acts, from the reform of the poor law and the creation of the Central Electricity Board in the 1920s, signalled a centralised mindset.[6] Still, at first, the Labour Party supported the idea of local government as the agent of post-war reconstruction – initial plans for the National Health Service were municipally based, for example. For pragmatic administrative reasons and because of the antipathy of key figures, however, the party reversed its policy.[7] Trends in government that had emerged in the interwar years were now even more apparent. The financing of local services continued to shift away from rates and trading incomes towards central grants, weakening the independence of municipalities and strengthening the control of central government, while municipal services such as gas and healthcare were nationalised and overseen by regional boards. In the reformist mood of the post-war period, local governments were often bypassed.[8] This is not to suggest that the local state was no longer important in the 'mixed economy of welfare'. But its agents were now implementers, supporters or 'publicisers' of central government instead of controllers of their own orbit.[9]

Voluntary associations had a similar experience. In the early 1940s the District Provident Society, for example, was an important part of organising the welfare relief of the war effort on the home front, and forecast that a need for its services would continue whatever form governmental shifts took.[10] When voluntarism came into direct conflict with new provision that was universal and comprehensive, however, it became clear that some aspects of voluntarism and state expansion could not co-exist, and the state invariably took over the

---

[5]   William A. Robson, 'The outlook', in Harold J. Laski, W. Ivor Jennings and William A. Robson (eds), A century of municipal progress, 1835–1935, London 1935, 463.

[6]   Peter Jones, From virtue to venality: corruption in the city, Manchester 2013, 43–7.

[7]   Alysa Levene, Martin Powell, John Stewart and Becky Taylor, Cradle to grave: municipal medicine in interwar England and Wales, Oxford 2011, 22–7; Jerry White, 'From Herbert Morrison to command and control: the decline of local democracy and its effect on public services', History Workshop Journal lix/1 (2005), 76; James A. Chandler, Explaining local government: local government in Britain since 1800, Manchester 2007, 169.

[8]   Doyle, 'The changing functions of urban government', 311; Davis, 'Central government and the towns', 282; Martin J. Daunton, 'Payment and participation: welfare and state-formation in Britain 1900–1951', Past & Present 150 (Feb. 1996), 169–216.

[9]   Peter Shapely, 'Governance in the post-war city: historical reflections on public-private partnerships in the UK', International Journal of Urban and Regional Research xxxvii/4 (2012), 1288–1304; Jacquie L'Etang, Public relations in Britain: a history of professional practice in the twentieth century, Mahwah, NJ 2004, 63–5.

[10]   'DPS annual report' (1941, 1943).

old roles.[11] Many associations continued to work alongside the Manchester Welfare Services Committee, formed in 1948, but they acknowledged that they were now directed by central government.[12] Negotiation of responsibility in the mixed economy of welfare continued, and local associations remained important, but they had, like municipal government, passed the highpoint of their role as the purveyors of welfare.[13] As the historian of the Manchester University Settlement put it in 1945: 'every social organism carries within itself the germ of its own decay', and so the 'self-dedicated Victorian philanthropists' had given way to the 'expanding army of trained and certificated officers of statutory authorities' that it had originally encouraged.[14] Voluntary culture was buoyant and expanded in new areas – such as animal welfare, heritage and consumer protection – but it was 'at the expense of local activism that focused on urban government'.[15]

The welfare state thus took away the independence of civic culture in cities such as Manchester. It also ideologically weakened the version of citizenship that saw rights and responsibilities from a local perspective. Interwar welfare had signified limited interventions in the lives and health of those on the margins of society, guiding the working classes to social citizenship.[16] Social democracy now articulated welfare provision as a universal legal right of citizenship given to those who made up a national community. Liberal conceptions of individual responsibility and self-improvement, formerly the cornerstones of civic urban culture and interwar welfare, were not just seen as inadequate but irrelevant: the rights of citizenship had become more important than the responsibilities.[17]

If people who continued to live in cities did think of themselves as part of a community, there were competing allegiances that meant that this was increasingly unlikely to be civic. For the labour movement, economic right claims about the redistribution of wealth and power – after the demoralising experience of mass unemployment – means testing and benefit cuts in the 1930s, shaped a sense of identity and belonging.[18] Class identification was generally important in how Britons thought about their relationship to society

---

[11] Finlayson, 'A moving frontier', 199.

[12] City of Manchester Welfare Services Committee, *1948–1958: a decade of civic welfare*, Manchester 1959; J. Gaddum, *Family Welfare Association of Manchester and Salford: a short history, 1833–1974*, Manchester 1974, 26–9; E. White, *A history of the Manchester and Salford Council of Social Service, 1919–1969*, Manchester 1969, 23–35.

[13] Kate Bradley, *Poverty, philanthropy and the state: charities and the working classes in London, 1918–1979*, Manchester 1999, 17; Daunton, 'Payment and participation', 215.

[14] Mary D. Stocks, *Fifty years in Every Street: the story of the Manchester University Settlement*, Manchester 1945, **1.**

[15] Jones, *From virtue to venality*, 40.

[16] David Gladstone, *The twentieth-century welfare state*, Basingstoke 1999, 31.

[17] For more discussion see Hulme, 'Putting the city back into citizenship', 48–9.

[18] Bourke, *Working class cultures in Britain*, 15, 19–21.

throughout the first half of the century, and, after the Second World War, it continued to exert influence due to the powerful position of trade unionism and an increased sense of entitlement for jobs, housing and healthcare.[19] The idea of 'community' as a determining force in working-class lives could be backward-looking nostalgia or forward-looking socialist utopianism, but it was nevertheless conducive to encouraging class-consciousness. For the working classes, the neighbourhood of their family, friends and fellow workers formed the basis for attachment – though the cohesiveness of working-class 'communities', both in old neighbourhoods and new estates, was complex.[20]

On the other hand, the mid-point of the century also saw the blossoming of national ideas of culture and belonging. The increasing sophistication of communication technologies, such as radio, film and then television, helped make the 'imagined' nation even more real than had been possible with the print culture that was so essential to creating the nation in the eighteenth and nineteenth century.[21] Second World War unity and duty, though partly a propaganda myth, encouraged these feelings.[22] Into the post-war period, in response to social and political instability, national identity also took on further racial characteristics. New Commonwealth immigration, particularly African-Caribbean and Asian, began to change the demographics of the country, and a racialised 'whiteness' became an essential part of 'Britishness': a way to reimagine the national community in a period of imperial decline. Inclusion and exclusion on grounds of race and ethnicity, though a feature of earlier periods, became even more important. Both the legality and experience of belonging in Britain was restructured, whether through legislation or everyday negotiations of (and discrimination against) racial difference.[23] For those who found their status as Britons questioned, unity and defence could be found through the formation of associations and protest movements that attempted – with various degrees of success – to promote a British citizenship that was not limited to whiteness. But the terms of citizenship discourse had clearly been affected by race.[24]

Changes within urban culture, both physically and culturally, were also combining to hamper local belonging. Increasingly suburbanised populations,

---

[19]   Ben Jones, *The working class in mid twentieth-century England: community, identity and social memory*, Manchester 2012, 198.

[20]   Bourke, *Working class cultures in Britain*, 25, 136-51; Jones, *The working class in mid twentieth-century England*, 120-47.

[21]   Anderson, *Imagined communities*.

[22]   Sonya Rose, 'Sex, citizenship, and the nation in World War II Britain', *American Historical Review* ciii/4 (1998), 1148. For a substantial analysis of this period, and the role of war particularly, see Richard Weight, *Patriots: national identity in Britain, 1940-2000*, Basingstoke 2002.

[23]   Chris Waters, '"Dark strangers" in our midst: discourses of race and nation in Britain, 1947-1963', *JBS* xxxvi/2 (1997), 207-38; Kathleen Paul, *Whitewashing Britain: race and citizenship in the postwar era*, Ithaca, NY 1997.

[24]   Kieran Connell, *Black Handsworth: race in 1980s Britain*, Berkeley, CA 2019.

both working- and middle- class, looked more to ideals of home and family than to civic duty or urban pride. Signs of this shift were already apparent in the interwar decades, especially in the more economically resilient parts of the country as the virtues of private middle-class life took on a new public significance, but the 1950s and 1960s saw an even clearer move to the urban margins.[25] People became more likely to see themselves as affluent consumers than active citizens, retreating to the less demanding private sphere as a new 'home-centred modernity' grew.[26] Governmental demoting, class politics, racial and patriotic discourse and growing suburban culture thus signalled that the city had lost some of its primacy in debates about citizenship and belonging. Civic leaders, none the less, tried to maintain an image of ambition and future progress – Manchester published a grand visionary plan for reconstruction in 1945, for example, like many other cities.[27] But results in actually revitalising the city in the 1950s and 1960s were mixed, reflecting urban vulnerability to factors such as economic dislocation and changing state policy. In a sense, the ideological underpinnings of this urban reform, despite having its roots in interwar planning, also expressed something different from the civic identity of that period. Just as with the broader shifts in citizenship ideology, urban planning was put into the service of regenerating a national society and through the acknowledgement of a certain standard of living that the new social-democratic state entailed.[28]

Manchester, in terms of a definable civic identity or unit of belonging, increasingly seemed less important. The muted reception of the centenary of the city charter in 1953 encapsulated this shift in urban culture, governance and citizenship. The few activities put on by the city council – a couple of concerts, an exhibition of charters and a civic service in the cathedral – were limply received. The *Times* noted that Manchester was not 'noticeably *en fete*', and bitingly reported that the few people who stopped to watch the mayor's procession to the cathedral were probably just 'going between stations' rather than turning out for what was 'hardly a jubilant demonstration'.[29] The local press blamed the two world wars and the Great Depression for damaging the

---

[25]   Alison Light, *Forever England: femininity, literature and conservatism between the wars*, London 1991, 10.

[26]   See Matthew Grant, '"Civil defence gives meaning to your leisure": citizenship, participation, and cultural change in Cold War recruitment propaganda, 1949–54', *Twentieth Century British History* xxii/1 (2011), 77–8, and, for home-centred modernity, Jones, *The working class in mid twentieth-century England*, 17.

[27]   R. Nicholas, *City of Manchester plan*, London 1945; Chris Perkins and Martin Dodge, 'Mapping the imagined future: the roles of visual representation in the 1945 City of Manchester Plan', *Bulletin of the John Rylands University Library of Manchester* xxxix (2012), 247–76.

[28]   James Greenhalgh, *Reconstructing modernity: space, power and governance in mid-twentieth century British cities*, Manchester 2018.

[29]   'Manchester 100 years a city', *The Times*, 30 Mar. 1953, 4; 'Achievements of 100 years', *The Times*, 25 Mar. 1953, 10.

dignity of the city, but also recognised that 'the tendency towards centralisation has weakened the power of every provincial city to stimulate and satisfy the creative imagination of its citizens'.[30] Local government had lost prestige and independence, and was met with a largely indifferent population. Nationally important events, such as the 1953 Coronation, were now more likely to be celebrated at the level of the street party or even individual television-owning house – in a strange sort of way a return to the more passive observation of nineteenth-century civic ritual.[31]

By the 1960s, according to a local professor of drama, the city centre was 'dead at night', with 'not enough theatres, or concert halls, or cafes', while, according to Alderman Richard Harper, the 'type of person' that might have formerly been a suitable city councillor 'had gone to live so far out of the city that their only interest in Manchester was how to get there in the morning and how to get out as quickly as possible in the evening'.[32] As a conference of architects in the city in 1960 put it, 'The very idea of the city as a unity of social and cultural values' was 'losing its appeal'.[33] The broader civic spirit that had been so evident in Manchester's 1926 and 1938 festivals had dissipated, and the city no longer seemed to be a natural home for citizenship.

The failure of urban community and the rise of the civil rights movement in the US

The statist developments of the 1930s set the basis for a longer-term strengthening of urban government in America. At the start of the decade Herbert Hoover implemented changes that tackled problems of public finance, with state legislatures giving municipalities more power to finance their own projects using anticipated income as collateral for borrowing. The Public Works Administration during Roosevelt's New Deal further encouraged this liberalisation of municipal finance. After the Second World War, when markets had recovered, local government was able to generate income from private capital rather than federal government, 'opening the floodgates' for local public enterprise.[34] Between 1945 and 1947 the newly created Chicago Transit Authority, for example, purchased the city's elevated railway system and street railways for around $87,000,000, finally achieving that of which municipal ownership advocates in the 1920s could only dream.[35] Even if city councils had become

---

30   'Manchester', MG, 26 Mar. 1953, 6.

31   Roberts, 'The evolution of civic ritual', 460–1,

32   'Why people are leaving city', MG, 29 Oct. 1962, 15; 'Councillors "not what they used to be"', MG, 2 Aug. 1963, 4.

33   'Problems of urban renewal', MG, 15 June 1960, 9.

34   Radford, 'From municipal socialism', 885–7.

35   City of Chicago, *Chicago's report to the people, 1933–1946*, Chicago, IL 1947. See also

more empowered, however, there were shifts taking place that were leading to a growth in national power, patriotic consciousness and a 'rights-based' narrative of citizenship that mostly bypassed the local.

The Second World War was particularly transformative. The rhetoric of mobilisation, both on the foreign and home fronts, insisted that the interests of individuals and groups had to give way to national need. Sovereignty was now clearly embodied in an increasingly leviathan federal government that was empowered to protect the collective good – superseding New Deal programmes in terms of authority, spending and impact. Americans now looked even more towards the nation and its government to fulfil the entitlements of citizenship. Big government thus managed to overcome traditions of individualism and decentralised governance by successfully infusing liberal values with an overt nationalism – an effect that continued when the Cold War took centre stage.[36] This new version of the American 'warfare state' did still depend on associational culture, though. Organisations such as settlements, in much the same way as they had during the Great Depression, saw the war as renewing the need for their activities. Association House, for example, maintained on the cusp of the American entry into the conflict that 'fundamentally, we must build internal defences against these foreign ideas that threaten our American system' – which included 'the masses of people in our big cities like Chicago' being 'educated to the privileges and responsibilities of American citizenship'.[37] After 1945 the federal government centralised the gathering of tax revenues and formulated policy, but delegated the implementation of its programmes to states, localities and private non-profit organisations. Nevertheless the federal state was now more clearly in control. By the late 1960s most social settlements were contracted with the Office of Economic Opportunity to provide neighbourhood services and programmes and showed a high degree of uniformity with the funding priorities of federal agencies.[38]

Broader urban problems also led to the decline of the city as the site of citizenship. By the 1940s Chicago had suffered a long period – through depression and war – without sufficient investment. Civic life continued, of course, but it seemed muted in comparison with its former ambition in the opening decades of the century. As one letter-writer to the *Tribune* observed in 1944 there were 'hundreds' of unoccupied, dilapidated or vermin-infested buildings in the city. Criticising the mayor, Kelly, he reminisced about the time when 'the "I Will" policy of Chicago got things done', and asked, 'where is the civic pride so evident when Mr Wacker headed the Chicago Plan

George Krambles and Arthur H. Peterson, *CTA at forty-five: a history of the first forty-five years of the Chicago Transit Authority*, Oak Park, IL 1993.

[36] James T. Sparrow, *Warfare state: World War II Americans and the age of big government*, Oxford 2011, 3–12.

[37] 'Board of directors minutes' (1939–40), 1, Association House of Chicago Records, box 2, MSS lot A.

[38] Hall, *Inventing the nonprofit sector*, 7.

Commission?'[39] Urban renewal programmes eventually began to reshape the city, with a new expressway system and high-rise public housing schemes controversially cutting apart the old neighbourhoods. But the white middle classes, and increasingly the working classes too, were already leaving. A conference on 'civic unity' in 1952 described how 'many Chicagoans are fleeing to the suburbs, discouraged, pessimistic, feeling hopeless because they believe that city and neighbourhood problems are not being met fast enough'.[40]

Hoping to find the American Dream, they swapped older industrial inner-city neighbourhoods for better (and cleaner) jobs and housing on the ever-expanding edges of the city, enabled by the rapid growth in car ownership, new roads and modern planned industrial parks. In the early 1950s Chicago's economy was still powerful, sharing in a broader period of growth for the US. But its depopulating inner area looked old and out of touch with post-war America – the 'busy, grimy industrial city of the past' coming into conflict with the vision of the 'modern and affordable' alternative of the suburbs, which accounted for 74 per cent of the US population growth between 1950 and 1970.[41] As had been the case in Britain, the retreat to a more suburban and 'private' sense of citizenship weakened civic participation and spirit.[42]

The result of these shifts could be seen in a civic celebration in Chicago in 1962. Ostensibly, this was a relatively unimportant date: the 125th anniversary of Chicago's incorporation as a city. Mayor Daley, however, with his 'director of special events', Jack Reilly, saw it as an opportunity for boosterism and to advertise the 'true image of Chicago' to the world.[43] In an echo of the Pageant of Progress just over forty years earlier, it was dubbed the Exposition of Progress and held on Navy Pier (formerly the Municipal Pier). The narrative and staging of the exposition was also similar: municipal exhibits; entertainments such as a beauty pageant; and a parade, led by the mayor, that included civic and ethnic organisations in Chicago (notably now including the city's growing Mexican community).[44] But, in scale and popularity, it paled in comparison to Big Bill's effort of 1921: it lasted only two rather than fourteen days; there were seventy exhibits compared to several hundred; and hundreds of marchers rather than thousands took a short route for the parade (from Wacker Drive to State and then south to Congress). The *Chicago Tribune*, which gave scant attention to the Exposition, was tellingly coy about the turnout of spectators, opting for a vague

[39] 'On civic betterment', *CT*, 7 July 1944, 10.

[40] Chicago Commission on Human Relations, 'Fourth Chicago conference on civic unity' (152), Metropolitan Housing and Planning Committee, Special Collections and University Archives at Library of the Health Sciences, UIC, folder 2, box 198a.

[41] Pacyga, *Chicago*, 321. For the broader picture see McDonald, *Urban America*, 65–76, 85–104.

[42] John D. Fairfield, *The public and its possibilities: triumphs and tragedies in the American city*, Philadelphia, PA 2010, 238–67.

[43] 'City to mark 125th year in progress fete', *CT*, 17 Apr. 1962, 16.

[44] 'Great city got start 125 years ago today', *CT*, 4 Mar. 1962, 1, 10.

'thousands'.[45] Perhaps most indicative of changes in urban culture, however, was the response from the suburbs. Reilly wrote to representative organisations to invite their participation, hoping that 'many of Chicago's neighbors, whose economic picture is largely dependent upon the city, will want to join in this celebration'.[46] The response of the Northwest Suburban Conference, which represented the majority of northwest suburban municipalities, was indicative: happy to take part, but only on what they called a 'nominal' basis.[47] Reilly needed the suburbs more than they needed the city.

In other ways the limitations of civic culture in the 1920s and 1930s had already begun to point towards the necessity of other models of citizenship. Idealistic narratives about both past and present progress, the foundation of interwar ideas of urban citizenship, downplayed Chicago's racial dynamics. An 'occasionally integrated public culture', as John McGreevy puts it, was not extended into residential communities.[48] Racist whites used property owners' associations and craft unions aggressively to enforce segregation, threatening violence and refusing to sell to African Americans. Around 50 to 80 per cent of Chicago was covered by racial deed restrictions and restrictive covenants by 1939.[49] The colour-line disproportionately condemned African Americans to unskilled work and residential segregation and set limits on political advancement. Well-established European-heritage groups, such as the Irish or Italians, transcended their own ethnicities to see themselves as 'white' – and demanded rights and privileges on that basis in violent opposition to sharing neighbourhoods with blacks.[50] White minorities could thus assimilate to the form of citizenship that gave them the rights to the city, while African Americans could not. Nowhere was this clearer than in the countless violent riotous responses from whites to the attempts by the Chicago Housing Authority to pursue a policy of neighbourhood integration for their projects. In-depth private reports shared by progressive civic organisations emphasised their inability to curb violent actions and detailed just how deep the animosity towards African Americans ran.[51]

---

[45]   'City birthday parade damp but lively', *CT*, 25 Aug. 1962, 47

[46]   'Chicago inviting suburbs to party', *Arlington Heights Herald* 12 July 1962, 13

[47]   '"Nominal" participation, *Arlington Heights Herald*, 19 July 1962, 93.

[48]   McGreevy, *Parish boundaries*, 4.

[49]   Wendy Plotkin, '"Hemmed in": the struggle against racial restrictive covenants and deed restrictions in post-WWII Chicago', *Journal of the Illinois State Historical Society* xciv/1 (2001), 32.

[50]   St Clair Drake and Horace R. Cayton, *Black metropolis: a study of negro life in a northern city* (1945), Chicago IL 1993, 756; Guglielmo, *White on arrival*, 146. See David R. Roediger, *Working towards whiteness: how America's immigrants became white, the strange journey from Ellis Island to the suburbs*, New York, NY 2005.

[51]   See, for example, Mayor's Commission on Human Relations, 'Memorandum on Fernwood Park Homes', Metropolitan Housing and Planning Committee, folder 3, box 198a. For context see Hirsch, *Making the second ghetto*, 40-67.

Given these obstacles, black Chicagoans turned toward other routes to realise their claims as citizens. The Bud Billiken Day Parade, for example, grew in popularity throughout the interwar period, and by the end of the decade the attendance reached 150,000. In 1934 it was combined with a new civic ritual: the election of an unofficial 'Mayor of Bronzeville', a popularity contest that nevertheless laid the groundwork for political action by declaring the neighbourhood's 'sovereignty' and drawing attention to 'political limitations at the municipal level'.[52] More generally the 1930s to 1950s saw the flowering of the 'Black Chicago Renaissance' in the arts. This movement did not just take place in the city, but through it too, utilising the associational networks of civic culture. Part of this renaissance and resistance depended on the conjoining of black consumerism with new politicised identities, as leisure and culture provided a vibrant hotbed for the development of dissent against white capitalism.[53] Political change at a wider level was also transforming the ideological discourse of citizenship at the local. Militant and Communist organisations in the 1930s enlisted an increasingly conscious working-class black population and worked alongside white liberal politicians, the progressive press and reform groups to tackle social and legal restrictions.[54] African Americans embraced the liberal democratic rhetoric of Roosevelt's New Deal and, despite the general unwillingness of New Dealers to address racism, began to articulate a rights-based narrative that became the basis of an emerging protest movement. This chimed with and worked through the increased activism and working-class consciousness of the organised labour movement.[55] Racial equality, the challenging of the *status quo* and civil rights thus gradually became more important than the attempts at cultural assimilation, self-help or the accommodation of segregation that had marked the 'economic nationalism' of black business leaders in the 1920s.[56]

During the Second World War, as economic opportunities grew, so too did civil rights demands. Notions of war duty coalesced with the liberal democratic language of the New Deal to form the basis for a new justification for entitlement to constitutional rights and equality. As the Chicago Council of Negro Organizations (a late 1930s federation that brought together over thirty of the South Side's organisations) put it in 1942: 'While we are offering our services and our lives for the winning of the war, we are still fighting for a working democracy at home.'[57] Catalysing this consciousness in Chicago

---

[52] Rutkoff and Scott, 'Pinkster in Chicago', 322–7.

[53] Davarian Baldwin, *Chicago's new negroes: modernity, the Great Migration, and black urban life*, Chapel Hill, NC 2007.

[54] Christopher R. Reed, *The Depression comes to the South Side: protest and politics in the black metropolis, 1930–1933*, Bloomington, IN 2011.

[55] Kimble Jr, *A New Deal for Bronzeville*, 1–8.

[56] Boyd, *Jim Crow nostalgia*, 27.

[57] *The Chicago Council of Negro Organizations, Monthly Newsletter* (Jan. 1942). See also Neil A. Wynn, *The Afro-American and the Second World War*, New York, NY 1993.

was the further growth of the black population, from 278,000 in the 1940s to 813,000 in the 1950s in a second 'Great Migration' from the south. In the same period, the overall population of the city only grew by about 150,000.[58] In 1942 the Congress of Racial Equality was formed in Chicago and began to challenge discrimination in restaurants and places of recreation. The Chicago sociologist St Clair Drake argued in 1945 that it was 'in the cities that the problem of the Negro in American life appears in its sharpest and most dramatic forms' and that it 'may be, too, that the cities will be the arena in which the "Negro problem" will finally be settled'.[59]

Optimism at the end of the 1950s about the economic future, then, could not disguise segregation, discrimination and inner-city deterioration. The interwar city had failed to become a cohesive community and, when combined with post-war trends, its legacy set the stage for racial conflict, riots and civil rights agitation in the 1950s and 1960s – especially as Daley's Democratic machine dismantled black political power.[60] The African American community did not, perhaps understandably, take part in his Exposition of Progress. The next year, however, a coalition of both black and white elites, a third of whom were from Chicago, hosted the Century of Negro Progress exposition in the city as one of the main events of the national centenary celebrations of the Emancipation Proclamation. The exposition, they argued, would demonstrate the 'true heritage, history and contribution of the Race' to the nation's 'democratic tradition and American experience'.[61] Demands for citizenship were strong within the festival, but its approach echoed the less contentious civic assimilation narrative propagated by Bronzeville's civic elite in the interwar period. Demonstrations of contributions to American society were more apparent than demands for equal rights. The Exposition was a failure, however, and did not attract large crowds. As Mabel Wilson has concluded, it showed how 'black Americans were [now] seeking [other] modes of direct action that would forge advances in social justice and equality rather than high-minded and well-worn platitudes on racial progress'.[62] Into the 1960s it was this direct struggle for 'inclusion in the body politic' that became the basis for 'a new understanding of citizenship'.[63] Chicago was a key site in the ensuing civil rights movement, with direct action against segregation in schools, housing and public spaces.[64] Civic elites had failed to articulate a convincing case for local belonging or urban pride as the qualification for citizenship, and their often racialised civic

---

[58]   Biles, 'Race and housing in Chicago', 32.

[59]   Drake and Cayton, *Black metropolis*, 756.

[60]   McDonald, *Urban America*, 133, 143-55; Kimble Jr, *A New Deal for Bronzeville*, 149.

[61]   See various reports in the CD, 6 Jan. 1962.

[62]   Mabel Wilson, *Negro building: black Americans in the world of fairs and museums*, Berkeley, CA 2012, 244.

[63]   Schudson, *The good citizen*, 231.

[64]   See J. R. Ralph, *Northern protest: Martin Luther King, Jr., Chicago, and the civil rights movement*, Cambridge, MA 1993.

hierarchy was now challenged by a growing belief that citizenship would have to be legally and constitutionally guaranteed by federal government through the courts: a 'new avenue of national citizen power'.[65] Those that were discriminated against consequently looked beyond the civic to find justice.

In both countries, what it meant to be a member of society in the post-war period arguably came to be understood as the 'right-bearing citizen of a territorial nation-state'.[66] In industrial cities, such as Manchester and Chicago, the urban and its government became the backdrop to processes of shaping citizenship rather than the frontline. But this epilogue of decline should not obscure the relative longevity of urban civic pride nor the importance that local ideas of citizenship had in structuring identities, interventions and practices of citizenship in the twentieth century. If anything, the downfall of the city as the site of citizenship emphasises its previous importance. The modern city was not simply a passive container for larger or broader discourses of citizenship, but a key aspect of how they were articulated, experienced and contested.[67] The legacy of the shock industrial city was long and powerful, and continued to affect what it meant to be a citizen in ways that many historians have often failed to appreciate. In their premature heralding of the rise of the national and, more recently, the global, they have neglected the vibrancy of civic life until at least the late 1930s.

Inclusion and exclusion in citizenship terms was complicated and messy. Those that were shaping urban culture – from local governments to voluntary associations – had to contend with cities that were diverse and changing all the time in this period of modernity. Broader twentieth-century developments in communication, democratisation and popular culture also altered the ideology and techniques of promoting urban citizenship. Undoubtedly, the sorts of civic communities that were constructed in the interwar period were thus qualitatively different from those of the supposed golden era of the late nineteenth-century Civic Gospel of Britain or the Progressivism of the US. But, as the concept was conceived by both governors and governed in the 1920s and 1930s, urban citizenship was not necessarily a pale reflection of pride and belonging in those preceding periods. It was, rather, the direct descendant of the energetic civic response of local elites to nineteenth-century urbanisation: a facet of citizenship culture and the city that continued to evolve in the long and complex period after the shock.

---

[65] Schudson, *The good citizen*, 232–58; Thomas J. Sugrue, *Sweet land of liberty: the forgotten struggle for civil rights in the North*, New York, NY 2008.

[66] Holston and Appadurai, 'Cities and citizenship', 187.

[67] Dennis, *Cities in modernity*, 1.

Bibliography

Unpublished primary sources

GREAT BRITAIN

Manchester, City Archives
Centenary Pageant, GB127.M740/2/8/2/39
Charter centenary celebrations, GB127.M68/21, GB127.M68/21/2–5
'Commemorative volume by Jewish community of the centenary of incorporation',
    GB127.MS.f.296.M150
Epitome of Proceedings of Committees 36 (1918–19), 352.042.M12
Ernest Emil Darwin Simon papers, GB127.M14/306
The Family Welfare Association of Manchester Ltd, GB127.M294
Housing Committee minutes, 1918–39, GB127.Council minutes/Housing
    Committee
Hulme Lads' Club, box 2, 5, 6, GB127.M716
Jewish Lads' Brigade, box 3, 6, GB127.M130
Lower Broughton, the Ascension, 1865–1979, GB127.L154
Manchester Civic Week, GB127.M740/2/8/3/2
Manchester Civic Week: official handbook, Manchester 1926, M68/11
Miscellaneous souvenirs of Manchester Civic Week, MSC942.7391
Newspaper cuttings, Manchester Civic Week, vols 1–6, 1926, F942.7389 M173
'Pageant Committee and Executive Committee minutes', GB127.M467/4/3
Records of the Manchester and Direct Branch of the Working Men's Club and
    Institute Limited, GB124.G20.13
Zion United Reformed Church, GB127.M187/24

UNITED STATES

Chicago, Harold Washington Library Centre Municipal Research Collection
Chicago Housing Authority, Cx.H84

Chicago History Museum
Association House of Chicago records, 1899–1972, boxes 1–4, MSS lot A
Benton House miscellaneous pamphlets, F38JW.B5Z
Benton House records, 1892–1980, boxes 1–3, MSS lot B
Charter Jubilee Committee, 'List of historical markers placed at various sites
    throughout the city' (1937), qF38.HN.C3
Chicago Boys and Girls Club records, 1901–69, box 1, MSS lot
Chicago Boys' Week Federation, Scrapbook of newspaper clippings, photographs,
    forms, posters, vols 1–9 (1923–6), F38JV.C4s

215

Chicago Commission on Citizenship Education, 'Local government in Chicago' (1932), F38E.C421

Chicago Housing Authority, *Bulletin*, 1, nos 4–5, no. 1 (Mar. 1941–Jan. 1943)

Chicago's Charter Jubilee bulletin of progress 1, nos 1–16 (6 Mar.–11 Aug. 1937), qF38CD.1937.C4.W7

'Conference of those interested in developing a more intelligent and efficient citizenship' (1923), F38AS.C4co

Frank W. McCulloch papers, 1931–88, boxes 1–6, MSS lot M

HD7288.78.U62

Miscellaneous pamphlets on the Adult Education Program of the Work Projects Administration, F38QF.C4A3z

Off-the-Street-Club miscellaneous pamphlets, F38JW.O3z

Pageant of Progress Exposition miscellaneous pamphlets, F38MZ 1921.P14

Vernon Bowyer papers, 1919–60, boxes 1–4, MSS

Chicago, University of Illinois at Chicago Special Collections and University Archives

Metropolitan Housing and Planning Committee

YMCA Wabash Records

Washington, DC, National Archives

Maps and plans of housing projects, PWA (1933–6), RG 196, 330\20\1\3–5

Official documents and publications

Anderson, Matthew (ed.), *How Manchester is managed*, Manchester 1925

Board of Education, *Report of the consultative committee on the education of the adolescent*, London 1926

— *Report of the consultative committee on secondary education*, London 1938

Central Housing Advisory Committee, *Management of municipal housing estates*, London 1945

Chicago Board of Education, *Suggestions to instructors on a course in citizenship*, Chicago, IL 1921

— *5th annual report of Montefiore School, 1933–34*, Chicago, IL 1934

Chicago Bureau of Recreation, *Annual report*, Chicago, IL 1926

Chicago Commission on Race Relations, *The negro in Chicago: a study of race relations and a race riot*, Chicago, IL 1922

Chicago Council of Social Agencies, *Social service year book, 1932*, Chicago, IL 1933

— *Social service year book, 1933*, Chicago, IL 1934

— *Social service year book, 1939*, Chicago, IL 1940

Chicago Recreation Commission, *Recreation and delinquency: a study of five selected Chicago communities*, Chicago, IL 1942

City of Chicago, *Chicago's report to the people, 1933–1946*, Chicago, IL 1947

City of Chicago Bureau of Parks, *Playgrounds and bathing beaches, rules and regulations*, Chicago, IL 1926

City of Manchester Welfare Services Committee, *1948–1958: a decade of civic welfare*, Manchester 1959

Committee on Civic Education of the Superintendent's Advisory Council of the Chicago Public Schools, *Education for citizenship*, Chicago, IL 1933

Kelly, Edward J., 'Report concerning Chicago's Charter Jubilee', *Journal of the Proceedings of the City Council of the City of Chicago*, Illinois (10 Nov. 1937), 4720–5.

Local Government Board, *Report of the Committee appointed by the president of the local government board and the secretary for Scotland to consider questions of building construction in connection with the provision of dwellings for the working classes in England and Wales and Scotland and report upon methods of securing economy and despatch in the provision of such dwellings*, London 1918

Manchester Education Committee, *General survey: 1914–24*, Manchester 1926

— *A survey of the facilities for adult education available in Manchester*, Manchester 1935

Ministry of Health, *About housing*, London 1939

— *The management of municipal housing estates*, London 1939

Nicholas, R., *City of Manchester Plan*, London 1945

Report of the Urbanism Committee to the National Resources Committee, *Our cities: their role in the national economy*, Washington, DC 1937

Tryon, Rolla M., *The social sciences as school subjects: report of the Commission on the Social Studies*, New York, NY 1935

Tyldesley Urban District Council, *The municipal tenants' handbook*, Gloucester 1939

United States Bureau of Education, *Report on the teaching of community civics* (bulletin no. 23, 1915)

Newspapers and periodicals

The American Citizen
Architecture (1926)
Arlington Heights Herald
Chicago Commerce (1921)
Chicago Daily News
Chicago Defender
Chicago Herald and Examiner
Chicago Illinois News
Chicago Jewish Chronicle
Chicago Jewish Tribune
Chicago Tribune
Christian World
The Citizen
Co-operative News
Daily Dispatch
Greater Chicago
Harper's
Literary Digest
Liverpool Post
Manchester Daily News
Manchester Dispatch
Manchester Evening Chronicle
Manchester Evening News
Manchester Guardian

New York Times
Poetry
Portsmouth Evening News
Public Opinion Quarterly
Southern Reporter
Sunday Chronicle
The Times
Walsall Observer
Yorkshire Evening Post

[Local newspapers collated in Chicago Boys' Week Federation, Scrapbook of newspaper clippings, photographs, forms, posters, vols 1-9 (1923-6), CHM, F38JV.C4s; and Newspaper cuttings, Manchester Civic Week, vols 1-6, 1926, MCA, F942.7389 M173]

Contemporary books and articles

Abbott, Edith, *The tenements of Chicago, 1908-1935* (1936), New York, NY 1970

Adams, Edwin W., *A community civics: a textbook in loyal citizenship*, Chicago, IL 1920

Addams, Jane, *Twenty years at Hull House*, New York, NY 1912

Ames, Edgar W. and Arvie Eldred, *Community civics*, New York, NY 1922

Ashley, R. L., *The new civics: a textbook for secondary schools*, New York, NY 1921

Association for Education in Citizenship, *Education for citizenship in secondary schools*, Oxford 1936

— *Experiments in practical training for citizenship*, Letchworth 1937

Baird, Thomas, 'Films and the public services in Great Britain', *Public Opinion Quarterly* ii (1938), 98

Banks, Isabella, *Manchester man*, London 1876

Barker, W. (ed.), *Your city: Manchester, 1838-1938*, Manchester 1938

Barnett, S. A. and Patrick Geddes *The ideal city* (1905-6), ed. Helen Meller, Leicester 1979

Bensman, Joseph and Arthur J. Vidich, 'Race, ethnicity and new forms of urban community' (1975), in Philip Kasinitz, *Metropolis: centre and symbol of our times*, New York, NY 1995, 196-203

Beresford, Charles, 'The future of the Anglo-Saxon race', *North American Review* clxxi (Dec. 1900), 802-10

Blakiston, C. H., *Elementary civics*, London 1920

Brindley, W. H. (ed.), *The soul of Manchester*, Manchester 1929

Brooks, Lee M., 'The urban community', *Social Forces* xvii/1 (1938), 119-28

Bureau of Education, *The social studies in secondary education* (bulletin no. 28, 1916)

Bureau of Engineering, Department of Public Works, City of Chicago, *A century of progress in water works*, Chicago, IL 1933

Burgess, Ernest W., 'The new community and its future', *Annals of the American Academy of Political and Social Science* cxlix (1930), 157-64

Carley, Joe, *Old friends, old times, 1908-1938: Manchester memories from the diaries of Joe Carley*, n.p. 1990

Chicago Association of Commerce, *Survey of Chicago: twenty-first anniversary of the Chicago Association of Commerce*, Chicago, IL 1925

Chicago Board of Education, *Adult Education Annual Report for 1937*, Chicago, IL 1938

Chicago Community Trust, *Americanization in Chicago*, Chicago, IL 1919

Chicago Council of Social Agencies, *Preliminary inquiry into boys' work in Chicago*, Chicago, IL 1921

Chicago Woman's Club, *Tenement housing conditions in the twentieth ward*, Chicago, IL 1912

Communist Party of Manchester, *100 years of struggle: Manchester's centenary, the real story*, Salford 1938

Cooke-Taylor, William, *Notes of a tour in the manufacturing districts of Lancashire*, London 1844

Co-operative Union Ltd, *Continued education for junior Co-operative employees: an account of the classes attended by junior employees in Manchester*, Manchester 1929

— *Ten year plan for Co-operative education*, Manchester 1935

Crawford, David Lindsay, *The city and the state*, Birmingham 1928

Cressey, P. G., *The taxi-dance hall: a sociological study in commercialized recreation and city life* (1932), New York, NY 1968

Dewey, John, 'The philosophy of Thomas Hill Green', *Andover Review* xi (1889), 337–55

— 'The school and social progress', in Dewey, *The school and society*, 19–46

— *The public and its problems: an essay in political enquiry*, Philadelphia, PA 2012 (1927)

—– (ed.), *The school and society*, Chicago, IL 1899

Dole, Charles F., *The new American citizen*, Boston, MA 1918

Drake, St Clair, 'Profiles: Chicago', *Journal of Educational Sociology* xvii/5 (Jan. 1944), 261–71

— and Horace R. Cayton, *Black metropolis: a study of negro life in a northern city* (1945), Chicago, IL 1993

Dunn, Arthur W., *The community and the citizen*, Boston, MA 1907

— *Community civics for city schools*, Boston, MA 1921

Eaton, Allen, *Immigrant gifts to American life: some experiments in appreciation of the contributions of our foreign-born citizens to American culture*, New York, NY 1932

Edwards, A. Trystan, 'The metropolitan idea', *Architecture* (Apr. 1926), 386

Engels, Friedrich, *The condition of the working class in England in 1844*, London 1892

Faucher, Léon, *Manchester in 1844: its present position and future prospects* (1844), London 1969

Fessler, M., 'Relation of voluntary to municipal bodies', in Chicago Association of Commerce, *First International Municipal Congress and Exposition*, Chicago, IL 1911, 57–60

Frazier, E. Franklin, *The negro family in the United States*, Chicago, IL 1939

Gaus, John M., *Great Britain: a study of civic loyalty*, Chicago, IL 1929

— 'Civic education in the English schools', *Annals of the American Academy of Political and Social Science* clxxxii (1935), 164–72

Gerson, A. J., 'The social studies in the grades, 1909–1929', *Historical Outlook* xx (1929), 269–72

Gill, Conrad, *Government and people: an introduction to the study of citizenship*, London 1921

Glick, Frank Ziegler, *The Illinois Emergency Relief Commission: a study of administrative and financial aspects of emergency relief*, Chicago, IL 1940

Gosnell, Harold F., *Machine politics: Chicago model*, Chicago, IL 1937

Gray, G. H., *Housing and citizenship: a study of low cost housing*, New York, NY 1946

Green, Thomas H., 'Liberal legislation and freedom of contract' (1861), in Thomas H. Green, *Lectures on the principles of political obligation and other writings*, ed. Paul Harris and John Morrow, Cambridge 1986, 194–212

Greenlaw, Edwin, 'The new significance of the community pageant', in *The community pageant: an agency for the promotion of democracy* (University of North Carolina extension leaflets, war information series, 16), Chapel Hill, NC 1918

Gruening, Ernest, *The public pays: a study of power propaganda*, New York, NY 1931

Hall, Newton M., *Civic righteousness and civic pride*, Boston, MA 1914

Harris, George Montagu, *Municipal government in Britain: a study of the practice of local government in ten of the larger British cities*, London 1939

Hatton, Sidney Frank, *London's bad boys*, London 1931

Hayward, Frank Herbert, *Reflections on civics in schools*, London 1934

Higham, Charles S. S., *The good citizen: an introduction to civics*, London 1934

Hill, Mabel and Philip Davis, *Civics for new Americans*, New York, NY 1916

Historical Pageant of Manchester: Heaton Park, Manchester 1926

Howe, Frederic C., *The city: the hope of democracy*, New York, NY 1905

— *The British city: the beginnings of democracy*, New York, NY 1907

Hull-House maps and papers: a presentation of nationalities and wages in a congested district of Chicago, New York 1895

Hunter, J. D., 'Family relief and service', in Chicago Council of Social Agencies, *Social service year book, 1932*, Chicago, IL 1933, 9–17

Hunter, Robert, *Tenement conditions in Chicago: report by the investigating committee of the City Homes Association*, Chicago 1901

Illinois Committee on Public Utility Information, *Chicago's genii, the public utilities*, Chicago, IL 1921

Irish Historical Productions, *The pageant of the Celt*, Chicago, IL 1933

James, H. E. O. and F. T. Moore, 'Adolescent leisure in a working-class district', *Occupational Psychology* xiv (1940), 132–45

Jewish People's Institute, *Community culture in an era of depression*, Chicago, IL 1932

— *The development of a social force in Chicago*, Chicago, IL 1934

Joad, C. E. M., 'The people's claim', in Clough Williams-Ellis (ed.), *Britain and the beast*, London 1937, 64–85

Kay-Shuttleworth, James, *The moral and physical condition of the working class employed in the cotton manufacture in Manchester*, London 1832

Leisure of the people, Manchester 1919

Lethaby, W. R., 'Architecture as form in civilisation', in Lethaby, *Form in civilization*, 1–16

— 'Towns to live in', in Lethaby, *Form in civilization*, 22–34

— *Form in civilization: collected papers on art and labour*, London 1922

Lewis, Lloyd Downs and Henry Justin Smith, *Chicago: the history of its reputation*, New York, NY 1929

Macadam, Elizabeth, *The new philanthropy: a study in the relations between the statutory and voluntary social services*, London 1934

McCarthy, Charles, Flora Swan and Jennie McMullin, *Elementary civics: the new civics*, Chicago, IL 1918

MacKay, Constance D'Arcy, *Patriotic drama in your town*, New York, NY 1918

MacKaye, Percy, *The civic theatre in relation to the redemption of leisure*, New York, NY 1912

— Community drama: its motive and method of neighborliness, Boston, MA 1917

Manchester and District Regional Survey Society, Social studies of a Manchester city ward: a study of the health of Ancoats and some suggestions for its improvement, Manchester 1928

Manchester Guardian yearbook, Manchester 1925, 1927

Manchester Historical Pageant, Manchester 1938.

Manchester and Salford Better Housing Council, Angel Meadow and Red Bank: report of a survey undertaken in part of St. Michael's and collegiate wards of the city of Manchester by the Red Bank Survey Group, Manchester 1931

— Some housing conditions in Chorlton-on-Medlock, Manchester 1931

Manchester and Salford Sanitary Association, Public health considered in reference to the physical and moral condition of the people, Manchester 1855

Marr, Thomas H., Housing conditions in Manchester and Salford: a report prepared for the Citizens' Association for the Improvement of the Unwholesome Dwellings and Surroundings of the People, Manchester 1904

Masterman, Charles F. G., The heart of the empire: discussions of problems of modern city life in England, London 1907

— How England is governed, London 1921

Mearns, Andrew, The bitter cry of outcast London, London 1883

Merriam, Charles E., Civic education in the United States, Chicago, IL 1934

Miers, Henry A., 'Some characteristics of Manchester men', in Brindley, The soul of Manchester, 33–7

Moody, Walter D., 'Public schools: teaching the child city building', in Chicago Association of Commerce, First International Municipal Congress and Exposition, Chicago, IL 1911, 91–2

— Wacker's manual of the Plan of Chicago, Chicago, IL 1920

Mumford, Lewis, The culture of cities, London 1938

Municipal Voter's League, Annual preliminary report, Chicago, IL 1916

National Association of Housing Officials, Housing yearbook, Chicago, IL 1939

National Auditions annual: a Century of Progress souvenir edition of the Afro-American Pageant, Chicago, IL 1934

Newman, George, The rise of preventive medicine, Oxford 1932

Newsholme, Arthur, 'Some conditions of social efficiency in relation to local public administration', Public Health xxii (1908), 403–15

North, Cecil C., 'The city as a community: an introduction to a research project', in Ernest W. Burgess (ed.), The urban community: selected papers from the proceedings of the American Sociological Society, 1925, Chicago, IL 1926, 233–7

Official guide: book of the Fair, 1933, Chicago, IL 1933

Official pictures of A Century of Progress Exposition, Chicago, IL 1933

Orwell, George, The road to Wigan Pier (1937), New York, NY 1958

Parker, Louis Napoleon, 'Historical pageants', Journal of the Society of Arts (22 Dec. 1905), 142–6

— Several of my lives, London 1928.

Peddie, J. R., The British citizen: a book for young readers, Glasgow 1920

Phillips, Gordon, 'Manchester and its critics', in Brindley, The soul of Manchester, 261–70

Phythian, Arthur T., The ethics of citizenship: a universal basis from which to determine progressively the rights and duties of citizenship, Manchester 1923

Pierce, Bessie L., Citizens' organizations and the civic training of youth, Chicago, IL 1933

— (ed.), *As others see Chicago: impressions of visitors, 1673–1933* (1933), Chicago, IL 2004

Pilkington, Margaret, 'Social service', in Brindley, *The soul of Manchester*, 233–44

Priestley, J. B., *English journey*, London 1934

Public Ownership League of America, *Proceedings of Public Ownership Conference* (bulletin no. 14, 1919)

Redford, Arthur, *The history of local government in Manchester*, III: The last half century, London 1940

Reilly, Charles, 'The face of Manchester', in Brindley, *The soul of Manchester*, 100–12

Rex, F., *General outline of the municipal government of the city of Chicago*, Chicago, IL 1937

Riis, Jacob, *Children of the tenements*, New York, NY 1903

Roberts, Peter, *Civics for coming Americans*, New York, NY 1917

Robson, William A., 'The outlook', in Harold J. Laski, W. Ivor Jennings and William A. Robson (eds), *A century of municipal progress, 1835–1935*, London 1935, 455–64

Romance of a people, Chicago, IL 1933

Simmel, Georg, 'The metropolis and mental life' (1903), in *On individuality and social forms: selected writings of Georg Simmel*, ed. Donald N. Levine, Chicago, IL 1971, 324–39

Simon, Ernest D., *A city council from within*, London 1926

—and E. M. Hubback, *Training for citizenship*, London 1935

Simon, Shena D., *A century of city government: Manchester, 1838–1938*, London 1938

Sinclair, Upton, *The jungle*, New York, NY 1906

Smith, Henry Justin, *Chicago's great century: 1833–1933*, Chicago, IL 1933

Smith, T. V. and Leonard White, *Chicago: an experiment in social science research*, Chicago, IL 1929

Spring, Howard, *Shabby tiger* (1934), London 1973

Stead, W. T., *If Christ came to Chicago: a plea for the union of all who love in the service of all who suffer*, Chicago, IL 1894

Strong, Josiah, *The twentieth century city*, New York, NY 1898

Taylor, G., *Chicago Commons through forty years*, Chicago, IL 1936

Thrasher, Frederick M., *The gang: a study of 1,313 gangs in Chicago* (1927), Chicago, IL 1936

Tocqueville, Alexis de, *Democracy in America* (1835), trans. Harvey C. Mansfield and Delba Winthrop, Chicago, IL 2000

— *Journeys to England and Ireland*, trans. George Lawrence and K. P. Mayer; ed. J. P. Mayer, London 1957

Trevelyan, Janet Penrose, *Evening play centres for children: the story of their origin and growth*, London 1920

Tryon, Rolla M., *The social sciences as school subjects: report of the Commission on the Social Studies*, New York, NY 1935

Twigg, H. J., *Junior co-operators and their organisation*, Manchester 1923

Wacker, C. H., *An appeal to business men: provide work now for the unemployed, relation of national prosperity to city planning, business and the Chicago plan*, Chicago, IL 1921

Wallace, Florence Magill, *Pageant building*, Springfield, IL 1918

Walter, Benjamin, 'Paris, capital of the nineteenth century' (1939), *Perspecta* xii (1969), 163–72

Webb, Sidney, *Socialism in England*, London 1890

Wells, Ida B. (ed.), *The reason why the colored American is not in the World's Columbian Exposition*, Chicago, IL 1893

West, Florence E., *Stepping stones to citizenship*, Exeter 1923

West Chicago Park Commissioners, *Illinois Centennial Pageant, 1818–1918*, Chicago, IL 1918

White, Ebe M., *Civics in progress: suggestions to teachers of the subject*, London 1929

Williams-Ellis, Clough, *England and the octopus*, London 1928

Wilson, Edmund, 'Hull House in 1932', *New Republic* lxxiii (25 Jan 1933), 287–90

Wilson, Richard, *The complete citizen: an introduction to the study of civics*, London 1920

Worts, Frederick R., *Citizenship: its meaning, privileges and duties*, London 1919

Zangwill, Israel, 'The melting pot' (1908)

Ziegler, S. H. and H. J. Wilds, *Our community: good citizenship in towns and cities*, Philadelphia, PA 1918

Zorbaugh, Warren, *The Gold Coast and the slum: a sociological study of Chicago's Near North Side* (1929), Chicago, IL 1983

Secondary sources

Aalen, Frederick H. A., 'English origins', in Ward, *The Garden City*, 28–51

Ahier, John, *Industry, children and the nation: an analysis of national identity in school textbooks*, London 1988

Amsterdam, Daniel, 'Before the roar: US unemployment relief after World War I and the long history of a paternalist welfare policy', *JAH* ci/4 (2015), 1123–43

— *Roaring metropolis: businessmen's campaign for a civic welfare state*, Philadelphia, PA 2016

Anderson, Ben, 'A liberal countryside? The Manchester Ramblers' Federation and the "social readjustment" of urban citizens, 1929–1936', *Urban History* xxxviii/1 (2011), 84–102

Anderson, Benedict, *Imagined communities: reflections on the origin and spread of nationalism*, London 1983

Anthony, Scott and James G. Mansell, 'Introduction: the documentary film movement and the spaces of British identity', *Twentieth Century British History* xxiii/1 (2012), 1–11

Argersinger, Jo Ann E., 'Contested visions of American democracy: citizenship, public housing, and the international arena', *JUH* xxxvi/6 (2010), 792–813

Ater, Renee, 'Making history: Meta Warrick Fuller's Ethiopia', *American Art* xvii/3 (2003), 12–31

Auerbach, Jeffrey A., *The Great Exhibition of 1851: a nation on display*, New Haven, CT 1999

Bachin, Robin, 'At the nexus of labor and leisure: baseball, nativism, and the 1919 Black Sox scandal', *Journal of Social History* xxxvi/4 (2003), 941–62

— *Building the South Side: urban space and civic culture in Chicago, 1890–1919*, Chicago, IL 2004

Baigent, Elizabeth and Ben Cowell (eds), *'Nobler imaginings and mightier struggles': Octavia Hill, social activism, and the remaking of British society*, London 2016

Baker, Jean H. (ed.), *Votes for women: the struggle for suffrage revisited*, Oxford 2002

Baker, Laura E., 'Civic ideals, mass culture, and the public: reconsidering the 1909 plan of Chicago', *JUH* xxxvi/6 (2010), 747–70

Baldwin, Davarian, *Chicago's new negroes: modernity, the great migration, and black urban life*, Chapel Hill, NC 2007

Bartie, Angela, Linda Fleming, Mark Freeman, Tom Hulme and Paul Readman, 'Performing the past: identity, civic culture and historical pageants in twentieth-century English small towns', in Luda Klusakova (ed.), *Small towns in the 20th and 21st centuries: heritage and development strategies*, Prague 2017, 24–51

— and Alexander Hutton, 'Historical pageants and the medieval past in twentieth-century England', *EHR* cxxxiii/563 (2018), 866–902

— and Charlotte Tupman, '"And those who live, how shall I tell their fame?" Historical pageants, collective remembrance and the First World War, 1919–1939', *Historical Research* xc/249 (2017), 636–61

Bassett, Melanie, 'Regional societies and the migrant Edwardian Royal Dockyard worker: locality, nation and empire', in Naomi Lloyd-Jones and Margaret M. Scull (eds), *Four nations approaches to modern 'British' history: a (dis)United Kingdom?* London 2018, 189–214

Beach, Abigail, 'Potential for participation: health centres and the idea of citizenship, c.1920–1940', in Lawrence and Mayer, *Regenerating England*, 203–30

Beaumont, Caitríona, 'Citizens not feminists: the boundary negotiated between citizenship and feminism by mainstream women's organisations in England, 1928–39', *Women's History Review* ix/2 (2000), 411–29

Beaven, Brad, *Leisure, citizenship and working-class men in Britain, 1850–1945*, Manchester 2005

— *Patriotism, popular culture and the city, 1870–1939*, Manchester 2012

— and John Griffiths, 'Creating the exemplary citizen: the changing notion of citizenship in Britain, 1870–1939', *Contemporary British History* xxii/2 (2008), 203–25

Beers, Laura, 'Education or manipulation? Labour, democracy, and the popular press in interwar Britain', *JBS* xlviii/1 (2009), 129–52

Bellah, Robert N., 'Civil religion in America', *Daedalus* xcvi/1 (1967), 40–55

Bender, Thomas, 'Intellectuals, cities, and citizenship in the United States: the 1890s and 1990s', *Citizenship Studies* iii/2 (1999), 203–20

— 'Reflections on the culture of urban modernity', in Çınar and Bender, *Urban imaginaries*, 267–78

Bentley, Michael, *Modernizing England's past: English historiography in the age of modernism, 1870–1970*, Cambridge 2005

Berman, Marshall, *All that is solid melts into air: the experience of modernity*, New York, NY 1982

Biagini, Eugenio, *Citizenship and community: liberals, radicals and collective identities in the British Isles 1865–1931* (1996), Cambridge 2002

— 'Introduction: citizenship, liberty and community', in Biagini, *Citizenship and community*, 1–18

— 'Liberalism and direct democracy: John Stuart Mill and the model of ancient Athens', in Biagini, *Citizenship and community*, 21–44

Biles, Roger, 'Race and housing in Chicago', *Journal of the Illinois State Historical Society* xciv/1 (2001), 31–8

Black, Iain S., 'Modernity and the search for the urban variable', *JUH* xxxii/3 (2006), 466–76

Bluestone, Daniel, *Constructing Chicago*, New Haven, CT 1993

Bodnar, John E., *Remaking America: public memory, commemoration, and patriotism in the twentieth century*, Princeton, NJ, 1992

Boehm, Lisa Krissoff, *Popular culture and the enduring myth of Chicago, 1871–1968*, London 2004

Boisseau, Tracey Jean, 'Once again in Chicago: revisioning women as workers at the Chicago Woman's World's Fairs of 1925–1928', *Women's History Review* xviii/2 (2009), 265–91

Bolotin, Norman and Christine Laing, *The World's Columbian Exposition: the Chicago World's Fair of 1893*, Urbana, IL 2002

Bourke, Joanna, *Working class cultures in Britain, 1890–1960: gender, class and ethnicity*, London 1997

Boyd, Kelly, *Manliness and the Boys' Story paper in Britain: a cultural history, 1855–1940*, Basingstoke 2003

Boyd, Michelle R., *Jim Crow nostalgia: reconstructing race in Bronzeville*, Minneapolis, MN 2008

Boyer, Paul, *Urban masses and moral order in America, 1820–1920*, Cambridge, MA 1978

Bradley, Kate, *Poverty, philanthropy and the state: charities and the working classes in London, 1918–1979*, Manchester 1999

Brett, Peter, 'Citizenship education in Britain in the shadow of the Great War', *Citizenship Teaching and Learning* viii/1 (2013), 55–74

Briggs, Asa, *Victorian cities* (1963), Berkeley, CA 1993

—'Foreword', to H. J. Dyos (ed.), *The study of urban history: the proceedings of an international round-table conference of the Urban History Group*, London 1968, p. v

— 'Saxons, Normans and Victorians', in *The collected essays of Asa Briggs*, i, Brighton 1985, 215–35

Brindle, Patrick and Madeleine Arnot, '"England expects every man to do his duty": the gendering of the citizenship textbook, 1940–1966', *Oxford Review of Education* xv/1 (1999), 103–23

Bukowski, Douglas, *Big Bill Thompson, Chicago, and the politics of image*, Urbana, IL 1998

Burchardt, Jeremy, *Paradise lost: rural idyll and social change in England since 1800*, London 2002

Burke, Peter, 'Performing history: the importance of occasions', *Rethinking History* ix/1 (2005), 35–52

Burton, Alan, *The British consumer co-operative movement and film, 1890s–1960s*, Manchester 2005

Cain, Louis P., *Sanitation strategy for a lakefront metropolis: the case of Chicago*, DeKalb, IL 1978

Capozzola, Christopher, *Uncle Sam wants you: World War I and the making of the modern citizen*, Oxford 2008

Capshaw Smith, Katharine, 'Constructing a shared history: black pageantry for children during the Harlem Renaissance', *Children's Literature* xxvii (1999), 40–63

Carpenter, James J., '"The development of a more intelligent citizenship": John Dewey and the social studies', *Education and Culture* xxii/2 (2006), 31–42

Carson, Mina, *Settlement folk: social thought and the American settlement movement, 1885–1930*, Chicago, IL 1990

Carter, Laura, 'The Quennells and the "history of everyday life" in England, c. 1918-69', *History Workshop Journal* lxxxi/1 (2016), 107-34

Carter, Matt, *T. H. Green and the development of ethical socialism*, Exeter 2003

Carter, Simon, *Rise and shine: sunlight, technology and health*, Oxford 2007

Cavallo, Dominick, *Muscles and morals: organized playgrounds and urban reform, 1880-1920*, Philadelphia, PA 1981

Certeau, Michel de, *The practice of everyday life*, Berkeley, CA 1984

Chandler, James A., *Explaining local government: local government in Britain since 1800*, Manchester 2007

Chorley, Katharine, *Manchester made them*, London 1950

Churchill, David S., 'Making broad shoulders: body-building and physical culture in Chicago, 1890-1920', *History of Education Quarterly* xlviii/3 (2008), 341-70

Çınar, Alev and Thomas Bender, 'The city: experience, imagination, and place', in Çınar and Bender, *Urban imaginaries*, pp. xi-xxvi

— and Thomas Bender (eds), *Urban imaginaries: locating the modern city*, Minneapolis, MN 2007

Clark, Anna, 'Gender, class and the nation: franchise reform in England, 1832-1928', in James Vernon (ed.), *Re-reading the constitution: new narratives in the political history of England's long nineteenth century*, Cambridge 1996, 239-53

Codell, Julie F., 'Ford Madox Brown, Carlyle, Macaulay and Bakhtin: the pratfalls and penultimates of history', *Art History* xxi/3 (1998), 324-66

Cohen, Lizabeth, *Making a new deal: industrial workers in Chicago, 1919-1939*, Cambridge 1992

Colley, Linda, *Britons: forging the nation, 1707-1837*, London 1994

Colls, Robert, *George Orwell: English rebel*, Oxford 2013

— and Philip Dodd (eds), *Englishness: culture and politics, 1880-1920*, Beckenham, 1986

Conkin, Paul K., *Puritans and pragmatists: eight eminent American thinkers*, Bloomington, IN 1968

Conn, Steven, *Americans against the city: anti-urbanism in the twentieth century*, Oxford 2014

Connell, Kieran, *Black Handsworth: race in 1980s Britain*, Berkeley, CA 2019

Corbould, Clare, *Becoming African Americans: black public life in Harlem, 1919-1939*, Cambridge, MA 2009

Cott, Nancy F., 'Across the great divide: women in politics before and after 1920', in Louise A. Tilly and Patricia Gurin (eds), *Women, politics, and change*, New York, NY 1990, 153-76

Cowman, Krista, '"From the housewife's point of view": female citizenship and the gendered domestic interior in post-First World War Britain, 1918-1928', *EHR* cxxx/543 (2015), 352-83

Cozens, Joseph, 'The making of the Peterloo martyrs, 1819 to the present', in Keith Laybourn and Quentin Outram (eds), *Secular martyrdom in Britain and Ireland: from Peterloo to the present*, Basingstoke 2018, 31-58

Craig, Douglas B., *Fireside politics: radio and political culture in the United States, 1920-1940*, Baltimore, MD 2000

Cronon, William, *Nature's metropolis: Chicago and the great West*, New York, NY 1991

Crook, Tom, 'Accommodating the outcast: common lodging houses and the limits of urban governance in Victorian and Edwardian London', *Urban History* xxv/3 (2008), 414-36

Damer, Sean, '"Engineers of the human machine": the social practice of council housing management in Glasgow, 1895-1939', *Urban Studies* xxxvii/11 (2000), 2007-26

Darling, Elizabeth, '"Enriching and enlarging the whole sphere of human activities": the work of the voluntary sector in housing reform in inter-war Britain', in Lawrence and Mayer, *Regenerating England*, 149-78

—'What the tenants think of Kensal House: experts' assumptions versus inhabitants' realities in the modern home', *Journal of Architectural Education* liii/3 (2000), 167-77

— 'A citizen as well as a housewife: new spaces of femininity in 1930s London', in Hilde Heynen and Gülsüm Baydar (eds), *Negotiating domesticity: spatial productions of gender*, London 2005, 49-64

Dauber, Michele Landis, *The sympathetic state: disaster relief and the origins of the American welfare state*, Chicago, IL 2013

Daunton, Martin J., 'Payment and participation: welfare and state-formation in Britain 1900-1951', *Past & Present* 150 (Feb. 1996), 169-216.

— (ed.), *The Cambridge urban history of Britain*, III: *1840-1950*, Cambridge 2001

Davies, Andrew, *The gangs of Manchester: the story of the Scuttlers, Britain's first youth cult*, Preston 2008

— Steven Fielding and Terry Wyke (eds), *Workers' worlds: cultures and communities in Manchester and Salford, 1880-1939*, Manchester 1992

Davis, Allen F., *American heroine: the life and legend of Jane Addams* (1973), Oxford 2000

Davis, John, 'Central government and the towns', in Daunton, *Cambridge urban history*, iii. 259-86

Dawson, Sandra Trudgen, 'Designing consumer society: citizens and housing plans during World War II', in Erika Rappaport, Mark J. Crowley and Sandra Trudgen Dawson (eds), *Consuming behaviours: identity, politics and pleasure in twentieth-century Britain*, London 2015, 179-96

Deloria, Philip J., *Playing Indian*, New Haven, CT 1998

Dennis, Richard, *Cities in modernity: representations and productions of metropolitan space, 1840-1930*, Cambridge 2008

Diamond, Andrew J., *Mean streets: Chicago youths and the everyday struggle for empowerment in the multiracial city, 1908-1969*, Los Angeles, CA 2009

Dickerson, Dennis C., *African American preachers and politics: the Careys of Chicago*, Jackson, Ms 2010

Doyle, Barry M., 'The changing functions of urban government: councillors, officials and pressure groups', in Daunton, *Cambridge urban history of Britain*, iii. 287-314

Doyle, Brian, 'The invention of English', in Colls and Dodd, *Englishness*, 113-40.

Driver, Felix, 'Moral geographies: social science and the urban environment in mid-nineteenth century England', *Transactions of the Institute of British Geographers* xiii/3 (1988), 275-87

Druick, Zoë, *Projecting Canada: government policy and documentary film at the National Film Board of Canada*, Montreal 2007

Dumenil, Lynne, *The modern temper: American culture and society in the 1920s*, New York, NY 1995

Dwyer, Peter, *Understanding social citizenship: themes and perspectives for policy and practice*, Bristol 2004

Dyos, H. J. (ed.), *The study of urban history: the proceedings of an international round-table conference of the Urban History Group*, London 1968

Edwards, Sian, *Youth movements, citizenship and the English countryside: creating good citizens, 1930–1960*, London 2018

Eisner, Marc Allen, *From warfare state to welfare state: World War I, compensatory state building, and the limits of the modern order*, University Park, PA 2000

Ellis, Jack C. and Betsy A. McLane, *A new history of documentary film*, London 2006

Elshtain, Jean B. (ed.), *The Jane Addams reader*, Chicago. IL 2002

Englander, David, *Poverty and poor law reform in Britain: from Chadwick to Booth, 1834–1914*, London 1998

English, Jim, 'Empire Day in Britain, 1904–1958', *HJ* xlix/1 (2006), 247–76

Erickson, Christine K. '"So much for men": conservative women and national defense in the 1920s and 1930s', *American Studies* xlv/1 (2004), 85–102

Ewen, Shane, *What is urban history?*, Cambridge 2016

Fahrmeir, Andreas and H. S. Jones, 'Space and belonging in modern Europe: citizenship(s) in localities, regions, and states', *European Review of History* xv/3 (2008), 243–53

Fairbanks, Robert B., 'Advocating city planning in the public schools: the Chicago and Dallas experiences, 1911–1928', in Robert B. Fairbanks, Patricia Mooney-Melvin and Zane L. Miller (eds), *Making sense of the city: local government, civic culture, and community life in urban America*, Columbus, OH 2007, 57–76

Fairfield, John D., *The public and its possibilities: triumphs and tragedies in the American city*, Philadelphia, PA 2010

Fallace, Thomas, 'John Dewey's influence on the origins of the social studies: an analysis of the historiography and new interpretation', *Review of Educational Research* lxxix/2 (2009), 601–24

Fanning, Charles, 'Dueling cultures: Ireland and Irish America at the Chicago World's Fairs of 1933 and 1934', *New Hibernia Review* xv/3 (2011), 94–110

Fass, Paula S., *The damned and the beautiful: American youth in the 1920s*, Oxford 1977

Faulks, Keith, *Citizenship*, London 2000

Findling, John E., *Chicago's great World's Fairs*, Manchester 1994

Fielding, Steven, 'A separate culture? Irish Catholics in working-class Manchester and Salford, c. 1890–1939', in Davies, Fielding and Wyke, *Workers' worlds*, 23–48

Finlayson, Geoffrey, 'A moving frontier: voluntarism and the state in British social welfare 1911–1949', *Twentieth Century British History* i/2 (1990), 183–206

Fitzpatrick, David, 'A curious middle place: the Irish in Britain, 1871–1921', in Roger Swift and Sheridan Gilley, *The Irish in Britain, 1815–1939*, London 1989, 10–59

Flanagan, Maureen A., *Seeing with their hearts: Chicago women and the vision of the good city, 1871–1933*, Princeton, NJ 2002

Floyd Jr, Samuel A., 'The negro renaissance: Harlem and Chicago flowerings', in Hine and McCluskey, *The black Chicago renaissance*, 21–43

Ford, Liam T. A., *Soldier Field: a stadium and its city*, Chicago, IL 2009

Fowler, David, *The first teenagers: the lifestyle of young wage-earners in interwar Britain*, London 1996

— *Youth culture in modern Britain, c. 1920–c. 1970*, Basingstoke 2008

Fraser, Nancy, 'Rethinking the public sphere: a contribution to the critique of actually existing democracy', *Social Text* xxv/xxvi (1990), 56–80

Fraser, W. Hamish, 'From civic gospel to municipal socialism', in Derek Fraser (ed.), *Cities, class and communication*, Hemel Hempstead 1990, 58–86.

Freeden, Michael, *The New Liberalism: an ideology of social reform*, Oxford 1978

Freeman, Mark, 'The provincial social survey in Edwardian Britain', *Historical Research* lxxv/187 (2002), 73–89

— '"Splendid display; pompous spectacle": historical pageants in twentieth-century Britain', *Social History* xxxviii/4 (2013), 423–55

Freund, Daniel, *American sunshine: diseases of darkness and the quest for natural light*, Chicago, IL 2012

Fuerst, J. S., *When public housing was paradise: building community in Chicago*, Westport, CT 2003

Gaddis, Vincent H., *Herbert Hoover, unemployment, and the public sphere: a conceptual history, 1919–1933*, Oxford 2005

Gaddum, J., *Family Welfare Association of Manchester and Salford: a short history, 1833–1974*, Manchester 1974

Gainor, J. Ellen, 'Introduction', to Jeffrey D. Mason and J. Ellen Gainor (eds), *Performing America: cultural nationalism in American theater*, Ann Arbor, MI 1999, 7–18

Ganz, Cheryl R., *The 1933 Chicago World's Fair: a century of progress*, Urbana, IL 2012

Garb, Margaret, 'Health, morality, and housing: the "tenement problem" in Chicago', *American Journal of Public Health* xciii/9 (2003), 1420–30

— *Freedom's ballot: African American political struggles in Chicago from abolition to the Great Migration*, Chicago, IL 2014

Garrard, John, '1850–1914: the rule and decline of a new squirearchy?', *Albion: A Quarterly Journal Concerned with British Studies* xxvii/4 (1995), 583–621

— 'English mayors: what are they for?', in John Garrard (ed.), *Heads of the local state: mayors, provosts and burgomasters since 1800*, Aldershot 2007, 11–28

Gavin, Lettie, *American women in World War I: they also served*, Niwot, CO, 1997

Georgiou, Dion, 'Redefining the carnivalesque: the construction of ritual, revelry and spectacle in British leisure practices through the idea and model of "carnival", 1870–1939', *Sport in History* xxxxv/3 (2015), 335–63

Gerstle, Gary, *American crucible: race and nation in the twentieth century*, Princeton, NJ 2001

— 'Race and nation in the United States, Mexico, and Cuba, 1880–1940', in Don H. Doyle (ed.), *Nationalism in the New World*, Athens, GA 2006, 272–304

Gidlow, Liette, *The big vote: gender, consumer culture, and the politics of exclusion, 1890s–1920s*, Baltimore, MD 2004

Giglio, James N., 'Voluntarism and public policy between World War I and the New Deal: Herbert Hoover and the American Child Health Association', *Presidential Studies Quarterly* xiii/3 (1983), 430–52

Gladstone, David, *The twentieth-century welfare state*, Basingstoke 1999

— (ed.), *Before Beveridge: welfare before the welfare state*, London 1999

Glassberg, David, *American historical pageantry: the uses of tradition in the early twentieth century*, Chapel Hill, NC 1990

— *Sense of history: the place of the past in American life*, Amherst, MA 2001

Glenn, Evelyn Nakano, *Unequal freedom: how race and gender shaped American citizenship and labor*, Cambridge, MA 2002

Goetz, Edward G., *New Deal ruins: race, economic justice, and public housing policy*, Ithaca, NY 2013

Gold, John R. and Stephen V. Ward, 'Of plans and planners: documentary film and the challenge of the urban future, 1935-52', in David B. Clarke (ed.), *The cinematic city*, London 1997, 61–86

Goldin, Claudia, *The race between education and technology*, Cambridge, MA 2008

Goldsmith, Mike and John Garrard, 'Urban governance: some reflections', in Morris and Trainor, *Urban governance*, 15-27

Goldstein, Erik, 'Diplomacy in the service of history: Anglo-American relations and the return of the Bradford History of Plymouth Colony, 1898', *Diplomacy and Statecraft* xxv/1 (2014), 26-40

Gordon, Colin, *New deals: business, labor, and politics in America, 1920–1935*, Cambridge 1994

Gordon, Peter and John White, *Philosophers as educational reformers: the influence of Idealism on British educational thought and practice*, London 1979

Gosling, George Campbell, 'Rethinking the gift relationship in the British history of voluntary action', *Historische Zeitschrift*, forthcoming.

Gotham, Kevin Fox and Krisa Brumley, 'Using space: agency and identity in a public-housing development', *City and Community* i/3 (2002), 267-89

Grant, Bruce, *Fight for a city: the story of the Union League Club of Chicago and its times 1880-1955*, Chicago, IL 1955

Grant, Colin, *Negro with a hat: the rise and fall of Marcus Garvey*, Oxford 2008

Grant, Matthew, '"Civil defence gives meaning to your leisure": citizenship, participation, and cultural change in Cold War recruitment propaganda, 1949-54', *Twentieth Century British History* xxii/1 (2011), 52-78

Gräser, Marcus, 'A Jeffersonian skepticism of urban democracy? The educated middle class and the problem of political power in Chicago, 1880-1940', in Ralf Roth and Robert Beachy (eds), *Who ran the cities: city elites and urban power structures in Europe and North America, 1750-1940*, London 2007, 213-28

Green, Harvey, *Fit for America: fitness, sport, and American society*, Baltimore, MD 1986

Greene, Victor, 'Dealing with diversity: Milwaukee's multiethnic festivals and urban identity, 1840-1940', *JUH* xxxi/6 (2005), 820-49

Greenhalgh, James, *Reconstructing modernity: space, power and governance in mid twentieth century British cities*, Manchester 2018

Greer, Colin, *The great school legend: a revisionist interpretation of American public education*, New York, NY 1972

Griffiths, John R., 'Civic communication in Britain: a study of the *Municipal Journal* c. 1893-1910', *JUH* xxxiv/5 (2008), 775-94

Grimley, Matthew, *Citizenship, community and the Church of England: liberal Anglican theories of the state between the wars*, Oxford 2004

Grossman, James R., *Land of hope: Chicago, black southerners, and the Great Migration*, Chicago, IL 1989

Grover, Kathryn (ed.), *Fitness in American culture: images of health, sport, and the body, 1830-1940*, New York, NY 1989

Guglielmo, T. A., *White on arrival: Italians, race, color, and power in Chicago, 1890-1945*, New York 2003

Gullace, Nicolleta C., 'The blood of our sons': men, women and the renegotiation of British citizenship during the Great War, Basingstoke 2002

Gunn, Simon, *The public culture of the Victorian middle class: ritual and authority in the English industrial city, 1840-1914*, Manchester 2000

— *History and cultural theory*, Harlow 2006

Gurney, P. J., '"Intersex" and "dirty girls": Mass-Observation and working-class sexuality in England in the 1930s', *Journal of the History of Sexuality* viii/3 (1997), 256–90

Guttenberg, Albert Z., *The language of planning: essays on the origins and ends of American planning thought*, Urbana, IL 1993

Habermas, Jürgen, *The structural transformation of the public sphere: an inquiry into a category of bourgeois society*, Cambridge, MA 1989

Hagedorn, Ann, *Savage peace: hope and fear in America, 1919*, New York, NY 2007

Hall, Catherine, *Civilising subjects: metropole and colony in the English imagination, 1830–1867*, Chicago, IL 2002

Hall, Peter, *Cities of tomorrow: an intellectual history of urban planning and design since 1880*, Chichester 2014

Hall, Peter Dobkin, *Inventing the nonprofit sector and other essays on philanthropy, voluntarism, and nonprofit organizations*, Baltimore, MD 1992

Haller, Mark, 'Urban vice and civic reform: Chicago in the early twentieth century', in Kenneth T. Jackson and Stanley K. Schultz (eds), *Cities in American history*, New York, NY 1972, 290–305

Halloran, S. Michael, 'Text and experience in a historical pageant: toward a rhetoric of spectacle', *Rhetoric Society Quarterly* xxxi/4 (2001), 5–17

Hamby, Alonzo, *For the survival of democracy: Franklin Roosevelt and the world crisis of the 1930s*, New York, NY 2004

Hammack, David C., 'Failure and resilience: pushing the limits in depression and wartime', in Lawrence J. Friedman and Mark D. McGarvie (eds), *Charity, philanthropy, and civility in American history*, Cambridge 2003, 263–80

Harris, Alexandra, *Romantic moderns: English writers, artists and the imagination from Virginia Woolf to John Piper*, London 2010

Harris, Bernard, *The health of the schoolchild: a history of the School Medical Service in England and Wales*, Buckingham 1995

— *The origins of the British welfare state: social welfare in England and Wales, 1800–1945*, Basingstoke 2004

Harris, John, 'State social work and social citizenship in Britain: from clientalism to consumerism', *British Journal of Social Work* xxix/1 (1999), 915–37

Harris, José, 'Political thought and the welfare state, 1870–1940: an intellectual framework for British social policy', *Past & Present* no. 135 (May 1992), 116–41

— *Private lives, public spirit: a social history of Britain, 1870–1914*, Oxford 1993

Harty, Kevin J., 'Robin Hood on film: moving beyond a swashbuckling stereotype', in Thomas Hahn (ed.), *Robin Hood in popular culture: violence, transgression, and justice*, Cambridge 2000, 87–100

Hawkins, Mike, *Social Darwinism in European and American thought, 1860–1945: nature as model and nature as threat*, Cambridge 1997

Hawkins, Robert, 'The city as stage: performance, identity, and cultural democracy', *JUH* xli/1 (2015), 157–64

Hawley, Ellis W., 'Herbert Hoover, the commerce secretariat, and the vision of an "associative state", 1921–1928', *JAH* lxi/1 (1974), 116–40

Hayes, Nick, 'Civic perceptions: housing and local decision-making in English cities in the 1920s', *Urban History* xxvii/2 (2000), 211–33

Heale, Michael, *The United States in the long twentieth century: politics and society since 1900*, London 2015

Heap, Chad, *Slumming: sexual and racial encounters in American nightlife, 1885–1940*, Chicago, IL 2009

Heater, Derek, *What is citizenship?* Cambridge 1999

— *A history of education for citizenship*, London 2004

— *Citizenship in Britain: a history*, Edinburgh 2006

Heathorn, Stephen, *For home, country, and race: constructing gender, class and Englishness in the elementary school, 1880–1914*, Toronto 2000

Heise, Thomas, *Urban underworlds: a geography of twentieth-century American literature and culture*, New Brunswick, NJ 2011

Herrick, M. J., *The Chicago schools: a social and political history*, Beverley Hills, CA 1971

Higham, John, 'Hanging together: divergent unities in American history', *JAH* lxi/1 (1974), 5–28

Higuchi, Hayumi, 'The Billiken Club: "race leaders" educating children (1921–1940)', *Transforming Anthology* xiii/2 (2005), 154–9

Hilton, Matthew and James McKay (eds), *The ages of voluntarism: how we got to the big society*, Oxford 2011

Hine, Darlene Clark, 'Introduction', to Hine and McCluskey, *The black Chicago renaissance*, pp. xv–xxxiii

— and John McCluskey, Jr (eds), *The black Chicago renaissance*, Urbana, IL 2012

Hirsch, Arnold, *Making the second ghetto: race and housing in Chicago, 1940–1960*, New York, NY 1983

Hobbs, Allyson, *A chosen exile: a history of racial passing in American life*, Cambridge, MA 2014

Hobsbawn, Eric, 'Introduction: inventing traditions', in Eric Hobsbawn and Terrence Ranger (eds), *The invention of tradition*, Cambridge 1984

Hodges, Adam J., *World War I and urban order: the local class politics of national mobilization*, Basingstoke 2016

Hofstadter, Richard, *Social Darwinism in American thought* (1944), Boston, MA 1964

Holcombe, Randall G., 'The growth of the federal government in the 1920s', *Cato Journal* xvi/2 (1996), 175–99

Hollow, Matthew, 'The age of affluence revisited: council estates and consumer society in Britain, 1950–1970', *Journal of Consumer Culture* xvi/1 (2016), 279–96

Holston, James and Arjun Appadurai, 'Cities and citizenship', *Public Culture* viii (1996), 187–204

Hudson, Cheryl, '"The negro in Chicago": harmony in conflict, 1919–22', *European Journal of American Culture* xxix/1 (2010), 53–67

Hughes, Anne and Karen Hunt, 'A culture transformed? Women's lives in Wythenshawe in the 1930s', in Davies, Fielding and Wyke, *Workers' worlds*, 23–48

Hulme, Tom, 'Putting the city back into citizenship: civics education and local government in Britain, 1918–1945', *Twentieth Century British History* xxvi/1 (2015), 26–51

— '"A nation of town criers": civic publicity and historical pageantry in interwar Britain', *Urban History* xliv/2 (2017), 270–92

— 'Urban materialities: state housing and the governing of the body', in Simon Gunn and Tom Hulme, *New approaches to governance and rule in urban Europe since 1500*, London forthcoming

Hunt, D. Bradford, 'What went wrong with public housing in Chicago? A history of the Robert Taylor Homes', *Journal of the Illinois State Historical Society* xciv/1 (2001), 96–123

— *Blueprint for disaster: the unravelling of Chicago public housing*, Chicago, IL 2009

Hunt, Lynn, *Measuring time, making history*, Budapest 2008

Hunt, Tristram, *Building Jerusalem: the rise and fall of the Victorian city*, London 2004

Isenberg, Alison, *Downtown America: a history of the place and the people who made it*, Chicago, IL 2005

Isin, Engin F., 'The city as the site of the social', in Engin F. Isin (ed.), *Recasting the social in citizenship*, Toronto 2008, 261–80

Jackson, Andrew J. H., 'Civic identity, municipal governance and provincial newspapers: the Lincoln of Bernard Gilbert, poet, critic and "booster"', 1914', *Urban History* xlii/1 (2015), 113–29

Jaher, Frederic Cople, *The urban establishment: upper strata in Boston, New York, Charleston, Chicago, and Los Angeles*, Urbana, IL 1982

Jarvis, David, 'British Conservatism and class politics in the 1920s', *EHR* cxi/440 (1996), 59–84

Jenkinson, Jacqueline, *Black 1919: riots, racism and resistance in imperial Britain*, Liverpool 2009

Jennings, Bernard, 'The friends and enemies of the WEA', in Roberts, *A ministry of enthusiasm*, 97–110

Jones, Ben, *The working class in mid twentieth-century England: community, identity and social memory*, Manchester 2012

Jones, Gareth Stedman, *Outcast London: a study in the relationship between classes in Victorian society* (1971), London 2013

Jones, Peter, *From virtue to venality: corruption in the city*, Manchester 2013

Joyce, Patrick, *Visions of the people: industrial England and the question of class, c.1848–1914*, Cambridge 1991

— *The rule of freedom: liberalism and the modern city*, London 2003

Judge, Roy, 'May Day and Merrie England', *Folklore* cii/2 (1991), 131–48

Kadish, Sharman, *A good Jew and a good Englishman: the Jewish Lads' and Girls' Brigade, 1895–1995*, London 1995

Kahan, Michael B., 'Urban America', in Christopher M. Nichols and Nancy C. Unger, *A companion to the Gilded Age and Progressive Era*, Chichester 2017, 31–43

Karpf, Juanita, 'Get the pageant habit: E. Azalia Hackley's festivals and pageants during the First World War years, 1914–1918', *Popular Music and Society* xxxiv/5 (2011), 517–56

Kasinitz, Philip, *Metropolis: centre and symbol of our times*, New York, NY 1995

Katz, Michael B., 'From urban as site to urban as place: reflections on (almost) a half-century of US urban history', *JUH* xli/4 (2015), 560–6

Kearney, Hugh, *The British Isles: a history of four nations*, Cambridge 1989

Kefford, Alistair, 'Housing the citizen-consumer in post-war Britain: the Parker Morris Report, affluence and the even briefer life of social democracy', *Twentieth Century British History* xxix/2 (2018), 225–58

Kennedy, David M., *Freedom from fear: the American people in depression and war, 1929–1945*, New York, NY 1999

Kenny, Nicholas and Rebecca Madgin, '"Every time I describe a city": urban history as comparative and transnational practice', in Nicholas Kenny and Rebecca Madgin (eds), *Cities beyond borders: comparative and transnational approaches to urban history*, Abingdon 2015, 3–26

Kent, Susan Kingsley, *Making peace: the reconstruction of gender in interwar Britain*, Princeton, NJ 1993

Kerber, Linda K., 'The meanings of citizenship', *JAH* lxxxiv/3 (1997), 833–54

Kidd, Alan, 'Introduction: the middle class in nineteenth-century Manchester', in Alan Kidd and Kenneth Roberts (eds), *City, class and culture: studies of social policy and cultural production in Victorian Manchester*, Manchester 1985, 1–25

— *Manchester* (1993), Edinburgh 2002

Kimble Jr, Lionel, *A New Deal for Bronzeville: housing, employment and civil rights in black Chicago, 1935–1955*, Carbondale, IL 2015

Kirschbaum, Erik, *Burning Beethoven: the eradication of German culture in the United States during World War I*, New York, NY 2015

Kivisto, Peter and Thomas Faist, *Citizenship: discourse, theory, and transnational prospects*, Oxford 2007

Kloppenberg, James, *Uncertain victory: social democracy and progressivism in European and American thought, 1870–1920*, Oxford 1996

Køhlert, Frederik Byrn, *The Chicago literary experience: writing the city, 1893–1953*, Copenhagen 2011

Koven, Seth, *Slumming: sexual and social politics in Victorian London*, Princeton, NJ 2004

Krambles, George and Arthur H. Peterson, *CTA at forty-five: a history of the first forty-five years of the Chicago Transit Authority*, Oak Park, IL 1993

Krasner, David, *A beautiful pageant: African American theatre, drama, and performance in the Harlem Renaissance, 1910–1927*, Basingstoke 2002

Kyvig, David E., *Daily life in the United States, 1920–1939: decades of promise and pain*, Westport, CT 2002

L'Etang, Jacquie, *Public relations in Britain: a history of professional practice in the twentieth century*, Mahwah, NJ 2004

Lasch-Quinn, Elisabeth, *Black neighbors: race and the limits of reform in the American settlement house movement, 1890–1945*, Chapel Hill, NC 1993

Law, Alex, 'The ghost of Patrick Geddes: civics as applied sociology', *Sociological Research Online* x/2 (2005), 1–14

Lawrence, Christopher and Anna-K. Mayer (eds), *Regenerating England: science, medicine and culture in interwar Britain*, Atlanta, GA 2000

Lees, Andrew, *Cities perceived: urban society in European and American thought, 1820–1940*, Manchester 1985

— and Lynn Hollen Lees, *Cities and the making of modern Europe, 1750–1914*, Cambridge 2007

Lefebvre, Henri, *The production of space*, Oxford 1991

Leighton, Denys, *The Greenian moment: T. H. Green, religion and political argument in Victorian Britain*, Exeter 2004

LeMahieu, D. L., *A culture for democracy: mass communication and the cultivated mind in Britain between the wars*, Oxford 1988

Lerner, Richard M. and Laurence Steinberg, 'The scientific study of adolescent development', in Richard M. Lerner and Laurence Steinberg (eds), *Handbook of adolescent psychology*, I: *Individual bases of adolescent development*, Hoboken, NJ 2009

Leuchtenburg, William E., *The perils of prosperity, 1914–1932*, Chicago, IL 1993

Levene, Alysa, Martin Powell, John Stewart and Becky Taylor, *Cradle to grave: municipal medicine in interwar England and Wales*, Oxford 2011

Lewis, Jane, 'The voluntary sector in the mixed economy of welfare', in Gladstone, *Before Beveridge*, 10–17

Light, Alison, *Forever England: femininity, literature and conservatism between the wars*, London 1991

Lloyd-Jones, Naomi and Margaret M. Scull, *Four nations approaches to modern 'British' history: a (dis)United Kingdom?*, London 2018

Lombardo, Timothy J., 'Making urban citizens: civility and civic virtue in the modern metropolis', *JUH* xli/1 (2014), 143–51

Lovett, Robert Mors and Oscar Ludmann, 'Hull-House, 1921–1937', in Allen F. Davis and Mary Lynn McCree (eds), *Eighty years at Hull-House*, Chicago, IL 1969, 166–72

Lowenthal, David, 'Past time, present place: landscape and memory', *Geographical Review* lxv/1 (1975), 1–36

Luckin, Bill, 'Revisiting the idea of degeneration in urban Britain, 1830–1900', *Urban History* xxxiii/2 (2006), 234–52

Lumsden, Linda J., *Rampant women: suffragists and the right of assembly*, Knoxville, TN 1997

McCarthy, Helen, 'Parties, voluntary associations, and democratic politics in interwar Britain', *HJ* l/4 (2007), 891–912

— *The British people and the League of Nations: democracy, citizenship and internationalism, c. 1918–45*, Manchester 2011

McCarthy, Kathleen D., *Noblesse oblige: charity and cultural philanthropy in Chicago, 1849–1929*, Chicago, IL 1982

McCarthy, Michael P., 'The new metropolis: Chicago, the annexation movement and progressive reform', in Michael H. Ebner and Eugene M. Tobin (eds), *The age of urban reform: new perspectives on the Progressive Era*, London 1977, 43–63

McDonald, John F., *Urban America: growth, crisis, and rebirth*, London 2008

— *Chicago: an economic history*, Abingdon 2016

McFarlane, Barbara, 'Homes fit for heroines: housing in the twenties', in Matrix (ed.), *Making space: women and the man-made environment*, London 1984, 26–36

McGreevy, John, *Parish boundaries: the Catholic encounter with race in the twentieth-century urban north*, Chicago, IL 1996

Mackay, Alice Jane and Pat Thane, 'The Englishwoman', in Colls and Dodd, *Englishness*, 217–54

Macleod, David I., *Building character in the American boy: the Boy Scouts, YMCA, and their forerunners, 1870–1920*, Madison, WI 1983

Mandler, Peter, 'Against "Englishness": English culture and the limits to rural nostalgia, 1850–1940', *Transactions of the Royal Historical Society* vii (1997), 155–75

— 'How modern is it?', *JBS* xlii/2 (2003), 271–82

Marsden, William E., *The school textbook: geography, history and social studies*, London 2001

Mason, Jeffrey D., 'American stages (curtain raiser)', in Jeffrey D. Mason and J. Ellen Gainor (eds), *Performing America: cultural nationalism in American theater*, Ann Arbor, MI 1999, 1–6.

Matless, David, 'Regional surveys and local knowledges: the geographical imagination in Britain, 1918–39', *Transactions of the Institute of British Geographers* xvii (1992), 464–80

— *Landscape and Englishness*, London 1998

Matthews, David, *Medievalism: a critical history*, Woodbridge 2015

Mattson, Kevin, *Creating a democratic public: the struggle for urban participatory democracy during the Progressive Era*, Philadelphia, PA 1998

Mayne, Alan, *The imagined slum: newspaper representation in three cities, 1870–1914*, Leicester 1993

Meacham, Standish, *Toynbee Hall and social reform, 1880–1914: the search for community*, London 1987

Meller, Helen, *Patrick Geddes: social evolutionist and city planner*, London 1990

Mettler, Suzanne, 'Social citizens of separate sovereignties: governance in the New Deal welfare state', in Sidney M. Milkis and Jerome M. Mileur (eds), *The New Deal and the triumph of Liberalism*, Amherst, MA 2002, 231-71

Metzger, Janice, *What would Jane say? City-building women and a tale of two Chicagos*, Chicago, IL 2009

Mitrani, Sam, 'Diversity, conflict, empowerment? The politics of black Chicago from abolition to Harold Washington', *JUH* xlii/5 (2016), 953-9

Molina, Natalia, *How race is made in America: immigration, citizenship, and the historical power of racial scripts*, Berkeley, CA 2014

Monger, David, *Patriotism and propaganda in First World War Britain: the National War Aims Committee and civilian morale*, Liverpool 2012

Morris, Jeremy, 'The strange death of Christian Britain: another look at the secularization debate', *HJ* xlvi/4 (2003), 963-76

Morris, R. J., 'Governance: two centuries of urban growth', in Morris and Trainor, *Urban governance*, 1-14

— 'Structure, culture and society in British towns', in Daunton, *Cambridge urban history of Britain*, iii. 395-426

— and R. H. Trainor (eds), *Urban governance: Britain and beyond since 1750*, London 2000

Moses, Lester G., *Wild West shows and the images of American Indians, 1883–1933*, Albuquerque, NM 1996

Most, Andrea, *Making Americans: Jews and the Broadway musical*, Cambridge, MA 2004

Moulton, Mo, *Ireland and the Irish in interwar England*, Cambridge 2014

Mrozek, Donald, 'Sport in American life: from national health to personal fulfilment, 1890-1940', in Grover, *Fitness in American culture*, 18-46

Mumford, Kevin, *Interzones: black/white sex districts in Chicago and New York in the early twentieth century*, New York, NY 1997

Murphy, Kate, *Fears and fantasies: modernity, gender, and the rural-urban divide*, London 2010

Murphy, Paul V., *The new era: American thought and culture in the 1920s*, Lanham, MD 2011

Neary, Timothy B., 'Black-belt Catholic space: African-American parishes in interwar Chicago', *US Catholic Historian* xviii/4 (2000), 76-91

Newton-Matza, Mitchell, *Jazz Age: people and perspectives*, Santa Barbara, CA 2009

Nicholas, Siân, 'From John Bull to John Citizen: images of national identity and citizenship on the wartime BBC', in Weight and Beach, *The right to belong*, 36-58

Norman, Alison, '"A highly favoured people": the planter narrative and the 1928 Grand Historic Pageant of Kentville, Nova Scotia', *Acadiensis* xxxviii/2 (2009), 116-40

Novak, William J., 'The myth of the "weak" American state', *American Historical Review* cxiii/3 (2008), 752–72

O'Leary, Cecilia E., *To die for: the paradox of American patriotism*, Princeton, NJ 1999

Olneck, Michael R., 'Americanization and the education of immigrants, 1900–1925: an analysis of symbolic action', *American Journal of Education* xcvii/4 (1989), 398–423

Otter, Sandra D., '"Thinking in communities": late nineteenth-century Liberals, Idealists and the retrieval of community', *Parliamentary History* xvi/1 (1997), 67–84

Pacyga, Dominic A, *Chicago: a biography*, Chicago, IL 2009

— *Slaughterhouse: Chicago's Union Stock Yard and the world it made*, Chicago, IL 2015

Parchami, Ali, *Hegemonic peace and empire: the Pax Romana, Britannica and Americana*, London 2009

Park, Roberta J., 'Healthy, moral, and strong: educational views of exercise and athletics in nineteenth-century America', in Grover, *Fitness in American culture*, 123–68

Patterson, James T., *Grand expectations: the United States, 1945–1974*, Oxford 1996

Paul, Kathleen, *Whitewashing Britain: race and citizenship in the postwar era*, Ithaca, NY 1997

Pearson, Geoffrey, *Hooligan: a history of respectable fears*, London 1983

Pegram, Thomas R., *One hundred percent American: the rebirth and decline of the Ku Klux Klan in the 1920s*, Chicago, IL 2011

Perkins, Chris and Martin Dodge, 'Mapping the imagined future: the roles of visual representation in the 1945 City of Manchester Plan', *Bulletin of the John Rylands University Library of Manchester* lxxxix (2012), 247–76

Philpott, Thomas L., *The slum and the ghetto: immigrants, blacks, and reformers in Chicago, 1890–1930*, Belmont, CA 1978

Pick, Daniel, *Faces of degeneration: a European disorder, c. 1848–c. 1918*, Cambridge 1989

Platt, Anthony M., 'The negro family in the United States, E. Franklin Frazier', in Gwendolyn Mink and Alice O'Connor, *Poverty in the United States: an encyclopaedia of history, politics and policy*, i, Santa Barbara, CA 2004, 495–7

Platt, Harold, *Shock cities: the environmental transformation and reform of Manchester and Chicago*, Chicago, IL 2005

Plotkin, Wendy, '"Hemmed in": the struggle against racial restrictive covenants and deed restrictions in post-WWII Chicago', *Journal of the Illinois State Historical Society* xciv/1 (2001), 39–69

Popkin, Sue J., *The hidden war: crime and the tragedy of public housing in Chicago*, New Brunswick, NJ 2000

Porter, Bernard, *Absent-minded imperialists: what the British really thought about empire*, Oxford 2004

Porter, Dorothy, '"Enemies of the race": biologism, environmentalism, and public health in Edwardian England', *Victorian Studies* xxxiv/2 (1991), 159–78

Prakash, Gyan, 'Introduction: imaging the modern city, darkly', in Gyan Prakash (ed.), *Noir urbanisms: dystopic images of the modern city*, Princeton, NJ 2010, 1–13

Proctor, Tammy M., *On my honour: Guides and Scouts in interwar Britain*, Philadelphia, PA 2002

Quandt, Jean B., *From the small town to the great community: the social thought of progressive intellectuals*, New Brunswick, NJ 1970

Radford, Gail, *Modern housing for America: policy struggles in the New Deal era*, Chicago, IL 1996

— 'From municipal socialism to public authorities: institutional factors in the shaping of American public enterprise', *JAH* xc/3 (2003), 863–90

Ralph, J. R., *Northern protest: Martin Luther King, Jr., Chicago, and the civil rights movement*, Cambridge, MA 1993

Ravetz, Alison, *Council housing and culture: the history of a social experiment*, London 2001

Rea, Anthony, *Manchester's Little Italy: memories of the Italian colony of Ancoats*, Manchester 1988

Readman, Paul, 'The place of the past in English culture c. 1890–1914', *Past & Present*, no. 186 (Feb. 2005), 147–99

— *Storied ground: landscape and the shaping of English national identity*, Cambridge 2018

Reed, Christopher R., *The Depression comes to the South Side: protest and politics in the black metropolis, 1930–1933*, Bloomington, IN 2011

Reiman, Richard A, *The New Deal and American youth: ideas and ideals in a depression decade*, Athens, GA 1992

Reuben, Julie A., 'Beyond politics: community civics and the redefinition of citizenship in the Progressive Era', *History of Education Quarterly* xxxvii/4 (1997), 399–420

Revell, Keith D., *Building Gotham: civic culture and public policy in New York City, 1898–1938*, Baltimore, MD 2003

Rieger, Bernhard and Martin Daunton,, 'Introduction', in Martin Daunton and Bernard Rieger (eds), *Meanings of modernity: Britain from the late-Victorian era to World War II*, Oxford 2001, 1–24

Riesman, David, 'Some observations on Lewis Mumford's *The city in history*', *Salmagundi* xlix (1980), 80–6

Ritvo, Harriet, *The dawn of green: Manchester, Thirlmere, and modern environmentalism*, Chicago, IL 2009

Roberts, Ben, 'Entertaining the community: the evolution of civic ritual and public celebration, 1860–1953', *Urban History* xliv/3 (2017), 444–63

Roberts, Robert, *The classic slum: Salford life in the first quarter of the century* (1971), Bungay 1983

Roberts, Stephen K., 'The evolution of the WEA in the West Midlands, 1905–26', in Roberts, *A ministry of enthusiasm*, 77–96

— (ed.), *A ministry of enthusiasm: centenary essays on the Workers' Educational Association*, London 2003

Rodger, Richard and Robert Colls, 'Civil society and British cities', in Robert Colls and Richard Rodger (eds), *Cities of ideas: civil society and urban governance in Britain, 1800–2000*, Farnham 2004, 1–20

Rodgers, Daniel T., *Atlantic crossings: social politics in a progressive age*, London 1998

Rodrick, Anne B., *Self-help and civic culture: citizenship in Victorian Birmingham*, Farnham 2004

Roediger, David R., *Working towards whiteness: how America's immigrants became white, the strange journey from Ellis Island to the suburbs*, New York, NY 2005

Rose, Jonathan, *The intellectual life of the British working classes*, Reading 2001

Rose, Michael E. and Anne Woods, *Everything went on at the Round House: a hundred years of the Manchester University Settlement*, Manchester 1995

Rose, Sonya, 'Sex, citizenship, and the nation in World War II Britain', *American Historical Review* ciii/4 (1998), 1147–76

— *Which people's war? National identity and citizenship in Britain, 1939–1945*, Oxford 2003

Rutkoff, Peter M. and William B., Scott, 'Pinkster in Chicago: Bud Billiken and the mayor of Bronzeville, 1930–1945', *Journal of African American History* lxxxix/4 (2004), 316–30

Ryan, Deborah Sugg, 'Staging the imperial city: the Pageant of London, 1911', in Felix Driver and David Gilbert (eds), *Imperial cities: landscape, display and identity*, Manchester 1999, 117–35

— '"Pageantitis": Frank Lascelles' 1907 Oxford Historical Pageant, visual spectacle and popular memory', *Visual Culture in Britain* viii/2 (2007), 63–82

Ryan, Mary, 'The American parade: representations of the nineteenth-century social order', in Lynne Hunt (ed.), *The new cultural history*, London 1989, 131–53

— *Civic wars: democracy and public life in the American city during the nineteenth century*, Berkeley, CA 1997

Rydell, Robert, 'The fan dance of science: American World's Fairs in the Great Depression', *Isis: A Journal of the History of Science* lxxvi (1985), 525–42

— *World of fairs: the Century-of-Progress Expositions*, Chicago, IL 1993

— '"Darkest Africa": African shows at America's world's fairs, 1893–1940', in Bernth Lindfors (ed.), *Africans on stage: studies in ethnological show business*, Bloomington, IN 1999, 135–55

Saler, Michael T., *The avant-garde in interwar England: medieval modernism and the London Underground*, Oxford 2001

Saunier, Pierre-Yves, 'Introduction', to Pierre-Yves Saunier and Shane Ewen (eds), *Another global city: historical explorations into the transnational municipal moment, 1850–2000*, Basingstoke 2008, 1–18

Savage, Jon, *Teenage: the creation of youth, 1875–1945*, London 2007

Savage, Mike, Alan Warde and Kevin Ward, *Urban sociology, capitalism and modernity*, Basingstoke 2003

Schaffer, Daniel, 'The American Garden City: lost ideals', in Ward, *The Garden City*, 127–45

Schlör, Joachin, *Nights in the big city: Paris, Berlin, London, 1840–1930*, London 1998

Scott, Neil, *People of Hulme: some Manchester memories*, Hulme 2003

Schottenhamel, George, 'How Big Bill Thompson won control of Chicago', *Journal of the Illinois State Historical Society* xlv (1952), 30–49

Schrenk, Lisa D., *Building a Century of Progress: the architecture of the 1933–34 Chicago World's Fair*, Minneapolis, MN 2007

Schudson, Michael, *The good citizen: a history of American civic life*, New York, NY 1998

Searle, Geoffrey R., *The quest for national efficiency: a study in British politics and political thought, 1899–1914*, Oxford 1971

Selig, Diana, *Americans all: the cultural gifts movement*, London 2008

Shackel, Paul A., 'Public memory and the search for power in American historical archaeology', *American Anthropologist* ciii/3 (2001), 655–70

Shafir, Gershon (ed.), *The citizenship debates: a reader*, Minneapolis, MN 1998

Shapely, Peter, *The politics of housing: power, consumers and urban culture*, Manchester 2007

— 'Governance in the post-war city: historical reflections on public-private partnerships in the UK', *International Journal of Urban and Regional Research* xxxvii/4 (2012), 1288–304

Sharpe, Pamela, 'Population and society, 1700–1840', in Peter Clark (ed.), *Cambridge urban history of Britain*, II: *1540–1840*, Cambridge 2000, 491–528

Sherington, G. E., 'The 1918 education act: origins, aims and development', *British Journal of Educational Studies* xxiv/1 (1976), 66–85

Shiman, Lilian Lewis, 'The Band of Hope movement: respectable recreation for working-class Children', *Victorian Studies* xvii/1 (1973), 49–74

Simonson, Mary, *Body knowledge: performance, intermediality, and American entertainment at the turn of the twentieth century*, Oxford 2013

Skocpol, Theda, 'The Tocqueville problem: civic engagement in American democracy', *Social Science History* xxi/4 (1997), 455–79

— Marshall Ganz and Ziad Munson, 'A nation of organizers: the institutional origins of civic voluntarism in the United States', *American Political Science Review* xciv/3 (2000), 527–46

Smith, Michael P. and Thomas Bender (eds), *City and nation: rethinking place and identity* (2001), New York, NY 2017

Smith, Rogers M., *Civic ideals: conflicting visions of citizenship in US history*, New Haven, CT 1997

Snape, Robert, *Leisure, voluntary action and social change in Britain, 1880–1939*, London 2018

Spann, Edward K., *Designing modern America: the Regional Planning Association of America and its members*, Columbus, OH 1996

Sparrow, James T., *Warfare state: World War II Americans and the age of big government*, Oxford 2011

Spear, Allan, *Black Chicago: the making of a negro ghetto, 1890–1920*, Chicago, IL 1967

Spinney, Robert G., *City of big shoulders: a history of Chicago*, DeKalb, IL 2000

Stange, Maren, *Symbols of ideal life: social documentary photography in America, 1890–1915*, Cambridge 1989

Stapleton, Julia, *Political intellectuals and public identities in Britain since 1850*, Manchester 2001

— 'Citizenship versus patriotism in twentieth-century England', *HJ* xlviii/1 (2005), 151–78

Stearns, Peter N., *Battleground of desire: the struggle for self-control in modern America*, New York, NY 1999

Stears, Marc, *Pluralists, and the problems of the state: ideologies of reform in the United States and Britain, 1906–1926*, Oxford 2002

Stevenson, John, *British society, 1914–1945*, London 1984

Stocks, Mary D., *Fifty years in Every Street: the story of the Manchester University Settlement*, Manchester 1945

— *Ernest Simon of Manchester*, Manchester 1963

Stovall, Mary E., 'The *Chicago Defender* in the Progressive Era', *Illinois Historical Journal* lxxxiii/3 (1990), 159–72

Stray, Chris, 'Paradigms regained: towards a historical sociology of the textbook', *Journal of Curriculum Studies* xxvi/1 (1994), 1–29

Strickland, Arvarh E., *History of the Chicago Urban League*, Urbana, IL 1966

Stuart, P. H., *Philanthropy, voluntarism, and innovation: settlement houses in twentieth-century America*, Indianapolis, IN 1992

Sturdy, Steve, 'Hippocrates and state medicine: George Newman outlines the founding policy of the Ministry of Health', in Christopher Lawrence and George Weisz (eds), *Greater than the parts: holism in biomedicine, 1920–1950*, Oxford 1998, 112–34

Sugrue, Thomas J., *Sweet land of liberty: the forgotten struggle for civil rights in the North*, New York, NY 2008

Sundstrom, Linea, 'The "Pageant of Paha Sapa": an origin myth of white settlement in the American West', *Great Plains Quarterly* xxviii/1 (2008), 3–26

Susman, Warren, 'Ritual fairs', *Chicago History* xii/3 (1983), 4–7

Teaford, Jon, *The twentieth-century American city: problem, promise and reality*, Baltimore, MD 1986

Tebbutt, Melanie, 'Rambling and manly identity in Derbyshire's Dark Peak, 1880s–1920s', *HJ* xlix/4 (2006), 1125–53

— *Being boys: youth, leisure and identity in the inter-war years*, Manchester 2012

Thane, Pat, *Foundations of the welfare state* (1982), Harlow 1996

Thomas, Zoe, 'Historical pageants, citizenship, and the performance of women's history before second-wave feminism', *Twentieth Century British History* xxviii/3 (2017), 319–43

Thompson, F. M. L., 'Social control in Victorian Britain', *Economic History Review* xxxiv/2 (1981), 189–208

Tinkler, Penny, *Constructing girlhood: popular magazines for girls growing up in England, 1920–1950*, Abingdon 1995

— and Cheryl Krasnick Warsh, 'Feminine modernity in interwar Britain and North America: corsets, cars, and cigarettes', *Journal of Women's History* xx/3 (2008), 113–43

Todd, Selina, 'Flappers and factory lads: youth and youth culture in interwar Britain', *History Compass* iv/2 (2006), 715–30

Toon, Elizabeth, 'Selling the public on public health: the Commonwealth and Milbank health demonstrations and the meaning of community health education', in Ellen C. Lagemann (ed.), *Philanthropic foundations: new scholarship, new possibilities*, Bloomington, IN 1999, 119–30

Trattner, Walter I., *From poor law to welfare state: a history of social welfare in America* (1974), New York, NY 1979

Trentmann, Frank, 'Materiality in the future of history: things, practices, and politics', *JBS* xlviii/2 (2009), 283–307

Treuherz, Julian, 'Ford Madox Brown and the Manchester murals', in John G. Archer (ed.), *Art and architecture in Victorian Manchester*, Manchester 1985, 162–207

Trolander, Judith Ann, *Settlement houses and the Great Depression*, Detroit, MI 1975

Tuttle Jr, William M., *Race riot: Chicago in the red summer of 1919*, New York, NY 1970

United Charities of Chicago, *Yesterday, today, 1857–1957*, Chicago, IL 1957

Vaillant, Derek, *Sounds of reform: progressivism and music in Chicago, 1873–1935*, Chapel Hill, NC 2003

Van Slyck, Abigail A., *A manufactured wilderness: summer camps and the shaping of American youth, 1890–1960*, Minneapolis, MN 2006

Vandrei, Martha, 'A Victorian invention? Thomas Thornycroft's "Boadicea group" and the idea of historical culture in Britain', *HJ* lvii/2 (2014), 485–508

Vernon, James, *Distant strangers: how Britain became modern*, Berkeley, CA 2014

— *Modern Britain: 1750 to the present*, Cambridge 2017

Wall, Wendy L., *Inventing the 'American way': the politics of consensus from the New Deal to the civil rights movement*, Oxford 2008

Wallis, Mick, 'Pageantry and the Popular Front: ideological production in the thirties', *New Theatre Quarterly* x/38 (1994), 132–56

Ward, David, *Poverty, ethnicity and the American city, 1840–1925: changing conceptions of the slum and the ghetto*, Cambridge 1989

Ward, Stephen V., 'The Garden City introduced', in Ward, *The Garden City*, 1–27

— *Selling places: the marketing and promotion of towns and cities, 1850–2000*, London 1998.

— (ed.), *The Garden City: past, present and future*, London 1992

Warner Jr, Sam Bass, *The urban wilderness: a history of the American city*, New York, NY 1972

Watanabe-O'Kelly, Helen and Anne Simon, *Festivals and ceremonies: bibliography of works relating to court, civic and religious festivals in Europe, 1500–1800*, London 2000

Waters, Chris, '"Dark strangers" in our midst: discourses of race and nation in Britain, 1947–1963', *JBS* xxxvi/2 (1997), 207–38

Weight, Richard, *Patriots: national identity in Britain, 1940–2000*, Basingstoke 2002

— and Abigail Beach (eds), *The right to belong: citizenship and national identity in Britain, 1930–1960*, London 1988

Welshman, John, 'Physical education and the School Medical Service in England and Wales, 1907–1939', *Social History of Medicine* ix/1 (1996), 31–48

Wendt, Lloyd, *Chicago Tribune: the rise of a great American newspaper*, Chicago, IL 1979

— and Herman Kogan, *Big Bill of Chicago* (1953), Evanston, IL 2005

Werner, Michael and Bénédicte Zimmerman, 'Beyond comparison: *histoire croisée* and the challenge of reflexivity', *History and Theory* xlv/1 (2006), 30–50

Wharton, James C., 'Eating to win: popular concepts of diet, strength, and energy in the early twentieth century', in Grover, *Fitness in American culture*, 86–122

White, E., *A history of the Manchester and Salford Council of Social Service, 1919–1969*, Manchester 1969

White, Jerry, 'From Herbert Morrison to command and control: the decline of local democracy and its effect on public services', *History Workshop Journal* lix/1 (2005), 73–82

White, Morton and Lucia White, *The intellectual versus the city: from Thomas Jefferson to Frank Lloyd Wright*, Cambridge, MA 1962

Whitfield, Stephen J., 'The politics of pageantry, 1936–1946', *American Jewish History* lxxxiv/3 (1996), 221–51

Whitmarsh, Guy, 'The politics of political education: an episode', *Journal of Curriculum Studies* vi/2 (1974), 133–42

Whyte, William, 'Building the nation in the town: architecture and identity in Britain', in Whyte and Zimmer, *Nationalism*, 204–33

— and Oliver Zimmer, 'Introduction', to Whyte and Zimmer, *Nationalism*, 1–16

— and Oliver Zimmer (eds), *Nationalism and the reshaping of urban communities in Europe, 1848–1914*, Basingstoke 2011

Wiener, Martin J., *English culture and the decline of the industrial spirit, 1850–1980*, Cambridge 1981

Wildman, Charlotte, 'Religious selfhoods and the city in inter-war Manchester', *Urban History* xxxviii/1 (2011), 103–23

— 'A City Speaks: the projection of civic identity in Manchester', *Twentieth Century British History* xxiii/1 (2012), 80–99

— 'Urban transformation in Liverpool and Manchester, 1918-1939', *HJ* lv/1 (2012), 119–43

— *Urban redevelopment and modernity in Liverpool and Manchester, 1918–1939*, London 2016.

Williams, Bill, 'The Jewish immigrant in Manchester: the contribution of oral history', *Oral History* vii/1 (1979), 43–53

Wilmer, S. E., *Theatre, society and the nation*, Cambridge 2004

Wilson, Mabel, *Negro building: black Americans in the world of fairs and museums*, Berkeley, CA 2012

Wilson, Trevor (ed.), *The political diaries of C. P. Scott, 1911–1928*, Cambridge 1970

Wohl, Richard, 'The country boy myth and its place in American urban culture: the nineteenth-century contribution', *Perspectives in American History* iii (1969), 107–21

Wolffe, John, *God and greater Britain: religion and national life in Britain and Ireland, 1843–1945*, London 1994

Woods, Michael, 'Performing power: local politics and the Taunton pageant of 1928', *Journal of Historical Geography* xxv/1 (1999), 57–74

Wukas, Mark, *The worn doorstep: informal history of Northwestern University Settlement Association, 1891–1991*, Chicago, IL 1991

Wynn, Neil A., *The Afro-American and the Second World War*, New York, NY 1993

Yoshino, Ayako, *Pageant fever: local history and consumerism in Edwardian England*, Tokyo 2011

Zeiger, Susan, *In Uncle Sam's service: women workers with the American Expeditionary Force, 1917–1919*, Philadelphia, PA 1999

Ziegler-McPherson, Christina A., *Americanization in the States: immigrant social welfare policy, citizenship and national identity in the United States, 1908–1929*, Gainesville, FL 2009

Zweiniger-Bargielowska, Ina, 'Building a British superman: physical culture in interwar Britain', *Journal of Contemporary History* xli/4 (2006), 595–610

— 'Raising a nation of "good animals": the new health society and health education campaigns in interwar Britain', *Social History of Medicine* xx/1 (2007), 73–89

— *Managing the body: beauty, health, and fitness in Britain, 1880–1939*, Oxford 2010

Zylstra, Geoff D., 'Productions of space, productions of power: studying space, urban design, and social relations', *JUH* xliii/3 (2017), 562–9

Unpublished dissertations

Adderley, S. D., 'Bureaucratic conceptions of citizenship in the voluntary sector (1919-1939): the case of the National Council of Social Service', PhD diss. Cardiff 2002

Carter, Laura Joyce, 'The "history of everyday life" and democratic culture in Britain, 1918-1968', PhD diss. Cambridge 2017

Haggith, Toby, '"Castles in the air": British film and the reconstruction of the built environment, 1939-51', PhD diss. Warwick 1998

Heathman, Katie Palmer, 'Revival: the transformative potential of English folksong and dance, 1890-1940', PhD diss. Leicester 2016

Hollow, Matthew, 'Housing needs: power, subjectivity and public housing in England, 1920-1970', DPhil. diss. Oxford 2011

Oldfield, Carolyn, 'Growing up good? Medical, social hygiene and youth perspectives on young women, 1918-1939', PhD diss. Warwick 2001

Satterfield, A. W., 'Publications disseminated by the US government during the early 20th century for the American housewife: a selected bibliography', MSc diss. Chapel Hill, NC 2005

Smith, J., 'The Manchester and Salford Women Citizens' Association: a study of women's citizenship, 1913-1948', PhD diss. Manchester 2007

Web-based sources

'Historical Pageants', SoundCloud,<https://www.soundcloud.com/tom-hulme-9>

'The Lancashire Cotton Pageant', *The Redress of the Past*, <http://www.historicalpageants.ac.uk/pageants/1111/>

'St Paul's Steps', *The Redress of the Past*, <http://www.historicalpageants.ac.uk/pageants/1318/>

'The Sherborne Pageant', *The Redress of the Past*, <http://www.historicalpageants.ac.uk/pageants/1193/>

'Sister's Pageant Memories', *The Redress of the Past*, <http://historicalpageants.ac.uk/publications/blog/sisters-pageant-memories/>

Cantwell, Christopher D., 'Religion in the American city, 1900-2000', *American History: Oxford research encyclopaedia*, Oxford 2016, <http://americanhistory.oxfordre.com/view/10.1093/acrefore/9780199329175.001.0001/acrefore-9780199329175-e-355>

Coolidge, Calvin, 'Address before the National Council of the Boy Scouts of America, Washington, D. C.', 1 May 1926: Gerhard Peters and John T. Woolley, 'The American Presidency Project', <http://www.presidency.ucsb.cdu/ws/?pid=395>

Day, Katie, 'Urban space and religion in the United States', *Religion: Oxford research encyclopaedia*, Oxford 2017, <http://religion.oxfordre.com/view/10.1093/acrefore/9780199340378.001.0001/acrefore-9780199340378-e-470>

'Festival Play', *Chicago Commerce* (Aug. 27 1921), available at the Great Chicago Fire and the web of memory, <https://www.greatchicagofire.org/commemorating-catastrophe-library/festival-play>

Nieboer, Ruth A., 'Arthur Dunn: civic visionary from the heartland', conference paper, Annual Meeting of the National Council for the Social Studies, San Antonio, Tx, 16-19 November 2000, <https://catalogue.nla.gov.au/Record/5676049>

Index

[Page numbers in bold indicate figures]

Abbott, Robert S., 38, 128, 130. *See also* *Chicago Defender.*
Addams, Jane, 24, 140, 161, 178
Addison, Christopher, 189
African American community: associational culture, 38-9, 87-8, 126-7, 129-30, 158, 161, 212; civic inclusion, 37-8, 86-8, 91, 98, 126-7, 155, 213-14; enfranchisement, 20-1; pan-Africanism, 127-9, 130; political consciousness, 98, 126-130, 211-14; racism (experience of), 37-8, 88, 126, 130, 157-8, 196-7, 211-13; segregation and housing, 38-9, 86, 88, 126, 211; urban migration, 37, 145, 212-13
American Citizenship Foundation, 150, 157
Americanisation, 7, 39-40, 41, 56, 97, 118, 153, 157
Ancient Greece: understandings of (Britain), 50, 54, 61-2
Association for Education in Citizenship (Britain), 44, 67

Black communities in Britain: experiences of, 5, 42-3, 206
Board of Education (Britain), 66, 142, 164
Boy Scouts (Britain, US), 139, 149, 150, 162, 183
Briggs, Asa, 2
British Documentary Film Movement, 33, 64, 187-8
British Empire, *see* imperialism
British Empire Exhibition (1924-5), 77
Brown, Ford Madox, 110, 132
Burgess, Ernest, 32, 144. *See also* Chicago School of Sociologists.
Burnham, Daniel, 65, 82. *See also* Burnham Plan of Chicago (1909).
Burnham Plan of Chicago (1909), 65, 76, 82, 120, 178, 209-10

Carey Sr, Archibald J., 87
central government (Britain, US): growth, 167-8, 174-5, 204-5, 209; ideology, 23-6, 50-2, 181-2, 185-90, 194-5, 204-5, 209; welfare, 167-8, 180-1
Century of Negro Progress (1962) (US), 213
charities (Britain, US), 170-6, 179-84. *See also* Chicago: local associations; Manchester: local associations.
Chicago: areas and neighbourhoods: Back of the Yards, 56, 56 n. 40; Fuller Park, 161; Gold Coast, 146; South Side. *See also* African American community.
Chicago: civic celebrations: Boys' Week, 152-7, **155**, **156**; Bud Billiken Day, 129-30, **131**, 212; Century of Progress (Chicago World's Fair) (1933-4), 73, 93-4, 124-7, 128-9, **129;** Chicago's 125th Anniversary (1962), 210-11; Chicago Jubilee (1937), 94-8, **95**; Pageant of Progress (1921-2), 1-2, 5, 74-6, **75**, 81-2, 83-4, 85-8, 90-2, 94, 105; Woman's World's Fair (Chicago), 91; World's Columbian Exposition (Chicago World's Fair) (1893), 73, 93, 120, 122, 177. *See also* urban festivals; women, associational culture, political campaigning.
Chicago: governmental departments, committees and commissions: Board of Education, 55-6, 76, 181; Chicago Housing Authority, 190, 211; Chicago Juvenile Court, 137; Chicago Transit Authority, 208; Commission on Citizenship Education (1932), 57; Commission on Race Relations (1922), 38; Department of Public Works, 76; Sanitary and Ship Canal, 56

Chicago: housing projects: Altgeld
   Gardens, 192; Ida B. Wells Homes, 197;
   Robert Taylor Homes, 197
Chicago: local associations: Association
   House, 40, **59**, 152, **154**, 181-2,
   182-3, 209; Chicago Association of
   Commerce, 161-2, 190; Chicago Boy
   Scouts, 183; Chicago Boys' Club,
   158, 137, 183; Chicago Boys' Clubs
   Federation, 152; Chicago Council of
   Negro Organizations, 212; Chicago
   Council of Social Agencies, 40, 146;
   Chicago Federation of Labour, 92;
   Chicago Historical Society, 40, 96,
   98; Chicago Real Estate Board, 37,
   211; Chicago Retail Lumber Dealers
   Association, 74-6; Chicago Urban
   League, 39, 181; Chicago Woman's
   Club, 162, 185; Chicago Workers'
   Committee on Unemployment, 180,
   182; City Club of Chicago, 177; Civic
   Federation of Chicago, 36, 177; House
   of Happiness, 182; Hull House, 24,
   140, 150, 178, 183; Jewish People's
   Institute, 150, 182; Loyal Order of the
   Moose, 90; Metropolitan Community
   Church Choir, 87; Municipal Voters
   League, 44, 177; Off-the-Street-Club,
   152; Reserve Officers Training Corps,
   153, **156**; Rotary Club, 152-3; Stock
   Yards Community Council, 56; Union
   League Boys Club, 150, 161; Union
   League Club of Chicago, 57, 150, 161;
   United Charities, 146, 162, 181. *See also*
   Boy Scouts; Jewish diaspora in Chicago;
   settlement movement.
Chicago, University of, 31, 35, 56, 67, 146
Chicago Black Renaissance, 128, 212. *See
   also* African American community.
Chicago Defender, 38, 69, 88, 126-7, 130,
   157
Chicago Race Riot (1919), 38, 84, 143
Chicago School of Sociologists, 31-3,
   144-7
Chinese diaspora in Chicago, 86-7
cinema (Britain, US), 30, 148-9, 151, 162
citizenship: concepts of (Britain, US):
   active, 9, 26, 54, 76, 90, 116, 189, 207;
   nested, 8, 8 n. 35, 63-4

City Beautiful Movement (US), 24, 74. *See
   also* Burnham Plan of Chicago.
civic architecture (Britain, US), 42, 73, 76,
   78-81, **80**, 82-3, 94, 102
civic culture (Britain, US), 9-10, 27, 41,
   56-7, 83, 131, 161-5, 185, 204-5, 206,
   211-12. *See also* middle classes.
civics (Britain, US): in Chicago, 55-9;
   in Manchester, 59-63; and national
   identity, 63-5; spread of, 50, 52; success
   or failure of, 65-9; textbooks, 53-4;
   theory of, 48-53, 54. *See also* historical
   pageantry; urban festivals.
civil rights (US), 21, 212-14. *See also*
   African American community.
class (Britain, US), *see* working classes;
   middle classes
clubs, *see* Chicago, local associations;
   Manchester, local associations
Communism: fear of (Britain, US), 7,
   43-4, 88, 116, 118, 181-2. *See also*
   working classes.
comparative history, theory of, 12-13, 13
   n. 59, 45
consumerism (Britain, US), 37, 72, 93,
   137-8, 138-9, 142-3, 195-6, 207, 212
Coolidge, Calvin, 91, 149
crime (Britain, US), *see* immorality
Cressey, P. G., 144. *See also* Chicago School
   of Sociologists.

Daley, Richard J., 210, 213
Dawes, Rufus C., 93-4, 126
Dawson, Charles, 128
degeneration, 22, 24, 138-9, 140, 177,
   184-5, 194. *See also* national efficiency;
   race suicide.
Dewey, John, 24, 51-2, 141
Drake, St Clair, 212
Du Bois, W. E. B., 127 and n. 103
Dunn, Arthur W., 50-1, 54, 55

economic depression (Britain, US): and
   central legislation, 172, 174, 180; civic
   response, 1-2, 57-8, 93-4, 96-7, 174,
   180-3; and industrial unrest, 43, 181-2;
   urban effects, 41-2, 162, 172, 179
education, *see* Association for Education
   in Citizenship; Board of Education

(Britain); Chicago: governmental departments, committees and commissions; civics; Manchester: governmental departments and committees; urban festivals; Workers' Educational Association

Edwards, Trystan, 31

Empire Day (Britain), 7, 64. *See also* imperialism.

Englishness, 7, 31. *See also* national identity.

Fabianism (Britain), 61, 171, 173

Fascism: fear of (Britain, US), 43-4, 67, 116. *See also* working classes, fear of.

First World War: effects of (Britain, US): and citizenship, 19-20, 116, 141; and crime, 164; and expansion of government, 168, 172; and migration, 37-8l and national identity, 37, 118-19; and understanding of historical progression, 110-12, 121

Frank, Waldo, 35

Frazier, E. Franklin, 145, 146. *See also* Chicago School of Sociologists.

Garden Cities (Britain, US), 4, 28-9, 33, 34. *See also* urban planning.

Geddes, Patrick, 49 and n. 7, 50, 65, 76, 90, 185

gender (Britain, US), 19-20, 28, 89-90, 137-8, 147-8, 188, 189. *See also* masculinity; women.

General Strike (1926) (Britain), 43, 104, 133

George, Walter Lionel, 35

Girl Guides (Britain, US), 141. *See also* youth.

Goldman, Solomon, 123, 126

Gray, G. H., 190

Great Chicago Fire (1871), 36, 82, 95, 119-20, 122, 177

Great Migration (US), *see* African American community

Green, Thomas Hill, 22, 50, 51-2, 54, 61, 62, 64, 104, 159

Greenlaw, Edwin, 118

Grierson, John, 33. *See also* British Documentary Film Movement.

Griffith, John, 27

Hall, Newton M., 74

Hammond, J. L., 43

Harlem Renaissance (New York), 127-8

Hatton, Sidney Frank, 149

Hayward, Franklin Harold, 76-7

Hill, Octavia, 191. *See also* housing, tenant management.

historical pageantry (Britain, US): Anglo-American cultural diplomacy, 117; democratisation of, 114-15, 120, 132-3; depictions of early modern history, 113; depictions of the First World War, 119; depictions of industrialisation, 113-14, 120, 122; depictions of medieval history, 112-3; depictions of municipal autonomy, 113; depictions of race and ethnicity, 120-4; depictions of religion, 112, 122-4; depictions of the Roman Empire, 112; development of the movement, 107-8, 108-9, 117-19; and modernity, 107-8, 110, 112, 119-20, 152-3; and patriotism, 113, 117-20; as political radicalism, 132-3; and the progressive movement, 117-18; as rural idealism, 113; success, 134-5; and women, 114-16. *See also* historical pageants.

historical pageants: Chicago Festival Play (1921), 119-21; Chicago Jubilee Pageant (1937), 122; Communist Party of Manchester Pageant (1938), 133; Illinois Centennial Pageant (1918, Arthur Hercz), 119; Illinois Centennial Pageant (1918, Chicago Park Commissioners), 119-120; Light of Ages (1937) (Chicago), 122-4; Manchester Historical Pageant (1926), 109-16, 134; Manchester Historical Pageant (1938), 109-16, **111, 116**, 131-2; O, Sing a New Song (1934) (Chicago), 126-7, 128-9, **129**; Oxford Pageant (1907), 117; Pageant of the Celt (1934) (Chicago), 124; Pageant of Industries (1926) (Manchester), 76; Romance of a People (1933) (Chicago), 125-6; Sherborne Historical Pageant, 108. *See also* historical pageantry.

Hoover, Herbert, 179, 208

housing (Britain, US): conditions, 184-5,

186, 187; gendered understandings, 185-7, 189, 191-2; government understandings of tenants, 185, 196; legislation, 188-90; reform movements, 24, 33, 185-88, 191; segregation by race and ethnicity, 36-8, 196-7, 211; tenant management, 191-4; tenant responses, 194-5. *See also* Chicago: housing projects; Manchester: housing estates; urban planning.
Howard, Ebenezer, 28. *See also* Garden Cities.
Howe, Frederic, 24-5, 26

Ickes, Harold, 32
idealism, 23, 50, 51-2, 61, 104
Illinois Committee on Public Utility Information, 68
Illinois Emergency Relief Commission, 180-1
Illinois Society of the Colonial Dames of America, 40-1
immorality: urban causes of, 27-30, 32-3, 36, 40, 92-3, 104, 140, 143-50, 170, 176-8
imperialism (Britain): celebration of, 7, 63-4, 73, 77; fear of decline, 5, 22, 41, 171, 206; and identity, 6-7, 8, 63-4, 73; and US, 117. *See also* national efficiency.
Insull, Samuel, 68, 122
Irish diaspora: in Chicago, 36-7, 98, 125, 161; in Manchester, 43, 89
Italian diaspora: in Chicago, 86, 158, 161, 211; in Manchester, 42, 89, 130-1

Jeffersonian small-town democracy (US), 25, 29
Jewish Agency for Palestine (US), 125-6. *See also*, Judaism.
Jewish diaspora: in Chicago, 38, 123, 125-6, 150, 157, 158, 181, 182; in Manchester, 42-3, 43-4, 89, 103-4, 148, 158, 159
Joad, C. E. M., 28
Judaism (Britain, US): worship, 103-4. *See also* historical pageantry, religion; historical pageants, Romance of a People; Jewish diaspora in Chicago; Jewish diaspora in Manchester.

Kelly, Edward, 97, 122, 123, 126, 209
Ku Klux Klan (US), 88, 157-8.

Lascelles, Frank, 110, 113
Lethaby, William Richard, 30-1
liberalism, ideology of (Britain), 22-3
Lindsay, David, 30
Linn, James Weber, 94
local government (Britain, US); apathy, 54, 61, 67, 92; co-operation with voluntary associations, 172-5, 179; corruption, 3, 4, 24, 26, 36, 44-5, 54-5, 177; decline of, 203-4, 207-8; growth of, 167-9, 171-2, 178-9; municipalisation, 4, 44, 54-5, 68, 171, 208; publicising of, 1-2, 33-4, 60, 75-6, 98-9. *See also* Chicago, governmental departments, committees and commissions; civic culture; civics; historical pageants; Manchester, governmental departments and committees; urban festivals; youth.

Macadam, Elizabeth, 175
Mackay, Constance D'Arcy, 118
MacKaye, Percy, 74
Manchester: areas: Ancoats, 22, 84, 151, **152**, 162-3; Hulme, 41, 149, 150-1, 162, 163; Miles Platting, 164, **186**
Manchester: civic celebrations: Manchester Centenary (1938), **99**, **101**, 100-5; Manchester Centenary Festival (1953), 207-8; Manchester Civic Week (1926), 1-2, 5, 43, 77-84, **82**, **83**, 89-92, 105. *See also* urban festivals.
Manchester: governmental departments and committees: Education Committee (Manchester), 164; Housing Committee, 190, 193; Welfare Services Committee, 205
Manchester: housing estates: Blackley, **192**; Gorton, 195; Wythenshawe, 102
Manchester: local associations: Ancoats Lads' Club, 162-3; Broughton Boy Scouts, 162; Broughton Girls' Friendly Society, 150; Co-operative Union, 158, 164; Council of Manchester and Salford Jews, 103; District Provident and Charity Organisation Society of Manchester and Salford (DPS),

170-5, 176, 204; Girls' Friendly Society of Eccles, 148, 150; Groves Lads' Club, 151, 159; Hulme Lads' Club, 150-1, 162, 163; Jewish Lads' Brigade, 103, 148, 158; Manchester Citizens' Association, 147, 149, 151, 163; Manchester and District Branch of the Working Men's Club and Institute Union, 62; Manchester Municipal Officers' Guild, 62-3; Manchester's Provident Dispensaries Association, 171-2; Manchester Ramblers' Federation, 150; Manchester and Salford Better Housing Council, 186-7, 191; Manchester and Salford Council of Social Service, 175; Manchester and Salford Ladies' Health Society, 171; Manchester and Salford Sanitary Association, 170; Manchester and Salford Women Citizens' Association, 90, 191; Manchester Surgical Aid Society, 170, 173; Manchester University Settlement, 22, 147, 150, **152**, 173, 205; Procter Gymnasium and Hulme Lads' Club (*see* Manchester: local associations, Hulme Lads' Club); Royal Patriotic Fund Corporation, 172; Soldiers' and Sailors' Families' Association, 172. *See also* Boy Scouts; Jewish diaspora in Manchester; settlement movement; Workers' Educational Association; youth.

Manchester, University of, 30, 42, 83, **152**

Manchester Guardian (role of), 43, 59-60, 61, 83, 103

Manchester Town Hall and Town Hall Extension, 79-80, **80**, 102, 131

Market, Morris, 35-6

masculinity (Britain, US), 27-8, 45, 144-5, 165. *See also* gender.

Mass Observation (Britain), 134, 148

middle classes (Britain, US): civic culture of, 22-3, 39, 102, 169-70, 172-4; suburbanisation, 25, 45, 141, 172, 206-7, 208, 210, 211

Miers, Henry A., 42

Mill, John Stuart, 23

Ministry of Health (Britain), 142, 189, 191-2. *See also* central government.

Monck, Nugent, 109, 113, 114-15

Mumford, Lewis, 28-9 and n. 44, 32, 34

municipal corruption (Britain, US), *see* local government

Municipal Reform Act: centenary of (Britain), 100, 203-4

Mitchell, Miles Ewart, 1, 2, 77-8, **82**, **83**

modernity: cities, as site of, 10-12, 29-30, 60, 198, 207; and gender, 137-8, 162-3; growth of interest in, 10; relationship to history, 11-12, 31, 78-9, 107; relationship to rural life, 27-31; transnational, 12-13. *See also* historical pageantry.

Moody, Walter, 65

National Association for the Advancement of Coloured People (US), 127

National Council of Social Service (Britain), 173-4, 175-6

national efficiency (Britain), 22-3, 54, 100-2, 139-42, 189

National Fitness Campaign (Britain), 141-2. *See also* national efficiency.

National Health Service (Britain), 204

national identity (Britain, US), 6-8, 19-20, 63-5, 102, 112-13, 117-18, 206, 209. *See also* Americanisation.

National Origins Quota (1924) (US), 21

National Unemployed Workers Movement (US), 43

National Youth Administration (US), 166

Native Americans, 120-1, 123

New Deal (US), 5, 32-3, 57-9, 97, 165-6, 167-8, 180-1, 184, 188, 189-90, 208-9, 212. *See also* central government.

New Liberalism (Britain), 23, 61, 66, 126. *See also* liberalism.

Newman, George, 142

North, Cecil C., 32

O'Hanlon, Sydney, 147 and n. 57

Orwell, George, 41-2 and n. 98

parades (Britain, US), *see* urban festivals

Park, Robert, 31-2, 145, 146. *See also* Chicago School of Sociologists.

Parker, Louis Napoleon, 108-9, 109-10, 113, 114, 116, 117

Passmore Edwards Settlement (London), 163-4. *See also* settlement movement.

Peterloo (Manchester), 131-3

Phillips, Gordon, 45

Phillips, Jacob, 104

Pierce, Bessie Louise, 35, 57-8

Platt, Harold, 2, 13

Polish diaspora: in Chicago, 36-7, 98, 125

population growth (Britain, US), 2-3, 4-5, 35, 36

Priestley, J. B., 41

processions, *see* urban festivals

Progressive movement (US), 24-5, 29, 35, 50-2, 54-5, 68, 74, 86, 117-18, 140, 161-2, 168-9, 177-9

Protestantism (Britain, US): and citizenship, 66, 103-4. *See also* historical pageantry; religion; YMCA; YWCA.

public housing (Britain, US), *see* housing

public ownership (Britain, US), *see* local government

public space: concept of, 9 and n. 40, 12, 78-85, 130-1

Public Works Administration (US), 188, 190, 208. *See also* New Deal.

race riot, *see* Salford, race riot (1919).

race suicide (US), 140.

racial conflict (Britain, US), 3-4, 4-5, 36-9, 87, 196-7, 206, 211-14. *See also* Chicago Race Riot.

racism, *see* African American community.

Regional Planning Association of America, 29, 34, 49 n. 7

Reilly, Charles, 41

Reilly, Jack, 210-11

religion (Britain, US): and civic pride and citizenship, 66, 88-9, 96-8, 103-4, 122-4; and community, 8, 36-7, 39, 56-7, 97-99, 103, 128, 158; failure of, 145, 147, 163; inter-faith ideal, 89, 122. *See also* Jewish diaspora in Chicago; Jewish diaspora in Manchester; Judaism; Protestantism; Roman Catholicism.

Report of the Urbanism Committee to the National Resources Committee (US), 32-3

ritual (Britain, US), 79-83. *See also* urban festivals.

Roberts, Adelbert, 87

Roberts, Robert, 147

Roman Catholicism (Britain, US): citizenship, 21, 96-7, 123, 155; fears of and discrimination against, 21, 24, 89, 96-7; neighbourhoods, 36-7. *See also* historical pageantry; Italian diaspora in Manchester; religion.

Roosevelt, F. D. R., 93, 97, 180, 208, 212. *See also* New Deal.

rural idealism (Britain, US), 5-6, 25, 28-9, 31, 145, 149-50.

Salford: race riot, 42-3

Sandburg, Carl, 45

Save-Our-Schools Committee (Illinois), 67

Scott, C. P., 59-60, 61. *See also* Manchester Guardian.

Second World War: socio-cultural effects of (Britain, US), 206, 208-9, 212-13

settlement movement (Britain, US), 22-5, 140, 147, 158, 171, 173, 178, 181, 183, 205, 209. *See also* Chicago, local associations; Manchester, local associations,

Shock City: Manchester and Chicago as, 2-3, 35-6, 41, 45, 169-70, 176-8; narrative of overcoming, 53-4, 56, 76, 78; theory, 2, 11-12

Simmel, Georg, 10, 31

Simon, E. D., 44, 45, 61-2, 67

Simon, Shena, 45

slums (Britain, US), *see* housing

Smith, Henry Justin, 92

social control, 51, 84 and n. 50, 107 and n. 2, 144, 146, 170, 170, 194

Social Darwinism (Britain), 139

social housing, *see* housing

Social Studies Movement (US), 50-2 and n. 12. *See also* civics.

societies, *see* Chicago, local associations; Manchester, local associations

sociology (Britain, US), 31-3, 35, 49, 61, 144-7, 163, 213. *See also* Chicago School of Sociologists.

Spring, Howard, 41

Stead, W. T., 3-4, 36, 177

suburbanisation (Britain, US), *see* middle classes; working classes

Tawney, R. H., 50, 62
Taylor, Robert R., 196-7
Thompson, William 'Big Bill', 1, 2, 44, 81, 84, 85, 88
Thrasher, Frederick, 145, 146, 148. *See also* Chicago School of Sociologists.
Tocqueville, Alexis de, 183
town planning (Britain, US), *see* urban planning
Toynbee Hall (London), 22, 140
trans-Atlantic exchange, 12-13, 24, 48-9, 51-2, 188, 189, 190-2

United States Film Service, 34
urban ecology (US), 32, 144. *See also* Chicago School of Sociologists.
urban festivals (Britain, US): and associational culture, 89-91, 97-8; and class, 84, 105-6; and community identity,, 84-6; economic motives, 74, 77-8; growth, 73-4, 76-7; as municipal education, 76-8, 81-2, **95**, **99**, 100-1, **101**; organisation, 74, 77, 94-6, 100; parades during, 80-4, **83**, 85-8, 89, 94, 98, 102-3, 129-31, 153, 155-6, 207-8, 210; progress narratives of, 74-8, **95**, 96; and race and ethnicity (Chicago), 84-9, 96-8, 105-6; success of, 91-2, 105-6, 256, 207-8, 210-11; urban planning and architecture, 76, 78-81, **80**; and women, 85, 89-90, 91. *See also* Chicago, civic celebrations; Manchester, civic celebrations.
urban planning (Britain, US): decentralisation, 5-6, 28-9, 34; international exchanges, 4, 29, 48-9, 187; promotion of, 30-1, 32-4, 55, 66-7, 78, 207; and regionalism, 29, 49, 70-1. *See also* Burnham Plan of Chicago; Garden Cities; housing.
urban variable, 19, 198

Vernon, James, 11, 12

Wallace, Florence Magill, 118
Wallas, Graham, 50, 61
Washington, Booker T., 39, 128
Webb, Beatrice, *see* Fabianism
Webb, Sidney, *see* Fabianism

Weisgal, Meyer, 126
Whiggish history (Britain), 79, 110-11
Whit walks (Britain), *see* Italian diaspora in Manchester
White, Ebe M., 49
Wildman, Charlotte, 27, 78-9
Williams, Eugene, 38. *See also* Chicago Race Riot (1919).
Williams-Ellis, Clough, 28, 66-7
women (Britain, US): associational culture, 7, 22, 24, 90-1, 103, 115, 130, 140, 151; citizenship, 19-20, 22, 89-91, 115; concerns about sexuality of, 137-8, 141, 143, 144-5, 147, 148; political campaigning, 83-4, 85, 113, 177, 186. *See also* gender; housing; youth.
Workers' Educational Association (WEA) (Britain), 62, 63
working classes (Britain, US): civic inclusion, 84, 97, 115-16; class consciousness of, 39-40, 92, 131-3, 205-6, 212; enfranchisement of, 19-20; fear of 3, 22, 36, 39-40, 43, 67, 113, 118, 141, 170; improvement of, 4, 9, 22-3, 24, 50, 62, 139-42; Labour movement and, 37, 39-40, 43, 74, 92, 184, 205-6; suburbanisation, 207, 210. *See also* housing; youth.
Works Progress Administration (US), 58, 180. *See also* New Deal.

Young Men's Christian Association (YMCA) (Britain, US), 56-7, 58, 130, 140, 150, 152, **153**, **156**, 158, 162, 164, 165-6. *See also* youth.
Young Women's Christian Association (YWCA) (Britain, US), 141, 183. *See also* youth.
youth (Britain, US): crime, 28, 137, 144, 145, 150, 161, 164; definition, 136-7; gender, 137-8, 141, 143-5, 147-8, 151-2; growth of associations for, 150-3, 158, 161; growth of governmental support for, 161-2, 163-4, 165-6; health, 141-3, 154; inculcation of co-operative spirit, 154-5, 158-60; race (Chicago), 143-4, 155-8

Zorbaugh, Harvey Warren, 146. *See also* Chicago School of Sociologists.